Civilization
&
Barbarity

Civilization & *Barbarity*

IN 20TH-CENTURY EUROPE

Gabriel Jackson

Humanity Books

an imprint of Prometheus Books
59 John Glenn Drive, Amherst, New York 14228-2197

Published 1999 by Humanity Books, an imprint of Prometheus Books

03 02 01 00 99   5 4 3 2 1

Library of Congress Cataloging-in-Publication Data

Jackson, Gabriel.
    Civilization & barbarity in 20th-century Europe / Gabriel Jackson.
        p.   cm.
    Includes bibliographical references and index.
    ISBN 1–57392–668–X (alk. paper) — ISBN 1–57392–645–0 (pbk. : alk. paper)
    1. Europe—Civilization—20th century. I. Title. II. Title: Civilization and
barbarity in twentieth-century Europe.
CB425.J32   1999
940.5—dc21   99–31854
                                                     CIP

Printed in the United States of America on acid-free paper

Contents

Maps

Preface

In the present century, Europe has inflicted on itself—and on much of the rest of the world—two immensely destructive wars. In the dictatorships of Hitler and Stalin, it has experienced two of the most brutal tyrannies of which we have historical evidence. In the genocide of the Jews, Gypsies, and available Slavs, the Nazis (principally Germans, but with considerable help from other followers) massacred human beings purely for who they were and not for what they had thought or done—or had allegedly thought or done. In the mass purges initiated by Lenin and gruesomely multiplied by Stalin, millions of human beings were exiled or murdered on the basis of fancied opposition and forced confessions. And in less imaginative and less publicized persecutions, patriotic nationalists of one stripe or another have victimized the minorities in their midst.

Yet this also has been a century of scientific and artistic miracles. Starting with the discovery of radioactivity in 1895, European physicists initiated what has become a worldwide explosion of creative work in the exact sciences. Europe also initiated surrealism and abstraction in modern art, and created a new musical vocabulary going far beyond the well-tempered scale of the era from Bach to Brahms. Finally, Europe has offered, in the form of the "welfare state" (as developed in Scandinavia after the First World War and generalized to most of noncommunist Europe after the Second World War), a higher standard of living and a wider choice of "lifestyles" to a larger proportion of its inhabitants than has any other complex society, past or present.

How can one understand the combination of such prodigious accomplishments and such devastating violence? And what can one learn from those contrasting events? As a historian, I have always thought that, regardless of one's personal tastes and interests, the understanding of any society requires a basic comprehen-

7

sion of its economic foundations, its political systems, and its shifting power rela-tionships. But in the present work, I am more concerned with moral, intellectual, and artistic legacies than I am with economic and political powers. Of course we must ask: What are the factors that produced European economic and scientific leadership? And what are the factors that produced such horrific wars and cultural conflict within the context of a single civilization?

But more important in terms of the future of humanity: What produced the vileness of Hitler and Stalin? The creative exuberance of Einstein and Picasso? The moral earnestness of Bertrand Russell and Boris Pasternak? If Europe as we know it today were suddenly to disappear by reason of a nuclear war, an epidemic disease, or some uncontrollable demographic or ecological change, what would be worth remembering? What would we consider important, both for Good and for Evil, as examples to emulate and as catastrophes to avoid?

It is precisely this sense of universal moral inquiry that has motivated me to write this book. I do not accept the current disparaging judgments of some multicul-turalists to the effect that European history, and Western civilization in general, are merely a monument to "dead white men." For me, Europe is a human culture, not a white-skinned biology. The liberation from race discrimination and imperialism, and the development and self-affirmation of Asian, African, and Latin American soci-eties, has naturally involved claims of uniqueness, often including a reverse racism in response to the long history of the "white man's burden."

I believe that human beings of any racial stock can produce an Einstein, a Mozart, or a Hitler. And we have ample evidence that people of all races value the contributions of European science, music, and the fine arts in exactly the same way as do people of European extraction. In terms of emotional and intellectual capac-ities we are all one human race, capable of reflecting upon—and learning from—the history of the extraordinary century which is the subject of this book.

A word about bibliography and footnotes. I owe a tremendous debt to the authors of the textbooks and general interpretations which I have used over a period of some forty years' teaching: such works as those of Carleton J. H. Hayes; Cyril Black and E. C. Helmreich; Chambers, Harris, and Bayley; Paul Beik and Laurence Lafore; R. R. Palmer, H. Stuart Hughes, Raymond Aron, Gordon Craig, Walter Laqueur, Arno Mayer, and William McNeill; the intellectual histories of Crane Brinton, Peter Gay, George Mosse, and Carl E. Schorske; the "Rise of Modern Europe" series edited by William L. Langer; the "Peuples et Civilisations" series edited by Maurice Crouzet; and the work of the postwar German historians Karl Dietrich Bracher, Martin Broszat, Hans Mommsen, and their disciples. Also invaluable to me have been the *New Grove Dictionary of Music and Musicians*, the "World of Art" series published by Thames and Hudson, the Oxford *Concise Sci-ence Dictionary*, and the 1987 revised Penguin edition of Isaac Asimov's *New Guide to Science*.

But this is a book of synthesis and interpretation. I have not footnoted my narrative of "mainstream" events, political and economic theories, treaties, constitutions, and legislation. Nor have I tried to give anything like equal treatment to each European nation or every decade. The notes refer to my sources concerning the smaller countries or to special areas and topics; most particularly, they direct the reader's attention to the articles in monthly and quarterly publications which are available in university libraries but whose article titles are not included in the "online" catalogues, as are the titles of all books.

I am especially grateful for the comments on chapter 5 by several scientist colleagues—the chemist Russell Doolittle and the physicist Norman Kroll of the University of California, San Diego, and Henry Linschitz, Rubenstein Professor of Chemistry, emeritus, of Brandeis University. Several humanist colleagues—Dan Aaron, Ralph Bennett, Mimi Berlin, Arno Mayer, Thomas Metzger, and André Schiffrin—have made suggestions probably more helpful to me than they realized when making them. Gerald Feldman and Richard Herr at UC Berkeley, and David Ringrose at UC San Diego, arranged colloquia which gave me valuable feedback while writing this book. My Barcelona friends Eduard Amorós and Antoni Rosell helped me mightily in computer matters; and Rick Szykowny of Humanity Books contributed clarity to my prose without distorting my interpretations. I received a travel grant from the Faculty Research Committee at UC San Diego (where I taught history and humanities for eighteen years). Finally, I am much indebted to the courteously offered bibliographical aid of the library staffs of UC Berkeley, UC San Diego, the Central University in Barcelona, and the Max Planck Institute in Göttingen.

Gabriel Jackson
Barcelona, March 1999

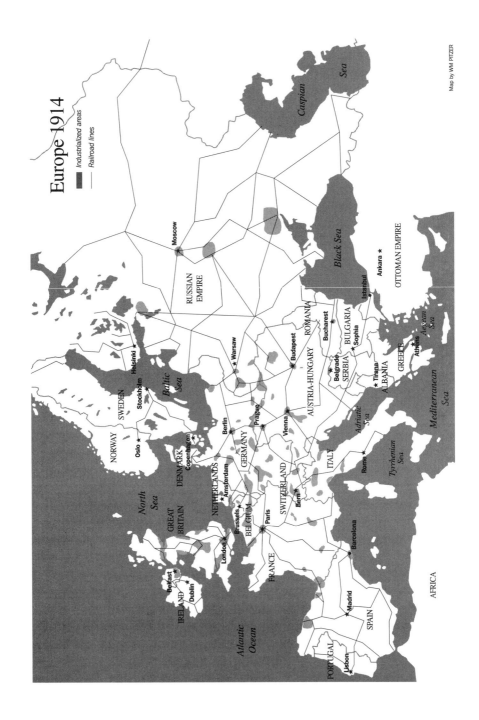

Europe 1914

Industrialized areas
Railroad lines

Map by WM PITZER

1

Europe before the First World War

*E*urope in 1914 was universally recognized as the most dynamic portion of the known world in terms of economic development, military prowess, scientific originality, and artistic variety. Such had been the case for at least two centuries. Indeed, the widespread intellectual assumptions that change, development, and "progress" were the very essence of Western history had only become dominant because of the evident dynamism of European culture in contrast with the relatively static economics, technology, and social organization of the other cultures—Asian, African, and American Indian—with which the Europeans had come into contact.

In order to illustrate that dynamism, and its essentially international character, we can do no better than to consider the course of the nineteenth-century industrial revolution: a revolution which spread rapidly and peacefully from its original centers in Britain and northwestern Europe to the shores of the Mediterranean Sea, and in general to the entire continent west of Russia and the Ottoman-dominated territories in the Balkan peninsula.

The first requisite for a peaceful industrial revolution had been fulfilled by the late-eighteenth-century improvements in agricultural productivity. These made it possible to feed the working population of the new industrial cities, and a few decades thereafter the development of railroads and steamships enabled the nations of Western Europe to import wheat from Russia and America. The European population quadrupled during the course of the nineteenth century, and was somewhat better fed and clothed in 1900 than it had been at the dawn of the previous century. And for those who were unable to benefit from the new economic developments (or who preferred more adventurous solutions), it was possible to emigrate and start a new life in the Americas and Australia.

With regard to relationships among the many European nationalities, the industrial revolution constituted an integrative experience. In the early decades English, Scottish, Welsh, and Belgian engineers, technicians, factory foremen, and accountants were frequently employed to assist French and German entrepreneurs in the establishment of iron works and textile factories, as well as in the construction of railroads (which circulated on the left, in honor of British habits). We can get a whiff of the euphoria associated with railroad building from the celebratory verses of a minor German poet, Karl Beck, around the year 1840:

> For these rails are bridal bracelets,
> Wedding rings of purest gold;
> States like lovers will exchange them,
> And the marriage tie will hold.[1]

By the second half of the century, the British and Belgians were joined by French, Swiss, Austrian, and German engineers and businessmen carrying the new technologies to Italy, the Iberian peninsula, and Scandinavia, and to scattered locations in Hungary, Poland, and European Russia.

This intra-European development was not as nakedly exploitative as was the roughly simultaneous colonization of Asia and Africa. French, German, Czech, Basque, Catalan, and Italian workers possessed most of the same artisan skills, knowledge of tools, experience of work discipline, and capacity for both organized work and organized protest as did the British and northwest European pioneers of the industrial revolution. The same can also be said for the business managers and accountants, so that within Europe all classes among the many nationalities learned quickly and were within a few years' time fully capable of continuing their own commercial and industrial development.

There was also a significant amount of permanent emigration within Europe, not only of peasants to the cities in their own countries, but of Poles to the farms of Prussia, the industry of the Ruhr, and the coal mines of France; of Italians to France, Switzerland, and Germany; of Serbian and Croatian stonecutters to the building trades of northern Europe; and of German farmers and technicians to Hungary, Romania, and imperial Russia, where their reputation for efficiency and productivity made them welcome immigrants from the point of view of the local governments.

Throughout these years, moreover, the freedom to travel through Europe was generally unhampered by the various unhappily familiar twentieth-century obstacles to freedom of commerce and personal movement, such as tariffs, currency restrictions, visas, and passports. Indeed, until approximately 1880, the tendency all over the continent was to lower tariffs and ease restrictions on the crossing of national borders. Major banking houses were international in their operations, capital passed freely over frontiers, and the gold standard made for confidence and fluidity in international payments. At the same time, however, this intra-European rapidity of the industrial revolution stands in marked contrast to the failure of economic and technological change to reach from nineteenth-century Europe into Africa, the Middle East, and all but the westernmost provinces of the Russian empire.

One evident (but by no means sufficient) reason for this limitation was the differences of religion between Europe and its neighbors. Throughout most of Europe, the beginning of the nineteenth century found the Roman Catholic and various Protestant churches living at peace with one another. The Protestants, with their insistence on the importance of reading the Bible, had created a substantially literate population in most of northern Europe, and the same was true to a slightly lesser degree in Catholic Bavaria, France, Austria, and northern Italy. Thus, with mixed populations living in the same territories, speaking the same languages, singing similar (if not identical) music, and distributing printed prayer books, the Protestant and Catholic churches were able competitively to influence each other's customs, ceremonies, and educational styles. Also, with the slow but steady decline in the importance of theological dogma for most of the population, intermarriage had become fairly common. As a result, by the dawn of the nineteenth century European culture had largely overcome the religious schisms of the Reformation era.

But there had been no such interaction between the Western forms of Christianity and the Islamic and Eastern Orthodox religions. The immense differences in belief, practices, and popular culture were certainly among the reasons why the industrial revolution—and most other forms of cultural interchange—stopped at the borders between Catholic-Protestant Europe and the worlds of Islam and Orthodox Russia. However, religion alone is not sufficient to explain why the industrial revolution occurred only in the territories of Western Christianity. Important economic and institutional differences having nothing to do with religion—or with human abilities as such—had developed over the centuries. These patterns were easily communicated within Christian Europe, but not so easily exported to the neighboring Islamic and Orthodox nations. To take but one example, the northern European climate required winter-proofed houses with glazed windows, fireplaces with adequate chimneys, and ovens capable of containing very high temperatures without burning the dwelling or smoking out its inhabitants. The building materials, the tempered metals, the tools, and the knowledge of how to use them had all become the common property of Europe several centuries before the industrial revolution.

Historical experience had also prepared the European population to exercise a moderate degree of personal initiative in relation to authority. The predominant system of territorial government, based on a centuries-long accumulation of feudal practices, involved courts, written contracts, and mutual obligations between rulers and ruled. However slender the rights of a European peasant on the eve of the industrial revolution, they were substantial indeed in comparison with those of a Russian serf or of any non-noble subject of the Ottoman and North African potentates. By 1800, many European peasants either owned their own land, tools, and buildings outright or held them on long-term leases that amounted to ownership so long as they paid their taxes.

European peasants also had the right to decide whether or not to marry and could therefore think in terms of a family economy. They could postpone marriage in order to accumulate resources, educate their sons and daughters in a trade, leave property to their children, migrate in search of economic opportunity, and so on. A high proportion of the population thus had a well-established sense of personal autonomy and responsibility, which was very important for the rapid, successful spread of the industrial revolution and especially for the development of a market economy. But these qualities, while not entirely absent in the neighboring Islamic and Orthodox societies, were still the exception rather than the rule.

The industrial revolution, the rapid development of the exact sciences, and the application of science in the form of new inventions mutually reinforced each other throughout the century. To quote a leading British economic historian:

> the Siemens-Martin steel-smelting process was developed by the collaboration of men from Germany, France, and Wales; the motor car by Lenoir, Hugon, and Otto in the 1860's, and Gottlieb Daimler and Karl Friedrich Benz in Germany and France; and oil-prospecting called forth the rapid drill (Germany, 1895), the diamond exploratory drill (Holland and USA, 1905–1915), the torsion balance (Hungary, 1890), the seismograph (Germany, 1919), and the rotary hydraulic drill (France, 1846; improved 1919–20).[2]

One further important factor tending to integrate Europe was the almost completely international atmosphere of artistic and musical life. Paris, London, and Rome were traditional centers for painters, sculptors, dancers, musicians, acrobats, and magicians. Vienna, Prague, Budapest, Munich, Berlin, and Warsaw enthusiastically joined them during the course of the nineteenth century. Milan from early in the century, and Barcelona in the last decades, were international centers of opera production. The great Hungarian pianist-composer Franz Liszt spent a decade as a theater and music director in the Duchy of Weimar, and throughout his long life he used a substantial part of his immense concert earnings to subsidize the development of talented younger artists. So far as we know, nobody asked to see their passports.[3]

But the industrial revolution, together with the rapid development of steamships, the telegraph, and especially of capital surpluses looking for profitable investment, led to increased interest in the less developed areas of the globe. At first there seemed to be plenty of opportunity for everyone: for the British in India, Burma, and China; for the Russians in Central Asia and Siberia; for agreed-upon spheres of interest in Persia and Afghanistan between Britain and Russia; for the Habsburg empire in southeastern Europe, where it appeared to be the natural heir of the Ottoman empire;

for France in both Africa and Asia; and for Spain and Portugal in Africa, all according roughly to their relative military and economic capacities.

Most of these areas, either because of the climate or existing large populations, were not important as areas for European emigration—the two significant exceptions being French settlement in Algeria and Russian settlements in Kazahkstan and Siberia. The serious competition for trade and investment was limited pretty much to England and France. At the same time, all the major European powers thought of themselves as bringing the benefits of Christianity and science to the less "civilized" portions of the globe. Generally speaking, their missionary, exploratory, and medical activities involved as much cooperation as rivalry.

As of 1871, however, the creation of an entirely new territorial power, the German Federal Empire, destroyed the existing equilibrium among the major states. In three short, relatively undestructive wars, the kingdom of Prussia seized the duchy of Schleswig from Denmark (1864), expelled the Habsburg empire from the existing German Federation (1866), and took Alsace and part of Lorraine from France (1870–71).

In the first of these splendid little wars, the Prussian Chancellor, Prince Otto von Bismarck, enlisted the cooperation of Austria. In the second, he quarreled with Austria on abstruse technical grounds about the interpretation of the new status of Schleswig. In the third instance, he doctored a reasonable-sounding telegram from his peacefully inclined sovereign, King William, to make it sound as though the latter had been insulted. This famous (or infamous) "Ems Dispatch" induced the ill and vain Napoleon III to declare war, which Bismarck had already decided was the necessary prelude to the Prussian unification of Germany. After a rapid military triumph, Bismarck not only annexed Alsace and imposed a five-billion-gold-franc indemnity on his wealthy victim, but proclaimed the new German Federal Empire in the Hall of Mirrors at Versailles. Thus he achieved the spectacular military, political, and financial humiliation of France, which had been the leading continental power for several centuries.

In the view of the overwhelming majority of German historians—and a substantial proportion of all European historians—Bismarck is considered a great statesman. For this writer too he appears to be an exemplar of moderation, especially in comparison with his successors, Kaiser William II and Adolf Hitler. He did indeed possess a rare combination of brutality and subtle intelligence, and I shall come soon to the moderation of which he was capable. But regardless of the praise or involuntary admiration that Bismarck is awarded in most histories, it is essential for one to realize, in attempting to understand the tragic history of twentieth-century Europe, that its single greatest power was born of a stunning combination of deceit and military prowess. Those three short wars created a fear and suspicion toward the new, united Germany that were gravely to affect the history of the following century.

Bismarck was thoroughly conscious of the terror that his swift victories had inspired, and he was conscious as well of the potential danger to Germany if those fears were not alleviated. To that end, he successfully reconciled the Austrians by supporting them economically and diplomatically in the Balkans. He established the *Dreikaiserbund* (Three Emperors' League) as the means to assuage Russian fears and to share with Russia and Austria the peaceful domination of Poland and the Balkans. He discreetly encouraged French imperialism in Africa and Southeast Asia. He repeatedly referred to the new Germany as a "satisfied" power. He was quietly persistent, but not aggressive, in acquiring African colonies, and he did nothing to challenge British sea power.

Bismarck also established himself as a kind of informal chairman of the "Concert of Europe." In 1878, he played the role of honest broker in a crisis involving the Ottomans, Russia, Austria, and the feisty young principality of Bulgaria. In 1884, he hosted the conference that established the immense Congo territory under the sovereignty of the small but wealthy kingdom of Belgium. He alternately prodded and flattered the English while establishing German colonies in southwest Africa, the Cameroons, and Tanganyika. Thus, by the late 1880s, all the desirable territories of Africa (and many of the richest portions of the Middle East and Asia) had been brought under European flags or had become "spheres of influence" of the European powers.

From 1862 to 1890, Bismarck guided the fortunes of Prussia and then of the new German Federal Empire. But in the latter year, the young Kaiser William II dismissed his grandfather's masterful but cautious chancellor. Henceforth, Germany no longer referred to itself as a "satisfied" power. On the contrary, the country vigorously expanded its imperial presence in Africa, joined in the general race for commercial concessions in China, and began to build a navy which was clearly intended to challenge British control of the seas. From 1890 to 1914, all diplomats and military officers (if not all politicians generally) knew that the major nations of Europe were engaged in an arms race and in the formation of ever tighter military alliances.

Since the First World War, dozens of competent historians have studied the course of late-nineteenth-century European imperialism, the formation of the military alliances, and the intimate relationship between these two processes. For intellectuals whose personal competitiveness rarely extends beyond the tennis court or the appointments and promotions committees within their university departments, there is an endless fascination to the threats, promises, military and naval feints, financial policies, and personal traits of the reigning princes, the important chancellors and foreign ministers, and the occasional key ambassadors whose judgments and motives entered into the making of these diplomatic and military decisions. No game of chess could be more complex, more suspenseful, than the study of the origins of what the people who lived through it referred to, in melancholy awe, as the "Great War"—especially as, once the carnage was over, all the major players were anxious in their official papers and memoirs to put the blame on the misunderstandings or the exaggerated ambitions of their enemies.

The story has already been effectively narrated from multiple points of view and thoroughly documented from several national archives. The details are much too complex to be treated briefly, but the main lines of development need to be discussed because, from about 1880, the internationalizing, cooperative aspects of the industrial revolution slowly but decisively gave way to an increasing, and potentially bellicose, nationalistic competition.

To summarize the interests of the great powers one by one: Britain was determined to maintain its domination of the seas and its leading role in world trade and investment. Its imperial possessions were important for reasons of both security and prestige, but Britain was perfectly prepared to share "the white man's burden" with other "advanced" nations. With respect to Europe, the British avoided binding military commitments but were always alert to the possible domination of the continent by a single power. Other things being equal, England liked to feel that it was favoring the development of political liberty and what we now call human rights in Italy, Greece, and the Balkans.

The French were likewise concerned, in both Africa and Southeast Asia, with trade, investment, and the "civilizing mission" of Christianity and French culture. Subliminally, the fact that England was more powerful economically and in the size of its empire, and that Germany had swiftly replaced France as the principal continental power, motivated the French all the more strongly to insist on their nation's extra-European imperial and cultural roles, and to defend the almost exclusive use of French as the language of diplomacy. The French also possessed the first republican, nonaristocratic empire since pre-Augustan Rome.

Russia was determined to maintain its control of Poland and Finland, to share in the spoils of the Ottoman empire's gradual dismemberment, and to be recognized as the special protector of both the recently constituted kingdom of Serbia and the principality of Bulgaria. This last aim brought Russia into constant, nagging conflict with Austria. The nation's extraordinary energies were also engaged in a steady expansion across Siberia, into Central Asia, and south to both the Caspian Sea and Afghanistan. Britain was anxious to limit any Russian advances toward India and China, but otherwise all the powers hoped that Russia's successes in Asia would lessen its concerns with the Balkans and the tottering Ottoman empire.

Austria-Hungary was the one remaining dynastic empire in Europe, the hyphen having been added in 1867 when Vienna granted sovereignty over the eastern half to the Magyars, with Budapest becoming a kind of co-capital. The Habsburg territories formed a natural geographic and economic unit; and while German was clearly the dominant language in politics, administration, and culture, careers were open to talent, as anyone can see who examines the names of the leading ministers, army officers, judges, intellectuals, and artists.

Nationalism was clearly a growing political force in nineteenth-century Europe. Italy and Germany had both achieved full unity in 1871. Greece, Serbia, Romania, and Bulgaria had all gained independence after centuries of Ottoman rule. Similarly, in 1867 Hungary was "liberated" from Austrian rule, thereby whetting the appetites of the Slovaks, Romanians, and Croats in its own territory, and those of the Poles, Czechs, and Slovenes in the Austrian half of the empire.

Thus, on the one hand, the Austro-German and Magyar rulers could hope to develop the industrial revolution, nurse the historic loyalty to the dynasty, and extend their political and cultural domination in the Balkans, while reconciling the smaller nationalities by means of partial autonomy, improved educational opportunity, and careers open to talent. But, on the other hand, nationalism seemed to offer the great panacea for centuries of subordination and, at times, of bitterly remembered persecution. Serbia and Bulgaria saw themselves as rival leaders of the new Balkan states living in the shadow of Austria and Russia. The Poles and Czechs had strongly organized nationalist parties, and the Slovenes and Croats became increasingly nationalistic in the last decades before 1914.

National and nationalist rivalries primarily, and imperialist rivalries secondarily, motivated the steady growth of the alliance system after the emergence of the newly unified Germany as the most powerful single nation on the continent. From 1872 to 1890, Bismarck maintained (in one form or other) the concept of the Three Emperors' League as a way of keeping the peace between Austria and Russia and securing his own eastern flanks in the face of a possible French war of revenge.

In 1879, Germany and Austria also formed the Dual Alliance, which henceforth became the most important military commitment of the two empires. In 1882, they added the recently unified Italy, partly to maintain the diplomatic isolation of France, partly to avoid conflicts between Italy and Austria which might destabilize the Balkans. Between 1882 and 1912, this Triple Alliance supported Italy in the acquisition of her African colonies: Tunis, Eritrea, Somaliland, and Libya.

In 1887, Bismarck forbade German banks to lend more money to the financially unstable tsarist empire, and this action inaugurated a rapprochement between Russia—Europe's most conservative monarchy—and republican, anticlerical France. In 1894, the two powers formed an alliance intended to protect both of them against Germany, an alliance which lasted until 1914. During this period France also invested heavily in Russian railroads, textiles, and metal industries.

Fear of Germany also led to a friendlier relationship between England and France. Until 1898 they had been partial allies and partial rivals in the occupation of Egypt. In the Fashoda crisis of that year, France acknowledged the primacy of Great Britain, after which the two powers began to coordinate their Mediterranean policies. The Entente Cordiale of 1904 included understandings about their interests in Morocco and initiated conversations about the disposition of their navies in case of war with Germany.

In 1907 Britain and Russia compromised on their imperial interests in Afghanistan; it thus became possible for Britain, Russia, and France to form the Triple Entente, which now faced the Triple Alliance of Germany, Austria-Hungary, and Italy. As might be expected, all the governments claimed their intentions were purely defensive, but the sober truth is that the loose concert of power which had existed from 1815 to 1870 had gradually been replaced by two powerful, hostile alliances.

If one focuses only on the formation of these mighty alliances and the accompanying increases in armaments, it will certainly appear that the war which began in August 1914 had become inevitable. But if one considers the internal political and cultural life of these same decades, it will appear that the nations were becoming increasingly aware of their own distinct interests, but not necessarily that they would soon embark upon such a destructive and suicidal war.

England was the most prosperous and stable of all the nations. The traditional class of landlords had compromised with the rising industrial capitalist class to share the general governing power in Parliament. Manhood suffrage, primary education, producer and consumer cooperatives, and the legalization of trade unions were all factors in the gradual, mostly peaceful improvement of the quality of life for most British citizens. Such problems as British rule in Ireland, the marked subordination of women both in the home and at work, and the deplorable living conditions in mining towns and industrial slums remained unresolved, but they were not problems that would involve England in war with her continental neighbors.

France of the Third Republic was led mostly by representatives of the small capitalist class. The failure of Napoleon III's Mexican intervention and the disastrous defeat in the Franco-Prussian war had left the French middle class without any appetite for military adventures. An excellent public-school system created an almost completely literate population and made French the dominant language, even though Bretons, Savoyards, Occitans, Basques, and Catalans continued to use their own vernaculars locally. French entrepreneurs concentrated on a varied, high-quality agriculture that was the envy of all Europe, as well as on small-scale industry and investments in the Iberian peninsula and North Africa. By the end of the century, they were also investing in government bonds and new industrial projects in Russia and the Balkans. With their combination of prosperity, personal liberty, and sophisticated culture, the French felt a pleasantly condescending attitude toward their Italian, Spanish, and Portuguese cousins, and toward the awakening Slavic peoples, many of whose intellectuals and artists preferred life in Paris to their unstable homelands. The French had not forgotten the loss of Alsace, but neither were the immense majority disposed to initiate a war in order to recover the lost province.

The situation within the Habsburg Empire was more complex. There were a half-dozen important languages spoken and a conscious resistance by the small nationalities to the imposition of German and Magyar. Standards of living and degrees of personal liberty varied much more greatly than in England or France. Austrians, Czechs, and city dwellers in Hungary, Slovenia, and Croatia enjoyed levels of literacy, health care, and municipal services comparable to those of Western Europe. But rural Hungary, Slovakia, and Bosnia-Herzegovina had pre-industrial societies ruled by feudal landlords and German or Magyar royal officials. The language question hampered the spread of literacy because any effort to establish primary schools would lead to demands for instruction in the local language as well as (or instead of) in German or Magyar.

Vienna and Budapest were comparable to Paris in the richness of their artistic and scientific culture. Relative to their very small numbers within the total population, Jews and recent converts from Judaism were extraordinarily prominent in the economic and cultural life of the two capitals. For those who admired individual merit and believed in the political heritage of the Dutch, English, and French revolutions, the large role of the Jews was not a problem.

However, the Jews (and the peasants) in most of the Habsburg lands had not been emancipated until 1848, and anti-Semitism was endemic among all the nationalities. For these reasons, both the Habsburg royalty and the Jewish community found it prudent to disguise the economic and professional prominence of the Jews. For example, in the second half of the nineteenth century, Budapest was the fastest-growing capital city in Europe, second only to America's grain capital, Minneapolis, for the production of its flour mills. It was also a growing banking center for European investments in Russia and Turkey. Its financial-commercial aristocracy consisted largely of Jewish and converted Jewish families who had been raised to the nobility and who had Magyarized their names, bought landed estates, and in general assimilated their way of life as completely as possible to that of the historic Magyar gentry. Of the 346 "noble" families officially listed toward the end of the war in 1918, 220 had been named since 1900.[4]

In foreign affairs the Austrian situation was also more complex than that of France. In relation to Germany and Western Europe, the empire was overwhelmingly interested in peaceful trade, investment, and varied cultural interchanges. In relation to its southeastern neighbors, the Habsburg administration wished to establish a kind of economic-military protectorate, a wish that divided the ruling classes of Serbia, Romania, and Bulgaria in their attitudes toward the "big brother" in Vienna. Toward Russia and Italy, the Austrian rulers felt a watchful hostility that was restrained only by German assurances of support in case of direct conflict in the Balkans. Thus, while Austria had no conceivable motives for war with Germany, France, or Great Britain, the conflict of her Balkan ambitions with those of Russia was ominous—and, indeed, turned out to be the detonating factor in the explosion of August 1914.

Just as the German Federal Empire was the most important military power in Europe from the moment of its creation, it was also the first nation to create a new "stake in society" for all its citizens. Under Bismarck's leadership, the new Germany established the first national system of old-age pensions and partial health insurance. The many separate German principalities shared a centuries-long tradition of subsidies to the arts and sciences and of state protection of forests and other natural resources. The new empire now added the general population to the protected list, both in the interests of economic productivity and public health and to combat the spread of subversive international doctrines such as socialism and anarchism. Indeed, the pioneering social-security system was intended to buy the loyalty of the new industrial working class without giving to Germans the full political and legal equality proclaimed by the French Revolution.

A final set of circumstances to be considered in outlining the situation of Europe before the First World War are the political, philosophical, and cultural movements which tended to create an all-European outlook rather than competitive nationalist visions. The French Enlightenment and the industrial revolution had given rise to great hopes for the liberty and prosperity not just of a restricted elite but of the populations generally. The nineteenth century was an era of hopeful "isms": liberalism (the word was coined at the Spanish Cortes of 1812), nationalism, republicanism (arising principally from the Jacobin tradition in the French Revolution), and several varieties of socialism, anarchism, and federalism. All of them promised a political structure that would do away with feudalism, "divine right" monarchy, and arbitrary landlord rule.

By the end of the century, nationalism, anarchism, and Marxian socialism were the most important of the "isms." Modern nationalism dates from the era of the French Revolution, but it is by no means easy to define because a sense of common loyalties and common culture certainly existed well before 1789: indisputably in the more developed countries such as England, France, and Holland, and to a degree also among Scots, Irish, Germans, Poles, Swedes, Danes, Czechs, and numerous Balkan, Italian, and Iberian peoples. In all these cases, the ruling classes—and a varying proportion of the general populace—were conscious of a common history, of shared dynastic and territorial loyalties, and of using roughly similar versions of the same language.

What was new from the time of the French Revolution was the leading role of the "Third Estate"—i.e., everybody who was not a priest or a titled landlord or royal servant. Revolutionary France survived the armed intervention of the dynastic states by means of the *levée en masse*, the creation of a new type of citizen army based upon an implicit bargain between rulers and ruled: defense of the revolutionary homeland in return for legal and political rights and, more generally, the replacement of class privileges by a citizenship common to all.

In the century following the French Revolution, the political institutions of all Europe west of Russia adopted in large measure the concepts of legal equality and the right to some degree of participation in government. Nationalism was now the conscious identification of the majority with a state that promised them personal rights and political dignity such as never had existed in the past. Until at least the mid-nineteenth century, its international implications were generous and optimistic.

Thus, the early theorists of nationalism—most prominently, Johann Gottfried Herder and Giuseppe Mazzini—preached a world in which the liberated nationalities would each contribute its arts and spiritual values to a peaceful, pluralistic Europe. There were indeed several instances in which nationalism played a generous, liberating role, such as with English aid in the liberation of Greece from Turkish rule; the general Western embrace of liberal nationalist emigrants from Germany, Austria, and Hungary after the failed revolutions of 1848; and both English and French aid in the unification of Italy under a constitutional monarchy.

Many late-nineteenth-century Czech, Slovene, and Croatian nationalists sought linguistic and administrative autonomy within the Habsburg empire rather than the destruction of that empire in favor of inevitably rival national states. Intellectuals all over Europe increasingly identified themselves with their mother tongue, but those of broad outlook agreed with the sentiment expressed by the great Danish educator Nikolai Grundtvig—to be a human being first, and a Dane (or whatever nationality) second.

Anarchism, like all the other "isms," included a number of different and partially competing theoretical formulations. The common denominator was the opposition to a centralized state and to all official or exclusive religions; there was also an emphasis not—as too often alleged—on an absence of all government but rather on local authority, power from the bottom up rather than the top down. (Anarchist emphasis on local authority often took the form of loyalty to a particular region, but this in itself was a counterforce to state-sponsored nationalism.) Anarchism was strongest among the artisans of Switzerland and the Jura mountains, and among both small peasants and new industrial workers in the Latin countries. It was also viewed sympathetically by cooperativists in the British isles and Scandinavia. The militants were frequently what the Spaniards called *obreros conscientes*: workers who read widely, invited university professors and scientists to give "adult education" lectures, and studied the applied sciences related to their industrial jobs with a view to replacing the bourgeoisie by democratically controlled worker enterprises.[5]

The anarchists substituted an optimistic faith in human perfectibility for traditional Christianity. They also advocated the study of Esperanto, an artificial language with a much simplified grammar and a vocabulary drawn from the Romance and Germanic languages so as to be easily learnable anywhere in western and northern Europe. And an important minority of anarchist thinkers and militants stressed the need for "direct action" (assassinations) as the means to eliminate landlord or capitalist oppression, based on the terribly simplistic idea that killing a particular minister or king would strike a lasting blow against historic oppressions. Without in any way minimizing the contradictions between such actions and the doctrines summarized above, I think it important to remember that the *pistoleros* were always a small minority, and that the philosophical anarchism which influenced millions of socially and educationally modest persons was an internationalist, generous-minded, antimilitary, and antiauthoritarian force in pre-1914 Europe.

Far more important than anarchism was Marxian socialism. Again, there were many doctrinal splits, personal and organizational rivalries, and a complete uncertainty as to exactly how to proceed once the rule of the bourgeoisie was overthrown. The common denominators among the competing strains of Marxian socialism included a recognition of the "positive" role of the bourgeoisie in creating the most productive economy in human history thus far; a belief in the historic task and human capacity of the industrial working class to take over the productive apparatus; a belief that both the needs of economic production and the recognized requirements of social justice would lead to the destruction of the bourgeois regimes; and the notion that those regimes would be replaced by a classless society—one in which the existing states would "wither away," since exploitation and the need for coercion would have been eliminated.

Such a doctrine, regardless of the details and the lacunae (such as whether the "inevitable" revolution would require lethal violence, or exactly how long it would take the state to "wither away"), was an internationalist doctrine, and one whose assumptions about human capacity and motivation were optimistic. In 1848, when they published the *Communist Manifesto*, the founding fathers of Marxian socialism, Karl Marx and Friedrich Engels, clearly believed that a strongly class-conscious industrial proletariat would have to exercise violence before the bourgeoisie would relinquish power. By the time of his death in 1895, however, Engels had come to believe there was a rational hope that the socialist parties of the Second International might achieve power through democratic elections, and that the transformation might thus occur without major violence.

One of the important non-Marxist intellectuals to note with approval the new attitude of Engels was the Czech philosopher (and later first president of the Czechoslovak Republic), Thomas Masaryk. Though Masaryk admired the Marxian analysis of the capitalist economy and shared the desire to improve the living conditions and educational opportunities of the industrial working class, he criticized Marxism for its dogmatic materialism and its underestimation of cultural factors. But in a long article on the "social question," published in Czech in 1898 and in German the following year, Masaryk noted with approval that the Marxists were becoming less deterministic regarding economic developments, more open to the importance of religious and cultural factors, and more flexible as to the possibilities of political democracy.[6]

In the first decade of the twentieth century, the socialist parties were indeed on their way toward achieving majority status in both Germany and the German-speaking portions of the Habsburg empire. Eduard Bernstein was the best-known theoretician of a revised Marxism, one which recognized that the living conditions of the working class had improved in the latter half of the nineteenth century and that education, recognized trade unions, and the gradual extension of political democracy would make it feasible to achieve socialism through peaceful methods. Marxian socialism and its Bernsteinian revision were less influential in the French socialist party and in the politically active trade unions in England, Poland, Bohemia, and Scandinavia (none of which had enacted old-age pension laws like those of Germany). But this internationalist, antimilitary socialism was sufficiently powerful in pre-1914 Europe that all the major powers worried seriously whether, in the event of war, the socialist parties and trade unions would support the national cause.

An important dissident voice in political philosophy during the first decade of the century was that of the French engineer Georges Sorel. Sorel agreed with Bernstein that the workers' living conditions had improved, but he did not share either the generally optimistic tradition of the French Enlightenment or the idea that trade unions and voting could bring about the socialist revolution. He thought of civilization as very precarious and, in words quite logical for a trained scientist, he defined it in terms analogous to the Second Law of Thermodynamics: "a state of tension and unyielding struggle to ward off forces of decay and destruction."[7]

The only way that civilization could be saved would be through the action of the proletariat, imagined as the successors to the Spartans, the early Christians, the soldiers of Oliver Cromwell, and the Grande Armée. Through the General Strike they would "enthrone a new civilization and a heroic morality on the ruins of the decaying bourgeois world." Since Sorel assumed that the bourgeois regime would already be tottering at the time of the proletarian initiative, the violence would lead to a quick triumph, not to civil war. Although Sorel became in time a traditionalist French patriot, the weight of his doctrine is not nationalistic; indeed, he lived to hail both Lenin and Mussolini in the first years after the Great War.

While Marxian socialism was the most important ideological influence among class-conscious industrial workers and secularized professionals, the Catholic Church during the papacy of Leo XIII (1878–1903) propounded a doctrine of "social Catholicism" which was equally influential among the conservative middle class, the churchgoing peasantry, and the substantial minority of urban workers who retained their religious attachments. His major encyclical, *Rerum Novarum* (1891), condemned the materialist philosophical basis of socialism and reaffirmed the rights of private property—but it also condemned the evils of unchecked, merciless economic competition and the increasing concentration of capital in a few hands. Indeed, the very use of the term "social Catholicism" (instead of "Christian charity") constituted an important adaptation to a society in which human beings could claim certain rights and not merely appeal to the charitable sentiments of their social superiors. As opposed to the materialist, atheist (in his view) trade unions associated with the socialist parties, Leo XIII advocated the establishment of "associations" to relieve poverty, speak for workers' legitimate interests within the factory, and provide medical, accident, and life insurance.

Ironically, in these views the pope had been anticipated by a portion of the German clergy which, in 1871, had formed the Center Party for the purpose of defending Catholic interests within the new German Federal Empire. During the following decades the Center Party advocated freedom of trade-union organization, the elimination of sales taxes on the minimum necessities of life, the adoption of income taxes, and of course the social-security laws instituted by Bismarck. As a result of these initiatives, the Center Party became the second-largest party in the Reichstag and received the votes of many moderate (and especially antimilitarist) voters who were not practicing Catholics.

The internationalist element which was prominent in both socialist and Christian thought was even more characteristic of the sciences. Surely one of the great glories of the late nineteenth century was the foundation of scientific (as against purely empirical and traditional) medicine. From the time of early Greek civilization, doctors were accustomed to relieving human suffering without regard to the tribal or religious affiliations of their patients. But their effectiveness had been severely limited—and much satirized in world literature—by their complete ignorance of what actually caused the diseases they were trying to cure. Almost all they could really do was to identify by their symptoms a handful of the commonest diseases, following which they could simply prescribe diet, rest, baths, and the use of traditional herbs.

As happens very frequently in the history of science, progress on similar problems was being made in several places at once. In the early 1850s, Ignaz Semmelweis, a Hungarian-Jewish doctor working in the municipal hospital of Vienna, recognized the infectious and contagious nature of childbed fever. Although Semmelweis didn't yet know what caused it, he drastically reduced its occurrence by insisting that obstetricians wash their hands before delivering babies. During the same years, the British surgeon Joseph Lister found a way to avoid the infections which so frequently accompanied surgery: He introduced the use of carbolic acid to wash his instruments, spray the walls of the operating room, and assure the cleanliness of his bandages.

But the key discovery was made in France by the chemist Louis Pasteur, who proved that a bacterium which he identified under the microscope was the specific cause of a silkworm disease that was plaguing the French textile industry. Bacteria were quickly recognized as the causative agents of various kinds of spoilage in the preparation of wines, beers, and dairy products. Pasteur and his collaborators went on to develop the process known as "pasteurization," the brief, intense heating of liquids to a temperative less than their boiling point, but one high enough to destroy the undesirable bacteria. A natural extension of the principle of pasteurization was the process of sterilizing by steam the bandages, bed clothes, uniforms, and other equipment used in hospitals.

Pasteur's studies of silkworm disease and cattle anthrax led him to announce in 1865 the germ theory of disease, which immediately became the foundation stone of scientific medicine. Pasteur's teams created vaccines for anthrax and rabies, and their work was followed up in chemical laboratories and hospitals all over Europe and America. German chemists, staining bacteria with the recently developed aniline dyes, were able to identify the specific causes of dozens of bacterial diseases. British and German chemists developed milder antiseptics to improve the conditions of surgery without subjecting both doctors and patients to the unpleasant smell of carbolic acid. The German doctor Robert Koch identified the bacterial causes of tuberculosis, human anthrax, and cholera. The Russian doctor Elie Metchnikoff, trained in both Russia and Germany, made crucial studies of the role of white blood cells in combatting infection. In 1904, Metchnikoff became subdirector of the Pasteur Institute in Paris and, in 1908, he and the German doctor Paul Ehrlich shared the Nobel Prize in physiology and medicine.

A second giant step in modern medicine was taken in 1909 with the creation of the first synthetic drug. After literally hundreds of experiments, Ehrlich and his Japanese assistant Sahachiro Hata found that salversan or "safe arsenic"—compound number 606 of their many years' efforts—cured syphilis. Thus, between 1865 and 1909 there came the rapid development of microbiology, the identification of bacterial diseases, the creation of vaccines, the spread of pasteurization and antiseptic surgery, and the beginnings of synthetic drug cures. Wherever Western missions, businesses, and military posts were established in Africa, Asia, and the Pacific, Western doctors followed, and it was the knowledge brought by these doctors that initiated the extraordinary decline in infant mortality all over the globe in the twentieth century.

It is, to be sure, also true that, in the rapidly growing community of microbiologists, there were many personality conflicts and rivalries over credit for discoveries. But in general, the international atmosphere was overwhelmingly one of cooperation, rapid uncensored publication, and the adoption of the new techniques by doctors everywhere. The main obstacles to the spread of effective medical treatment were economic and technical, not nationalistic—which explains why, at the same time that disciples of Pasteur and Koch were identifying and treating bacterial diseases in tropical Africa, cholera continued to threaten Europe.[8]

Thus far, in speaking of "isms" and of the new science of medicine, I have been treating subjects that contribute, on the whole, to an optimistic or "progressive" view of human development which embodies the philosophical optimism of the eighteenth-century Enlightenment. But there were always major currents of thought with negative implications. Of these, perhaps the most widespread was "social Darwinism," the application to human civilization of some of the seeming implications of Charles Darwin's theory of biological evolution, a theory that had been the subject of passionate debate from the moment of its appearance in 1859.

The underlying principle of Darwin's theory was that living species had been slowly differentiated and modified by an accumulation of slight changes in their hereditary structure. Just why these changes should occur Darwin did not know and did not pretend to say, but he believed that the survival of each slight mutation depended on the relative advantage it offered to the organism in adapting itself to its given environment. Since only a small proportion of the creatures born actually survived to live out their natural "lifespan," the implication was that those which survived were the "fittest" in the struggle for food and adequate living conditions.

Darwin himself, and most of the colleagues who defended his work, carefully avoided any teleological or moral speculations as to the success or disappearance of particular species. But it was not long before political philosophers and social scientists began to use analogies based on the imagery of the evolutionary debate. Crudely put, if middle-class people who lived within their incomes, disciplined their children, were apparently faithful to their wives, and went to church on Sunday also managed to accumulate more wealth and property than those who lived more careless lives, they must be better adapted to survive and to count themselves among the "fittest." Similarly, if certain peoples—let us say the English, with their excellent system of government and their successful worldwide empire, or the Germans, with their immensely productive industries and great universities—were also the most powerful on the world stage, this must be clear evidence of their superiority in terms of adaptation and fitness.

In this way, a theory which had been created to explain objectively the slow, long-term development of species became a rationalization for class exploitation and racism; and a theory which avoided all moral judgments was distorted to justify concepts of superiority and inferiority that were clearly intended to serve the interests of those in power, both within a given nation and upon the international stage. Many distinguished scientists and leading intellectuals believed they were merely being realistic when they preached "the white man's burden"—the superiority and, consequently, the political-imperial responsibility of the Anglo-Saxon or Germanic peoples. But this arrogant, pseudoscientific concept of racial superiority was then used to rationalize the massacre of black Africans in the last two decades of the nineteenth century. On numerous occasions during the conquests of Central Africa, Tanganyika, the Congo, and the Sudan, British, French, Belgian, and German military units wiped out entire villages by arson. Faced with "revolt" on the part of native warriors armed with spears, they killed thousands by means of the recently invented Maxim machine gun, while suffering mere dozens of casualties themselves. Their exploits, reported in European journals of the day, provoked many readers to express their horror at such conduct by fellow Europeans, while many others either openly justified the slaughters on grounds of spreading "civilization" or expressed a resigned, complacent sorrow at the "mysterious ways" of the Lord.[9]

The first decade of the twentieth century also witnessed the foundation of the new science of genetics. The Austrian monk Gregor Mendel made the first scientific studies of plant heredity in the 1860s, but his discoveries received less publicity than the average doctoral thesis in the exact sciences would receive today. Mendel's work was rediscovered at the turn of the century, however, and led immediately to the multiplication of experiments in plant, insect, and animal heredity and the rapid development of genetics.

As in the case of Darwinian evolution, the presumed human implications of the new science became highly politicized. Perhaps intelligence, honesty, and good character, like good bone structure or good looks, depended upon one's genes. Perhaps humans could be bred like peas (Mendel's preferred plant) or fruit flies (used by the American zoologist T. H. Morgan) to emphasize particularly desirable traits—provided, of course, one could agree on the list of such traits.

Exactly the same prejudices that were active in social Darwinism thus came to characterize the propaganda for that subdivision of genetics known as "eugenics." Ideally, one would keep the poor and less intelligent from reproducing and encourage the gifted—especially those "Aryan" or "Anglo-Saxon" or "Germanic" individuals who constituted the "highest" forms of racial type. With the full knowledge of the genetic code (and its limitations) that will likely be known by the twenty-first century, it may indeed become possible to develop a beneficent, carefully controlled form of eugenics. But in the early twentieth century, eugenics was only a dangerous pseudoscience preached by persons with strong class and racial prejudices.

In the last decades of the nineteenth century, there also developed a deep current of general pessimism concerning the future of European civilization. Baudelaire, Nietzsche, and Dostoyevsky are but three of the truly great writers to whom the hopes of such doctrines as anarchism, socialism, and social Catholicism (or its evangelical cousins in the Protestant countries) seemed completely utopian. I leave the discussion of their influence for a later chapter, because it was to be considerably greater in the twentieth century than during their lifetimes. Even so, any effort to assess the mood of Europe before the First World War must include the fact that a considerable number of the great artists and thinkers in the decades before 1914 were convinced of the basic irrationality and sinfulness (or in secular terms, capacity for violence and cruelty) of the human species. For the most part, their intentions were neither racist nor nationalist, but their ideas made war more "thinkable" because of the way in which they undermined existing forms of idealism and hope.

I conclude this opening chapter with a few brief references to pan-European cultural and political phenomena of the early twentieth century. Not only the biological sciences (bacteriology, evolution, and genetics) but also the physical sciences were particularly flourishing in the years before 1914. Because of the clear continuity from c. 1895 to the present, I leave the detailed discussion of such discoveries for a later chapter; but the discovery of radioactivity, and the beginnings of both quantum physics and relativity theory, all occur before the First World War.

The Nobel Prizes, first awarded in 1901, became immediately the most prestigious of international awards in science and literature. Feelings of national pride were evident among many of the winners, but the nationalism involved was more like that of Herder and Mazzini—the celebration of national diversity—than the nationalism of competitive alliances and arms races.

Music and the fine arts also remained completely international in spirit. Wagner's genius as both composer and stage innovator was recognized even by those who disliked his well-known anti-Semitism. The great Austrian-Jewish composer and orchestral conductor Gustav Mahler was as highly regarded in Paris, Amsterdam, London, and New York as he was in Vienna. The Norwegian Edvard Grieg, the Finn Jean Sibelius, and the Czechs Antonin Dvorak and Bedřich Smetana were all celebrated as contributors to the "concert of nations" as conceived by Herder and Mazzini. The Russians Alexander Scriabin and Igor Stravinsky, and the Frenchmen Claude Debussy and Maurice Ravel, mutually admired and influenced each other's novel developments in music and ballet. Such seminal works in the musical revolution of the twentieth century as Arnold Schoenberg's *Pierrot Lunaire* and Stravinsky's *Rite of Spring* premiered in 1912 and 1913, respectively.

Art during the same years was both international and highly experimental, with the development in France and Spain of cubism and collage, and a new aesthetic interest in machines, fabrics, metals, and industrial landscapes in the futurist art of largely Italian and Russian painters. Both painting and sculpture began to show the influence of the African and South Pacific cultures with which Europe came into contact as a result of late-nineteenth-century commerce and exploration. African rhythms and percussion instruments also made their appearance in European music, though their principal influence came after the First World War.

In addition to their emphasis on machines and industry, futurist pronouncements included naive invocations of violence as a necessary, healthy, masculine form of creative energy. The leading spirit of Italian futurism, Filippo Tommaso Marinetti, was present as a journalist during the Bulgarian siege of Adrianapolis in the Balkan War of 1912. In the following year he enjoyed a tremendous theatrical success in several European capitals with a one-man show entitled *Zang Tumb Tuum*, a monologue (with sound effects) that recounted the mobilization, the siege warfare, and the horrible fate of war prisoners abandoned and dying in the tropical heat.[10] There is no way of knowing how many in Marinetti's audience had the slightest notion of the vast "improvements" in the firepower of rifles, machine guns, and artillery being made by the major nations—improvements that would be employed all over Europe to deadly effect a few years later.

A significant (though, in practical terms, unsuccessful) effort to arrest the arms race was undertaken in the two international peace conferences held at the Hague in 1899 and 1907. Called by the Russian tsar after an informal sounding of the main European governments, these conferences offered an opportunity, outside the framework of the military alliance system, to seek ways to reduce international tension. Although they did not produce any disarmament agreements, they did result in the establishment of an international court of arbitration at the Hague, one which survives to this day. The court's decisions are not binding on the sovereign states; but someday—when and if the necessary forms of limited world government have been achieved—the Hague conferences will be remembered as their beginning.

More important for the immediate future were the agreements concerning the treatment of prisoners of war, including stipulations that they not be required by interrogators to reveal more than their name and rank, and that they be properly fed and housed, given appropriate medical care, and permitted to send and receive mail. Unfortunately, the agreements applied only to international war between uniformed armies and not to civil wars or revolutions. Even so, they did much to mitigate the horrors of the two world wars in the twentieth century, and they were crucial early steps in the development of internationally recognized human rights.

Returning to the pre-1914 situation, attitudes concerning the second Hague conference in 1907 indicated how little support existed for disarmament. In England, a vocal minority of members of Parliament urged the British government to introduce disarmament proposals. But the admiralty would hear nothing about reduction of the recently introduced dreadnought construction program, and the spokesman for the Social Democratic Federation stated that class war was more threatening than international war, and that "bourgeois pacifism" was mere paternalism. As for the Germans, Chancellor Heinrich von Bülow ridiculed the idea of disarmament before a laughing Reichstag.[11]

Thus, in the early years of the twentieth century, the optimistic trends of industrial and scientific development, the growth of parliamentary and trade-union democracy, and the importance of internationalist political and religious movements, all gave promise of continuing the predominantly peaceful tendencies of the previous century. But there were also strong currents of pessimism in intellectual and artistic circles, and an arms race that presented a constant threat of utter catastrophe—a threat of which the rulers and their cabinets in all countries were fully aware.

ENDNOTES

1. Quoted in T. S. Hamerow, *Restoration, Revolution, Reaction: Economics and Politics in Germany, 1815–1871* (New York, 1958), p. 8.

2. Sidney Pollard, *European Economic Integration, 1815–1970*, London: Thames and Hudson, 1974, p. 90. I have depended heavily in these paragraphs on chapters I–V of Pollard and on chapters 1–7 of E. L. Jones, *The European Miracle* (Cambridge University Press, 1981).

3. Alan Walker, *Franz Liszt: Volume One, The Virtuoso Years* and *Volume Two, The Weimar Years* (New York: Knopf, 1983 and 1989).

4. Wm. O. McCagg Jr., "Hungary's 'Feudalized' Bourgeoisie," *The Journal of Modern History*, March 1972, 65–78.

5. For a classic autobiography of an *obrero consciente* of the late nineteenth century, see Anselmo Lorenzo, *El proletariado militante* (Mexico, D. F.). Also Gerald Brenan, *The Spanish Labyrinth* (Cambridge University Press, 1950—and deservedly kept in print since then), especially chapters 2, 7, and 8, which concern both the Spanish anarchists and their European background.

6. Erazim Kohak, "Masaryk's Revision of Marxism, 'The Social Question'," *The Journal of the History of Ideas*, v. XXV, no. 4, 1964, 519–42.

7. The quoted phrases in these paragraphs on Sorel come from the excellent article by J. L. Talmon, "The Legacy of Georges Sorel," *Encounter*, February 1970, 47–60.

8. For a single dramatic instance, see Frank M. Snowden, "Cholera in Barletta, 1910," *Past and Present*, August 1991, 67–103. The author points to the difference between the scientific knowledge available and the lack of political will, technical resources, and resident physicians to purify the water supply and treat patients.

9. See Sven Lindqvist, *Exterminate All the Brutes* (New York: The New Press, 1996), for a succinct treatment of such incidents and a rich bibliography on their contemporary reporting in the European press.

10. Marjorie Perloff, *The Futurist Movement* (Chicago: University of Chicago Press, 1986), pp. 59–61.

11. A. J. A. Morris, "English Radicals and the Hague Conference," *The Journal of Modern History*, September 1971, 367–93.

2

The First World War

We have seen that, in the first years of the twentieth century, the arts and sciences were especially flourishing, European trade and culture dominated the globe, and European peoples could move from country to city, or emigrate, virtually without legal restrictions. For the majority of citizens, economic and political prospects were hopeful and careers were increasingly open to talent, even in countries with very conservative governments and social structures. Why then did Europe apparently stumble helplessly into a suicidal war?

One reason was ignorance on the part of the general population. Europe in 1914 had not yet entered the age of mass communication, of hourly radio and TV bulletins from all points on the globe. The small proportion of persons who read the newspapers knew that there were international tensions over Morocco and in the Balkans, and that England and Germany were engaged in an ominous race to build superbattleships known as "dreadnoughts." But no one imagined an immediate threat of general war because of these tensions; and, in any event, foreign and military policy were the preserves of very limited elites in all governments.

Also, with the exception of a minority of military planners, no one foresaw how devastatingly destructive a new war would be. Napoleon's battles, and those of the victorious Prussian armies in 1866 and 1870, had been fought rapidly, with great devastation to the armies themselves but relatively little damage outside the area of battle. The Crimean War and the American Civil War had both involved tremendous casualties and ghastly suffering of both the armies and the civilian population from disease, hunger, and "scorched earth" tactics. But few Europeans had a physical sense of what war had been like on the distant shores of the Black Sea or in the Atlantic coast states of America. And all general staffs still dreamed in terms of horse-cavalry reconnaissance and swift, decisive battles destroying the bulk of the (trapped or surrounded) enemy.

The tightening bonds of the Triple Alliance and the Triple Entente did indeed substantially increase the danger of general war in the decade before 1914. The alliances, which were intended to maintain a balance of power and to protect each member in case of aggression, also meant that any serious local conflict would become general unless the aggrieved governments' allies counseled restraint and sought compromise rather than confrontation. Unfortunately, as of 1907, the German army had only one strategic plan in case of war with Russia: the Schlieffen Plan (named for the German chief of staff), which required the quick conquest of France in order to free up the forces necessary to face the Russian "hordes" (as they were openly referred to by large sectors of German opinion) in the east. This plan, along with the simultaneously excitable and indecisive temperament of Kaiser William II (and of many of his staff officers), meant that German authorities accepted in advance the high probability that any war on the continent could not be localized.

In the Balkans, the Austrian annexation of Bosnia-Herzegovina in 1908 simultaneously challenged Serbia, Russia, and Turkey. Russia had lost a short war with Japan but was now rearming rapidly, and it was natural to suppose that difficulties in Asia would motivate the Russians to take more interest in the Balkans. In addition, Turkey—long since written off as "the sick man of Europe"—underwent a revolution in 1908 that brought vigorous modernizing officers to power and suggested a potential revival of Turkish authority in the Balkans.

Serbia, Bulgaria, and Romania each had ambitions to expand its territory at the expense of Austria, Turkey, or one another. In the two Balkan wars of 1912 and 1913, they exchanged territories and "compensated" each other like European princes in the seventeenth and eighteenth centuries, with one important difference: whereas in the earlier period many of the ethnic populations did not yet think in terms of nationality and sovereignty, in the Balkans as of 1908 there were Serbs, Slovenes, Croats, Albanians, Montenegrins, Macedonians, Greeks, Bulgarians, and Romanians, all with a developing sense of national uniqueness and overlapping ethnic-linguistic-territorial claims.

In the two Balkan wars, Germany and England combined their good offices to restrain the appetites of the young Balkan kingdoms and to assuage the worries of both Russia and Austria. These two strongest world powers were also seeking, in 1912 and 1913, to reassure each other on naval and colonial issues. They did not reach any formal agreements, but the diplomatic atmosphere among the major powers was less tense during those years than it had been from 1908 to 1911, a fact which left both diplomats and newspaper readers unprepared for the sudden crisis in July 1914.

Western opinion perhaps did not realize how much resentment the Bosnian annexation of 1908 and the territorial settlements imposed by the great powers in 1913 had created in the Balkan countries. In particular, full Habsburg rule in Bosnia had crushed recent Serbian hopes of acquiring that territory, and the new, mostly Muslim kingdom of Albania had been created in 1911 in large measure to keep Serbia from expanding to the Adriatic coast. Secret societies in Serbia were prepared to fight the Habsburg empire through terrorism, and when the heir to the throne, Franz Ferdinand, visited Sarajevo on June 28, 1914, he and his wife were assassinated by a young Serb patriot.

Events now moved rapidly. The Austrian military authorities consulted their German allies, and the latter, on July 6, assured Austria of their full support while at the same time counseling caution. The Austrians knew, however, that Germany would have to support them whether they were cautious or not. In addition, neither Germany nor Austria had ever clearly established the principle of civilian supremacy in government. The military leaders in both countries enjoyed great social prestige and could, if they wished, overrule (or simply ignore) the wishes of the civilian leaders. Although they preferred to have civilian consent if possible, they did not consider themselves bound to obey prime ministers.

For example, the Austrian general staff did accept civilian advice to postpone an ultimatum to Serbia. Due to the fact that the fervently patriotic French president, Raymond Poincaré, was visiting his Russian allies during mid-July, the military waited until Poincaré had embarked for home before delivering, on July 23, an ultimatum which was intended to be unacceptable. (They also included a demand for full acceptance within 48 hours.) But on July 25, the Serbs delivered a reply so conciliatory that even the kaiser, in one of his famous marginal comments, scribbled that now there was no cause for war. Both the Austrian and German military leadership, however, had decided otherwise—the Austrians because they wanted to "crush" the upstart Serbia, the Germans because they foresaw a general war approaching anyway and considered that Germany was better prepared now, relative to France and Russia, than it would be a few years later.

Thus, on July 26 both the British and German fleets concentrated in their home waters. The German Chancellor Bethmann-Hollweg talked hopefully about localizing the crisis, and the British Foreign Minister Sir Edward Grey offered to mediate—a proposal which was not welcome to the military in either Vienna or Berlin. Austria, affirming the Serbian answer to be unsatisfactory (and hoping to forestall European intervention), declared war on Serbia on July 28. Serbia's "big brother" Russia announced the beginnings of mobilization on July 29. Since mobilization was understood to be the last step before war, the Germans demanded that Russia rescind the orders. When this did not occur, Germany mobilized on August 1, and France did likewise.

It was now crucial for Germany to execute the Schlieffen Plan. On August 2 the Germans asked neutral Belgium for permission to cross its territory in order to invade France. The Belgian refusal did not deter the German invasion, which then became the political and moral justification for the English to declare war on August 4. The determination of Austria to destroy Serbian pretensions, and the dependence of Germany on the Schlieffen Plan, meant that, in the space of one short week, the "local" crisis resulting from the assassination of the Archduke Franz Ferdinand had expanded into a general European war.

One further psychological factor may well have contributed to the speed of the fatal explosion. Serious poets and philosophers had for several decades been exalting heroism, sacrifice, and bloodshed as requirements to restore the health of a civilization which—in their armchair views—had become too pacific, too "bourgeois," too dominated by commercial interests. Most ordinary citizens did not read these musings, but the Boy Scout movement in England, the hiking clubs in Germany and Austria, and the "pan-German" and "pan-Slav" organizations transmitted such ideas to their members and also accustomed young males to the wearing of paramilitary uniforms and to a species of voluntarily assumed military discipline.

In addition, many ardently patriotic instructors in the secondary schools of all European countries had helped to create a highly self-righteous mentality that was reflected in the parliamentary and the national debates during those first days of August. Legislators, journalists, clerics, and civilian leaders from all walks of life contributed to the wildly enthusiastic demonstrations that accompanied the declarations of war and the departure of the first troop trains.

The war for which the European nations were psychologically and materially prepared would have lasted about three months. The actual war lasted for fifty-one months, from August 4, 1914, to November 11, 1918. Because of imperialist interests it soon became a world war, with important actions occurring in the Middle East, parts of Africa and Asia, and on all the oceans. But the decisive actions took place on the European continent and in the Atlantic ocean within a few hundred miles of the British isles. For that reason, along with the fact that Europe is the subject of my book, I will discuss the war primarily in European terms, treating first the military outlines and then, in more detail, its multiple effects on civilian life.

Until late 1915, the Central Powers were relatively more successful than the Allies. The Germans occupied most of Belgium by the end of August and came within striking distance of Paris in early September. But the quick triumph of 1870 was not to be repeated. French morale was stronger than it had been in the Franco-Prussian war, and the Russian invasion of East Prussia forced Germany to abandon a crucial feature of the Schlieffen Plan. That is to say, instead of being able to concentrate an overwhelming body of infantry on the right wing which was supposed to sweep west and south of Paris, Germany had to transfer more troops to reinforce its eastern front in late August.

The German army defeated the Russians at Tannenberg (August 26–29) and at the Masurian Lakes (September 10–14), but it was stopped by a French counteroffensive in the Battle of the Marne (September 5–9, 1914). During the following month, the Franco-British and German armies tried unsuccessfully to outflank each other in northern France and Belgium. By the end of October they were facing each other, short of essential supplies, in hastily dug trenches from the North Sea coast to the Swiss border. Those positions were not to vary more than a few miles in one direction or the other until the summer of 1918.

Austria was not successful in its repeated invasions of Serbia, and Italy chose at first to remain neutral rather than join its Triple Alliance allies. However, Turkey closed the Dardanelles (the only entrance to the Black Sea) in August 1914 and joined the Central Powers in November. Germany was ultimately, though not easily, successful against the Russians in Poland, occupying Warsaw on the first anniversary of the war (August 4, 1915). Bulgaria declared war on Serbia in September 1915, and between them Germany, Austria, and Bulgaria now occupied Serbia and its tiny ally Montenegro.

Italy came in on the side of the Allies in May 1915, but neither its early actions nor the costly efforts by Australian and New Zealand expeditionary troops (the "Anzacs") to capture the Dardanelles were successful. During the course of the year, France suffered two million casualties and England one half million in several unsuccessful offensives launched against the German lines in France. The Anzacs withdrew from the Dardanelles on December 20, 1915, and, generally speaking, by the end of 1915 the Central Powers had achieved markedly better results on land than had their enemies.

At sea the British had virtually eliminated German commerce and established a tight blockade of the European coast by the end of 1914. At the same time, the German navy achieved complete control of the Baltic Sea. Under existing international law, it was legal for Britain to prevent the arrival of war materials at German ports, but the British also blockaded food, which brought them into diplomatic conflict with such otherwise friendly neutrals as Holland, Denmark, and Sweden.

Meanwhile the Germans had rushed construction of a new weapon, the submarine, with which they hoped to sink a high proportion of the British and neutral freighters whose cargoes were vital to the survival of the island kingdom. Since submarines were themselves highly vulnerable, their own survival depended on their sinking ships without warning. Thus the German counterblockade was much more obviously brutal than the British surface blockade. During 1915–16, German submarines sank approximately 1,700 ships, including large passenger liners such as the *Lusitania*, but in deference to American public opinion they temporarily gave up "unrestricted" sinkings in May 1916.

From the beginning of 1916 to late 1917, the war appeared to be a stalemate, without decisive gains for either side and without the prospect of technical innovations that might break the deadlock. From February 21 to December 18, 1916, the Germans tried to grind down the French army, which was partially surrounded in the salient of Verdun. Morale was more important than military strategy in the French determination to resist in the unfavorable geographic position. The battle cost 550,000 French and 450,000 German casualties. The British tried to relieve the pressure with the Somme offensive in the summer and fall, at the cost of 800,000 casualties for a gain of one hundred non-strategic square miles.

Nineteen-sixteen also witnessed the war's one important naval action, the Battle of Jutland in the North Sea on May 31. The Germans inflicted slightly more damage than the English, but since they also had the smaller navy they decided to risk no further surface engagements. Romania, encouraged by Russian successes in mid-1916, joined the Allies in September. Austro-German armies quickly occupied Romania by the end of November and also brought the Russians to a halt. Wherever fronts were fluid, the German army continued to show its superiority; and in December, following the formal surrender of Romania, Germany offered a "peace" with substantial German annexations—an offer that was immediately rejected by the Allies.

In 1917, further land battles in France produced enormous casualties in return for insignificant, temporary advances. On February 1, Germany announced the resumption of unrestricted submarine warfare. The admirals and generals knew that this would likely bring the United States into the war, but they gambled on the possibility of starving England into submission before American intervention would become militarily significant—or before the British blockade could starve the civilian population of Germany. The renewed submarine offensive sank a total of some 2,600 merchant ships in 1917, but the British had worked rapidly since early 1915 to develop new defenses, including hydrophones (which could determine the distance and direction of a propeller up to fourteen miles), anti-submarine mines, and the early use of ultrasonic waves to determine, by echo effect, the provenance of similar waves bouncing off the hulls of ships which might be targeted.[1] The admiralty also reluctantly accepted the civilian government's demand to escort ships by convoy. This combination of new defenses drastically reduced the effectiveness of German submarines by late 1917.

*   *   *

Also during 1917, Britain and her Arab allies in the Middle East scored important successes against the Turks, occupying Baghdad in March and Jerusalem in December. But in late October, the Italian effort to push back the Austrians ended in a disastrous retreat at Caporetto (immortalized in Ernest Hemingway's novel *A Farewell to Arms*). Thus, stalemate remained the apparently endless prospect until at least November.

But the last full year of war (November 1917 to November 1918), was characterized by the sudden possibility of German victory and a desperate race against the clock by the military dictatorship of Generals Paul von Hindenburg and Erich Ludendorff. The Russian revolution of March 1917 had weakened Russian military participation, but the provisional government of Alexander Kerensky intended to keep Russia in the war on the Allied side. However, with the Bolshevik revolution of November, Russia withdrew from the fighting and in, March 1918, signed a Draconian peace, the Treaty of Brest-Litovsk, which ceded to Germany control of all of Poland, the Baltic coast, and the Ukraine.

By this time, American troops were arriving in large numbers in France and the convoy system had defeated the submarines. Germany raced to transfer troops and raise food supplies and raw materials from her recently conquered eastern territories. The idea was to break the stalemate in Western Europe and knock France out of the war before American intervention shifted the balance of resources decisively in favor of the Allies. Between March 21 and July 20, the Germans initiated four local offensives and once more came within striking distance of Paris. But when the Allies counterattacked in late July—this time with fresh American troops taking part—the exhausted German army began a rapid, final retreat. The German generals now obliged the nation's civilian government to sue for peace, to ensure that an armistice was signed before Allied troops were able to pursue the German army onto German soil.

What was life like for those who manned the trenches and fought the battles in northern France in the years 1915–1917? Rather than chronicle the many deadlocked local actions, I will focus on the general characteristics of those battles, which bear such names as the Aisne, the Somme, Verdun, Ypres, and Passchendaele. First of all, the defense had immense advantages: deep trenches, barbed-wire entanglements, machine-gun emplacements in concrete pillboxes, and magazine-loading rifles (which greatly increased the speed and accuracy of previous models); plus periscopes, flares, and telephone systems that made it possible to observe the slightest enemy movements across the few hundred yards of "no man's land" between the entrenched armies. Any attempt to pierce the enemy lines had to be preceded by an intensive artillery barrage, the purpose of which was to destroy the enemy wire and at least partially disorganize the trench system, the machine-gun defenses, and the supply roads on which reinforcements would depend. But in fact, such barrages—often lasting a few days—would clearly signal the area in which the attack was to come, and would also reduce to mud the roads which the attackers themselves needed to use in the event they actually pierced the enemy front.

Generally speaking, the men lived in fear and boredom during the long months between infantry battles. They were well-clothed and well-fed, and hygiene was so much superior to that of past wars that, for the first time in history, more men were killed during wartime by bullets than by diseases. Moreover, since the actions were being fought on French soil, the Allies were more motivated than the Germans to initiate local offenses on short fronts in the hope of pushing the enemy back. The Germans, on the other hand, were exploiting foreign soil, and whenever they retreated they took with them whatever cattle, horses, and crops they could commandeer, and frequently booby-trapped public buildings and destroyed local water supplies. No one can understand the vengeful nature of the Treaty of Versailles without remembering the degree of willful destruction practiced by the German army, especially in its final retreat from northern France and Belgium in the fall of 1918.

In the three years I am discussing, anywhere from 20,000 to 50,000 casualties could be suffered in a few days of "over the top" infantry charges in order to capture a few square miles of land. Casualties would lie where they had fallen until the two sides arranged a brief truce for the purpose of collecting their wounded and dead. Newspapers would recount such "successes" for their readers, but the British, French, and German people quickly learned how costly and indecisive were these reported "victories." Despite the horrific casualties, the top English and French generals maintained their attack psychology in the face of all contrary experience. The British commanding general, Douglas Haig, had been a cavalry officer in South Africa and was married to one of the Queen's ladies-in-waiting, and thus became virtually unremovable until the highly intelligent and strong-willed Prime Minister David Lloyd George was able to deprive him of supreme command in late 1917.

The French Marshall, Joseph-Jacques-Césaire Joffre, had earned the gratitude of his countrymen by saving their capital in the Battle of the Marne. But in 1915 and 1916, Joffre ordered numerous local offensives which gained no strategic ground and bled an army that had already suffered more casualties than anyone had imagined possible in August 1914. He was replaced by General Robert-Georges Nivelle, whose own offensives in the spring of 1917 caused even higher casualty rates than those of his predecessor, and whose "over the top" orders led to mutinies of which the Germans remained miraculously ignorant. From mid-1917, Generals Philippe Pétain and Ferdinand Foch restored sanity to the French war effort, rebuilding the morale, supplies, and communications that enabled the French to resist the German offensives of spring 1918 and to cooperate, for the most part amicably, with their British and American allies in the final victorious expulsion of the German army in September 1918.

There were relatively few technological innovations during the stalemate years. Poison gas was introduced by the Germans in April 1915 and occasionally used by each side, but the rapid provision of gas masks to all frontline troops—coupled with the undependability of winds—kept gas from ever being a decisive weapon. The British-invented tank was introduced in small numbers at the Somme in September 1916 and used in larger numbers to breach the German lines in November 1917, but its vulnerable caterpillar treads, lack of speed, and heavy armor, plus roads that had often been converted into mud by friendly artillery fire, prevented the tank from being a major weapon.

The Great War was the last West European war in which horses played a vital role. Both sides depended on them to bring artillery, food, ammunition, mail, and medical supplies from the railheads across the churned-up local roads and to the trenches.[2] In fact, a shortage of horses was one of the reasons why the German invaders had outrun their supply trains by the time they reached the Marne River in September 1914. Unlike horses, airplanes played a limited role. They were important for reconnaissance, and the "dog fights" and occasional spectacular air raids on towns indicated what the future held in store. But aircraft did not materially affect the outcome of the First World War.[3]

A medical novelty of the war was the new phenomenon known as "shell shock": the very serious psychological and behavioral effects produced in men who were exposed to heavy artillery fire for long periods of time. It affected officers more than enlisted men, volunteers more than drafted troops, and men cowering in the trenches more than men moving on open ground. The victims of "shell shock" were thus the men who had the largest emotional commitment to the cause yet at the same time were physically frustrated from doing battle personally. Thousands of them had to be hospitalized for a wide variety of neuroses, nightmares, and phobias, many of them for years after the fighting had ended.[4]

Altogether, the four-year war produced about 10,000,000 battle deaths, 20,000,000 seriously wounded (for decades after the war, one-armed or one-legged veterans sold lottery tickets or cigarettes in the streets of all major European cities), 5,000,000 widows, 9,000,000 orphans, and 10,000,000 refugees.[5] In view of such carnage, any sane observer must ask: What war aims could have justified such sacrifices? Actually, just as no power had been prepared for a long war, none, except perhaps Austria, had a clear idea of its war aims from the start. In Austria's case, its aims were perfectly consistent with its actions and proclamations of the prewar decade. The Austrians insisted that Serbia be prevented from becoming the leader of a group of independent Balkan states, and Austria fought literally to survive as a multinational, multilingual empire being threatened by national independence movements.

Germany took the initiative to save its one reliable ally and to prevent Russia from expanding beyond its existing European borders. The general fear of a Slav empire growing in both population and economic strength was widespread enough to affect both the Social Democrats and the Catholic Center Party, the two groups which might have threatened opposition. At least at the outset, they both accepted the military rationale that Germany was fighting to defend the gates of Europe against potential barbarism. France fought to save its Russian ally and to recover Alsace-Lorraine. Britain fought to restore the independence and neutrality of Belgium and to prevent German domination of the continent. Russia aimed to expand in the Balkans at the expense of Austria and Turkey, but by late 1916 both its government and its army were literally falling apart, and the two revolutions of 1917 left Russia without any clear foreign policy.

Thus, it is at least possible to imagine that if the original aims of the principal combatants—Germany, France, and England—had remained the same, the mediating efforts of President Woodrow Wilson in late 1916, and those of Pope Benedict XV in 1917, might have achieved peace with a less-than-total victory for either side. Such was certainly the hope of both the Wilson administration and the papacy. It was also the hope of the majority of Social Democrats and Catholic Centrists in Germany, of the patiently suffering civilian populations of France, Belgium, and Britain, and of leading British intellectuals such as J. A. Hobson, H. N. Brailsford, George Bernard Shaw, and Bertrand Russell. But those original aims, which had been used to obtain parliamentary consent for the war budgets in 1914 and to create sympathetic attitudes among the neutrals, were destined to change over the course of the war, making a negotiated peace impossible.

Germany's victories in the east in 1915 and 1916 led it to proclaim an "independent" Poland under joint German and Austrian auspices; and when American diplomats sounded out their conditions for peace in late 1916, the Germans made it clear that they expected to retain Alsace-Lorraine and to dominate both Belgium and the Baltic coast. Such expanded aims were necessary in order to restore the flagging enthusiasm of the German public, but of course the sacrifices which fueled these demands also made the French and English all the more determined not to accept continued German rule in Belgium and Alsace.

In addition, the Allies had brought Italy into the war after a process of competitive bidding with her erstwhile Triple Alliance partners. In a secret treaty whose existence came to plague the Versailles peace conference, England and France offered Italy the South Tyrol, the Istrian peninsula, the Dalmatian coast (to be taken from the crumbling Habsburg empire), plus various Mediterranean islands and slices of territory still belonging to the crumbling Ottoman empire— islands and territories that were equally coveted by Greece, whose king was pro-German but whose pro-Allied government had cooperated with the Anglo-French landings in Salonika in the summer of 1915.

Besides incompatible war aims which implied a fight to the finish, the contest also produced deep fissures in the European intellectual and artistic world—fissures which can clearly be seen in the October 1914 literary debate between the great French writer Romain Rolland and the equally prestigious German novelist Thomas Mann.

Rolland was in principle a pacifist who moved to Switzerland at the outbreak of war; he was later to be highly instrumental in facilitating International Red Cross access to prisoner-of-war camps and a regular and efficient exchange of mail between the prisoners and their families. In October 1914, Rolland still hoped for a quick restoration of peace, and in an article significantly entitled "Above the Battle" he appealed to "Slavs hastening to the aid of your race, Englishmen fighting for honor and right, intrepid Belgians who dared to oppose the Teutonic colossus . . . Germans fighting to defend the birthplace and philosophy of Kant against the Cossack avalanche." Phrases of pseudoracial identity abound throughout Rolland's essay, and in his concern with preserving the treasures of art he confessed to preferring Russia to Germany, because (in his opinion) Germany had

given the world no great art since Wagner, whereas Russia had more recently produced Tolstoy and Dostoyevsky. Thus sadly and reluctantly, Rolland concluded, he
felt compelled to prefer the Allied cause to that of Germany.

Rolland's claim to be "above the battle" while taking the Allied side was
answered by an angry and impassioned Thomas Mann, who informed him that "the
present war is a war of *Kultur* vs. Civilization." Civilization he defined by the words
Vernunft, Aufklärung, Sanftheit, Geist (reason, enlightenment, gentleness, spirit);
Kultur he defined as "a sublimation of the daemonic . . . a spiritual organization of
the world . . . above morality, above reason, above science." In a short poem of his
own composition, Mann proclaimed that men deteriorate in peace, that law is a lev-
elling force which only benefits the weak, and that war brings out strength.[6]

Put bluntly, Mann's position was that France represented a tired, overly intellectual civilization which had too long dominated Europe, whereas Germany represented the youthful, energetic, heroic future. Dozens of German professors, scientists, and writers supported such claims to a particular Germanic superiority, and
dozens of British and French intellectuals proudly defended the Enlightenment,
the French Revolution, and Anglo-Saxon liberalism against the Germans. The
sanest voice in those years was that of Bertrand Russell, the British logician and
philosopher who realized immediately that a long war would destroy European civilization. He refused the racist cultural claims to superiority of any given nationality, took an active pacifist position, and went to jail for his pains.[7]

If we turn from the intellectuals to the general civilian population, we can see in
all countries a gradual evolution from naive enthusiasm through self-righteous patriotism to fatalism and war weariness. Thousands of French and Belgian farm families
close to the stationary fronts saw their lands and buildings destroyed, and normal
civilian life to a distance of at least fifty miles from the lines was also disrupted by
military transport, reconnaissance, and alleged or actual espionage. But away from
the front lines, civilians saw little physical action except for occasional air raids.

The big changes took place cumulatively. Food production fell by about one-
third on the continent due to the fact that so many farmers were at the front. By the
end of the war, diet was monotonous everywhere and many areas of the Central
Powers and revolutionary Russia were close to starvation. The armies' needs for
fuel meant that coal, wood, and oil were rationed in all countries, including the
neutrals, and the populations endured the cold of winter with little or no household
heating. Civilian goods of all kinds became scarce and of low quality.

France, Germany, Austria, and (to only a slightly lesser degree) England struggled increasingly with the problem of how to balance the needs of war production
and normal civilian life. Women managed farms and took factory jobs in unprecedented numbers, thereby initiating an unplanned socio-economic revolution in
twentieth-century Europe. By mid-1916, it was clear to all governments that price
controls, rationing, and careful allocation of raw materials were essential. In

France, Eduard Herriot—mayor of Lyons and biographer of Beethoven—became the first of a series of ministers working to coordinate the efforts of businessmen with military planners and civilian administrators. In Germany, the brilliant industrialist Walther Rathenau received full authority to direct the war economy. In both France and Germany, prisoners of war were used as factory and mine workers under minimally humane conditions that reflected the well-intentioned resolutions passed at the Hague conferences of 1899 and 1907.

In England, the principle of civilian supremacy was never in doubt. This is not to say that important generals and admirals did not use all the influence they could muster, by whatever methods. But that influence had to be channeled through the civilian cabinet, and all policy decisions were made by the prime minister and his cabinet representing a parliamentary majority. In France, the military had more direct influence in politics than in England, but the civilian government made the key decisions.

In Germany, the kaiser had constitutional powers much greater than those of the French president or the British king. Military budgets had not required the consent of the Reichstag even before the war, and there was hardly a pretense of parliamentary control once the war began. As of early 1917, Generals Hindenburg and Ludendorff completely dominated the civilian cabinet and the kaiser. Social Democratic and Centrist calls for a negotiated peace led to promises of democratic reform after the war, but could not substantially affect the Hindenburg-Ludendorff dictatorship. In Austria, the military dominated from the start, and it came increasingly under German control as the war lengthened.

One of the interesting aspects of the war in the East, obscured in Western consciousness and later historiography by the drama of the Russian revolutions and the German collapse, was the beginning of the liberation of peoples who had been ruled for centuries by the three dynastic empires: the Romanovs, the Habsburgs, and the Hohenzollerns. Since the late eighteenth century, the national territory of the once-powerful and still very proud Polish people had been divided among the three dynastic empires. Less powerful but equally tenacious small peoples—the Lithuanians, Latvians, and Estonians—had been incorporated into the Russian empire during the eighteenth century; and the Finns had been transferred from Swedish to Russian sovereignty in 1809.[8] Moreover, there was no natural frontier dividing these peoples from the Russians. Indeed, the Russian capital, St. Petersburg, was located in the far northwest corner of the empire, just across a narrow bay from Finland and less than one hundred miles east of the coastal plains of Estonia. What distinguished the Latvians, Estonians, and Finns from their Slavic neighbors were cultural factors: the Lutheran religion; high rates of literacy (as of 1900, well over 90 percent in the Baltic provinces as against an average of 30 percent for the empire as a whole); spoken languages to which they remained obstinately faithful despite all efforts at Russification; many centuries of seaborne commerce and fishing in the Baltic; and many centuries of German, Danish, and Swedish influence. Indeed, until the late nineteenth century, the majority of landlords and urban professional classes in Latvia and Estonia were German and in Finland, Swedish.

During the second half of the nineteenth century, much as in the Austro-Hungarian empire, industrialization created native working classes and greatly reduced the German or Scandinavian share of business and professional activity. Revived national consciousness included the creation of grammars and dictionaries for the vernacular languages, the demand that these be taught in the schools and universities, and general demands for "home rule"—if not for full independence. But the revival of national consciousness also took the form of Slavic nationalism among the Russian minorities in the Baltic provinces, and of course increased the desire of the German communities to retain their distinctive culture (which in any case they had been permitted to do). Thus, the new cultural nationalism created new psychological problems for all the peoples.

Until the late nineteenth century, Russian rule had been relatively benign out of deference to the prosperity created by the hard-working Baltic populations, and thanks to informal power-sharing arrangements with the German landlords and bourgeoisie. But the pressure of competing nationalisms and of the secular "Western" cultures led the Russian government, in the two decades before the First World War, to attempt the linguistic and administrative Russification of Finland and the Baltic provinces. In particular, the Russian revolution of 1905 had been echoed not only among the industrial workers of the area but included estate burnings and lynchings of German landlords in Estonia and Latvia. The savage class war provoked a savage reaction, with the Russian military and local German aristocracy cooperating to repress the Baltic workers and peasants.

As of 1914, Poland, the Baltic provinces, and Finland all had middle-class political organizations advocating some form of home rule, and all had social democratic parties which looked to the German and Austrian social democratic parties for spiritual leadership. Thus, when the war began, the psychological situation in Eastern Europe was very different from that in the West. The Germans were not invading nations with a long history of independence and a culture fully as rich as that of the attackers. They were invading the homelands of peoples with a strong consciousness of their own history and values, who had had both good and bad experiences with German landlords, merchants, and doctors, and who now saw an opportunity to play off Russian power against German power—but who tended, on the whole, to admire German culture and to prefer German rule to Russian if they had the choice.

In Poland, all three ruling powers were anxious to show their goodwill toward their subjects. There were Polish troops in all three imperial armies, and they were seen off at the railway stations with the same sort of enthusiasm as the first French and German contingents leaving Paris and Berlin. Austria-Hungary, far more conscious of national sensibilities than either the Russians or Germans, had established Polish language schools and administration as of 1870. Of the many semipolitical, semiconspiratorial groups active in Poland, the most important were the National Democrats led by Roman Dmowski, and a loose conglomeration of socialist and patriotic forces led by Josef Pilsudski, former editor of one of Poland's first socialist newspapers and a former political exile in Siberia.[9]

A social conservative and a pragmatist, Dmowski noted that Russia was the ally of the Western democracies and took a pro-Allied stance. He hoped that Russia could be induced to concede real national autonomy and that the Allies, after defeating the Central Powers in Poland, would aid his party in negotiations with Russia. But England and France were anxious not to ruffle the feathers of imperial Russia, and so they treated Polish affairs as an internal Russian matter during the years 1914–1916 (the last years that a coherent imperial government still existed in Russia).

Pilsudski, having been exiled in Siberia and having witnessed the ferocious repression of the Left after the revolution of 1905, decided that only well-organized military force could destroy the Russian autocracy, which he saw as the great enemy of Polish liberty. He was also better disposed than Dmowski toward the large Ukrainian, Lithuanian, and Jewish minorities which shared the soil of Poland. He viewed the Austrians as the least obnoxious of the three occupying powers. As of 1908, he began to organize and train his "Polish Legions" (named in memory of the units that had fought on Napoleon's side a century earlier) in the Carpathian mountains. He was named a brigadier general by the Austrians, in whose ranks his legions fought during the years 1914–1916.

The war in the East never became stalemated as it did in the West. The Russian invasion of East Prussia in August 1914 had not only been repulsed by the Germans, but the latter had by late 1915 occupied virtually all Poland, plus Lithuania and part of Latvia. The Russians enjoyed a brief success in 1916 against the Austrian army—much less well trained and disciplined than that of Germany—but by the end of 1916 the German army, and Austrian divisions interlarded with German troops, completely dominated the historic territory that the Polish patriots hoped somehow to liberate.

Also during that triumphal year 1916, the Germans—or rather the German military, with their complete domination of the kaiser—were planning in some form either to establish satellite states or annex most of the Polish, Lithuanian, and west Latvian territories (Courland) which they had been administering since the summer of 1915. With the kaiser's blessing, and without consulting the Reichstag, the military began to distribute confiscated Lithuanian farmlands to German settlers. The Center and Social Democratic parties, acutely worried about the moral isolation of imperial Germany (of which they had become aware through their Swedish contacts), advocated independence rather than annexation; but they were politically powerless.

The March revolution then disorganized the Russian army sufficiently so that the Germans were able, with relative ease, to occupy the port of Riga, Latvia north of the Daugava river, and the whole of Estonia. Seeing the opportunity to detach all the Baltic territories and Finland from a greatly weakened Russia, Germany also trained and used a few thousand Baltic and Finnish volunteers, recruited from among those socially conservative classes who admired German economic efficiency and had educated their sons in German universities.

The Germans also considered the possibility of establishing local pro-German governments in the East. They authorized an Estonian National Council in the spring of 1917 and Estonian armed units in July. They allowed the Lithuanian National Association to discuss a future constitution in September, and accepted the Lithuanian declaration of independence in February 1918 (by which date the Bolsheviks had also offered independence). And, with remarkable political intelligence, the Germans offered the military governorship of Poland to General Pilsudski, whose surprising refusal to become their glorified satrap led to his being put under house arrest (though in conditions much pleasanter than those of Siberia).

The Western allies were anxious to keep Russia in the war, and the provisional government was anxious to secure their economic aid for the eventual reconstruction of postwar Russia. But the best cadres of the Russian army had been destroyed by late 1916, the countryside was full of deserters, the civil administration was chaotic or absent, and the general population had long since lost the patriotic enthusiasm of late 1914. The provisional government was unable to provide coherent political or military leadership, and a wide variety of revolutionary "Soviets" (local municipal and factory councils) were demanding "socialist" solutions in the main cities.

In these circumstances, the principal Bolshevik leader, Vladimir Lenin, suddenly realized that the Swiss exile which he had imagined would last indefinitely— if not for his entire lifetime—might come to a glorious end, and that his well-organized, tightly disciplined revolutionary "vanguard" might seize power and initiate the world socialist revolution. The Germans saw it as clearly in their interest to increase the chaos in Russia, and they did not remotely suppose that Lenin and his followers could establish a stable government. They provided a sealed train which carried Lenin from Switzerland to St. Petersburg in the spring of 1917.

The Bolsheviks won the temporary support of the Russian population with the slogan "peace, bread, land to the people." They also promised the right of self-determination to the constituent peoples of the Russian empire. When they seized power in November 1917, "peace" and "self-determination" were the parts of their program on which they could act immediately. The Bolsheviks announced Russian withdrawal from the "imperialist" war, and in the ensuing three months they recognized the right to independence of Finland, the Baltic countries, Poland, the Ukraine, and Transcaucasia. Simultaneously they were negotiating peace at the city of Brest-Litovsk, headquarters of the German Eastern armies. The Bolsheviks were of course the incomparably weaker party in terms of existing power, and they had announced their commitment to peace before the bargaining began. Still, the Germans were surprised by the cheeky proposal of a peace without indemnities and annexations—something they had already refused to such respectable inter-locutors as President Wilson and Pope Benedict XV. Who were these scruffy intel-lectuals (Leon Trotsky and Lev Kamenev among the more prominent) whose coup d'état had been made possible only by German money and German transport? Quite possibly the Germans were unaware of the force of world revolutionary hopes—hopes, nevertheless, which Lenin had to persuade his own closest col-leagues to forego temporarily at the end of 1917.

At the same time the Germans were truly desperate to obtain grain and raw materials from the disintegrating empire, and to obtain a dependable truce that would allow them to transfer the bulk of their troops to France. On the one hand, they were drunk with the giddy prospect of a new Eastern empire of their own; on the other, the German and Austro-Hungarian populations were near starvation, Austrian military discipline depended entirely on the presence of German cadres, and the Americans were training millions of fresh troops whose deployment in a matter of months would make German victory impossible on the crucial Western front.

Within the Bolshevik leadership, Lenin was struggling to convince his colleagues that the Draconian conditions laid down by the Germans would have to be accepted. The most important thing was to establish a base for the later world revolution. The Germans were not preventing the Bolsheviks from consolidating their power in the heartland of Russia, and the Bolsheviks would be swept away if they did not make good on their promise of peace. The Bolsheviks' chief strategist, Leon Trotsky, invented the disingenuous formula "no peace, no war." The Germans were not impressed, and decided to resume their march eastward. During February 1918 they occupied most of the Ukraine, including the main cities of Kiev, Kharkov, and Rostov.[10]

On March 3 the Bolsheviks signed the Treaty of Brest-Litovsk. By its terms they surrendered all claims to Finland, the Baltic provinces, the Ukraine, and much of the Caucasus. German industry was to enjoy a kind of extraterritorial status in Russia itself, including non-payment of tariffs, subsidized transport, use of German currency, unrestricted repatriation of profits, and so forth. Moreover, the lands detached from Russia were three times the size of Germany itself. They included one-quarter of Russia's total population and industry and three-quarters of her known coal and iron reserves.

Once the peace with Russia was concluded, the available grain and troops were rushed westward, and the Germans launched their desperate Western offen-sive on March 21—a gamble that seemed potentially successful until the month of July. Meanwhile the conservative political forces in Lithuania, Latvia, Estonia, and Finland all negotiated to acquire princely cousins of the kaiser as constitutional monarchs, thereby guaranteeing social stability and future German friendship toward their newly independent states.

Finnish politics during 1917 and 1918 manifested a particularly complex and ultimately successful balancing act between imperial (later Bolshevik) Russia, imperial Germany, and the Western allies. When the March revolution clearly reduced the weight of Russia but also threatened an unpredictable future, the German government privately assured Prime Minister Pehr Evind Svinhufvud that Finnish independence would be in the interest of Germany (though they gave no guarantees). In July the Germans decided to send substantial armaments to Finland, the arrival of which coincided with the first weeks of the Bolshevik revolution and also with the return of General Gustav Mannerheim. Mannerheim was Finland's leading military figure, a general of the imperial Russian army, married to the daughter of a Russian general, and recipient also on this occasion of a sealed train to carry him from the Ukraine to Helsinki.

At this moment Svinhufvud and most conservatives assumed that German troops would be necessary to drive the Russian occupying forces out of Finland. The Social Democrats wanted to negotiate with the Bolsheviks, who were already proclaiming their readiness to accept Finnish independence. General Mannerheim welcomed German arms, but preferred not to have German troops possibly complicating the achievement of independence.

On December 31 Svinhufvud conferred with Lenin, and on January 4 the Soviet government recognized Finnish independence—a move which was later gratefully remembered by Finnish conservatives as well as by the entire Left. But as it happened, revolutionary Finnish militia occupied Helsinki on January 28, and a three-month civil war opposed the Bolshevik sympathizers to the conservative and constitutional democratic forces led by Mannerheim. Faced with potential communist revolution, Mannerheim agreed to the German occupation of the Aaland Islands, and on April 6, 1918, welcomed the Baltic division of the German army to "liberated" Helsinki, where their order and discipline made a good impression on the much-frightened middle classes.

Still thinking that the Germans were going to win the war, the conservatives negotiated with Prince Friedrich Karl of Hesse as their favored candidate for the eventual throne. The Germans confirmed the Finnish choice on October 9—the very day on which Hindenburg and Ludendorff ordered the civilian government to sue for peace. A month later the kaiser fled to Holland, Germany surrendered, and the Finnish provisional government appealed successfully to the victorious Allies to confirm the existence of the independent republic of Finland.

The defeat of the Germans in the West caught the Polish, Baltic, and Finnish leaders by surprise, but just as the Eastern front had never been as deadlocked as the Western, so the attitude of the victorious Allies was not as categorical toward Germany in the East as it was in the West. The armistice specified that German troops were to remain in the Baltic provinces to help maintain "order"—i.e., protect the new regimes against possible Bolshevik action. At the last minute, when vacating Warsaw, the Germans released Pilsudski and put him in charge of the city, a move that was accepted by the Allies and which made possible a minimally unified Polish government in the first years of independence.

Thus, the ups and downs of the war in the East, the political savvy of the Baltic and Finnish independence leaders, the anti-imperialist self-determination doctrine of the Bolsheviks and their imperative need for peace, and the (at least at times) intelligent wartime administration of the Germans, followed by their complete military defeat—all combined to permit the beginnings of political independence for peoples who had had to accept Romanov or Hohenzollern imperial rule for centuries past.

ENDNOTES

1. Roy M. MacLeod and E. K. Andrews, "Scientific Advice in the War at Sea," *The Journal of Contemporary History*, 1971, no. 2, 3–41.

2. John Singleton, "Britain's Military Use of Horses, 1914–1918," *Past and Present*, May 1993, 178–203.

3. Phillippe Bernard, "Stratégie aérienne pendant la premiére guerre mondiale," *Revue d'historie moderne et contemporaine*, July 1969, 350–74.

4. Norman Felton, *Shellshock and its Aftermath* (London, 1926).

5. Numerical totals from Brian Bond, *War and Society in Europe, 1870–1970* (New York: St. Martin's Press, 1983), p. 100.

6. Romain Rolland, *Above the Battle* (Geneva, 1914), includes English versions of both his and Mann's essays, together with citations of other leading intellectuals on both sides in the first days of the war. See also L. W. Fuller, "German Intellectuals and the War of 1914," *The Journal of Modern History*, June 1942, 145–60.

7. Bertrand Russell, *Justice in Wartime* (London, 1917, reprint 1971 by the Bertrand Russell Peace Foundation).

8. My accounts of the Baltic provinces depend principally on John Hiden and Patrick Salmon, *The Baltic Nations and Europe* (London: Longmans, 1991); and of Finland, on Marvin Rintala, *Three Generations, The Extreme Right Wing in Finnish Politics* (The Hague: Mouton, 1962). Despite the title, Rintala gives full information about all the political groups in early-twentieth-century Finland.

9. On Polish politics, and the roles of Dmowski and Pilsudski, I have depended principally on Norman Davies, *God's Playground: A History of Poland* (New York: Columbia University Press, 1982), v. II, chapter 18 and *passim*; and on Waclaw Jedrzejewicz, *Pilsudski* (New York: Hippocrene Books, 1982).

10. Richard Pipes, *The Russian Revolution* (New York: Vintage Books, 1991), pp. 208–40, 572–95, and *passim*.

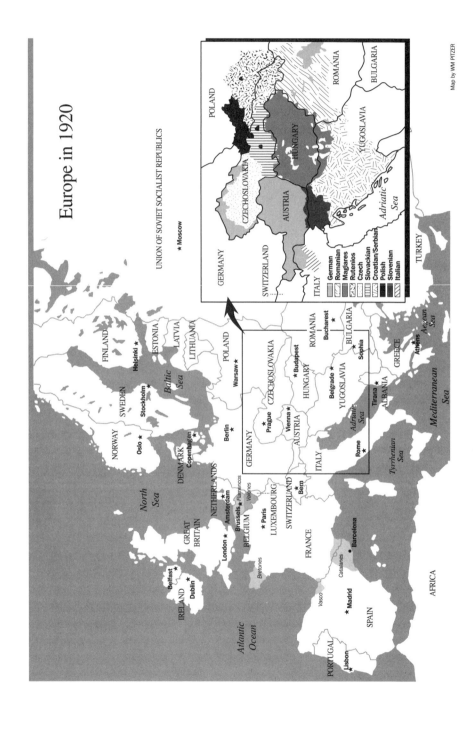

Europe in 1920

UNION OF SOVIET SOCIALIST REPUBLICS

★ Moscow

Map by WM PITZER

GERMANY

SWITZERLAND

ITALY

POLAND

CZECHOSLOVAKIA

AUSTRIA

HUNGARY

YUGOSLAVIA

ROMANIA

BULGARIA

Adriatic Sea

German
Romanian
Magiares
Rutenios
Czech
Slovackian
Croatian/Serbian
Polish
Slovenian
Italian

NORWAY

SWEDEN

FINLAND

ESTONIA

LATVIA

LITHUANIA

Baltic Sea

Helsinki ★

Stockholm ★

Oslo ★

Copenhagen ★

DENMARK

Berlin ★

POLAND

Warsaw ★

GERMANY

NETHERLANDS

Amsterdam ★

Flamencos

Valones

Brussels ★

BELGIUM

LUXEMBOURG

London ★

GREAT BRITAIN

Belfast ★

Dublin ★

IRELAND

North Sea

Bretones

Atlantic Ocean

Vasco

Catalanes

★ Madrid

SPAIN

Barcelona ●

PORTUGAL

Lisbon ★

Paris ★

FRANCE

SWITZERLAND

Bern ★

Prague ★

CZECHOSLOVAKIA

Vienna ★

AUSTRIA

HUNGARY

Budapest ★

Rome ★

ITALY

Adriatic Sea

Tyrrhenian Sea

YUGOSLAVIA

Belgrade ★

Tirana ★

ALBANIA

Sophia ●

BULGARIA

ROMANIA

Bucharest ★

GREECE

Athens ★

Aegean Sea

Mediterranean Sea

TURKEY

AFRICA

3

Uncertain Peace and Recovery

In the West, the victory of the Allied powers—Great Britain, France, and the United States—was the victory of nations that shared the institutions of capitalism, political liberty, and civilian supremacy in government. This victory came at a price, however: England, France, and Belgium experienced sensations of sheer physical exhaustion and powerful desires for the return of "normalcy," understood as a resumption of the peaceful pursuits and the economic progress which had been characteristic of the prewar decades.

The mood was much the same among their neutral neighbors. Thus while Switzerland, Spain, Holland, Denmark, Norway, and Sweden had all suffered somewhat from the blockade and from the four-year interruption of international trade, their populations were predominantly pleased with the military victory of nations whose general ideals and institutions they shared. There were shortages of food and consumer goods to be made up; roads, harbors, and bridges to be repaired; and a virulent epidemic of influenza to be coped with. Nevertheless, from Gibraltar to Spitzbergen and from England to Switzerland, it was not unreasonable to anticipate the rapid restoration of normal civilian life.

But east of Switzerland and Italy there was no normalcy to restore. Imperial Russia had been replaced by a Bolshevik government that controlled the bulk of central Russia, but was also fighting a multi-front civil war against the military forces of the old regime as well as various nationalist groups seeking to free themselves entirely from Russian sovereignty. In Germany the kaiser had abdicated and a republic had been proclaimed, but the great majority of the middle classes, the peasants, the military, the professionals, and the civil servants had remained loyal to the empire until the moment of collapse, so that there was nothing resembling unanimous support for the nascent republic.

In all the Central and East European territories which had been ruled by the three defunct empires, national committees of varying ideology and authority were establishing their claims to create new republics in Poland, Lithuania, Latvia, Estonia, and Finland to the north, and in Czechoslovakia, Austria, and Hungary in the traditional Habsburg lands. In the Balkans, the existing kingdoms of Romania, Bulgaria, and Greece were completely dependent upon the intentions of the Allies, and representatives of Slovene, Croat, Montenegrin, and Macedonian communities were negotiating to transform the existing kingdom of Serbia into the multinational kingdom of Yugoslavia.

In these circumstances the subject peoples of Central and Eastern Europe and the Balkan peninsula took very seriously the text of the "Fourteen Points" that Woodrow Wilson had proposed on January 8, 1918, as the basis for future world peace. Their representatives of course knew that confidential discussions were taking place within the Allied camp and that secret agreements had already been made; also that the United States had only entered the war eight months before the president's speech. Nevertheless, it was universally recognized that without the contribution of the United States it would have been impossible for France and England alone to defeat Germany, and that consequently the voice of America would be fully equal to that of the original Western powers.

Particularly relevant for the stateless peoples were Points X, XI, and XIII of Wilson's document. Point X declared that "the peoples of Austria-Hungary, whose place among the nations we wish to see safeguarded and assured, should be accorded the freest opportunity of autonomous development." The phrase "whose place among the nations" did not in itself guarantee existence as a sovereign state, but it most certainly implied self-government and international recognition in some form.

Point XIII called for "an independent Polish state . . . which should include the territories inhabited by indisputably Polish populations, which should be assured a free and secure access to the sea. . . ." In this case Wilson was unmistakably proposing full statehood. Also, since there was no way to provide access to the sea without including some German-populated territory, he was making it clear that if there were a conflict between ethnic lines and economic viability, the latter interest would prevail. Similarly, in Point XI, which dealt with Balkan affairs, Serbia was to be "accorded free and secure access to the sea." This latter statement was crucial for those who were planning to establish a new South Slav kingdom under the existing Serbian dynasty; it was also a potential obstacle for the Italians, who felt that the secret agreements they negotiated with the Allies had given them a clear claim to the Adriatic coastal territories of the Habsburg empire.

All the peoples of the Habsburg empire, plus a few other stateless nationalities such as the Irish and the Catalans, sent delegations to the Versailles conference in the hope of achieving national independence. But the overwhelming preoccupation of the conference during the first six months of 1919 was to impose peace upon a defeated Germany. The Fourteen Points said nothing about Germany, and in the interest of hastening a German surrender, the Allied authorities allowed the German people to hope that Wilsonian principles would be applied to their future as well. But in fact, the victors were to treat Germany as a defeated enemy who was to be kept militarily impotent and would be required to pay the immense costs of the recently terminated war.

The decisions regarding Germany were made by the American President Woodrow Wilson, the British Prime Minister David Lloyd George, and the French Prime Minister Georges Clemenceau, with the consent (but only minor participation) of the Italian Prime Minister Vittorio Orlando. No German delegates were invited to take part in the discussions. Similarly, there had been some informal contact with the Bolsheviks, but no real prospect of including them. The Communist government had repudiated all tsarist debts and had greatly embarrassed the Allies by publishing the many secret treaties whose contradictory promises would soon poison relations among the victors. Bolshevik revolutionary propaganda was of course anathema to all the Western capitalist governments, and the Allies were supporting the anti-communist forces in the Russian civil war. Thus all decisions concerning Germany depended upon the interaction between the three Allied leaders and their close advisors.

Wilson was both an idealist and an experienced, hard-headed politician. The political side of him knew very well that unrestricted submarine warfare, the general Anglo-Saxon cultural heritage of North America, and the enshrined memories of French aid to the revolutionary armies of George Washington all meant that American opinion would be overwhelmingly favorable to England and France as against Germany. On the other hand, Wilson's idealistic side was determined to establish a new League of Nations, to create a world of "open covenants of peace, openly arrived at" (Point I of the Fourteen Points), to reduce the armaments of all nations "to the lowest point consistent with domestic safety" (Point IV), and to make possible self-government and a sense of international justice, not only for all the European peoples in the immediate future, but also—in a matter of decades— for all the non-European peoples presently under colonial rule. Like many people of high ideals, Wilson was utterly convinced of the purity of his own motives, and he irritated others by his inability to hide his sense of moral superiority.

Lloyd George represented an England that had not been threatened so severely since the time of Napoleon. He had just won re-election with such slogans as "Hang the Kaiser" (though he and his ministers were in fact glad that the kaiser had fled to Holland, a country from which he could not be legally extradited), and with demands that Germany be "squeezed till the pips squeak." As for the aged, immensely dignified, and immensely pessimistic Clemenceau, he represented a country that had been twice occupied by German armies during his lifetime, a country one-tenth of whose territory had been reduced to ruins by four years of artillery bombardments and several months of further destruction by the retreating Germans, a country whose birthrate and economic resources would be totally inadequate if Germany were ever again to be in a position to invade. Thus, although there were moments of bitter conflict among the three statesmen, between the Franco-British determination that Germany should literally pay the total costs of the long war and the Wilsonian moral revulsion against German militarism, there was no doubt that a strongly punitive peace would be imposed upon Germany.

By the Treaty of Versailles, signed on June 28, 1919 (the fifth anniversary of the assassination of the Archduke Franz Ferdinand in Sarajevo), Germany gave up all its African colonies, its Pacific Islands, and its commercial/military concessions in China. Germany also renounced the many territorial and commercial concessions made by Russia in the March 1918 Treaty of Brest-Litovsk. Alsace-Lorraine was restored to France, and a Polish "corridor" was created out of territories where incontestably the majority of inhabitants considered themselves German. The historic border between Germany and the Habsburg empire now became the border between Germany and the new republic of Czechoslovakia. The mixed German-Czech population in the so-called Sudetenland was not consulted as to its preferences.

However, the victors wisely did not try to decide all territorial questions in six months. Both Lloyd George and Wilson were anxious to avoid the creation of a permanently resentful Germany, and the American president saw an opportunity to apply the principle of self-determination once the main French and Polish demands had been satisfied. In February and March of 1920, internationally supervised plebiscites divided the mixed-population area of Schleswig peacefully between Denmark and Germany. And in the spring of 1921, less amicable plebiscites—albeit honestly conducted and internationally supervised—divided Upper Silesia between Germany and Poland.

The city of Danzig, which constituted Poland's main port on the Baltic, was principally German in terms of both its population and existing commercial facilities. In 1920 it became a Free City under the new League of Nations, with a high commissioner to arbitrate disputes between Polish and German interests. The league also supervised plebiscites in 1920 in which the majority of the citizens of Marienwerder and Allenstein voted to belong to East Prussia rather than to Poland.

France also demanded the annexation of the Saar on grounds that its coal mines would be legitimate compensation for the destruction of French mines during the war. However, the great majority of the region's population was German. Hence the Allies decided to cede the mines to France and to have the territory itself be administered by the League of Nations for fifteen years, at the end of which time the inhabitants would vote on whether they wished French, German, or continued league sovereignty.

The Danzig and Saar arrangements under the League of Nations, and the successful plebiscites in Schleswig, Silesia, Marienweder, and Allenstein, show that the Allies were ready to experiment with internationalist, consensual solutions to both national and economic issues. Their attitude was partly a matter of common sense, partly an opportunity to give a practical function to the new League of Nations. If Hitler had not come to power in 1933 openly determined to destroy all the peace treaties, it is quite possible that those arrangements could have been modified by consent and the wounds of the punitive peace thereby healed. History is of course a matter of factual sequences, not of hypotheses, but in a world which must learn to live at peace or destroy itself, the examples discussed in this chapter are worth remembering.

Thus the determination of the frontiers between Germany and its neighbors was not really arbitrary except for the Polish corridor and the northern border of Czechoslovakia. On the other hand, the attempted financial settlement—in particular the total of cash reparations demanded—was a case of economic insanity, well recognized at the time but apparently impossible to avoid after the French and British governments had repeatedly promised their peoples that Germany would be forced to pay for the entire war.

The Versailles treaty did not set a figure for reparations, and in late 1919 the most inflamed politicians were invoking the sum of sixty-four billion dollars, intended to cover not only the direct damage to French and Belgian soil and productive facilities, but also the full armaments costs of the Allies, the estimated cost of pensions for war widows and veterans, and so forth. By April 1921 they had reduced the total to thirty-two billion dollars, and had also decided that Germany would be capable of paying a maximum of five hundred million dollars in annual installments.

Five hundred million dollars would total about 1.6 percent of thirty-two billion —in other words, less than the value of normal interest payments, say 4 to 5 percent on the principal. This meant that even if the Germans paid the installments faithfully, the total theoretical size of their debt would continue to increase. In the face of such absurdity, the Germans dragged their heels about delivering even the amounts they could pay. In 1923, France occupied part of the industrial Ruhr in order to force compliance—a move which cost them more than the reparations they were enabled forcibly to collect. Germany suffered a completely unprecedented hyperinflation, and an international conference was called to scale down the 1921 reparations figures. In 1924 the Dawes Plan, and in 1929 the Young Plan (named for their principal American negotiators), drastically reduced the total indebtedness and provided Germany with American loans whose total was greater than the sums paid in reparations until 1931, at which time the whole system broke down.

Between 1919 and 1924, a number of further treaties granted an unprecedented degree of self-rule to the former subjects of the dynastic empires. Poland, Czechoslovakia, Romania, Yugoslavia, and the new Baltic republics all had their borders drawn along national lines and their dignity recognized by membership in the League of Nations. With the important exception of the Baltic states, they also had their security guaranteed by mutual-defense treaties with France, which in the early 1920s was the dominant military power on the continent.

All these states, seeking to emulate the West, drew up parliamentary democratic constitutions and held free elections. But they also erected mutual tariff barriers in what had been a virtual free-trade area under the Habsburgs or the Romanovs. They all had territorial disagreements with their neighbors—disagreements that often seemed incomprehensible to their Western protectors and which led in several cases to military conflicts near the frontiers. Likewise, they all had national minorities within their borders, and Jews against whom prejudice and occasional violence were endemic. There were substantial minorities of Ukrainians, Germans, and Lithuanians in Poland; of Hungarians in Czechoslovakia, Romania, and Yugoslavia; of Bulgarians in Romania and Yugoslavia; of Slovenes and Austrians in Italy; of Albanians in Yugoslavia; of Macedonians in Yugoslavia, Bulgaria, and Greece; of Greeks in Turkey; and of Turks in Greece and Bulgaria. The peace treaties all contained clauses protecting these minorities, but such clauses were much resented since they had not been written into the constitutions of Belgium, France, and Great Britain, nations in which national and religious prejudice were not unknown.

Nevertheless, the Covenant of the League of Nations, and the minorities clauses in the various peace treaties, represented positive steps in the long effort to establish social justice on an international basis. They would have been inconceivable without the initiative of Wilson and the acknowledgment by all the Allied powers that world peace depended upon justice, not revenge. Wilson himself knew very little about the ethnic and national makeup of the Europe he was remolding, but there are moments in history when great principles must find a bold (if fallible) spokesman. During 1919, in the windows of farm cottages on both sides of the armistice lines, the peasants lit candles and said prayers for "Meester Veelson." They worshiped what he stood for, if not everything that he did.

Thus, in the immediate postwar years from 1919 to 1924, Central-Eastern Europe and the Balkans witnessed the establishment of a number of new states whose borders had been drawn mostly according to the principles of national self-determination, with the preference in mixed areas being given to the former subject nationalities as against the Germans, Austrians, and Hungarians. Because of the irreversible mixture of peoples in the area, all these states perforce included new national minorities, and all of them pledged to protect the rights of those minorities as well as the rights of the Jews. All these states had capitalist economies and parliamentary constitutions, and all of them looked to the West for military security and mutually prosperous commercial relations.

THE RUSSIAN REVOLUTION

Contemporary historical developments in the former Russian empire were entirely different from those taking place under Wilsonian and Allied auspices in Central-Eastern Europe. In November 1917, the Bolshevik seizure of power effectively separated Russia from capitalist Europe and inaugurated the most thoroughgoing political and social transformation attempted anywhere in Europe since the French Revolution of 1789. Nothing about European history since 1917 can be understood without reference to the Russian Revolution, and so it is essential at this point to consider the background of that cataclysmic event.

In the decades preceding the Great War, the Russian empire was a congeries of overwhelmingly peasant and nomadic peoples loosely held together by dynastic loyalty to the tsar, by the Russian Orthodox Church in the European portions of the empire, and by a series of military and administrative posts established across the northern Eurasian continent (some one-seventh of the land surface of the planet earth) during the course of the eighteenth and nineteenth centuries. The empire was characterized by immense distances and a sparse population, which made it possible for very different cultures to coexist peacefully by ignoring each other most of the time. In the Caucasus mountains, and across central Asia and Siberia, the variety of nationalities, economic subcultures, religions, and languages was infinitely greater than the differences in Europe west of Russia.

The European West, because its territories are relatively small and its populations relatively homogeneous, has never fully appreciated the *human* breadth of the Russian (and earlier of the Spanish and Portuguese) empires. The Russians were not racist like the Anglo-Saxon and North European settlers of America, who eliminated the native Indians without ever considering the possibility of their peaceable assimilation into a loose federation of admittedly very distinct technical levels of culture. The Russians intermarried wherever they settled, and for all the backwardness of the imperial autocracy, its soldiers and administrators must have had human qualities which elicited a modicum of consent from very disparate peoples.

As of 1900, European-style culture in Russia—including urban areas with paved central squares, stone churches and town halls, commercial buildings and organized markets—was limited to the western border regions, the main river valleys, and the cities of St. Petersburg, Moscow, Kiev, and Odessa. Also as of 1900, industrial capitalism was developing in the main cities, and the peasants—who had been emancipated from serfdom in 1861—were gradually being transformed into a class of European-style farmers who either owned their land or held it on sharecropping leases.

Two characteristics of the late-nineteenth-century situation were especially germane to the future of Russia. One was that, in spite of economic backwardness and autocratic government, the best of Russian fine arts, literature, music, higher education, and sciences were fully equal to the best of the corresponding European accomplishments. The other was that the educated classes were profoundly divided on the question of Russia's future in a world of railways, international commerce, telegraphic communication, and the constantly increasing interdependence of nations on a worldwide scale.

Should Russia do everything possible to adopt all the methods and techniques of Western capitalism, plus parliamentary government and increasingly secular culture? Or were there aspects of the Orthodox religion and of a pre-capitalist peasant culture which were morally superior to the competitive secular West, and which should be treasured as basic ingredients of the Russian future? Those who held the first position were known as "Westernizers," and those who held the second were known as "Slavophiles."

The parties that created the Russian revolutions—especially the second, "Bolshevik" revolution—were mostly (but not entirely) Westernizers. When the tsar abdicated in March 1917, the Constitutional Democrats ("Cadets") hoped to reorganize Russia as a parliamentary monarchy or republic on the model of England or France. The largest Left party, the Socialist Revolutionaries, were Westernizers in the sense that they accepted the development of industrial capitalism, but they were Slavophiles in the sense that they exalted the spiritual qualities of the *mir*, the villages which exercised *collective* responsibility for peasant agriculture. They also were the heirs of "The People's Will," the idealistic student groups who, in the 1870s, had gone to live among the peasants as teachers and artisans, who had also assassinated Tsar Alexander II, and who by 1914 had added well over one hundred high government officials and civil servants to the list of liquidated "oppressors."

The Social Democratic Party, divided tactically and personally into two competing wings, hoped that the world war would be followed by a world socialist revolution, in which England and Germany would play the leading roles and in which Russia would collaborate to the best of its possibilities. The larger wing of the party favored Western parliamentary democracy and maintained friendly relations with the German Social Democrats, and with various Polish and Jewish trade-union and socialist groups in Poland. The minority wing despised parliamentary democracy and were themselves partly heirs to the secretive, violent traditions of the People's Will.

As of 1915–16, with the Germans triumphant in Eastern Europe, the Russian Social Democrats were working in underground cells or living in European exile without any expectation that the revolution might occur in the proximate future. But the tsar's abdication without resistance—and the extraordinary total collapse of the existing state—offered a sudden opportunity. It was in these circumstances, from March to November of 1917 (I use the Western rather than the Russian Orthodox calendar), that the theoretical certainty and organizing genius of

Vladimir Ilych Lenin, together with the Dantonian "audacity" of Leon Trotsky, literally made history.

Lenin had always insisted on being very much "first among equals" in the leadership of his faction within the Social Democratic Party. One of his more revealing tactical victories was to attach the name "Bolsheviks" (majority) to his group. He adopted the name after a particular vote in which they had indeed won the majority, but throughout most of the decade before the revolution, as well as during the spring and summer of 1917, the Bolsheviks were actually less numerous than their rivals, whom they left with the label "Mensheviks" (minority).

Lenin was a man who exuded certainty—at least in all relations with his close associates. He saw the collapse of Tsarism as a unique opportunity to launch a *world* socialist revolution using "backward" Russia as a springboard, a first territorial base. But he was fully confident that the war would also lead to the collapse of the other capitalist governments, with the revolution then spreading to the most industrialized countries, the ones whose economic maturity would make them the spearhead of world revolution, namely Germany and England.

He was also a man who had no qualms about using the resources of the existing system to advance the interests of the revolution. "Radical chic" millionaires had long been among the contributors to the Lenin-controlled Bolshevik treasury and press. His partisans engaged in illegal currency transactions and on several occasions even robbed banks (once under the leadership of the future "Father of Peoples," Joseph Stalin). Indeed, at the start of the war in August 1914, Lenin and his close associate Grigory Zinoviev were technically aliens in the Austrian sector of Poland; but through the good offices of the Austrian police, they were enabled to leave for neutral Switzerland.

Sympathizers living in Germany financed the publication in Stockholm of several works of Lenin and Bukharin, which were then smuggled into Russia. When the tsarist regime collapsed and the Bolshevik press began to call for a separate peace, the Germans found it worthwhile to supply a special train to carry Lenin and several associates from Switzerland to the Baltic coast, and thence by ferry to Sweden. The provisional government itself provided the entry visas for both Lenin and Trotsky, the latter returning from a period of journalistic activity in Canada and the United States.[1]

In the months from March to November the Russian provisional government, headed by the Left Socialist Revolutionary leader Alexander Kerensky, pledged to keep Russia in the war on the side of the Allies. Kerensky's government also planned to endow Russia with a democratic constitution, and tried to maintain good relations with an officer corps that was much more conservative and monarchist than the Duma (legislative) majority. The democratic Left, composed of the Socialist Revolutionary Party (SR's) and the Mensheviks, also solicited the cooperation of the Bolsheviks.

But Lenin had a clear program of his own, worked out in April, at the time of his return from Switzerland to Petrograd. (The capital had dropped the "St." from its name in 1914 and would be called Petrograd until 1924, when it was renamed Leningrad in honor of the recently deceased maximum Bolshevik leader. After the demise of the Soviet Union in 1991, it reassumed its historic name of St. Petersburg.) Lenin's program was summed up in the slogans "Peace," "Land to the Peasants," and "All Power to the Soviets." The first point put him at odds with all the other political parties, since they had voted to remain in the war. The second point enabled him to make inroads into the support of the Socialist Revolutionaries, especially since the latter were afraid to alienate the Allies, and perhaps completely disorganize the already chaotic domestic situation, by openly advocating peasant seizure of the land.

The third point enabled the Bolsheviks to give their own minority program the appearance of representing the will of the "workers and peasants." The Soviets were locally chosen committees which controlled (and spoke for) individual factories, groups of enlisted men, sailors on particular ships or naval bases, and so on. These Soviets, strongest near the big cities of Petrograd and Moscow, had SR-Menshevik majorities, which put them to the left of the provisional government. Moreover, their leaders were old comrades-in-arms who had shared prison and exile with the Bolsheviks; they were therefore loath to break with them despite crucial differences of program and ethics.

Lenin as the organizer and theoretician, and Trotsky as his main spokesman, took full advantage of the remaining goodwill of the other Left parties, and at the same time gradually increased their own proportion of popular support by proposing slogans which were indeed close to the wishes of the majority. The soldiers were sick of war and deserting in droves. The peasants assumed they would become the owners of the land they were encouraged to seize. Government by Soviets would replace the weak provisional government and enable the small but disciplined Bolshevik minority to govern in the name of popular organs.

A major factor weakening the provisional government was the mutual (and largely justified) suspicion between Prime Minister Kerensky and the commanding general on the Petrograd front, Lavr Georgevich Kornilov. With the government paralyzed, the Bolsheviks almost seized power in July and actually did so in November, though without the mass heroics depicted in the films of Sergei Eisenstein (made more than a decade later at the behest of—and in fear of—Stalin). The November revolution was a successful coup d'état: occupation of the main public buildings, post office, and radio stations by surprise and without resistance, and surrender of the Winter Palace by Duma deputies who wanted to avoid a bloodbath and still had no real idea what to expect from the Bolsheviks.

The Bolsheviks themselves hoped for a revolution in which they would be the executives, but in which the Left as a whole would offer willing collaboration. They permitted elections for a constituent assembly; but when those elections produced an SR-Menshevik majority, they closed it without ceremony on January 18, 1918. Thereafter it took them three years of civil war, resistance to international intervention, and the defeat of a foolhardy invasion of Poland before they firmly seated their own authority in Russia and accepted a peace treaty which ceded substantial Belorussian and Ukrainian populations to the new Poland.

But Lenin was eminently successful with the main portions of his initial program. He bought peace with Germany through the Treaty of Brest-Litovsk (though his support of the treaty often put him in the minority within his own party). He ably used the services of his longtime colleagues Zinoviev and Kamenev to organize the municipal governments of Petrograd and Moscow. He gained control of heavy industry and many military units near Petrograd through Soviets which either had Bolshevik majorities or accepted Bolshevik leadership in the absence of other clear proposals.

Lenin put his recent convert, the former Menshevik Trotsky, in charge of the Red Army. Trotsky's energy, persuasive power in critical situations, and successful use of both tsarist career officers and those promoted from within the ranks were crucial to the eventual Bolshevik military victory. Lenin also put his Georgian follower, Josef Stalin, in charge of nationalities, and the latter developed what was to be the permanent policy of the Bolshevik governments: cultivate the folklore and language of each nationality, but make sure that real power is in the hands of men loyal to central Bolshevik authority. Lenin also encouraged the peasants to take and cultivate the land, and left for the future any explanations about the extent to which they would (or would not) legally own it. Finally, whenever possible, he clothed his decisions in popular legitimacy via confirmation by enthusiastic voice votes in the Soviets.

Lenin's personal gifts enabled him to convince his own colleagues and to win considerable popular support. But economic chaos, civil war, and the lack of any "world revolution" soon forced him to adopt policies of "war communism" and mass terror. In these decisions also, his personal character was of some importance. Without being either vain or cruel in the normal meanings of those words, Lenin was absolutely sure of his personal indispensability (not a rare trait among great leaders) and of the correctness of the Bolshevik program, not only for the Russian people but for the workers and peasants of the entire world. Thus, although the first months after the November coup seemed like a species of honeymoon for the revolution, on August 30, 1918, the assassination of the police chief Uritsky and the attempted assassination of Lenin himself induced him, like the Jacobins of old, to defend the revolution through terror. Here too, no sadism, no floods of emotion seemed to motivate Lenin (though "smash" was one of his favorite verbs)—just the rapid physical elimination of many of his presumed enemies. The government announced on September 3 that in reprisal for Uritsky's death it had executed five hundred class enemies in Petrograd and four hundred in Yaroslavl.[2] Concentration camps were set up to "re-educate" recalcitrant bourgeois and "lumpen proletariat." The government never hid its readiness to imprison or execute, and Lenin justified the state terror on the grounds that far fewer people died that way than in the wars of the capitalist powers.

The policy of war communism was introduced to counter the prevailing chaos and to provide decisive leadership (in contrast to the alleged shilly-shallying of the SR's and the Mensheviks). Under war communism, all land, commerce, and industry were fully nationalized. Food rationing was introduced in accordance with class principles that awarded larger rations to industrial workers than to white-collar employees and "bourgeois." Foreign trade became a state monopoly, while domestically the government welcomed the failure of banks and the substitution of barter for a money economy. The properties of the Orthodox Church were confiscated, but the churches themselves remained open. Grain was requisitioned, but the government tried to leave the peasants with enough of their total produce so that they would not become disillusioned with the revolution. The Bolsheviks also tolerated a considerable black market in both food and consumer goods.

The period of war communism, from the summer of 1918 to March 1921, corresponds to the period of civil war and international intervention. The Soviet government faced a number of armed challenges: from peasant nationalist and anarchist groups in the Ukraine and Caucasus; from counterrevolutionary armies supported by the monarchists, the French, the Japanese, and to a lesser degree the British and Americans; from Czech legionnaires, ex-prisoners of war who had been friendly to the provisional government but who were anti-Bolshevik; and from German units which had been explicitly authorized by the Allies to defend the Baltic provinces against any Soviet move to recover sovereignty in the area.

The organization of the Red Army was Leon Trotsky's stellar contribution to the revolution. As of November 1917, the Bolsheviks could call upon approximately one hundred thousand "Red Guards" whom they used to seize and patrol government buildings in Petrograd and Moscow. But these poorly trained and undisciplined volunteer troops were by no means numerous enough to extend Bolshevik control beyond the capital cities. Through conscription, some two to three million soldiers were trained in the years 1918–1920. Shortages of arms and uniforms, as well as a shortage of real battles (as against minor skirmishes), meant that in fact there were rarely more than about one hundred thousand soldiers in actual combat. The Party, led by Western-oriented intellectuals, had to accept the fact that in spring the recruits would desert in order to take part in the planting, and in September a sizeable percentage would return to their units and help defend the government which had given them land.

The cultural gap between the top Bolshevik leadership and the mass of Russian peasants was, as I suggested earlier in relation to the imperial regime, far greater than such contrasts in Western Europe, and the genius of Trotsky and his staff in dealing humanely with their illiterate compatriots has never been fully appreciated in the West. The Red Army combined literacy and sanitation courses with military training. It taught that looting, anti-Semitic pogroms, and rape were not acceptable practices for a disciplined army, and it shot considerable numbers of looters and rapists in order to prove the point.

Trotsky employed about fifty thousand tsarist officers attracted by his outstanding ability and by the fact that the Red Army, regardless of ideologies, was defending the heartland of historic Russia against chaotic internal forces and foreign invaders. These officers in turn created a new class of noncommissioned and commissioned officers from the most talented of the worker and peasant conscripts. Trotsky for the most part did not interfere with their professional judgments, but established a corps of "political commissars" to guard against treason on the part of those who had, after all, come from the ranks of the upper classes. Despite typhus, smallpox, cholera, influenza, dysentery, and various forms of venereal disease, the Red Army by November 1920 managed to defeat the combined efforts of counter-revolutionaries, Ukrainian separatists, and European and Japanese interventions.[3]

In the eyes of the suffering population, victory in the civil war ended the justification for war communism and terror. SR's, Mensheviks, and anarchists began to agitate more openly. In particular, the sailors of the naval base at Kronstadt—ideal proletarians from the Bolshevik point of view—called for new elections to the Soviets, with free preliminary campaigning for all parties and a secret ballot. The government treated the demands as a counterrevolutionary plot to destabilize the country while they were seeking international diplomatic recognition. After two weeks of fruitless negotiations, crack Red Army units crossed the ice on the night of March 17, 1921, captured the besieged naval base, and executed hundreds of sailor-prisoners.

But at the same time as he repressed rebellion pitilessly, Lenin understood the message. Within days he announced the adoption of a New Economic Policy (NEP). Local retail trade and the use of currency were to be restored. Factories and shops with less than twenty employees were denationalized, and private initiative was to be permitted in retail trade, housing, and the professions. Grain requisitioning was replaced by a fixed tax in kind, and the peasants were permitted to sell their surplus in open markets. A money economy was restored, and a new state banking system with a gold-backed ruble was to be the basis of commercial transactions.

As Lenin explained matters to the tenth party congress, the country longed simply to heal its wounds. The government must pay heed to the needs of the overwhelming peasant majority. Limited capitalism, including foreign investment, was necessary, and need not endanger the future of socialism so long as the government held on to "the commanding heights"—that is to say, controlled the natural resources, the transportation and communication networks, the armed forces, and the large industrial plants. But although Lenin was willing to be flexible in economic matters, he would not restore a free press or the Menshevik and SR party organizations.

By 1928, the Russian economy under the NEP had recovered to its prewar levels. In the meantime, the Bolsheviks lost their maximum leader: Lenin suffered a stroke in 1922 and died in January 1924. His successful economic policies remained in force, but it took approximately five years for the party to decide on its future leadership. One of the great ironies of revolutionary history—not fully recognized by the major participants at the time—was that while the Bolsheviks saw themselves as fulfilling the impersonal will of History, their triumph in the years from 1917 to 1921 most certainly had depended on the powerfully directed voluntarism of their supreme leader, V. I. Lenin.

Beginnings of the Weimar Republic

During the same years that the most "backward" of the great powers was being transformed according to the will of the Bolsheviks, the most economically and scientifically advanced of the great powers was fitfully groping to recover from defeat in the world war. At the beginning of any discussion of the ill-fated Weimar Republic, it is important to note the tremendous difference in political atmosphere between Russia and Germany. In Russia, the reformist and leftist parties did not feel humiliated by the defeat of the tsarist armies. On the contrary, they looked upon it as a golden opportunity to remake their homeland. Also, the tsarist officer corps had no such control over the civilian government as was the case in Germany.

As a matter of fact, German civilian disenchantment with the war had become quite clear in 1917. A wing of the Social Democratic Party insisted publicly on a peace without annexations and on the democratizing of the imperial constitution. They formed a new party, the Independent Social Democratic Party, small but prestigious through the quality of its membership. And to the left of that party, the followers of the antiwar socialist intellectuals Karl Liebknecht and Rosa Luxemburg formed the "Spartacus League" (named for the most famous slave revolt within the Roman Empire). Nevertheless, until the last day of the war and beyond, the professional military told the civilian government what to do in all matters crucial to its interests and, as the only force capable of maintaining public order, it held any civilian government hostage to its tolerance.

In late September, the generals decided that the military situation was hopeless and that peace must be arranged rapidly before any fighting should occur on German soil. They ordered the last imperial chancellor, Prince Maximilian of

Baden, to sue for an armistice. The latter attempted to stave off total defeat by informing President Wilson on October 4 that Germany accepted the Fourteen Points as a basis for peace. Meanwhile, important political personalities tried to get the kaiser to abdicate in favor of one of his sons so that the federal empire would not be destroyed by the military defeat. The Allies informed Prince Maximilian that only a complete surrender would be acceptable, and the kaiser refused to step down until too late—abdicating and fleeing to neutral Holland on November 8.

During this same month of October, several mutinies occurred and included equalitarian demands of a kind previously unheard of in the disciplined history of the German armed forces. Thus, the sailors at the Kiel Naval Base—while continuing to observe the "Keep off the grass" signs—demanded that in the future, "The form of address, *Herr Kapitän*, should occur only at the beginning of the sentence, thereafter superiors may be addressed as '*Sie*' " (the polite form of "you").[4] More important than the mutinies was the simple, massive disintegration of the armed forces, as hundreds of thousands of soldiers and sailors began to walk home without seeking permission, and as workers in the main cities—inspired by the example of the Bolshevik revolution a year earlier—formed Soviets which in many districts became the only form of municipal authority. On November 7, 1918, the Bavarian section of the Independent Social Democratic Party proclaimed a Bavarian republic with the clear intention of decentralizing and radicalizing the political system of any future Germany.

In these circumstances, the only civilian members of a "legitimate" government available to act in the name of all Germany were the Social Democratic (SD) and Center deputies in the Reichstag. On November 9 in Berlin, the SD leaders Friedrich Ebert and Philipp Scheidemann proclaimed a republic, and the Centrist deputy Matthias Erzberger delivered the surrender note to the Allies. As provisional president and prime minister, respectively, Ebert and Scheidemann depended unhappily on the support of the Berlin Soviets and of those generals who accepted a republic as the only institutional authority available (for the moment) to deal with the Allies.

Some weeks later, on January 6, 1919, the Spartacus League attempted to push the fledgling republic toward Soviet-style communism with a mostly unarmed rising that tried to take control of the Berlin city council. The provisional government had no dependable police force to turn to, and they felt (probably quite correctly) that their whole future depended on their ability to maintain "law and order" in the streets of defeated Germany. They thus turned to the Freikorps, privately financed units of the demobilizing army, to repress the Spartacus revolt—a task which these troops performed with great brutality, including the assassinations of Liebknecht and Luxemburg. At the same time, the Bavarian republic was paralyzed by internal quarrels among its totally inexperienced ministers and its impassioned theoreticians. Its founder-president, Kurt Eisner, was assassinated in February 1919, and his most radical followers established a "Soviet" republic which the provisional government suppressed in May with the use of both army and Freikorps units.

Thus was the German republic born of the complete military defeat and internal disintegration of the German empire, and thus was it dependent on the most reactionary military forces to establish its authority in the streets. Then, too, the generals had carefully stage-managed the armistice, and the later signing of the Treaty of Versailles, in such a way as to implicate civilians, and civilians only. In the case of the treaty, as in that of the armistice, the provisional republican government tried to have the terms softened and indicated frankly—in the one public statement they were allowed to make—that Germany could never accept the clause assigning total responsibility for the war to German aggression. But the Allies, as we have seen, were in no mood to make concessions, and the civilian delegation had to sign the treaty, including the war-guilt clause.

As for the army, it had to surrender its heavy weapons, but neither the German nor Allied governments interfered with the personal liberty or the hierarchical authority of the officer corps. The tactics of the generals in relation to the civilian authorities laid the basis for two important legends of the postwar era: one, that the army had never been defeated in battle, and two, that it had been "stabbed in the back" by the "civilians," understood to mean socialists, communists, and Jews. In addition, the complete dependence of the new government on the existing armed forces meant that the monarchist core of the army, the police, and the civil services generally would remain untouched by the republican "revolution."

Despite all these troubles, there was a great fund of knowledge and goodwill in the ranks of the majority of civilians, who for two decades already had been voting for the SD and Center parties and calling for a more democratic constitution. Between February and August 1919 in the city of Weimar (associated with the great cultural figures of J. S. Bach, Goethe, Schiller, Franz Liszt, and Friedrich Nietzsche), an elected constituent assembly hammered out the fundamental charter of republican Germany.

The emperor was replaced by a president elected by universal suffrage. The Reichstag also was to be elected by universal *equal* suffrage of all citizens over the age of twenty. (The imperial Reichstag had been chosen by a weighted system of manhood suffrage that gave more votes to the wealthier classes). The chancellor and his cabinet were to be responsible to the legislative majority, as in any true parliamentary system. In an effort to make the Reichstag reflect as accurately as possible the state of public opinion, the constituent assembly adopted proportional representation, allotting one deputy for every sixty thousand votes—a feature which meant that the number of deputies would vary according to the number of persons actually voting.

Germany remained a federal state, with an upper chamber, the Reichsrat, representing the *Länder* (states). The Reichsrat could veto laws, in which case the lower house would have to muster a two-thirds majority to override the veto. But instead of letting matters come to direct conflict, the Reichstag leadership developed the habit of consulting the Reichsrat before passing legislation affecting the rights of the *Länder*. The constitution also included new social rights—such things as adequate housing, independent trade unions, freedom of peaceable assembly, and the care of war veterans and their families. The Weimar republic also extended one of the educational features of the existing constitution which to me, as an American, has always seemed particularly enlightened. Germany, like the United States, was a country with many churches. Whereas the U.S. has constitutionally erected a wall of separation between church and state, the German republic decided explicitly to use public funds for all schools in proportion to the percentages of each church (including the Jews) in a given area.

The intent of the constitution makers was clearly to create what we now would call a democratic welfare state with a mixed economy, and the Weimar assembly approved the final document in August 1919 by a vote of 262–75. But at the same time, the liberal–Centrist–Social Democratic majority was very careful not to interfere with the historic rights of the civil service, the university and secondary school teaching corps, the judiciary, the police, and the armed forces. All these groups were monarchist at heart. Professors and teachers continued to glorify the empire and its military traditions. Judges handed down heavy sentences against leftist strikers but treated right-wing violence very leniently, including such outrages as the assassinations of the Independent Socialist leader Hugo Haase and the (Jewish) Minister of Foreign Affairs Walther Rathenau. The police cracked leftist skulls preferentially in the numerous street demonstrations of the Weimar era, and always found it difficult to identify reactionary hoodlums.

Turning to the international aspects of the situation, France still insisted on full payment of the immense reparations, backed in lukewarm fashion by the Anglo-Saxon powers—one of whom, the United States, had rejected the vision of its own president as embodied in the Versailles treaty and the League of Nations. Even more so than the Allies, Germany had financed its war effort by the liberal use of the printing press. Now the combination of peace, a new government with little authority among the professional and business classes, and the loss of the entire gold reserve in reparations payments led to hyperinflation. When the French invaded the Ruhr because of nondelivery of expected reparations in kind (mostly coal and iron), the German mark collapsed to the point where prices changed hourly to keep up with "exchange" rates of hundreds of thousands, and then even millions, to the dollar.

But financial insanity does not, fortunately, do away with the underlying basis of a developed economy. A country's real wealth consists of its natural resources, its industrial and agricultural facilities, and the educational level and economic skills of its population. Germany was richly endowed in all these forms of wealth, and its factories and mines had not suffered the wartime damage which the equivalent facilities had suffered in Belgium and France.

The solution to the runaway inflation was largely the work of the Social Democratic Minister of Finance, Rudolph Hilferding. On January 1, 1924, he introduced the new *rentenmark*, based not on metallic reserves (which had virtually disappeared) but on a blanket mortgage on the national wealth—in effect, on confidence in the productive capacity of the entire German economy. The *rentenmark* initiated a form of noninflationary stability which has been characteristic of the peacetime German economy ever since. In 1924 also, the Dawes plan scaled back the total of future reparations payments and gave Germany substantial American loans, thereby contributing much to the new stability of German finances.

A Brief Glimpse of Normalcy

If one were to choose a date by which it could be said that the majority of Europeans felt they had "recovered" from the Great War and its revolutionary aftermath, it would be the year 1925 or 1926. By this time, the *rentenmark* had restored financial stability in Germany; the New Economic Policy had restored agricultural production and local commerce and industry in Russia; the new Central European republics had stabilized their internal administrations; and the Western Allies and the prosperous neutrals had all recovered their prewar standard of living and were moving ahead in both prosperity and political democracy.

The memory of so many deaths and physical privations during the war, combined with the daily sight of so many one-armed or one-legged veterans who would otherwise have been healthy men in their thirties, produced a new sensibility to all kinds of injustice and ill luck. In England, France, the Low Countries, and Scandinavia, suffrage now became truly universal for both sexes, strikers' rights and trade-union liberties were strengthened, and public education and subsidized health care were extended in formerly neglected areas. In Belgium, Holland, and Sweden, these changes involved a diminution of royal authority, and in all three countries a new balance between crown and parliament was peacefully achieved.

Most important to the feeling of renewed stability were changes in mood that augured a more peaceful future. Before 1914, Great Britain had been nervously reactive to both the industrial and naval challenges of imperial Germany. After the war, England adjusted itself peaceably to the fact that the United States had replaced it as the world's principal creditor and that Japan had greatly increased its own relative political and economic influence in the Pacific. The British also recognized that the recovery of their erstwhile enemy Germany was in fact essential to their own industrial and commercial prosperity. Finally, via a series of mostly amicable imperial conferences, the British accepted the transformation of their empire into the commonwealth, with all that this implied as to the virtual independence of Canada, Australia, and New Zealand.

Official France could not really free itself from the fear of Germany, but by the mid-1920s the country had rebuilt the prosperous agriculture and industry of the northeast. France was also electrifying its railways, paving rural roads, and modernizing the machinery of its mines and factories. Much as before 1914, Europeans in general thought of French consumer goods, clothes, cuisine, fine arts, and aesthetic objects of all kinds as models of high quality. The combination of war deaths and low birth rates had created a notable labor shortage in France, however, and the ranks were replenished in the 1920s by the immigration of some three million Italians, Spaniards, and Poles.

In the nineteenth century, France had traditionally given refuge to political exiles from the dynastic empires to the east. The French attitude toward immigrants was complex and reflected that unique combination of national pride and universalist ideals which was the heritage of the French Revolution. Workers were needed, and the immigrants could be paid less than fellow Frenchmen, though they would still be better off than they had been in the less developed countries of their origin. Artists, intellectuals, and exiled political leaders contributed to the extraordinary vitality of French cultural life, especially in Paris, and their mere presence confirmed the French in their feeling that France was the finest possible place for a civilized human being to live (if not, then why were they all coming here?). The bureaucracy did not make it easy for immigrant workers to become citizens, but the immigrants' children went to French schools, to be educated in the Cartesian tradition of clarity and the Enlightenment traditions of tolerance and equal opportunity. On balance, therefore, the assimilation of the Slav and Latin immigrants was a success, due to the strongly universalist ideals prevalent in a France which had recovered its prosperity and its world reputation.

Let us now pause to look at the situation of the prosperous neutrals. Sweden before 1914 had modeled its government and civil service very much on that of Germany. Respect for education and competence, in Sweden as in Germany, also entailed a strong sense of class distinction. Government took a clearly paternalistic attitude toward the ordinary citizen, as illustrated, for example, by the fact that one could relinquish membership in the national (Lutheran) church only if one simultaneously joined another Christian community.

By 1914, in Sweden as in Germany, the Social Democratic Party was the largest single party and the one which most insisted on democratic reforms. Two factors were particularly important in launching the famous Swedish "middle way" between Anglo-Saxon capitalism and Marxian socialism. One was that, as of 1920, the SD Party advocated not a general nationalization of the economy but rather a combination of social ownership of the natural resources with industrial capitalism and producer and consumer cooperatives. The other was that the arrival of universal suffrage and proportional representation also coincided happily with a readiness of the temperamentally authoritarian King Gustav V to accept true parliamentary government. The victory of the British parliamentary monarchy over the authoritarian German monarchy naturally encouraged this development.[5]

The evolution of Denmark showed how even a small country with few natural resources and a dangerous geographical location could achieve economic prosperity and democratic stability. Denmark had lost one-third of its territory to Bismarckian Prussia in 1864 and, in the last decades of the nineteenth century, Russian, Argentine, and American wheat had taken away its traditional agricultural markets. But the Folk Schools and the cooperative movement supplied the advice which enabled Danish farmers to switch from grain to dairy farming. Also, in the absence of large grazing acreage, they nurtured the lowly pig and became quality producers and exporters of butter, cheese, and ham.

During the war, the British blockade caused Denmark substantial trade losses, and life on a narrow peninsula cutting off the British-dominated North Sea from the German-dominated Baltic Sea required the Danes to practice the most exquisite neutrality. After the war, however, Denmark's marine engineers, Diesel motors, highly developed cement industry (there was always plenty of sand available), and capacity for dealing pleasantly with very different customers enabled it to build quays for the new Polish port of Gdynia, help modernize the port facilities of defeated Germany, build the Maas tunnel for its Dutch neighbors in Rotterdam, and supply ships for the new Soviet Union.[6]

Full parliamentary government and recognition of the bargaining rights of free trade unions had been achieved between 1899 and 1901, and universal suffrage in Denmark dated from 1915. After the war, governments sensitive to the needs of a small-scale economy regularly subsidized both private and cooperative enterprises in fishing, house construction, and various crafts. As in Sweden and Norway, the Social Democrats in Denmark did not demand that all the "means of production" be socialized, but rather that natural resources and public utilities be socially controlled, and that the state take major responsibility for old-age pensions and health and education facilities.

In the solution of their national problems, the Scandinavian countries had several natural advantages. One was relatively small populations (three million each in Denmark and Norway and six million in Sweden, c. 1920) speaking one language (though with significant regional dialects) and belonging overwhelmingly to one church (97 percent Lutheran). At the same time, tiny minorities of Jews and other Europeans were easily assimilated in the cities, where traditional Lutheran membership was combined with a tolerance of other beliefs.

The situation was more difficult in the newly created republic of Czechoslovakia. Only 65 percent of the roughly fourteen million total population were listed as "Czechoslovaks" by a government which was loath to "recognize" the Czechs and Slovaks as separate nationalities. They did indeed speak the same language, but the Czechs had belonged to the Austrian half of the Habsburg empire—indeed, had become the most industrialized portion of the entire empire by 1914—and also enjoyed higher standards of living and education than had the Slovaks. If one were to try to separate the two groups, the ethnic Slovaks would come to something like 20 percent of the national population.

In addition, there were 23 percent Germans, concentrated in the Sudetenland near the German frontier and in the principal cities of Prague and Pilsen; plus 5 percent Magyars, 3.5 percent Ruthenians (first cousins of the Ukrainians), and 2.5 percent Jews. It goes without saying that all such figures are only approximate: One cannot determine precisely whether people truly know—or care to acknowledge—their ethnic ancestry, or whether they are being categorized by civil servants with motives to maximize or minimize various groups. But with all due allowance for approximate numbers, it is clear that "Czechoslovaks" constituted only two-thirds of the population, and that if one treats them as separate nationalities, then the numerically and economically dominant Czechs constituted less than half the total.

Religious differences were less striking, but still very important. Seventy-six percent were Roman Catholics, but the Czechs, for whom the Protestant martyr Jan Hus is a national hero, were, so to speak, anti-Vatican Catholics, whereas the Slovaks and Magyars were among the most ultramontane communicants. And the Slovak People's Party of Father Hlinka was demagogically anti-Czech and anti-Semitic. The Ruthenians, plus a few ethnic Poles concentrated in the easternmost tip of Czechoslovakia, belonged to the Uniate Church, which was Eastern Orthodox in rite but which acknowledged the authority of the Pope. The 7 percent of Protestants were divided among a dozen sects. It is hard to evaluate the importance of anti-Semitism, or of the mutual suspicions that existed, both between Catholics and Protestants and within the Catholic community because of the Hussite tradition. But Czechoslovakia was somewhat more tolerant than its neighbors Poland and Hungary, and much less spiritually united than were the Scandinavian countries.[7]

The Czechoslovak constitution, like that of republican Germany, created a strong presidency, but lodged sovereignty in a parliament elected by universal suffrage with proportional representation. This feature encouraged the existence of numerous small parties, and the legislatures between 1920 and 1935 included about fifteen separate parties, of which only the Czechoslovak Agrarians, the Czechoslovak Social Democrats, and the Communists ever polled more than 10 percent at any one time. But with the exception of small ultranationalist German, Slovak, and Magyar formations, all the parties were willing to participate in coalitions and make the necessary compromises to live in peace.

The Czechoslovaks knew they were a small nation surrounded by potentially stronger enemies. They knew that their existence owed much to the goodwill of Woodrow Wilson and the astute pre-Versailles diplomacy of Thomas Masaryk and Edvard Benes. They knew that tolerance, workmanship, sobriety, and punctuality all contribute mightily to prosperity. They had not been humiliated like the Germans, and they willingly (if nervously) assumed their dependence on French economic and diplomatic leadership.

A series of coalition governments compiled an impressive legislative record: land reform (made easier by the fact that most of the large landlords had been nobles or upper bourgeoisie intimately linked to the personnel of the defunct empire); the eight-hour day; health and unemployment insurance; school building and teacher training in the local languages of each region; wide administrative autonomy for the Germans; special efforts to train Slovak-speaking officials and to develop roads and other infrastructure in Slovakia; and subsidies to leading industries such as armaments, porcelain, glass, leather, and quality steel.[8]

The attitude of the Sudeten Germans was particularly important. At first, as part of the ruling minority for centuries past, they were in no mood to accept the formerly subject Czechs as masters. They hoped that the application of Wilsonian principles would mean that their territory would be attached either to Germany or to Austria. But the proposed northern frontier of Czechoslovakia had been the Habsburg imperial frontier for centuries; it made sense both geographically and economically, and the Allies were in any case favoring the new states over the defeated Germans wherever the ethnic borders were doubtful. On sober reflection, however, Sudeten industrialists began to think that they might be better off with tariff protection against revived Austrian and German industry. Also, as part of a "victor" nation, they were not saddled with reparations—and in the inflationary years 1921–23, they were indeed lucky not to be part of the Weimar republic. Thus, for approximately the decade from 1925 to 1935 (at which latter time the Nazi agitation became important), the Sudeten Germans collaborated in the democratic government of the multinational Czech republic.

Essential to the democratic character and stability of that republic was the nature of its founder-president, Thomas Masaryk, who remained in office till 1935. Masaryk was the son of a Slovak serf who had become a professor of philosophy, lived for a time and married in the United States, and was a confirmed admirer of the "melting pot" concept of democracy. He was also a Czech nationalist who in 1876 had had the courage to declare false certain forged manuscripts which had long been used in nationalist propaganda. Masaryk had even risked being killed by a mob in order to protect a Jewish peddler from the sort of anti-Semitic violence that occurred in all parts of Eastern Europe.[9] Similarly, when in 1919 a mob took over the building of the Old German Theater in Prague, the recently inaugurated Masaryk announced that he would not appear in any Czech theater until the property rights of the German theater had been amicably settled.[10]

Individuals can of course play only a limited role in history, but those who are the founders of a state leave a larger imprint than most. If one compares the Weimar Republic with Czechoslovakia, one sees that the first president of the former—Friedrich Ebert—was a man who had only reluctantly become a republican and who both felt and was made to feel socially inferior to the reactionary military officers and civil servants who surrounded him. And the second president of the Weimar Republic was the same Marshal Hindenburg who had been co-dictator during the war and who was eventually to turn over the republic to Hitler. Thus it was the combination of Masaryk's character with the Wilsonian-French interest in the construction of new democratic states in Central Europe that gave Czechoslovakia a much happier start than that of post-imperial Germany.

Important also in the post-Versailles pacification of Europe were the Locarno Treaties, negotiated in 1925, and the acceptance of Germany as a member of the League of Nations in 1926. At Locarno, Germany, France, Belgium, Great Britain, and Italy guaranteed the western borders of Germany against any changes other than through mutual consent. This revised in a most important fashion the *diktat* of Versailles. In the latter case, a prostrate Germany had been ordered without discussion to sign. At Locarno, the internationally recognized republican Germany gave a diplomatic pledge to the countries it had invaded in 1914, and that pledge was solemnly confirmed by France, Belgium, Britain, and Italy. On the other hand, Germany still refused to guarantee her Polish border, and she signed a mutual-defense pact with the European pariah, Soviet Russia. In the absence of German guarantees, Poland (as well as the "Little Entente" nations of Czechoslovakia, Romania, and Yugoslavia) hoped that bilateral defense treaties with France would protect them against any future German aggression. Thus the Locarno pacts confirmed the existence of the same fault line between Western and Central-Eastern Europe that was evident in 1919: good prospects for normalcy in the West, uncertainty and fear in the East.

A final important factor in the tentative pacification of Europe were the activities of the League of Nations. The League has been famous more for its shortcomings than for its successes. The United States never joined, the disarmament conferences were mere verbiage without significant acts, the mandate system was largely a fig leaf disguising old-style imperialism, the sanctions against aggressors were defied by both the fascists and the Soviets in the 1930s, and so forth. But there were also very positive elements (such as the previously mentioned administration of Danzig) that contributed by example to a necessary future in which humankind learns to substitute negotiated agreements for "sovereign" military action.

The League of Nations established a World Court whose judges were to be of different nationalities and were selected by groups of nations rather than by individual states. During the interwar years the court settled numerous questions of interpretation in commercial agreements and treaty clauses. The conflicts brought to its jurisdiction were obviously not the main-power conflicts of the era, but their resolution provided an all-important example of how to advance beyond the traditional anarchy of international relations. The World Court proceedings showed that just and peaceful solutions could be arrived at without violence.

The International Labor Organization encouraged the development of worldwide standards on such matters as sanitary and lighting conditions in factories, mines, and ships; special conditions for pregnant women; strict limitation and eventual elimination of child labor; and unemployment insurance and paid vacations. The ILO's annual conferences were attended by delegates from over sixty nations, and its publications drew on the earlier German, Austrian, and Scandinavian experience of protective labor legislation; moreover, Germany and Austria—though denied membership in the league itself till 1926—were members of the ILO from the start. Membership in the ILO helped the socialist trade unions of Spain to maintain a considerable degree of prestige and bargaining power during the mild dictatorship of General Primo de Rivera, and also to cultivate personal and institutional relations with the democratic unions of more economically developed small nations, such as Czechoslovakia and Holland.[11]

The League of Nations also took action against famine and disease, and in its first two years of existence it helped some 430,000 refugees of twenty-seven different nationalities to go home. In 1920 it named the Norwegian explorer Fridtjof Nansen High Commissioner for Refugees, and his office created the so-called Nansen passport to protect the basic rights of thousands of stateless persons in the 1920s. He and the wealthy American engineer (and future president) Herbert Hoover also cooperated in the relief of famine in Russia and the Ukraine in 1921, thereby offering a compelling example of the concern for human welfare triumphing over the dislike of a particular political system.

From my discussions with younger colleagues, I know that many of them think of the two world wars as essentially one great war with a twenty years' truce separating its two military phases. While it is true that the economic and psychological recovery described in this chapter was evident principally in Western Europe and Scandinavia, it is also true that, by 1928, Germany had been virtually freed of the real burden of reparations and had been accepted in the League of Nations. Likewise, Soviet Russia had recovered from the devastation of war, revolution, and civil war from 1914 to 1921, and had established normal diplomatic relations with all the major nations except the United States. Moreover, the Locarno Pacts and the various administrative and mediating functions of the League of Nations were beginning to develop the internationalist habits alongside those of pure national sovereignty. Unless we are going to view history backward—with all later triumphs and catastrophes treated as inevitable emanations of the mind of History (or of God)—we should properly acknowledge the hopeful, if fragile, developments of the first decade following the Great War.

ENDNOTES

1. My account of the Bolshevik seizure of power is based principally on Richard Pipes, *The Russian Revolution* (New York: Vintage Books, Random House, 1991), chapters 8–11; regarding the finances in particular, see Joel Carmichael, "German Money and Bolshevik Honor," *Encounter*, March, 1974, 81–90.

2. My accounts of the civil war and war communism are based principally upon W. H. Chamberlin, *The Russian Revolution, 1917–1921*, and Leon Trotsky, *History of the Russian Revolution* (both available in several editions since 1934); as well as Geoffrey Hosking, *The First Socialist Society*, enlarged edition (Harvard University Press, 1990).

3. Orlando Figes, "The Red Army and Mass Mobilization during the Russian Civil War, 1918–1920," *Past and Present*, November 1990, 168–211.

4. Rudoph Coper, *Failure of a Revolution: Germany 1918–1919*, p. 68. Long out of print, reissued by Cambridge University Press, 1955.

5. O. F. Ander, *The Building of Modern Sweden* (Rock Island, Ill., 1958), chapter 10 and *passim*.

6. J. Danstrup, *A History of Denmark* (Copenhagen: Wivors, 1949).

7. For ethnic, religious, and political statistics I have depended on Joseph Rothschild, *East Central Europe between the Two World Wars* (Seattle and London: University of Washington Press, 1977), 87–116.

8. Hugh Seton-Watson, *Eastern Europe Between the Wars, 1918–1941*, chapters on Czechoslovakia; and S. Harrison Thomson, *Czechoslovakia in European History*, chapters 10–13.

9. J. S. Roucek, editor, *Central Eastern Europe, Crucible of World Wars*, 1946, 83–85.

10. V. Mares, *Current History*, September, 1952.

11. Anthony D. McIvor, *Spanish Labor Policy during the Dictablanda of Primo de Rivera* (Ann Arbor, Mich.: University Microfilms International, 1982), chapter III and *passim*.

4

Fascism and the Wave
of Conservative Dictatorships

*f*ascism is not a subject about which it is easy to write clearly. Its founding father, Benito Mussolini, made a point of saying that he had created the doctrine as he went along, and it never did receive a theoretical formulation comparable to the doctrines of socialism, communism, or anarchism. But Mussolini became a partial model for several dictators in the period between the two world wars, and in any case, with or without the help of coherent theories (so dear to the hearts of social scientists), it is important to understand the wave of belligerently anticommunist, antisocialist, and implicitly antidemocratic dictatorships that ruled many of the smaller, less prosperous European nations in the 1920s and 1930s.

As for the terms themselves, analysts over the past three quarters of a century have used the noun *fascism*, and especially the adjective *fascist*, in at least four different senses. Sometimes the words refer to the one-party nationalist and anticommunist movement created in Italy by Benito Mussolini immediately after the First World War. Sometimes they refer to the dictatorships of Mussolini in Italy and Hitler in Germany—by far the most powerful personal dictatorships exercised west of Russia in the interwar period. In a third usage they refer to numerous right-wing dictatorships in Europe and Latin America that imitated various features of Mussolini's regime, but which lacked the essential institutions that distinguished his rule from a traditional military or conservative dictatorship.

Finally, since the defeat of the Axis Powers in World War II, there have been no regimes in either Europe or Latin America that choose to identify themselves as "fascist," but there have been numerous marginal political movements which exhibit the same antidemocratic, militarist, racist, and ultranationalist traits that were characteristic of Italy and Germany in the 1930s. The adjective continues to be applied—quite accurately, in my opinion—to the sentiments and the sporadic violence of these groups; and in discussing European politics after 1945, I will refer to the "fascist heritage" of the Far Right. But if we want to understand the actual right-wing dictatorships of the period between the two world wars, it is desirable not to apply the word indiscriminately in so many different contexts.

I propose to use the words "fascism" and "fascist" in the first and narrowest definition given above. Without in any sense being an apologist for Mussolini, I believe that Hitler was so much more monstrously evil that a simple sense of proportion compels me not to use the same terms to characterize both men, and I will use the words "Nazism" and "Nazi" when referring to Hitler's regime. At the same time, most of Mussolini's admiring imitators did not try (or were not able) to organize the mass parties and mass propaganda machines which gave a distinct flavor, and a degree of international prestige, to Mussolini's exercise of power.

Fascism arose as a "revolutionary" response to the particular situation of Italy after the Great War. Mussolini had been a socialist newspaper editor before he became an Italian nationalist. He was also a keen observer of the Bolshevik revolution, and the Fascist Party developed a hierarchical organization and exercised a monopoly of political power in forms roughly similar to those of the Communist Party in the Soviet Union. However, Mussolini was not dreaming of a world revolution, but rather of ways to energize a disappointed country with a confused and fearful governing class.

We must remember that in the secret treaties of 1915, Italy had been promised the Habsburg territories of Istria and the Dalmatian coast, plus Mediterranean islands belonging to Turkey and coveted by Greece. At Versailles, the Italians had been awarded the South Tyrol (along with a German population) in order to have a defensible Alpine frontier, but their other expectations had been disappointed. Although Italy was a "victorious" power, its armies had more often than not been defeated in combat with Austro-German troops. This lack of military glory exacerbated Italy's existing prewar feeling of being a "have-not" power, of having received only scraps during the late-nineteenth-century European banquet of African territories.

Such were the sentiments of the ruling classes and, in 1919, the factory workers and poorer peasants were inspired by the beginnings of "their" revolution in distant Russia. Peasants demanded ownership of the land which they had been cultivating as sharecroppers or day laborers. The Socialist Party was polemically split between those who took a reserved attitude toward the Bolshevik coup and those who saw Communist Russia as the spearhead of world revolution and wanted to join the Third International. The inner-party debate also included the question whether the time had come to organize the management of Italian industry by worker Soviets.[1]

In August 1920, industrial workers in Milan and Turin occupied the factories in which they were employed. The hope was to maintain quality production and work discipline in a manner that would prove the ability of the workers to initiate a socialist revolution in the heart of Europe. The effort only lasted a few weeks, and it became immediately obvious that while the workers understood the care and use of their own machines, they were in no position to renew supplies, establish (or reestablish) marketing mechanisms, and so on.

The failure of the factory occupations tended to reduce the combativeness of the workers, but an unintended result of the experience—crucial for the development of fascism—was to frighten the middle classes and landlords to the point where they felt unable to maintain their own authority through the existing parliamentary system. Even more worrisome, the parties which had dominated politics in the newly united Italy between 1870 and the First World War had no credible programs or energetic leaders to offer in the present critical situation.

As of 1920–21, there were two large parties in Italy: the Socialists, internally split but with a vocal, militant wing that would found the Communist Party in 1921; and the *Partito Popolari*, representing a mass of dissatisfied peasants and workers who accepted Catholic leadership while looking for an antibourgeois redistribution of power and property. To the local oligarchs and conservative industrialists, it must have felt as though "history" might indeed sweep them away.

At this anxious moment, the man who claimed he could save the possessing classes from communism, and who also claimed that he would restore Italian national pride and military prowess (rhetorically invoking the Roman Empire and the using the slogan "Mare Nostrum"), was Benito Mussolini.

The son of a small-town shoemaker and anarchist sympathizer (a man who had named one son in memory of the Mexican liberator-president Benito Juarez, and the other in memory of the medieval freethinker Arnold of Brescia), Mussolini had been a prominent socialist journalist in the decade prior to 1914, revolutionary and anti-imperialist in orientation. He was not an abstract, intense thinker and polemicist like Lenin or Trotsky, but rather an earthy, flamboyant character, the anonymous author of such pulp works as a pamphlet entitled *God Does Not Exist* and a novel entitled *The Cardinal's Mistress*. He had read both Marx and Sorel and was considered able (if somewhat crude) by the intellectuals and socially prominent people he courted. Mussolini shared the futurist enthusiasm for airplanes and fast cars. He was a teetotaler, a nonsmoker, an energetic orator with convincing gestures and phrases, and a man without any sense of humor.[2]

In 1914, the Italian socialists—in contrast with those of France and Germany—advocated neutrality. Mussolini broke with them, calling instead for a temporary truce with capitalism and urging the defense of Italy against its hereditary enemy Austria. (He was supported in this position by two future leaders of the Italian Communist Party, Antonio Gramsci and Palmiro Togliatti.) From this time on, Mussolini replaced the class war and the socialist revolution as themes of his oratory with an emotional advocacy of national renewal and dignity through patriotism and war.

He founded his party, with the name *fascio di combattimento*, in 1919, and in the early years he was more a first among equals than a supreme overlord. The party organization was a series of regional fiefs controlled by local leaders. What they had in common were groups of semi-armed *arditi* or *squadristi*—squads of bully boys who were used to intimidate, beat up, or even kill the spokesmen of left-wing causes. But Mussolini was the principal unifying figure: as an orator, as one who had read a great deal more than his co-leaders, as one who assiduously courted top political and social figures, and as one who articulated the resentments of the war veterans and the motives of the frightened and confused middle classes.[3]

His party was not successful in electoral terms until *after* he had been named prime minister. Thus it won no seats in the parliamentary election of 1919, and only thirty-five seats (as against 139 for the socialists and Communists and 108 for the *Partito Popolari*) in 1921. However, the *arditi* soon became famous for destroying socialist presses, raiding leftist municipal offices, and beating up militant workers and peasants. By the end of 1920, there were some three hundred thousand fascists in Italy, and Mussolini was receiving substantial financial contributions from worried industrialists. An older leader of much greater prestige, the poet Gabriele D'Annunzio, had seized the contested city of Fiume and held power there for almost a year, dressing his local militia in black shirts and reading his floridly phrased decrees from the balcony of the city hall. Mussolini adopted the black shirts and the balcony oratory and made them dramatic, publicity-catching features of his political technique.

In October 1922, after five weak parliamentary governments had failed to solve the postwar depression or banish the specter of "Bolshevik" revolution—a specter carefully cultivated by Mussolini—the king and the aged parliamentary leader, Giovanni Giolitti, invited him to become prime minister of a coalition cabinet. The establishment of Mussolini's dictatorship took place quite gradually. There were Giolittian liberals and *Popolari* ministers until mid-1924. Italy's most prestigious philosopher, Benedetto Croce, endorsed the new government, as did the founder of the futurist movement, Filippo Marinetti; and Giovanni Gentile was to become the nearest thing to an official philosopher of fascism.

But from beginning to end, Mussolini's personality and methods were much more important than any doctrine. In the first full year of power, the new prime minister conducted a truculent (but not excessively risky) foreign policy. In November 1920, D'Annunzio had been expelled from Fiume and Italy had signed a treaty with Yugoslavia recognizing it as a free city. In the course of 1923, Mussolini orchestrated a series of urban disorders which enabled him to press for concessions from the weak Yugoslav monarchy. Ultimately he extracted a new diplomatic settlement in January 1924, whereby the city was annexed to Italy and its suburbs to Yugoslavia. This was carefully publicized as both a just solution on an ethnic, "Wilsonian" basis and a manifestation of Italy's new determination to exercise her "rights." And in the Tyrol, where the majority of villages were German-speaking, Mussolini instituted an aggressive policy of Italianization—of the schools, civil services, town and street names, and so on. In this way, he appealed to national pride while risking only the displeasure of the extremely weak Austrian republic.

In the summer of 1923, several Italian officers were mysteriously killed while serving on a boundary commission along the disputed Greek-Albanian border. Mussolini, somewhat in the fashion of Austria-Hungary at the time of the Sarajevo assassination, sent an ultimatum to Greece and, in the absence of a fully satisfactory reply, bombarded the Greek island of Corfu. Europe was intimidated: Great Power diplomats and League of Nations officials got together to mollify (to avoid use of the 1930s term "appease") Italy, which withdrew from Corfu in return for financial compensation from Greece. It was the new prime minister's opportunity to show the public that when Mussolini took the initiative, the world responded respectfully. He also took advantage of the crisis to repudiate a pledge made by the (insufficiently patriotic) Giolitti government in 1920—a pledge to accept Greek sovereignty over the Dodecanese Islands, formerly belonging to Turkey but mostly Greek in population. The weakness of Greece, and the relative indifference of the major powers, gave Mussolini another easy victory in the form of annexation of the islands.

Only in 1924 did he launch a full internal dictatorship. The fascist assassination of the socialist parliamentary leader Giacomo Matteoti in June of that year placed Mussolini in the position of having either to resign or defy the united protests of all the traditional parliamentary parties. After some months' hesitation, he chose the latter alternative and announced that henceforth, the fascist regime was a one-party political dictatorship. In its consolidation of power, Mussolini's fascist government administered castor oil as a form of torture, established prison islands, and sent various prominent intellectuals to live in supervised internal exile. Among the intellectual monuments to his brutal (but only sporadically murderous) dictatorship are the famous autobiography *Christ Stopped at Eboli* by the exiled Dr. Carlo Levi and the prison journals and letters of Antonio Gramsci, the most intellectually impressive communist leader outside of Russia.

Mussolini courted international as well as domestic opinion. A former newspaper editor, he became one of the first great "image makers" of the century of (mis)information. Tightening up on the rather lax public services, Mussolini let it be known in "advanced" countries such as England that he had "made the trains run on time." He also had photos taken of himself, bared to the waist, wielding a shovel in the draining of the Pontine marshes, which had been famous for malaria in Roman imperial history and which now would provide cultivatable land for several hundred Italian peasant families. In leisurely conversations with the internationally bestselling biographer Emil Ludwig, Mussolini expounded at some length on his methods of "sculpting" the raw material of the nation which it was his onerous (but honored) task to lead.

His most important domestic accomplishment was the solution of the legal and cultural position of the Roman Catholic Church in the Kingdom of Italy, a position which had been controversial since the unification of the state in 1870. Most of the leading politicians and parties had been anticlerical, and the parliamentary monarchy had confiscated most of the Church's large landholdings, and abolished its secular authority in territories which it had governed since the Middle Ages. Popes referred to themselves dramatically as "prisoners" of the godless state, and the mutual hostility of Church and political elite had left unanswered important questions concerning the church's role in education, marriage, and armed forces.

Mussolini knew that Pope Pius XI, who had been the bishop of Milan at the time when the fascist *squadristi* were "saving" the respectable middle class from the imagined terrors of communism, looked favorably upon his government. As pope he had in fact ordered the *Partito Popolari* to disband, thereby removing the Left Catholic opposition to Mussolini's consolidation of power. For four years, the fascist government and the Church negotiated a solution to their longstanding quarrels culminating in the Lateran Treaties of 1929.

By the terms of the Lateran Treaties, Italy recognized the Vatican city as a sovereign state—free to receive ambassadors and thus to communicate in diplomatic confidence with other sovereign states—and granted a large endowment to compensate for the seizure of Church lands and urban real estate. It abolished civil marriage and—while protecting the individual rights of non-Catholics—it recognized Roman Catholicism as the official religion of the state and its armed forces. It also gave the Church control of the curriculum and teacher training in the primary and secondary schools. The Lateran Treaty settlement was to outlive Mussolini himself, and was at the time a source of considerable international prestige for his regime.

Several other features of Mussolini's domestic regime deserve mention. One was his claim to have overcome the class struggle in economic affairs. Beginning in 1927, Mussolini established "corporations" in the different branches of industry and agriculture wherein representatives of the owners and the workers—in the mediating presence of government officials—established salaries and working conditions without resort to strikes. On this last point, Mussolini's efforts were a "success": There were indeed very few strikes after the *arditi* had destroyed the headquarters and terrorized the leaders of various unions, and after the most stubborn opponents of the new government had been jailed or exiled. But in fact, Mussolini was not much interested in economics—nor could he ever really exercise full control over the ruling elites (as against the ordinary citizens)—so that the corporations were more important as a boost to his international "image" than as a real factor in Italian economic decisions.

Something that very much did interest Mussolini was the idea of creating a more "masculine," disciplined Italy, one patterned along the lines of the ancient

Roman military. With this in mind, he sponsored the *ballila* youth groups, which provided uniforms, rudimentary military training, and athletic activities to boys and teenagers. However, the *ballila* brought the fascists into conflict with the Church over the spiritual nurture of young men, and Mussolini became adept at satisfying the anti-clerical impulses of many local fascist chiefs, while at the same time preventing the Church from establishing the monopoly to which it aspired in everything concerned with education. And since one of the presumed signs of masculine potency was to produce lots of children (males preferred), Mussolini regularly pinned medals on the breasts of particularly fecund mothers.

Mussolini also sought, with moderate success, to reinforce Italy's diplomatic presence in Central Europe and the Mediterranean. In 1926 he concluded a treaty with Albania, which soon became a virtual satellite, and also a treaty of friendship with Romania, intended to lessen her dependence on France and offer her an example of intelligent dictatorial government. This was followed in 1927 by a treaty with Hungary, and expressions of sympathy with her revisionist desires; in 1928 by treaties with Greece and Turkey, which closed old wounds in relation to both those countries. Also from c. 1928, and until Hitler indicated his intent to absorb that country, Mussolini was the friendly patron of the clerical dictatorships in Austria. The Italian dictator also enjoyed his role as one of the guarantors of the Locarno agreements and professed active friendship toward both republican France and the conservative dictatorships of Spain and Portugal.

If we pause now to list those features of Mussolini's regime which were distinctive, it seems to me they were the following: the one-party state; the claim to have overcome class struggle within the capitalist system; the emphasis on masculinity, military training, and expansion; the combined propaganda/social/community organizations such as the *ballila*; and the complete control of press and radio with a view to creating an image of national unity, anticommunism, and controlled imperial purpose. These are the features which constituted "fascism" as against the garden variety of conservative dictatorship. It is in fact Mussolini's penchant for publicity—and his pose as the "model" for numerous nondemocratic European governments—that has led to the use of the term *fascist* to describe those governments. But in fact, if one carefully considers, in their own terms, the histories of the small nations of Central and Eastern Europe, the Balkans, and the Iberian peninsula during the interwar years, they reveal a set of characteristics which are quite different from those of Mussolini's Italy.

All these small states were either dynastic monarchies with the tentative beginnings of constitutional liberty (Spain, Romania, Yugoslavia, Bulgaria, Greece, and Albania), or republics tending to be presidential and centralist, though committed in principle to Western-style parliamentary liberty, full freedom of expression, and considerate treatment of minorities (Austria, Poland, Portugal, Lithuania, Latvia, Estonia, and Finland). Alongside the varied and idiosyncratic histories which I will illustrate shortly, they shared the following important traits. First, they all lacked the independent, highly developed, and educated business and professional middle classes which characterized Great Britain, France, the Low Countries, and Scandinavia. Instead, their economic and professional elites were recruited from a handful of extended families, with some careers open to talent in the case of distinguished individuals. Moreover, within those elites there were too many lawyers and notaries, too few doctors and engineers—although at the highest levels, their artists and scientists were on a par with the world's best.

Second, all these countries were primarily agricultural, and their prosperity depended on European and world market prices. They all had high birth rates (with consequent underemployment in the villages) and developed mostly inefficient industries that were protected by high tariffs and restrictions upon foreign investment or ownership. Their industries were not competitive in world markets, nor did they employ enough persons to solve the problems of rural unemployment. Each of these nations hoped for French investments and export sales during the 1920s, and all of them, regardless of their ideological sentiments, tended to enter the German economic orbit in the mid-1930s, when Hitler sought their agricultural and mining exports in exchange for a degree of industrial modernization along German lines.

Third, all these countries were afraid of the Soviet Union, recalling as they did the expansionist history of the Russian empire and listening to the confident calls of its new leaders for world revolution. Their elites feared the loss of property and privileges, their peasants the imposition of atheism and the collectivization of their harvests and their small landholdings. And they all felt a combination of admiration and fear toward Nazi Germany: admiration for its technological prowess and educational and professional standards, and fear of its racist rhetoric and increasing military threats.

Fourth, with the exception of the Iberian countries, all these states were themselves characterized by endemic anti-Semitism. The Jews were seen as city people, and the normal peasant distrust toward merchants, lawyers, and bureaucrats was increased by the fact that Jews constituted so high a proportion of the business and professional classes. Moreover, bureaucrats and teachers came from the dominant nationalities, and they were often able to find easy answers to fundamental problems by blaming "the Jews."

Finally, all these countries had numerous national minorities whose rights to equal citizenship were supposed to be constitutionally guaranteed, but all of them pursued policies of forced assimilation and tried to prevent either their own courts or the League of Nations from interfering in their coercive efforts. In all of them, small fascist-style parties developed which appealed especially to unemployed military men, underpaid civil servants, and nationalist university students. But except for the Nazi wartime occupation, these countries all continued to be ruled by their traditional elites, and the smallness of these elites made individual personalities much more important than in the peacetime politics of the larger prosperous democracies.

As mentioned earlier, these were the important similarities shared by the numerous nondemocratic countries in Europe between the two world wars. But there were also important differences, and even the most cursory overview of fascist and conservative governments must take into account the varied national character of those regimes. To take a few examples (and to begin with the country I know best, Spain) when King Alfonso XIII visited Italy in 1924, he told his fellow monarch, Victor Emmanuel III: "I too have my Mussolini." The king was referring was to General Miguel Primo de Rivera, who had taken power in September 1923, eleven months after Mussolini had been called to office in Italy. The naming of the general, however, had not been a royal-parliamentary decision as in Italy, but rather a *pronunciamiento*, the type of relatively nonviolent military takeover which had been characteristic of Spanish politics all through the nineteenth century.

Spain in 1923 was very much still suffering the aftereffects of the Great War and the two Russian revolutions. The Spanish had been neutral in the first World War, with the upper classes, the military, and the Church generally sympathetic to the Central Powers, and the increasingly important middle classes and socialists sympathetic to the Allies. The war had been an economic bonanza, with the opportunity to sell food, raw materials, textiles, and leather and metal goods to both sides, and to gain even more spectacular profits from the transshipment of arms and raw material circumventing the blockade. Insatiable demand and rising prices benefited both the industrial-commercial classes and industrial labor, and Barcelona in particular became a center for espionage, smuggling, bourgeois new wealth, and labor militancy.[4]

The Spain in which this boom occurred was formally a constitutional monarchy with two principal parties (Conservative and Liberal) alternating in power according to the published results of nationwide elections. But in fact, outside the few large cities, the election returns were manufactured in the Department of the Interior. Middle-class liberals who had long accepted the falsified returns now demanded an end to the *pucherazos* (the stuffing of the ballot boxes) and to *caciquismo* (the domination of rural and small-town politics by a handful of wealthy persons buying votes, controlling scarce employment, and suppressing all opposition).

The fact that the Western Allies had recovered from the early German victories, thereby demonstrating the military capacity of democracy when confronted with the fabled prowess of Prussia, and that Woodrow Wilson had brought the United States into the war with a program to "make the world safe for democracy," added to the optimism of Iberian liberals. Then, too, both Spanish liberals and socialists had been greatly heartened by the first Russian revolution, and a significant proportion of the socialists were at least cautiously sympathetic toward the second (Bolshevik) revolution.[5]

As had been the case several times in Spanish history, the profits of a sudden boom were not invested in the technical improvement of the national economy but instead were rapidly spent on real estate and high living. These profits were also squandered on a complex four-way war of strikes, lockouts, and assassinations (about seven hundred killings in all between 1916 and 1923) involving the Catalan bourgeoisie, the Spanish army and police, the anarcho-syndicalist labor leaders, and the leaders of smaller Catholic or strike-breaking collectives. Thus, in the immediate postwar era, Spain's unrepresentative parliamentary governments were completely unable to cope with the social forces and the hopes released as a result of the war. Liberals demanded honest elections, socialists demanded land reform and school building for a largely illiterate population, and socialist and anarcho-syndicalist unions competed with each other both in organization efforts and in demands for the significant improvement of wages and working conditions.

These circumstances would surely in themselves have led to a profound crisis in the operation of the semi-constitutional monarchy. But the specific problem that precipitated the *pronunciamiento* of 1923 concerned Spanish military rule in North Africa. One of the many diplomatic conferences carving up Africa for the benefit of European powers had, in 1905, divided the ancient kingdom of Morocco between France (the larger zone) and Spain. Moroccan resistance to both occupying powers had been much more persistent than anticipated, and in 1921 an expedition which was supposed to end the "rebellion" once and for all— and which involved the prestige and the personal intervention of the Spanish king (who, like William II of Germany, enjoyed meddling in military decisions) ended in disaster. Parliamentary inquiries dragged on inconclusively for two years, and when it appeared that the king's role would be revealed, the moment seemed appropriate to restrain the parliament—something not too difficult to accomplish, given the internal divisions of the parties and the high degree of postwar social tension.[6]

General Primo de Rivera, who was not personally implicated in the 1921 disaster, assumed power at the king's request and justified himself to most of Spanish public opinion on the grounds that public order must be restored. In Primo's view the parliament was completely unrepresentative of the *pueblo sano* (his healthy fellow citizens, as Primo like to think of them). He was not particularly fond of intellectuals, either—and they were indeed his principal early critics. Primo closed the Madrid Ateneo and removed Spain's most renowned philosopher, Miguel de Unamuno, from the rectorship of the University of Salamanca. He also enjoyed polemical jousting, and in one of his many informal communiques, he explained to the irate Unamuno that "I believe that a dash of Hellenic culture does not confer the right to intervene in everything human and divine, nor to talk rubbish about all other problems."[7]

Like many of Spain's principal military and political leaders, General Primo de Rivera came from an Andalusian landowning family. There was indeed a kind of

unspoken division of labor in the semiconstitutional monarch, with industrial, financial, and commercial development largely in the hands of Basques and Catalans, and
military and political power in the hands of Castilians and Andalusians. But Primo's
family had not been especially wealthy, and Primo himself was neither a cruel man
nor a "capitalist oppressor." Like Mussolini, he wished to establish a nonparliamen-
tary government that would reconcile class interests in the name of patriotism. In partial imitation of Mussolini, he founded a *Unión Patriótica* which was intended to
serve as the one legal political party. But the results were disappointing—Primo's
Unión never achieved coherent leadership or popular enthusiasm.

Much more important in practical terms, Primo invited the collaboration of the
Unión General de Trabajadores (the socialist trade-union federation, known by its
initials as the UGT), and he showed his good faith by resolving the wage demands
of the Asturian coal miners substantially in their favor. On the other hand, as a
Spanish nationalist, he used a heavy hand in the repression of Catalan nationalist
activity, and as a general restoring "law and order" on behalf of the propertied
classes, he disarmed and imprisoned anarcho-syndicalist activists. Despite these
crackdowns, however, the fact remains that nonviolent forms of anarchist culture—
such things as the study of Esperanto, the practice of vegetarianism and nudism,
abstinence from alcohol and tobacco, unofficial marriages, and education in birth
control—flourished in Catalonia in the 1920s.[8]

Neither knowledgeable of nor greatly interested in economics, Primo followed
conservative developmental formulae. On the recommendation of civilian advisers,
he used the gold reserve to defend the peseta against its constant downward trend
in foreign exchange quotations, and he gave high tariff protections to Spanish
industry. But in the practical interest of establishing an efficient telephone system
in Spain, he allowed the American Telephone and Telegraph Company to operate
on very favorable conditions of management, and to repatriate all its profits.
Despite these occasional concessions, however, Primo was in no sense ready to let
his country be dominated by foreign capitalist powers. He supported his economics
minister, José Calvo Sotelo, when the latter established *Campsa* (the national petroleum monopoly) and imported massive quantities from Soviet Russia rather than
allow European and American corporations to dictate terms to Spain.

In general, Primo did not interfere with the traditional practice of *caciquismo*
in rural politics, and his government, far from being anti-clerical, decreed that the
titles awarded by private Catholic universities would be considered equal to those
from the state school. He was also most respectful to the Church in all public ceremonies. He faced difficulties with the artillery corps, but on the whole maintained
good relations with the military, based not only on his creditable personal record,
but also because in 1926 he negotiated the settlement which brought peace to
Spanish Morocco. He was not sensitive to the need for land reform, but invested in
railway development and in *política hidráulica* (the building of dams, artificial

lakes, and irrigation canals) in the general conviction that a transportation network and improved water supplies would surely benefit the entire nation.[9] These public works involved a good deal of bribery, but Primo himself was not one of the numerous twentieth-century dictators who have deposited as much of their nation's wealth as possible in private Swiss bank accounts.

He was positively rare among dictators of any age or continent in his sincere wish that the dictatorship be temporary. He talked constantly about amending the constitution of 1876 in order to restore a workable parliamentary monarchy. He had no faith in democratic elections, but he did believe that he needed the consent of the Church, the king, and the military leadership in order to rule. Indeed, when the generals withdrew their confidence in late 1929, Primo resigned (though reasons of ill health also came into play). In any event, in our cruel century we can gratefully recall a dictator who managed without concentration camps or bloody purges and even retired voluntarily.[10]

Another example of conservative dictatorship with occasional fascist trappings was the regency of Admiral Miklos Horthy in Hungary. Since the Hungarian elite was obdurately monarchist, and the Allies would not permit a Habsburg ruler, postwar Hungary was neither a republic nor a monarchy. In terms of territory and population, the successor state to the eastern half of the defunct Habsburg empire was the greatest single loser of the Great War. The total number of dead, wounded, and prisoners of war had amounted to approximately three-fifths of the prewar male population. By the Treaty of Trianon in June 1920, Hungary surrendered two-thirds of its 1914 territory to Romania (Transylvania), Czechoslovakia (Slovakia), and Yugoslavia (the Banat). These cessions included about half of the nation's total economic resources and population, and divided what had been a natural economic unit. As with German, Austrian, and Bulgarian frontiers, the principles of national self-determination were impossible to apply in practice and so were interpreted by the Allies in favor of the new states. One million Magyars remained in Czechoslovakia, 1,700,000 Magyars became Romanian subjects, and about half a million became Yugoslav subjects.

The desperate Hungarians made two completely unsuccessful attempts to escape the above-mentioned fate. From October 1918 to March 1919, the liberal aristocrat Mikaly Karolyi attempted to lay the basis of a Western-style democracy, including the partial distribution to the peasants of his own inherited lands (a gesture which confirmed his fellow aristocrats in the view that he was a traitor to Hungary's only legitimate ruling class). From late March to the end of July 1919, Bela Kun, a left-wing journalist who had participated in the Bolshevik revolution, tried to establish a Soviet republic. He pinned his hopes for success on Soviet material aid, which was not forthcoming; on the spread of the "world revolution," which did not occur; and on negotiations with the Western Allies, also not forthcoming.

By the spring of 1920 the traditional landlord ruling class had returned to power and was still fantasizing the restoration of the Habsburg dynasty as the legitimate government. The Allies vetoed any Habsburg candidacy, however, and recognized the government of the *Regent* Miklos Horthy, last admiral of the Austro-Hungarian Navy, which had been based at Trieste (a city now being contested by Italy and Yugoslavia). Throughout the interwar years, Hungary remained a regency under Horthy. The admiral's regime was ideologically (but helplessly) irredentist and depended on the support of patriotic war veterans, but it realistically accepted the need to integrate the nation peacefully into the new Europe. The prime minister throughout the 1920s was the conservative Calvinist aristocrat Count István Bethlen, who governed moderately on behalf of an establishment which included the Magyar landlords, the military, the state bureaucracy, the clergy (both Catholic and Calvinist), and the banks. The government party was guaranteed an automatic majority by the fact that outside the main cities, all the voting was done by raising hands in open assemblies. Socialists, trade unionists, and miscellaneous opposition groups were allowed to campaign for internal reforms as long as they accepted the revisionist foreign policy of the government and did not agitate for a secret ballot in the countryside. Horthy and Bethlen shared the polite social anti-Semitism of the traditional Magyar ruling class, but worked cordially with the important Jewish economic and professional classes in Budapest.

The 1920s witnessed a substantial recovery in Hungary in the areas of agriculture and light industry (textiles, paper, leather, and ceramics). But there was no effective land reform, educational advance, or change in the standard of living. The peasants depended principally on traditional sharecropping and remained largely illiterate, their homes without electricity and their roads mostly unpaved. In 1922 Hungary was admitted to the League of Nations, and in 1924 it received a League-sponsored "reconstruction" loan. The money was used, however, mostly to pay off Habsburg-era debts and to strengthen the banking and currency systems—actions which benefited the small urban elite, but which did not alter the primitive lives of the great majority of Hungarians.

In the depression of 1930–32, agricultural prices collapsed and all the Central European states (somewhat imitating Italy) tried vainly to save themselves through policies of "autarchy"—restricting imports and devaluing their currencies for temporary export advantage in what the economist John Maynard Keynes described as a "beggar thy neighbor" policy. By 1935, the beginnings of German rearmament and the system of bilateral trade agreements sponsored by the Nazis made Hungary increasingly dependent on Germany as both an agricultural and industrial market.[11]

In 1932, Count Bethlen was replaced as prime minister by a military officer of genuine fascist sentiments, Gyula Gömbös. The new prime minister had been an admirer of Mussolini and Hitler throughout the 1920s. He was antilegitimist (anti-Habsburg) and represented the non-noble war veterans and retired or unemployed civil servants who were fiercely patriotic, generally anti-Semitic, and bitterly resentful toward the traditional aristocracy. In imitation of his mentors, Gömbös led a paramilitary organization of some sixty thousand "vanguard fighters" but he was never remotely able to dominate Hungary as a fascist dictator. Magyar nationalism conflicted with the pro-Hitler sentiments of the local German minorities and also with the interests of Austria in the Burgenland. Gömbös did not share the dramatic or oratorical skills of Mussolini or Hitler; moreover, he needed the economic aid of the urban Jewish community, and decided to view as "brothers" those Jews who identified themselves with Magyar nationalism. He died unexpectedly in 1936.

In general, up to the time when Hitler directly occupied the country in 1944, Hungary's government was conservative, with the executive easily dominating a nonrepresentative parliament and a submissive judiciary. But it permitted free speech and publication, if and when the contents did not threaten the government's authority. Nor did Hungary's leaders "mobilize" the masses by oratory or single-party organization. They utilized anti-Semitism to limit the role of the Jews, but conscientiously avoided the rabble-rousing anti-Semitism of the Nazis.[12]

If Hungary was the greatest loser in the first World War, the greatest winners were Romania and Yugoslavia. Both nations emerged with greatly expanded territories in 1919, and both were anointed with the favor that the British normally award to stable monarchies, and which the Americans—who deprived themselves of the pleasures of monarchy in 1776—also unconsciously feel toward royal regimes.

The "Kingdom of Serbs, Croats, and Slovenes," as it was called in 1919 (later to become "Yugoslavia" in 1929), consisted of the prewar Serbian and Montenegrin monarchies, plus territories taken from the now-defunct Habsburg and Ottoman empires. The Croats (23 percent of the population) and especially the Slovenes (with only 8 1/2 percent of the population) had enjoyed somewhat higher living standards and government services than had the Serbs (43 percent). But the Serbian military and civil-service establishments became the effective rulers of the entire kingdom, and the dynastic authority of King Alexander was extended without consultation to all the non-Serbian areas and populations.

Most historians credit Alexander with personal integrity and a sincere desire to justly rule his enlarged realm of sixteen million subjects, in which the Serbs constituted less than half the population. But he and his small circle of Serbian intimates were incapable of thinking in multinational terms, and subsequent history suggests that no one individual or party would have been capable of truly unifying the extraordinarily diverse peoples. Serbs and Croats spoke the same language, but they belonged to different churches and had been culturally dominated for centuries by two very different empires. The Slovene and the Bosnian Muslim elites achieved some favorable treatment by becoming bilingual and making pragmatic compromises with the Serbian administration, police, and military. But there were also German, Magyar, and Romanian peasants and townspeople in the northern (formerly Habsburg) territories who felt themselves to be culturally superior to the Serbs. There were the Macedonians, who constituted a separate nationality—one which had not been recognized in the postwar settlements with a state of its own, but had been divided among Greece, Bulgaria, and Yugoslavia. There were also gypsies and Albanians, neither of them in any sense a threat to the state, but not easily assimilable either. Finally there were the Jews, not marked out for ill treatment, but also not assimilable to a dominant Serbian culture.[13]

The new kingdom, with the partial exception of Slovenia and the Dalmatian coast, suffered the general economic problems of the Balkan peninsula: primitive methods in both agriculture and industry; lack of transport, communication, and health infrastructures; 40 percent illiteracy; high birth and disease rates, high rural unemployment; and venality and corruption in both civil and military appointments, on which the small middle class heavily depended for survival. In these circumstances, the "triune" kingdom was never able to function as a constitutional monarchy. Falsified elections, physical violence on the floor of parliament, and police abuses against political opponents and critical journalists were prevalent from the start. Further complicating this situation was the fact that all the political parties—except for the illegal and persecuted communist party—represented regional nationalist interests.

One of the great dilemmas of Yugoslav history—and of Central-Eastern European and Balkan history in general—is the extent to which ethnic, religious, and national hatreds are truly prevalent in the mixed populations, and the extent to which these sentiments are propagandistically whipped up to "divide and conquer" on behalf of a dynasty, a dictator, or a political party. I have no minute knowledge of any of the countries discussed in this chapter except Spain, but I have read enough to know that the leading scholars in the field have come to diametrically opposed conclusions as to the profundity and tenacity of ethnic tensions.

I am inclined to believe that, in conditions of peace and with the economy operating at what are normal levels for the area involved, the great majority of members of all ethnic groups prefer to live amicably with their "different" neighbors. They may not want to intermarry with them, they may prefer, if feasible, to do business with "their own kind," but they are generally prepared to live and let live. However, when a crisis occurs—and especially if there is no widely respected political authority to resolve or mediate a crisis—then, in conditions of complete uncertainty, people instinctively identify themselves with their own group, at which point paranoia and violence can flare up rapidly. In the history of this entire area of mixed nationalities there are long periods of peace and cultural interpenetration punctuated by riots, massacres, and civil wars.

To return to Yugoslavia specifically, in 1928 Stepan Radich, charismatic leader of the Croatian Peasant Party, was shot during a session of parliament and died a slow and painful death over the next several weeks. It was not the first or last such incident, but it was the most important because it seemed to symbolize the martyrdom of the second largest people in the triune kingdom, and because of Radich's complex personal relationship to the king. The next year King Alexander suspended the inoperative constitution, renamed the country Yugoslavia in a mighty effort to *will* the unity of his dominions, and announced a royal dictatorship. In 1934, agents of the Italian and Hungarian governments assassinated Alexander in Marseilles at the start of what was to be an "image-improving" visit to France (at that time the patron of the Little Entente nations, Czechoslovakia, Romania, and Yugoslavia). As can be seen in even this brief discussion of the triune kingdom, Alexander's regime was clearly a royal dictatorship with a few constitutional trappings, but not a "fascist" regime.

Romania began its interwar history with the acquisition of prosperous former Habsburg territories in Transylvania and Bukovina, and with less prosperous acquisitions from Russia (Bessarabia) and Bulgaria (southern Dobruja). Compared with Yugoslavia it had two great advantages: its dynasty and civil service were already well established, and its population (totalling eighteen million) was 70 percent Romanian. In addition, Romania between 1917 and 1927 carried through the largest land reform to occur anywhere in Europe west of Russia. Over one million peasant families received one to ten hectares (roughly two and a half acres), thereby strengthening the patriotic basis for conservative royal rule in a country with high rates of illiteracy, tuberculosis, venereal disease, and other symptoms of extreme poverty. But in economic terms, the results were disappointing. There were few machines, few paved roads, and virtually no educational services or agricultural credit. The cattle population was greatly reduced by the plowing of what had been grazing lands prior to the reform. The high birth rate and the lack of technological improvement meant that neither productivity nor the standard of living improved, and Romania's villages, like those of Hungary and Yugoslavia, suffered constant high unemployment.

Corrupt elections, nepotism in appointments, and police harassment of the opposition were normal aspects of political life in Romania, which was theoretically a constitutional monarchy and enjoyed particular Western sympathy due to the Roman linguistic and archaeological heritage of the kingdom. Romania's nationality problems were less serious than those of Yugoslavia. There were Magyar and Ukrainian minorities which resented being placed under Romanian sovereignty, but they were a relatively small percentage of the population. The most important minority from a cultural and economic point of view, the Germans, had had compact communities in Transylvania and Bucharest for centuries, and were treated favorably by the government.[14]

Anti-Semitism was endemic in Romania (as elsewhere in the region), and the cultural contrast between the Jews and their neighbors was greater than in Poland, Austria, or Yugoslavia. The first two countries had business and professional classes of their own, and in Yugoslavia there were plenty of Greek and Muslim shopkeepers as well as Jews. But in Romania, although the Jews constituted only 4 percent of the population, they numbered one-third to one-half of all city dwellers and were prominent in all the liberal professions. Moreover, in the provinces acquired in 1919 (Bukovina and Bessarabia), the Jews were more solidly orthodox and unassimilated than in Hungary or Austria or Czechoslovakia. They wore their traditional caftans and black hats in the streets, and many of the store signs were in the Hebrew alphabet (the alphabet of written Yiddish).

A significant fascist party, the "Iron Guard," did develop in Romania in the late 1920s, and its appeal was quite similar to that of Mussolini's early fascism. The Iron Guard bemoaned the corruption, the lack of governmental initiative, and the lack of dignity and energy on the part of bureaucrats. It called for social justice and sometimes offered an example by helping peasants to harvest their crops or repair roads and dams. The Iron Guard made its appeals—a mixture of Romanian patriotism, anti-Semitism, fear and scorn of communist Russia—to the classes which felt most marginalized by the royal government: the lower rank military officers, the civil servants, and the peasants who were barely able to feed their families despite the land reform.

Between 1930 and 1940, the country was ruled by a particularly manipulative, opportunist king, Carol II. He developed (partly in imitation of the Yugoslav King Alexander, whose few admirable qualities he lacked) a royal dictatorship with a central "romanianizing" administration and much rhetoric about the Orthodox Church, the family, and the work ethic. He sometimes used the Iron Guard's vigilantes and sometimes repressed them as rivals of his own brutal police. In December 1933, the Iron Guard assassinated one of Romania's few uncorrupt premiers with the known connivance of the police and the probable connivance of the king; and in November 1938, the king had the founder of the Iron Guard murdered in prison.

In that five-year interval Hitler had replaced Mussolini as the most important European dictator. The Iron Guard became increasingly sympathetic to the Nazis, and Carol II also attempted to curry favor with Hitler. As a result, the role of the Iron Guard came to depend not on its strength as a local political movement but on the Nazi dictator's views. In September 1940 Carol was forced into exile and the Iron Guard now seemed completely triumphant. But their violence turned out to be too disorderly for Hitler, and in January 1941 he installed a military dictatorship which was to rule at his behest until the end of World War II.

If we compare what happened in Romania with events in Italy and Spain, we see that in the latter cases the king actually named and supported the dictator (and in the case of Italy and Mussolini the king of course accepted, willingly or not, the one-party state and the fascist propaganda apparatus). But Carol tried to play off the Romanian fascists against his own corrupt and violent police. Neither he nor Hitler ever consistently backed the Iron Guard, and thus the government of

Romania was essentially a royal dictatorship succeeded by a military dictatorship. To put it another way, while the interrelationship—at times collaborative, at times hostile—between a corrupt monarchy and a fascist movement was a constant factor in Romanian politics from 1927 to 1944, fascism never dominated the country.

Any chapter devoted to the interwar history of the tier of small countries located between Greece and Finland must yield a dreary impression of inevitable drift from attempted constitutionalism and partial democracy to oppressive authoritarian regimes. In the cases of Greece, Bulgaria, Poland, and the Baltic countries (which I am not treating separately), all these countries had clear constitutional intentions in 1919, and all of them were dictatorships before the onset of World War II. The degrees of corruption and cruelty, doctrinal clarity, and party or dynastic loyalty may differ greatly, but the overall trend is unmistakable.

All the more interesting, then, is the counterexample of Finland, a country which might easily have become a military dictatorship in 1918 and might easily have gone fascist at any time between 1928 and 1932, but which instead resolved its long political crisis in favor of constitutional, democratic governance. Crucial to this happy outcome were the moral and constitutional scruples of the three statesmen who dominated Finland (population three and a half million) during the first fifteen years of its independent existence.

In January 1918, the conservative parliamentary Prime Minister Pehr Evind Svinhufvud successfully negotiated Finnish independence with the revolutionary government of Vladimir Lenin. The Bolsheviks had promised independence to the peoples of the tsarist empire who desired it, and they honored this promise in the single case of Finland. The independence was recognized, of course, at a time when Lenin was fully confident that a world revolution would soon sweep away all existing sovereignties, but the fact remains that he signed and fulfilled a treaty with a Finnish prime minister who was still hoping to create a constitutional monarchy under a German prince. An early challenge to these arrangements came in late January 1918, when the pro-Bolshevik Finnish militia tried to seize Helsinki as a step toward creating a communist nation. They were defeated by late April of 1918 by Finnish troops under the command of General Gustav Mannerheim, who had been the highest-ranking Finnish officer in the Russian imperial army. Mannerheim was careful to limit the extent of German "aid" to his campaign, and he passed up any opportunity to become a dictator on behalf of Finland's most rabid reactionaries.

With the surrender of Germany in November 1918, Finland sued for Allied recognition as a republic and endowed itself with a democratic constitution whose main author was the liberal law professor J. K. Stahlberg. During the 1920s, the founding fathers of the republic—the liberal Stahlberg and the conservative Svinhufvud—both endorsed several amnesties of the communists imprisoned in 1918, and both also favored basic social legislation along the lines of the much-admired (and recently deceased) German empire.

Finnish elections were honestly conducted, though marred to some extent by sporadic violence between the communists and the anti-communists. In general, the Left received about 40 percent of the vote—two-thirds for the social democrats and one third for the communists—and the several Centrist parties received closer to 50 percent. The Far Right called repeatedly for the suppression of the communist party, but both Stahlberg and Svinhufvud opposed such a measure.

The year 1929 saw the rise of a native fascist party, the "Lapua movement" (named for a town in which the communist headquarters had been vandalized), which sought for the repeal of social legislation and the legal suppression of the communist party. In the presidential election of 1931, the movement's votes supplied a small margin of victory for Svinhufvud over Stahlberg, and the Lapuan leadership expected the victorious conservative to establish an anticommunist presidential dictatorship. When Svinhufvud failed to do so, the Lapuan leadership called for a "Finnish Hitler" and prepared a march on Helsinki (modeled on Mussolini's march on Rome some ten years earlier). But Svinhufvud accepted the challenge, ordered the army to prevent the march, and arrested the handful of marchers who refused to lay down their arms. Thus the three most powerful Finnish leaders—Mannerheim, Svinhufvud, and Stahlberg—steadily supported constitutional government and honest elections that included candidates from the communist party. The difference between their behavior and that of President von Hindenburg of Germany in 1933 cannot but tempt one to wonder how different twentieth-century history might have been if German conservatives had faced up to Hitler's verbal and street violence instead of facilitating his destruction of the Weimar Republic. In any case, these three Finnish statesmen share the credit for saving their nation from the depressing fate of Germany and all the rest of Central-Eastern, Balkan, and Baltic Europe. These acts of true integrity and political courage occurred in the worst years of the world depression, and when all their immediate neighbors except Sweden had become dictatorships.[15]

ENDNOTES

1. My discussion of the Left parties and the factory occupations is based principally upon Alistair Davidson, *Antonio Gramsci* (London: Merlin Press, 1977); also Thomas R. Bates, "Antonio Gramsci and the Bolshevization of the PCI," *The Journal of Contemporary History*, July 1976, 115–31.

2. On Mussolini the man, see Carleton Beals, *Rome or Death*, The Century Co., 1923; and G. A. Borhese, *Goliath: The March of Fascism* (New York: The Viking Press, 1937). Also Clarence Yarrow, "The Forging of Fascist Doctrine," *Journal of the History of Ideas*, 1942, no. 2, 159–81.

3. See S. J. Woolf, ed. *Fascism in Europe*, London: Methuen, 1981, especially the chapter on Italy by Woolf (chapter three) and the interpretive comments by H. R. Trevor-Roper in the chapter entitled "The Phenomenon of Fascism."

4. Gerald K. Meaker, *The Revolutionary Left in Spain, 1914–1923*, Stanford University Press, 1974.

5. In addition to the Meaker work cited above, see Colin C. Winston, "El sindicalismo libre, 1919–1931," *Historia 16*, December 1978, 73–81; and Stanley C. Payne, *The Spanish Revolution* (New York: Norton, 1970), pp. 40–57.

6. Carolyn P. Boyd, *Praetorina Politics in Liberal Spain* (University of North Carolina Press, 1979).

7. Quoted in my *Approximación a la España contemporanea, 1898–1975* (Barcelona: Grijalbo, 1980), p. 69 (my translation of the General's prose).

8. Dolors Marin i Silvestre, *De la llibertat per conèixer, al coneixement de la llibertat* (Ph.D. thesis in contemporary history, The University of Barcelona, 1995), gives a wealth of detail on the social-intellectual life of anarchist families and "affinity groups."

9. See Manuel Lorenzo Pardo, *La conquista del Ebro*, Saragoss, 1931, the account by the first engineer-executive of the Ebro valley hydraulic program; and Juan Velarde Fuertes, *Política economica de la dictadura* (Madrid: Guadiana, 1973).

10. My overall judgments are based on Raymond Carr, *Spain, 1808–1975*, chapter XIV; Shlomo Ben Ami, *The Origins of the Second Republic in Spain*, Oxford University Press, 1978, whose principal subject matter is the Primo dictatorship; and my own above-cited *Approximaxción*.

11. Jörg K. Hoensch, *A History of Modern Hungary*, Longmans, 1988; and Joseph Rothschild, *East Central Europe Between the Two World Wars* (University of Washington Press, 1974), chapter 4.

12. N. M. Nagy-Talavera, *The Green Shirts and Others: A History of Fascism in Hungary and Romania* (Stanford: The Hoover Institute, 1969).

13. For the factual background, see Rothschild, chapter 5; Barbara Jelavich, *History of the Balkans*, vol. 2, Cambridge University Press, 1983; and Fred Singleton, *A Short History of the Yugoslav Peoples* (Cambridge University Press, 1985). Especially recommended for the atmosphere of Serb-Croat personal and cultural relations as experienced by a great journalist and essayist is Rebecca West, *Black Lamb and Gray Falcon* (New York: The Viking Press, 1941).

14. On Romania, see the above-cited works by Rothschild, Jelavich, and Nagy-Talavera.

15. Eino Jutikkala and Kauko Pirinen, *A History of Finland* (New York: Praeger, 1974); Marvin Rintala, *Three Generations, the Extreme Right Wing in Finnish Politics* (Indiana University Press and The Hague: Meuton, 1962); Jean-Jacques Fol, "La montée du fascisme en Finlande, 1922–1932," *Revue d'historie moderne et contemporaine*, January 1971; and William J. Stover, "Finnish Military Politics Between the Two World Wars," *The Journal of Contemporary History*, October 1977.

5

The Scientific Revolution, 1895–1939

*P*rogress in the exact sciences has been continuous since the seventeenth century, the century in which Galileo, Kepler, Descartes, Newton, and Leibniz laid the foundations of modern physics, astronomy, and mathematics. Over the course of the late eighteenth and nineteenth centuries, the development of exact knowledge spread from physics and astronomy to chemistry, biology, geology, and medicine. And from the mid–nineteenth century onward, top-quality work was being done in North America and Asia as well as Europe.

The two most important motors of progress at all times were the successful application of mathematics to new areas, and the improvement of measuring instruments and of laboratory equipment in general. Mathematics enabled scientists to give the most exact, precise description of their results and to hypothesize (and hence inspire new experiments to discover) what might happen under a variety of conditions different from those already analyzed. Improved equipment in the form of telescopes, microscopes, balances, clocks, thermometers, and measuring rods; insulation from extraneous noise, light, and vibrations; ever more precise control of temperatures, pressures, and chemical environments; and the ability to create more complete vacuums—all these advances made it possible to see farther into space and to observe smaller and smaller units of matter, both at rest and in motion.

Until late in the nineteenth century, all physical phenomena appeared to be explicable in terms of—or at least potentially consistent with—the foundational laws of seventeenth-century physics. The relative simplicity of these laws, involving nothing more complex than quadratic and cubic equations, also gave rise to great optimism about the ultimate comprehensibility of the universe. If the motions of all the heavenly bodies could be accurately foreseen for thousands of years to come; if the trajectories of all projectiles could be accurately plotted in advance; if Newton's falling apple and all the galaxies obeyed the same gravitational laws—it seemed possible in principle that all phenomena, both inorganic and organic, might eventually be brought under analogous, mathematically and conceptually simple laws.

Thus it was that, from the age of Newton to the end of the nineteenth century, many great intellects, scientific and humanistic, religious and secular, shared a nonlogical but virtually unshakable faith in the emerging comprehensibility of the universe. Both the stern God of the Old Testament and the loving Son who had sacrificed himself to redeem the sins of mankind tended to be replaced (if only unconsciously) by the Great Engineer, the Benign Clockmaker who had set the universe in motion and who now looked on with fatherly pride while men of genius gradually discovered His laws.

The success of the Newtonian system also encouraged another belief—that observation and experiment in chemistry and biology would eventually reveal a substructure of Newtonian laws governing those sciences as well. In the era of the French Revolution, some even dared to hope that human society, if scientifically studied, would yield fairly simple, deterministic laws which would enable mankind finally to resolve age-old problems of war and poverty. The entire European faith in "progress" was thus intimately bound up with the continuing success of Newtonian science.

Among scientists themselves, however, doubts about the completeness of the Newtonian synthesis began to accumulate from about the middle of the nineteenth century. The study of gases now obliged them to think in statistical terms, to study the *average* behavior of masses of units rather than the specific behavior of individual units. On the other hand, the kinetic theory of gases did not contravene the concept of continuity, and its laws were mathematically comparable to the existing Newtonian laws.

In the same decades, the study of electricity and magnetism made it necessary to introduce a major new concept, that of the electromagnetic field of force. The field concept was more complex than that of Newtonian gravity, which acted at a distance, in a straight line, between the centers of massive material bodies. The field was constituted by energy rather than by material objects, and its changes of energy were propagated as transverse waves traveling in all directions through empty space at the speed of light, with the electric and magnetic lines of forces lying on planes perpendicular to the direction of propagation. Nevertheless, the field laws developed by the Scottish mathematician Clerk Maxwell did not contradict the principles of determinism and continuity of action (essential aspects of the Newtonian heritage), nor did they contradict the belief—firmly established at the beginning of the century— that light consisted of, and was propagated in the form of, waves.

By the late nineteenth century, however, there were clearly problems with the idea that light consisted *only* of waves. Waves need a medium, such as air or water, in which to travel, and so the conviction that light consisted of waves made it necessary to hypothesize a medium for their transmission across the immensity of "empty" space. This medium was called "the ether." As long as instruments for measuring the speed of light could not yield more than the most approximate estimates, there was no way of measuring the effect of the ether, either on light waves or on the earth, which must also be moving through it.

But by 1887 it was possible to measure very accurately the velocity of light, and an experiment was set up specifically to detect the effects of the ether on the motion of the earth. The speed of light was measured simultaneously in the direction of the earth's movement and at right angles to it. No matter how slight the effects of the ether, it was assumed that the light reflected back from a beam sent out in the direction of the earth's movement would return slightly sooner than light reflected from a beam at right angles to the earth's movement. When the measurements were made, however, absolutely no difference of velocity was detected.

Did this mean that the ether did not exist? Not necessarily. The Irish physicist George Fitzgerald hypothesized that a large body traveling very rapidly might be slightly foreshortened in the direction of its travel, and that such foreshortening—which would include the interferometer measuring the velocity of light—might be just enough to cancel the anticipated effect of the ether. And the Dutch physicist Hendrick Anton Lorentz hypothesized, from his experiments with cathode rays, that a flying particle which was foreshortened in the direction of its travel would also increase its mass. Fitzgerald's equation for the foreshortening and Lorentz's equation for the increased mass gave fully compatible results, thereby saving the ether theory for the moment; they were also soon to become important as the "Lorentz-Fitzgerald transformation" equations in connection with the special theory of relativity.[1]

Another of the widely believed, but not finally proven, assumptions of nineteenth-century physics and chemistry was the atomic theory: that the fundamental units of matter were the presumably undividable atoms of the approximately eighty distinct chemical elements which had been identified and classified in the course of the century. But by 1900 this theory was challenged by phenomena which clearly indicated that stable, undividable atoms were not the smallest units of matter (leaving aside the vague implications of the word "fundamental"). Both X-rays, discovered in 1895 by the German chemist Wilhelm Röntgen, and radioactive elements, discovered in 1898 by the Polish-French chemist Marie Sklodowska and her physicist husband Pierre Curie, could not be accounted for in terms of the indivisible atoms and stable molecular compounds which had been analyzed by nineteenth-century atomic chemistry. In 1897, the English chemist J. J. Thomson proved the existence of an almost massless, electrically charged particle, the electron, whose relation to existing atoms and molecules was completely undefined.

But the most dramatic new problem, one that demanded a clear break with tradition, was the phenomenon of black body radiation being studied principally in Germany and England. The English physicists Rayleigh and Jeans tried unsuccessfully to calculate the observed spectra of black body radiation in terms of the *continuous* changes in frequency and energy levels which they expected to find for the energy being emitted. Facing the same problem, the German physicist Max Planck—breaking with both his past experience and his intuitive belief in continuity—decided that the observed radiation *must* be occurring in discontinuous packets of energy, which he referred to as "quanta," and for the minimal units of discontinuous change, he produced the mathematical formula which has been the cornerstone of quantum physics ever since its publication in 1900. At some point in the course of this highly original work, whose implications both exhilarated and disturbed him, Planck told his adult son that he had discovered something comparable in importance to the discoveries of Isaac Newton.

He had indeed, and in the thirty years following the announcement of Planck's constant, an entirely new physics was created. This new physics did not invalidate Newtonian physics in its application to the macrophenomena of the earth and the solar system. But the rapidly developing quantum theory, as well as the theories of special relativity (1905) and general relativity (1915), were essential to describe both the atomic and subatomic phenomena previously unknown and—at the other extreme of magnitude—the nature of the millions of galaxies beyond the solar system, the number, immensity, and distance of which were literally unsuspected until the advent of the giant telescopes (and more especially the radio telescopes) of the present century.

Within a few years of 1900, the physics of the era from 1600 to 1900 was being called "classical physics," and the physics of quanta and relativity was being called "modern physics" (a terminology which I shall henceforth adopt). As an indication of the contrasts between science and the humanities, I note that when I was studying for my doctorate in the French university system in 1950, "modern history" meant the period from c. 1500 to 1789 (the date of the French Revolution), and everything since 1789 was labeled "contemporary history." Changes in human behavior occurring much more slowly than changes in scientific knowledge, it is not at all inappropriate that the "modern" era, which began five centuries ago for historians, begins with the twentieth century for physicists.

Indeed, modern physics has cut loose from the entire assumed framework of classical physics. For Newton, space was the infinite sensorium of God; for Einstein space was what we measure with a yardstick. Not that Einstein is an atheist. To the contrary: like the great seventeenth-century Jewish thinker Baruch Spinoza, Einstein believed in a completely deterministic universe which coincided with what we call "God"; and also like Spinoza, he based his broad personal tolerance and his patience with stumbling humanity on a conviction of the inevitability of things as they occur. But as a scientist, Einstein dispensed with all absolute frames and insisted on sticking to humanly observable facts: Space is what you measure with a ruler, and time is what you measure with a clock.

Shortly after Planck's discovery of the quantum nature of black body radiation, another German physicist, Phillip Lenard, noticed that when light strikes the surface of certain metals, electrons are emitted from that surface—a phenomenon known as the photoelectric effect. The short, high-frequency waves at the blue end of the spectrum caused the metallic surface to emit electrons of greater energy than did the long, low-frequency waves at the red end. But how could light waves, short or long, cause a metallic surface to emit electrons? In 1905, Einstein suggested an answer: that in some sense light must also be a corpuscle, a species of tiny projectile capable of bombarding the metal atoms and sometimes detaching a position of their electrons. The higher frequency (hence greater energy) of blue light explained its greater effectiveness in producing the photoelectric effect. Thus the quantum interpretation which Planck had applied to radiation provided the answer to the photo-electric effect, an answer which could not have been given if light were thought of solely as a wave.

Lenard was awarded the Nobel Prize in 1905 for his crucial experiments, and Einstein was awarded the Nobel Prize in 1921 for his theoretical explanation of the photoelectric effect. In the late 1920s, and into the Nazi era, Lenard became the spokesman for "German" physics—good, solid experimental physics—and Einstein's theoretical contributions were stigmatized as "Jewish" physics. Thus did anti-intellectualism and anti-Semitism combine within the Nazi mentality, a combination which has been frequent in many groups besides the Nazis, and to which I will return in discussing the 1930s.

In that same year, the *annus mirabilis* of Einstein's creative genius, he also announced the special theory of relativity. He asserted that the increased mass and foreshortened length of particles, which had been hypothesized by Fitzgerald and Lorentz, would apply to all bodies, small or large, moving with velocities approaching that of light; and that the velocity of light in a vacuum (whatever its exact particle/wave nature) would be constant regardless of the velocity of the source emitting the light. In addition, Einstein's theory proposed that there were no such things as absolute space and time, that (as his great predecessor Galileo had demonstrated in the seventeenth century) all spatial and temporal measurements must be *relative* to some chosen frame of reference.

It has often been said that Einstein was led to relativity by pondering the problems posed by the Michelson-Morley experiment of 1887. That critical experiment had indeed proven the constancy of the speed of light, and had found no trace whatsoever of the ether that scientists had been talking about since the time of Christian Huygens and the original wave theory of light in the seventeenth century. Since Einstein's theory spelled out the startling implications of the constant velocity of light, it is certainly understandable to assume that he might have been mulling over the Michelson-Morley result.

But Einstein, who was very scrupulous about crediting the work of colleagues, made no mention of this experiment in his paper announcing special relativity. From biographical studies it seems that as early as his teens, Einstein had been considering the implications for physics if the velocity of light were constant under all circumstances, that there could be no such thing as one light beam being accelerated to "catch up" with another. Perhaps even more important, both he and Max Planck considered the laws of thermodynamics to be the most firmly established of all physical laws—even more so than those of Newton. (Indeed, when Planck was asked how he had ever imagined anything as foreign to common sense and scientific tradition as the quantum theory, he replied that he was desperate to find an explanation which would not contradict the laws of thermodynamics.) The first law of thermodynamics is the law of the conservation of energy, and in a certain sense the famous Einstein formula stating that energy equals mass times the square of the velocity of light ($E=mc^2$) is a generalization of that law, far more powerful in its implications than the idea of the conservation of energy had been before anyone imagined that all forms of *matter* could be treated as equivalent to energy.

In the biographies, letters, and autobiographies of the great scientists of the early twentieth century, one can appreciate the combination of exhilaration and puzzlement which spread through the community of physicists, chemists, and astronomers as the implications of Planck's and Einstein's discoveries were understood and applied to a myriad of new phenomena, both below the threshold of the solid nineteenth-century atom and beyond the limited (not to say minuscule) observed universe of c. 1900. But although intellectually the beginnings of quantum and relativity theory were the most revolutionary developments at the start of the new century, it can be argued that the discovery of the various types of radiation, and the developments in chemistry and the understanding of atomic structure, were more immediately influential in the activities of most practicing scientists.

In the following paragraphs I shall try to give some idea of the experimentation, hypotheses, and discussion occurring between 1900 and the outbreak of the First World War. In France, the Curies smashed rocks and painstakingly swirled through tons of pitchblend supplied by Austrian physicists from the uranium mines of Bohemia. Marie Curie continued this work even after the unexpected death (in a traffic accident) of her husband, Pierre, in 1906. She worked in a simple shed— nothing that would be called a laboratory in any high school or college today—and destroyed her health while successfully separating and identifying usable quantities of radium and bits of other radioactive elements. (Of course, no one had any idea at the time of the health hazards of working with such materials.) Miraculously, Curie survived to the age of 67; her cookbooks were still radioactive in the 1980s.

In England the most active experimenter was Ernest Rutherford, an immensely energetic New Zealander who had arrived in England as a scholarship student and had worked successively at Cambridge, McGill University in Montreal, and Manchester University. Rutherford was a born "chairman" of team research—generous in his encouragement of graduate students, quick to recognize great talent, and able to listen to ideas other than his own (not a terribly frequent trait among great academics). His laboratory in Manchester also benefited from his friendship with Sir Arthur Schuster, a German-English chemist whose private wealth enabled him to buy the latest equipment.

As of 1900 the technique of spectrum analysis, developed largely in Germany, had identified many new chemical elements and predicted the existence of others, but it had not offered any clear picture of atomic structure. J. J. Thomson, discoverer of the electron, hypothesized that the atom was a porous, pudding-like sphere in which the electrons were embedded like raisins (his image). But increasing experience with the several forms of radiation and the puzzling behavior of radioactive elements both seemed to contradict this. Thus there was a great deal of experimentation and continued theorizing about the structure of atoms which nobody had yet "seen"—and whose very existence was contested by such prestigious scientists as the Austrian physicist Ernest Mach and the German chemist Wilhelm Oswald.[2]

Five years after Röntgen's discovery of X-rays in 1895, physicists and chemists had distinguished many forms of radiation. In addition to X-rays, which were immediately useful in medicine, there were alpha rays, soon to be identified as the nuclei of helium (with atomic weight 4 and a positive electric charge); beta rays, soon to be identified as electrons; and gamma rays, similar in their properties to X-rays, but more energetic and hence more penetrating. (Gamma rays were present also in outer space and hence became increasingly important in twentieth-century astronomy.) As of approximately 1908, Ernest Rutherford discovered that the atom was not a raisin pudding–like structure but rather consisted of a highly concentrated, positively charged center surrounded by a "cloud" of virtually weightless electrons. His crucial experiment involved the bombardment of heavy metal foil (gold and lead) with the recently discovered, positively charged alpha rays. The vast majority of the rays—99.9 percent—passed through the foil without detectable deflection; but a tiny remainder bounced back toward the source of radiation. Rutherford reasoned that this was occurring because the positively charged alpha particles were on a collision course with a very positively charged point in space. This repulsion of like charges indicated the positive charge of the concentrated center (or "nucleus") of the atom.

During these same years, chemists were identifying new elements whose place in the periodic table had been predicted but whose actual existence had not yet been proved. Several puzzling phenomena were also being observed by ever-more-precise experimental chemists. One was that radioactive elements apparently decomposed into other elements. Another was that there could be several substances of slightly different atomic weight which were nevertheless virtually indistinguishable as to chemical properties.

A chemist in Rutherford's Manchester laboratory, Frederick Soddy, took the lead in describing and weighing many such substances. He christened them "isotopes," meaning that they occupied the same position in the periodic table. It became clear as an experimental matter that when a nucleus lost an alpha particle it would shift down two steps in the periodic table, and that when it lost a beta particle it would move up one step (shifts which became known as the radioactive displacement law). But no one had a clear explanation as to why some radioactive decay produced a different element, while other substances showed differences of atomic weight yet retained the same chemical properties.

Possible explanations of the isotope phenomenon came with the work of a young Danish physicist who spent part of the year 1912 as a student in Rutherford's lab. Neils Bohr possessed the same ebullient, energetic, communicative personality as did his mentor, but he was more interested in physical theory. Often arguing (politely) with a skeptical Rutherford, Bohr created the first models of the atom as a kind of miniature planetary system. In a fundamental paper published in 1913, the young physicist successfully applied the new quantum theory in his model of the hydrogen atom (structurally the simplest of all elements). He explained the energy levels of the different electron orbits, their stability, and the discontinuous jumps between orbits by the use of Planck's constant. Equally important for the future of chemistry was Bohr's hypothesis that the chemical properties of an element were determined principally by its outermost shell of electrons.

But while the most significant work in the understanding of atomic structure was being done in England, Rutherford's lab did not exercise a monopoly on interesting experiments and fascinating theoretical speculations. Excitement and experimentation were also proceeding on the European continent and in North America and Japan as well. In Belgium, for example, a wealthy chemist named Ernest Solvay (who had made a fortune from the invention of an industrial process for producing bicarbonate of soda) decided to subsidize international meetings in Brussels, complete with a reception and dinner with the king and queen, of the world's leading physicists and chemists. Planck, Thomson, Rutherford, the Curies, Einstein, and about twenty other luminaries exchanged ideas and created a strong sense of the international, collaborative character of science. The informal chairman was Hendrick Lorentz, the Dutch scientist famous for the transformation equations which had entered importantly into Einstein's theories, as well as for his diplomatic ability to assuage the personal and national sensibilities of some of the distinguished participants.

The discussions reflected both the rapid expansion of knowledge and the uncertainty as to the status of "classical" physics. Planck spoke almost apologetically about the application of his quantum concepts. Rutherford, like most experimental scientists, was anxious to hold on to the classical framework. Einstein said in 1909 (but doubtless had been thinking for years already) that the next great task of physics would be to construct a satisfactory theory accounting for both the wave and corpuscular properties of light and of electromagnetic phenomena in general. Bohr modeled circular and elliptical orbits obeying Newtonian and Maxwellian equations wherever possible, and introduced quantum ideas (as had Planck himself) only when no classical explanation was available.

The declarations of war in 1914 drastically reduced (but did not entirely suspend) progress in pure science. Thomson, Rutherford, and the great majority of their colleagues devoted their energies to war work. Marie Curie mounted a radiological service in the hospitals near the French front. German scientific leaders—with the notable exception of Einstein—publicly endorsed German war aims and turned over all their resources to war-related research. But the Great War did not produce a complete break in the internationalist traditions of science. Rutherford corresponded with his Austrian colleague Stefan Meyer and with his former student Hans Geiger, who had returned to Germany and was serving the German government. Thus, when the British government proposed in 1918 to confiscate, as enemy property, a precious quantity of radium bromide that Meyer had lent the Manchester lab. Rutherford insisted that it be paid for, after which he sent the money to Vienna for use in repairing and re-equipping Professor Meyer's institute. Similarly, when one of Rutherford's students, James Chadwick, was taken prisoner during the war, Geiger arranged for him to resume his research in Germany.

As a way of illustrating the difference between the German and Austrian empires and the later brief Nazi empire, we may note that the Jewish pacifist Einstein spent the war years working quietly in Germany, and that he announced his general theory of relativity in 1915; also that the radical Jewish psychologist Sigmund Freud worked undisturbed in Vienna and had two sons serving in the Austrian army. It is true that the accumulated Allied bitterness toward the Central Powers, due especially to the occupation of Belgium and to unrestricted submarine warfare, was such that not until 1927 were the Germans and Austrians again invited to the Solvay conferences, but most individual relationships were quickly resumed in 1919.

The period between the two world wars was as rich in new advances as were the years 1895–1905. In announcing the general theory of relativity, Einstein suggested possible observations with which to test its validity. One such possibility was that light rays from beyond the solar system would be bent slightly when passing through the gravitational field of the sun. But assembling equipment and the necessary scientists would have to wait for the restoration of peace; it would also be highly desirable to have a full eclipse of the sun. As it happened, an eclipse was conveniently due in the summer of 1919, the first full year of peace, and would be visible from the island of Principe off the west coast of Africa. The British Royal

Astronomical Society sent an expedition, and its photos showed, as predicted, the bending of light rays. Thus were the delighted British able to announce the first confirmation of the fantastic new theory hatched by a German Jewish physicist during the recent war.

Meanwhile, theoretical physicists were anxious to solve the puzzles of the new quantum theory, and work proceeded with special intensity in Munich (Arnold Sommerfeld, younger colleagues, and pupils); in Göttingen (Max Born, younger colleagues, and pupils); and in Copenhagen (Neils Bohr, plus colleagues, pupils, and distinguished visitors). Einstein also played an important role, despite his philosophical objections to quantum theory. He endorsed the work of an unknown young Indian physicist, S. N. Bose, which offered new proofs of the quantum nature of radiation, and in 1924 he published his own findings concerning the quantum behavior of gas molecules.

In 1905, as part of his discussion of the photoelectric effect, Einstein observed that light would have to be a corpuscle if it was to detach atoms from a metal surface; and in 1909, as mentioned earlier, he called for a theory that would account for both the wave and corpuscular behavior of light. In 1924, Louis de Broglie, the younger brother of a well-known physicist and a happy collaborator in the family-owned laboratory, noted that the quantum equation included a frequency—a property of waves but not of corpuscles—and set out to interpret the quantum data in terms of "waves of matter." When Einstein's French friends Paul Langevin and Marie Curie sent him de Broglie's first theoretical papers, Einstein gave his strong endorsement.

Also in the mid-1920s, the brilliant young German physicist Werner Heisenberg created a "matrix mechanics" which made it possible to interpret mathematically the discontinuous quantum reactions without trying to "visualize" them. His English colleague P. M. Dirac contributed importantly to the clearer mathematical formulation of matrix mechanics. And simultaneously a young Austrian physicist, Erwin Schrödinger, developed a "wave equation" which was mathematically equivalent to the more abstract Heisenberg method and could be applied to classical as well as quantum-wave phenomena.

The equations of de Broglie, Heisenberg, Dirac, and Schrödinger all worked beautifully to explain the experimental data of atomic and molecular physics. They superseded the approximations and classical-quantum combinations of the early Bohr theories (much to the quasipaternal delight of Bohr himself). But because quantum physics contradicted all common sense and human intuition—as well annulling the classical laws at the micro level—its interpretation (as against its practical success) was very puzzling for most scientists, and has remained so to the present day.

Any effort to understand the implications of quantum mechanics must start from an appreciation of the experimental situation and the seminal ideas enunciated in the 1920s by Heisenberg and Bohr themselves. The balance which weighs a few grams of matter, or the light which shines above it, does not appreciably affect the condition or behavior of that matter. Thus for centuries, under classical conditions, the experimenter could plausibly separate himself and his instruments from the phenomena he was examining. He was the Cartesian being ("I think, therefore I am"), the conscious subject examining the "objective" world outside himself. But when he began to experiment with immeasurably smaller objects, his light beams and rulers inevitably altered the state of the object itself. He could no longer observe or measure without, by the very action itself, altering the object of observation or measurement.

Heisenberg summarized this limitation with his "principle of uncertainty": that it is impossible simultaneously to know the position and the momentum of a particle. You can be precise about one or the other, but not both at the same time. Matrix mechanics and Schrödinger's wave equation showed that it was possible to have two entirely different mathematical systems of interpretation which nevertheless gave the same results. At the very least it seemed that scientists would have to give up the idea of spatially visualizable images of the behavior of "matter" (whatever that was). As a result, Neils Bohr and his colleagues worked out what they called the doctrine of "complementarity," also referred to as "the Copenhagen interpretation." Treating atomic events as waves yielded part of the truth, and treating them as particles yielded part of the truth. The undoubted utility and dependability of the results was, for the time being at least, more important than a fully consistent interpretation.[3]

The older generation of physicists—such men as Planck and Einstein—were extremely loath to give up the full determinism of their classical heritage. But the younger generation—and virtually all physicists since the 1930s—have fully accepted the idea that at the micro, molecular, and submolecular level, the observed behavior of particles is statistical, highly probablistic and not fully determined; also that it cannot (and need not) be pictured. As a result the new atomic world ushered in by quantum physics yielded no such relatively simple relationships as those enshrined in the Newtonian laws. The necessary mathematics was much more complex than in classical physics. Old friends like squares, cubes, and *pi* still played a role, but there was a host of new "constants" with values running into the tenth powers (plus and minus); also complex magnetic effects, particle "spin" (discovered in the mid-1920s), and previously unknown attractive forces that were crucial to physical and chemical interactions but at the same time different from the more familiar forces of gravitation and electromagnetism. Thus in 1932 Werner Heisenberg showed the necessity of a "strong" nuclear force acting within the dimensions of single atoms and molecules, and in 1934 the young Italian physicist Enrico Fermi announced the presence of a "weak" nuclear force.

Also, in 1932 came the discovery of new particles: the neutron (almost the twin of the proton, but electrically neutral); the positron (the positively charged equivalent of the electron); the neutrino (a tiny neutral particle necessary to the energy exchanges of quantum chemistry, though not "seen" until 1956); and deuterium (a heavy isotope of hydrogen with atomic weight 2). In 1934 the second Curie couple, Irene Curie (Marie's daughter) and her husband Frederic Joliot-Curie, discovered artificial radioactivity, and during the thirties large numbers of new isotopes, with countless industrial and medical uses, were created in the laboratory. It was by now abundantly clear that the electrons and protons of the Rutherford-Bohr atom were only the first of an indefinite number of subatomic particles. Hence the 1930s witnessed the development of a variety of new laboratory methods for separating such particles from their host atoms or ions. The most successful of these, the cyclotron, was inaugurated at the University of California at Berkeley in 1939. And early in that year—just months before the outbreak of the Second World War—atomic fission was discovered almost simultaneously by small teams of French and German chemists.

Before leaving the field of physics and chemistry to discuss other aspects of science in the years from 1895 to 1939, it is worth emphasizing why this period deserves to be called revolutionary. During the era 1600–1900 classical physicists, and the educated public who followed their work, believed overwhelmingly in the full continuity and predictability of both material and energy forces (thought of as separate but interdependent, somewhat by analogy to the accepted Christian notions of body and soul). They also believed that God's (or Nature's) laws might require the understanding of algebra and calculus, but were still comprehensible by analogy to everyday experience and three-dimensional geometry.

But modern physicists live in a different world. Working with quantum theory and relativity, they have accepted discontinuity, have seen that matter and energy are equivalent to each other, have enthroned probability in place of determinism, and have accepted the idea that "events" in "space-time" can be described mathematically but cannot be pictured in "common sense" terms. The qualitative difference between the classical and modern situations is immense, and its philosophical implications have destroyed both the comfortable image of the great clockmaker God, and the austere but beautiful determinism of the Newtonian-Laplace astronomical equations (to say nothing of the Einsteinian faith that "God does not play dice with the universe," his reason for never accepting as final the truths of quantum mechanics).

Actually, Einstein's famous objection is not really an accurate picture of the new situation. Probabilistic laws at a subatomic level, coinciding in their practical operation with virtually deterministic solutions at the macro level, leave us with fully predictable consequences that have been used in all manner of electronic and nuclear devices. In short, the laws of quantum physics are just as dependable as those of classical physics. Einstein's lament does not mean that the universe is governed by chance; it means that he—and his admired predecessors such as Kepler and Maxwell, as well as Descartes and Newton—possessed a *religious* faith in full determinism as the only intellectually and aesthetically pleasing basis for understanding the universe. We still do not have a complete theoretical framework for such a comprehension (and perhaps we never will), but dependable laws of probability are very different from a universe of chance.

*   *   *

Another element of the scientific revolution at the turn of the twentieth century was the foundation of genetics, the science of biological heredity. In a general way it had always been obvious that offspring resemble their parents, and in many past societies stockbreeders had mated pairs of animals with particular desired traits which they hoped to perpetuate in their flocks. In an approximate fashion, they had succeeded in increasing the frequency of such traits, but no one had any idea how heredity actually worked.

The first scientific experiments to yield the beginnings of such knowledge were made c. 1860 by a teaching monk in a monastery near the Slovak city of Brno. Romanticized versions of the life of Gregor Mendel paint him as an obscure but gifted amateur, and it is indeed true that he lacked the doctoral degrees, the honorary citations, the national and international prizes, and the giant ego of many a modern scientific conquistador—so much so that when the publication of his results made no stir in the scientific world, he did not press the matter. But if we want to understand the triumphs of European science, we should look beneath the legends.

In mid-nineteenth-century Austria, with its small middle class and only the most rudimentary beginnings of a public-school system, the Church was one of the few institutions which could offer education to the talented children of non-wealthy families. To benefit from the Church's educational opportunities one did not have to have a religious vocation; one simply had to be a conforming believer of good character and high intelligence. In return for this church-sponsored education, the recipient would gladly serve the Church in ways that his superiors would determine.

As a boy Mendel's talents had been recognized by the local priest (who himself had a nursery of fruit trees). He recommended Mendel to the head of the local monastery, who in turn sent the young man to the University of Vienna. There Mendel learned of the atomic theory—that the basic constituents of matter were thought to be discrete units—and also that the behavior of some forms of matter, notably gas molecules, was being treated statistically.

Meanwhile local stock breeders in the Brno area were trying to find a way to improve their breeds, as had their opposite numbers in England and France. They took the problem to the monks—the best educated men they knew—and Abbot Knapp assigned the problem to his gifted, Vienna-educated protege. Mendel went to work cross-pollinating different strains of sweetpeas, and decided to concentrate on the reproduction of single visible traits, such as the difference between smooth seeds and crinkled seeds or between yellow plants and green plants.

Mendel kept careful records of his results over a number of generations, and his observations led him to hypothesize that for each separate trait there were two contributions of some kind to heredity, one deriving from each parent. He also noted that the separate traits were inherited independently of each other (i.e., that the round or crinkled seed could be found with either the yellow or the green plant). By counting up the results over a number of generations, he also observed that one trait was dominant over the other—in this case, that yellow dominated green. This mean that if Mendel crossed a yellow plant with a yellow plant, he got yellow plants; but if he crossed yellow with green or green with yellow, he got more yellow plants. Only when he crossed green with green did he get green progeny. Thus did he hit upon the discrete mechanism of heredity and discover the proportions in which one could expect to see a trait inherited, depending upon whether it was the "dominant" or the "recessive" trait.

Mendel published his results in 1866. Although they were not appreciated at the time, they were rediscovered simultaneously in 1900 by three young biologists, the Dutchman Henry DeVries, the German Karl Correns, and the Austrian Erich von Tschermak. In an ethical gesture that has not always characterized the progress of science, all three investigators acknowledged, in their separate publications, that they were rediscovering laws of proportional inheritance which had earlier been discovered by Gregor Mendel.

Several new factors have been responsible for the spectacular development of genetics since the dawn of the twentieth century. One was the fact that, by 1900, microscopes were capable of seeing chromosomes, the large masses of cells which included hereditary material. When the American chemist Walter Sutton noticed that chromosomes always come in pairs, that observation suggested immediately a relationship to Mendel's analysis. Without being able to explain the exact nature of the hereditary material, Danish and Dutch botanists began to call them genes, and several German chemists noted that inheritance seemed to depend upon a specific chemical substance, the nucleic acid which had first been identified in 1869.

New attention to a possible science of heredity was also motivated by its potential relationship to the Darwinian doctrine of evolution through natural selection. Evolution was said to take place through the accumulation of slight changes which made a plant or animal better adapted to survive in its specific environment. How the changes occurred, and under what conditions such "adaptations" were heritable, were debatable questions. The German biologist August Weismann developed the germ plasm theory of heredity, which insisted on the unbroken continuity of the germ plasm from generation to generation and the consequent non-heritability of traits acquired during the lifetime of the individual. Hugo DeVries, a student of plant heredity, emphasized that mutations (i.e., specific, discrete changes in the hereditary structure) were the principal means by which new species occurred. Thus the new science of genetics became essential to all research in evolutionary biology.

But the most important single development was the work of the American biologist T. H. Morgan and his students at Columbia University from about 1906 until the late 1920s. Morgan found in fruit flies the ideal genus for the study of heredity. Fruit flies multiplied rapidly and in great numbers. They were easy to feed, safe to handle, and had easily identifiable hereditary traits which could be studied in greater detail (and in much more sophisticated statistical fashion) than those of garden plants. Though the exact physicochemical processes of heredity were not to be discovered until the 1950s, the work of Morgan and his colleagues provided a fully adequate explanation of its mechanisms.

The revolutionary development of physical and biological sciences in the decades under discussion was accompanied by equally novel developments in the social sciences. But before discussing a few aspects of those sciences, I think it important to examine the term "social science." In the late nineteenth century, it was the ambition of investigators and thinkers in the relatively new fields of sociology, anthropology, political science, economics, and psychology to establish methods and achieve results which would be as precise as those of the exact sciences. It was a laudable ambition, and it helped to reduce the elements of personal idiosyncrasy and ideological or religious influence in the study of social phenomena. It encouraged an objective, nonjudgmental, open-ended, statistical approach; and like the established sciences, each social science defined its area of study and separated, as completely as practicable, the phenomena it was studying from the rest of human activity. But there is one essential element of exact science which cannot be matched in social science, namely the laboratory experiment, which can be repeated in order to confirm results and the precise implications of those results. The social sciences deal with human behavior in the aggregate; and since human beings are infinitely complex, with no two individuals exactly alike—much less tribes, nationalities, social classes, or professional groups—it is impossible to achieve an exactitude comparable to the results of an experiment in chemistry or physics.

The supreme accomplishment of the social sciences was to create a whole new area of human investigation. Previous European civilizations—and the civilizations of Egypt, the Middle East, and Asia—had all been the possession of very small elites. The great mass of human beings had been objects of exploitation or of pity, and their needs had occasionally been considered in terms of the power interests and prosperity of the governing elite. But prior to the eighteenth-century Enlightenment, the American and the French revolutions, and the proclamation of the Rights of Man, intellectuals had concerned themselves entirely with the activities of the elite minority. Now some of the finest minds of the era accumulated and interpreted data concerning the activities of all classes of human beings, and anthropologists in particular produced accurate descriptions and structural analyses of the many African, American Indian, and Pacific island cultures which had never been systematically studied by anybody.

Most intellectually impressive, in my opinion, and perhaps most influential throughout the twentieth century of all the European pioneers of sociology, was the German Max Weber. Weber was deeply influenced by the analysis of capitalism and class divisions that had been the great work of Karl Marx. But the scientific elements in Marx's work were partially vitiated by its teleological element: his certainty that capitalism would inevitably be succeeded by socialism and his determination to read all the evidence in the light of that supposedly scientific prediction.

In Weber's view, capitalism was not a purely modern European phenomenon, and he had no teleological convictions as to how long it would last and what might become of it in the future. Capitalism was (as Marx had said) the most productive economic system yet created by man. It had existed in the Egyptian, Roman, and Hellenic worlds, but its success had been greatly limited by the power of priestly castes, military establishments, and royal or state bureaucracies who had priorities other than the encouragement of rational economic life. Weber attributed the great success of modern capitalism to what he called "the protestant spirit," the emphasis on individual responsibility which was characteristic of the Protestant reformation, particularly in its Calvinist form. The capitalist entrepreneur sought an anti-traditional, innovative mastery of material forces; in this sense his outlook was more open-minded and flexible than that of priests, soldiers, and bureaucrats. And the great success of capitalism was also due to the fact that the entrepreneurial classes were powerful enough to compete with the likes of Prussian landlords and military castes for control of the state.

At the same time, the modern capitalist economy required the rational use of resources and the rational organization of labor and markets. This in turn required bureaucracy, in the sense that public functions had to be carried out according to sensible, predictable rules. Both large businesses and governments were so complex that their organization could no longer depend on unique individual qualities. Executives, managers, and administrators had to be replaceable without causing arbitrary changes in the operation of the whole complex. White-collar employees and industrial workers also had to be trained to use the machines which increasingly did the actual productive work. Thus bureaucracy was a necessary danger— necessary to the smooth operation of a complex society, and dangerous because bureaucrats are the inevitable enemies of novelty. In Weber's ideal, a successful capitalist system combined maximum rationality of the economic processes with the continuing initiative of creative businessmen and scientists.[4]

Although he avoided the grandiose predictions of a Hegel or Marx, Weber frequently expressed his views on the problems of Germany and Europe. He wanted to emancipate the Prussian peasants from the domination of the landlord aristocracy, and in the decade prior to the First World War (as well as during the war itself), he advocated free trade unions, parliamentary responsibility (which did not exist in the German empire), and universal suffrage. Since he believed that civil servants ought not to dominate policy, and that also the great mass of people lacked the knowledge to make wise decisions, Weber advocated a kind of *Führerdemokratie* in which the leader of the parliamentary majority, or the president in a republic, would determine policy. (The other key features of this democracy would be accountability, the regularity of elections, and the ability of the voters to elect someone else when they were dissatisfied.) Weber died in 1920—only the second year in the life of the Weimar Republic—but he was already very disappointed in its failure, in his view, to produce a leadership adequate to Germany's postwar problems.

Weber also favored imperialism on the grounds that the development of imperial markets and administration would offer economic opportunity and upward mobility and thus would loosen the hierarchical structure of German society. Between c. 1900 and 1914 he seems to have pictured as his ideal a world with a half-dozen competing imperial powers which would somehow not go to war with each other.[5] Like most intellectuals and political leaders of the era, he thought in terms of democratizing European life without feeling any strong concern for what imperialism meant to the non-European subject peoples. But except for his blindness (or indifference) to the needs of non-European peoples, Weber's analysis of the problems of an advanced industrial society seem as pertinent today as when he was writing. How to combine capitalist initiative with the predictable administration of a complex society; how to provide economic opportunity without confiscatory revolutions; how to consult the will of all citizens without putting in their hands decisions they are not capable of making; how to find leaders who can balance the legitimate interests of the capitalists, the urban and rural working population, and the bureaucrats—all these problems are as pressing today for the developed nations of the world as they were for Germany in 1900.

There is one more aspect of the early-twentieth-century scientific revolution which I think it essential to treat in this chapter, namely the effort to study scientifically the instinctual and nonrational portions of human behavior. I should say at once that it is even harder in psychology to achieve scientific precision than in the other social sciences. Even a Max Weber, who could be considerably more scientific than a Karl Marx because he was not trying to convince the world of the inevitability of a future revolution, had emotional preferences and ethical concerns which inevitably colored his collection and interpretation of data. The same holds true for all the social scientists of whose work I have any knowledge.

The great students of human psychology—Sigmund Freud, Carl. Jung, Alfred Adler, Karl Abraham, Richard von Kraft-Ebbing, Havelock Ellis, and Gregorio Marañon, among others—were all men of passionate temperament, dealing boldly with the problems of highly neurotic patients and working in a territory for which there were no previous maps. For this reason, we should not be surprised that they made mistakes; that many of their definitions had to be constantly reworked; that they could not confirm their theories with repeatable experiments which could be verified or falsified by other investigators; or that they could not arrive at laws for unique billion-celled human beings which would compare to laws governing the behavior of atomic particles or fruit fly genes.

Perhaps the most important of these new psychologists—certainly the best known and the most controversial—was Sigmund Freud.[6] Freud's original work and public career coincided almost exactly with the period under discussion in this chapter. It was around 1895 that he became dissatisfied with the use of cocaine and hypnosis as the principal methods for treating neuroses—methods which he had been using as the junior colleague of important psychologists in Paris and Vienna. But from his earliest practice Freud was convinced that the conscious, reasoning portion of the mind accounted for only a small proportion of total mental activity, that there was a huge area of unconscious and irrational drives, and that consciousness was just the tip of the iceberg. Thus c. 1895, Freud began to develop what we now know as psychoanalysis. Instead of being drugged or hypnotized, the patient was invited to lie down, relax completely, and say whatever came into his mind. The accumulation of these verbal free associations would enable doctor and patient together to recover partial memories of early childhood fantasies and traumas which Freud believed were at the root of his patients' non-organic illnesses.

Freud was a man of wide literary culture and a copious and excellent writer. His works are full of apt references to Cervantes, Shakespeare, Goethe, Schiller, Heine, and Dostoyevsky, among others. As a Jew he had benefitted from the liberalization of the Habsburg monarchy during his student days and had suffered from the entrenched anti-Semitism of the university and medical establishments. As a student he had translated the essays of John Stuart Mill. Emile Zola was one of his intellectual heroes at the time of the Dreyfus case, and several of his lifelong friends were prominent Austrian Social Democrats.

Freud himself had briefly considered studying law and entering politics, but one of the strong (if not always conscious) motives for the development of psychoanalysis was to resolve within the mind—to bring to consciousness and resolution—conflicts which would otherwise be expressed as political or professional or familial, and so would consume (or waste) the unconscious energies whose expression they were. Thus Freud was a man of moderately leftist sympathies who became convinced, by c. 1900, that he had discovered an important new method for resolving inner conflicts and adapting people "healthily" to the world as it is.

The titles of his first landmark books show the direction of his thinking: *The Interpretation of Dreams* (1900), *The Psychopathology of Everyday Life* (1901), *Three Theories of Sexuality* (1905) and *Wit and Its Relation to the Unconscious* (1905). He was pretty much boycotted by his Austrian colleagues, but he had immense reserves of both stoicism and humor, as well as prodigious capacities as an organizer and persuader. From 1906 to the end of his life, he dominated a growing international movement which trained and licensed analysts, published both scholarly researches and popular expositions, and held international congresses (except for the years of the first World War).

In an effort to understand what may be considered scientific in Freud's work, I will try to summarize his main tenets and procedures and then discuss the caveats and alternatives offered by other depth psychologists. Freud believed that most mental activity was unconscious, and that character was formed in the first five or six years of life—for better or for worse—principally as a result of the dynamic interrelationships between children and parent figures (usually, but not necessarily, the biological parents). The creative energy of successful human beings, from scientific and artistic geniuses through ordinary well-adapted farmers, businessmen, artisans, housewives, and mothers (little was said of industrial workers), as well as the energy of hysteria and neuroses, is sexual energy.

The sexual drive is at first not focussed ("polymorphous"). It strives for pleasure but discovers, upon emerging from infancy, that the world is not organized for its pleasure, whereat it gradually accepts the "reality principle"—the necessity for work, for limits on pleasure, for adaptation to the demands of others, and so forth. If the interdynamics are such that the child cannot accept the limitations which society imposes, the adult will suffer neuroses of varying severity with regard to his capacity to live a "normal" life. Most particular to Freud's theory was the importance of the Oedipus complex. He was convinced that infants inevitably wish to take, as their first and preferred "sexual object," the parent of the opposite sex, and that the capacity for adult heterosexual love—and for friendship and harmonious social interaction generally—depended on the successful transfer of this sexual energy from the parent to one's contemporaries of the opposite sex.

Over the years he developed a general map of the human mind divided as id, ego, and superego. The id was the realm of the unconscious, the preconscious, the instinctual drives of the basically sexual libido. The ego was the conscious, partly rational, reasoning and verbalizing portion of the territory. The superego was composed of the ethical ideals, the self-censorship, the necessary repression, the partly conscious and partly unconscious codes which adjusted the pleasure principle to the requirements of the reality principle. The ideal of analysis, whether engaged in as therapy or as a means to greater self-knowledge (a worthy aim in itself), was to maximize the area of the ego, to understand the force of one's instinctual drives, and to understand the sources of one's ideals, one's "conscience."

Freud was a scientific radical and a cultural conservative. It took truly defiant courage to preach in turn-of-the-century Europe that all emotional, intellectual, and artistic life was fueled primarily by sexual energy. At the same time, Freud was a typical late-nineteenth-century middle-class husband and father. He didn't marry till he could support a wife and children. He sympathized with his homosexual patients but he never accepted homosexuality as a "normal" expression of sexuality. He did not approve of any artificial methods of birth control and practiced abstention after having six children in nine years. He applied a combination of affection, humor, and the reality principle to the raising of those children, two of whom served voluntarily in the Austrian army during the first World War, and all of whom led reasonably successful, well-adjusted lives as adults.

Freud himself had been a jingoistic patriot in 1914, hoping that Austria would deliver a well-deserved chastisement to "upstart" Serbia. A year later, as the heavy casualties mounted and the civilian hunger increased during the course of obviously stalemated and suicidal war, Freud pondered a new theory of instinctual drives. By the end of the war he was convinced that not all the unconscious energies were sexual, hence fundamentally creative and motivated by a desire to live; alongside the life instinct, Eros, Freud now discerned a death instinct, Thanatos.

Freud had always been something of a stoic, particularly in his response to personal and professional disappointments. During the 1920s he often spoke publicly in favor of the League of Nations, and he joined such international figures as Einstein, Roman Rolland, and Bertrand Russell in statements concerning the necessity for disarmament and international peace. In 1930 he published a short work addressed to the general public (but by no means elementary in its style) entitled *Civilization and Its Discontents*, in which he pessimistically and stoically explained that civilization—absolutely necessary to the survival of the human race—nevertheless depended, and must always depend, on a degree of repression, on a combination of self-imposed and socially imposed renunciations of instinctual gratification. He retained his lifelong atheist views, offering men no hope but that of sublimation of the instincts and stoic acceptance of the inevitable. His own seventeen–year battle with cancer of the jaw illustrated magnificently what he meant by stoicism. He left open the question whether Eros or Thanatos would prove the stronger in time.

From Vienna Freud observed the rise and triumph of the Nazis in Germany. When they burned his books, he sardonically remarked to his disciple and biographer Ernest Jones: "What progress we are making. In the Middle Ages they would have burned me. Now they are content with burning my books." He was fortunate enough not to see the moment arrive when indeed they would have also burned him. Shortly after the Nazi occupation of Austria in March 1938, Freud was able to emigrate to his admired England, and there he died in September 1939, in the first weeks of Hitler's war and before the start of the Holocaust.

If we expand our view from Freud's psychology to modern depth psychology in general, certain things seem to be generally agreed upon in practice (if not always acknowledged in theory). All psychiatrists, psychoanalysts, psychologists, and licensed psychotherapists all over the Western world, and in parts of the rest of the globe, agree that the "talking cure" is better than cocaine or hypnosis. All agree that the rational portion of the mind is but a small portion of the total; also that there is a large, incompletely defined area of mental illnesses which cause great suffering (though these illnesses are not in themselves as grave as literal insanity), and whose symptoms can be greatly relieved by a course of hourly therapeutic conversations with an experienced, qualified psychologist. Almost all believe that as therapeutic drugs become more precise in their effects, they will gradually obviate the need for much of the time-consuming therapy now taking place. (Indeed, this last point was a hope explicitly voiced to by Freud during his own lifetime.) And almost all agree that sexual energy, and the early relationship to parental figures play crucial roles in the development of personality.

But as we all know, the psychoanalytic movement was riven by personal and theoretical rivalries from its earliest years. The theoretical ones had to do largely with Freud's insistence on the overwhelming importance of sexuality and the Oedipus complex. Carl Jung substituted, for much of Freud's archaic sexual libido, the concept of a collective unconscious shared by all human beings—his ideal of therapy was to harmonize the conscious adult motives with the influence of that collective unconscious. In place of Freud's concept of libido, Alfred Adler substituted the drive for power, for mastery of one's environment, and he attributed many neuroses to either the "inferiority" or the "superiority complex" (terms which he coined). But even Adler and Jung—and all the other schools of depth psychology which reject specific aspects of Freud's doctrines—still acknowledge the importance of the unconscious and the need to treat neuroses via therapeutic conversation sessions between patient and analyst.

To me, then, it seems that, despite all the theoretical splits and the strongly negative criticisms (embodied, for example, in the books by Fisher, Greenberg, and Crews, cited in my bibliographical endnote), the depth psychology inaugurated by Freud, and revised and fought over ever since by theoreticians and practicing therapists, constitutes a form of accumulating knowledge—and providing for the relief of suffering—that is worthy to be included in a chapter on European science, even if imprecision of psychology prevents it from being "science" in the sense of laboratory-testable or statistical truth. In the words of the distinguished American psychologist Jerome S. Bruner, Freud "made man comprehensible without at the same time making him contemptible."

ENDNOTES

1. My discussions of modern science in this chapter depend principally on George Gamow, *Thirty Years that Shook Physics* (New York: Doubleday, 1966); Heinz R. Pagels, *The Cosmic Code* (Bantam Books, 1983); J. C. Polkinghorne, *The Quantum World* (Princeton Science Library, 1989); and Emilio Segrè, *From X-Rays to Quarks* (San Francisco: W. H. Freeman, 1980).

2. Lewis S. Feuer, *Einstein and the Generations of Science*, Second Edition (New Brunswick, N.J.: Transaction, 1982), pp. 29–40; Gerald Holton, "Mach, Einstein, and the Search for Reality," *Daedalus*, spring 1968.

3. Gerald Holton, "The Roots of Complementarity," *Daedalus*, fall 1970.

4. Jürgen Kocka, "Otto Hintze, Max Weber, und das Problem der Bürokatie," and W. J. Mommsen, "Die antinomische Strukter des politischen Denken Max Webers," both in *Historische Zeitschrift*, no. 233, 1981.

5. Richard Bellamy, "Liberalism and Nationalism in the Thought of Max Weber," *History of European Ideas*, 1992, 499–507.

6. Given the controversial nature of Freud's legacy, I want to specify in greater detail than usual the readings on which the following pages are based. These include the major biographies of Ernst Jones and Peter Gay; plus Paul Roazen, *Freud and His Followers* (New York: A. A. Knopf, 1971); Seymour Fisher and Roger P. Greenburg, *The Scientific Credibility of Freud's Theories and Therapy* (New York: Columbia University Press, 1985); and Judith M. Hughes, *From Freud's Consulting Room* (Harvard University Press, 1994); Jerome S. Bruner, "The Freudian Conception of Man and the Continuity of Nature," *Daedalus*, winter 1958, 77–84; Philip Rieff, "Freud's Political Psychology," *Journal of the History of Ideas*, April 1956; Angus McLaren, "Conception and its Discontents," *Journal of Social History*, summer, 1979, 513–27; two articles by Carl E. Schorske, "Politics and Patricide in Freud's *Interpretation of Dreams*," *The American Historical Review*, April 1973, 328–347; and "Freud's Egyptian Dig," *The New York Review of Books*, 27 May 1993; and Frederick Crews, "The Unknown Freud" and "The Revenge of the Repressed," *The New York Review of Books*, 18 November 1993, and 17 November 1994, respectively, plus the many letters concerning both articles.

6

The Fine Arts and Music, 1895–1939

Parallel with the revolutionary developments in the sciences, the period from the mid-1890s to the outbreak of the Second World War witnessed equally astonishing innovations in the fine arts and music: in the visual arts, a revolt against the classical rules of design, perspective, proportion, and color; in music, the discarding of tonality and the traditional rules of voice leading, harmony, and modulation; in the dance, new forms of expressive mobility of the human body; and (the most important innovation of all for the general population) the invention of an entirely new art form—cinema or "the movies."

Until the mid-nineteenth century, the fine arts had almost exclusively served the tastes of royalty and the landed aristocracy. For centuries, painters had supplied portraits of their patrons and rulers, landscapes and still lifes to cover the spacious walls of their dwellings, and Biblical scenes for their churches and private chapels. Paintings and sculpture,were expected to be realistic representations of objects, in three-dimensional perspective, with arms, legs, and facial features reflecting, in accurate shape and proportion, what the normal human eye observed, and using an accepted pallet of colors that corresponded roughly with the visual experience of the untrained eye.

The growth of urban middle-class prosperity created a new class of patrons in the course of the nineteenth century and thus new opportunities for individual artists. Not that middle-class merchants and bankers were less conservative in their taste than were the traditional ruling classes whose manners they tended to imitate. But as newcomers to high culture, they were less confident of their personal judgment than were the existing aristocracy. At the same time, as self-made men, they were often capable of recognizing the merits of other self-made men. Some of them were willing to take a chance on the work of impressionist painters:

The outlines might be distressingly vague but the objects were still recognizable, and the paintings discovered beauty in such things as railroad stations, canal barges, and industrial smoke—things which had never before been thought of as "art objects." Some of them also had sons and daughters who decided to become artists rather than enter the family business. While this fact gave rise to many generational crises, there were also numerous instances in which middle-class families supported the creative efforts of those members who were revolting against the "tyranny" of bourgeois standards. We should not be misled by the fact that modern literature is full of novels and autobiographies bitterly satirizing the philistinism of the middle classes. Most of their authors come from the middle class, and without the admittedly grudging, often uncomprehending support of their families, they would never have had the chance to become writers and artists in the first place. In the arts as in economic development and political liberty, the rise of the middle classes provided far more diversified opportunity than did any aristocratic society, no matter how admirable its traditional culture.

Generically speaking, the artistic and musical revolutions were fueled by a deeply felt desire to overpower traditional constraints, decorum, and "good taste." Painters, sculptors, and composers were determined to express their artistic impulses more spontaneously, more dramatically, and to include in their work all kinds of new elements that had not been thought of previously as belonging to the realm of the aesthetic.

To begin with the visual arts: the spiritual and technical fathers of twentieth-century European art were the Provençal French painter Paul Cézanne, the French painter (though of Peruvian ancestry) Paul Gauguin, the Dutch painter Vincent Van Gogh, and the Norwegian Edvard Munch. Cézanne, in the effort to convey more feeling of volume, internal weight, and dignity to his subjects be they persons or landscapes or household articles, geometrized his brush strokes in ways that, twenty years later, would lead directly to cubism. Gauguin turned from the overly familiar European countryside to the geography and civilization of the South Sea islanders. Van Gogh painted miners and the rural and urban poor with a new empathy and dramatic force; he also painted landscapes that never sold during his lifetime, but whose fierce colors and brush strokes would transform the way twentieth-century artists would paint such subjects. And Munch brought to portraiture the expressions of depression and anxiety which have become more prevalent—or at least have attracted more attention—in the twentieth century than in earlier eras.

With all these artists, spiritual travail was intimately related to their technical innovations. Cézanne and Gauguin were both in revolt against the middle-class respectability of their backgrounds. The former took refuge in spiritual communion with the luminous landscapes of southern France—most especially a single mountain, the Mont-Saint Victoire, which he painted or sketched hundreds of times over the decades. Gauguin left his family and work (as a Paris bank officer) to paint first the rural life of Brittany and later that of Tahiti. Van Gogh was tortured by religious doubts and by the cruelty of the capitalist economy as he observed it among the poor. Munch could easily have devoted his talents to conventionally pleasing landscapes and portraiture, but his intuition and sympathies led him to portray the unhappy and the repressed, and to develop a pallet appropriate to that subject matter.

Yet the newest elements in European art came from outside the continent. In the latter half of the nineteenth century, imperial rivalries in Africa, Asia, and the Pacific gradually acquainted the European public with non-European cultures. Most contacts took the form of native encounters with European military posts, trading stations, and Christian missions, schools, and hospitals; there were also explorers, geographers, cartographers, ethnologists, and (increasingly in the twentieth century) anthropologists. Many of these individuals were consciously seeking an escape from accelerating urban and industrial development. They fully appreciated—and in some cases, idealized—the less hurried, less competitive nature of nonwhite societies.[1]

To Europe they sent (or returned with) samples of the richly varied art work they found in Africa, the South Pacific islands, and the Northwest Indian and Eskimo territories of Northern Canada and Alaska. These samples included wood, stone, and ivory sculpture; masks combining textiles, bird feathers, animal teeth, snake skins, and precious stones; ritual ornaments and charms; sculpted chairs, canoes, tunics, staves, and cloths whose ritual significance they could only guess at, but whose beauty was manifest. In British, French, and German ethnographic museums, and in the import shops of the great cities, artists could study these previously unknown art objects.

From the time of the Renaissance until 1900, all European art had been fully representational. The impressionists, like the four artists mentioned above, had expanded the subject matter and varied the techniques of traditional art, but their aims remained descriptive and representational. African sculpture combined recognizable images of humans and animals with abstract, geometrical symbols. It was largely monochrome, achieving its effects through volume, geometry, and surface carving rather than through color or miscellaneous materials.

Between 1906 and 1914, the example of African sculpture combined with the painting techniques of Cézanne to create cubism, whose principal early exponents were Pablo Picasso and Georges Braques. Like all young artists at the turn of the century, the future cubists were searching for new ways to depict human activity, human emotion, human transcendence of the purely physical. The problem they confronted was how to advance beyond the inherited tradition—so strong in perspective, so accurate in descriptive detail, so limited in expressive capacity precisely because it "imitated" nature so entirely?

African, Melanesian, and Northwest Pacific art offered a stunning variety of new possibilities. These anonymous artists were expressing ideas, concepts, and metaphysical meanings as much as (or more than) creating recognizable figures. The Europeans did not know—and for the most part, did not attempt to understand (except for the anthropologists)—the religious and ritual meanings. What they saw was a marvelous combination of the representational and the abstract: triangles representing noses, single or concentric circles representing eyes, nostrils, breasts, bellybuttons, and vaginas; ovals and squares representing heads; bits of stone and ivory representing teeth or eyes; graceful curves suggesting movement or ritual gesture; string or grass or feathers representing hair, and so on. Depending on the combination of these abstract forms, the effects could be magical, joyous, dignified, playful, terrifying, or comic. And the anonymity inspired the same kind of respect as did European medieval traditions: respect for a great talent being devoted without personal egotism to the expression of communal values.

African sculpture, with its emphasis on volume and abstraction in the service of ritual expression, was enormously influential in the development of cubism. Melanesian and Northwest Indian art—more decorative and prone to include organic materials such as grasses and feathers—exerted tremendous influence on surrealist art in the interwar period. Whatever their branch or school, however, all the painters and sculptors of the early twentieth century (except those who specialized in portraits of bank presidents and university rectors) were deeply influenced by both African and Pacific art.

Two other movements not directly connected to cubism or to African-Pacific art arose during the decade preceding the First World War. In France, "Fauvism" (wildness), and in the German-speaking countries and Belgium, "expressionism," broke the constraints of traditional art by giving the dominant role to color rather than to perspective and proportion. The Fauvists (Matisse, Vlaminck, Rouault, Dérain) drew heavy outlines, in strong color, as a way of emphasizing both volume and emotional expression. They did not hesitate to exaggerate or deform specific features in their paintings in order to achieve more decorative or more emotional effects. They might paint flesh in totally unrealistic colors such as green or yellow or blue, not to suggest ill health but to heighten both the geometric and the expressive power of contrasted colors.[2]

Fauvism was a purely painterly movement, but expressionism was inspired by broader philosophical concerns. Its founding fathers (Kirchner, Bleyl, Heckel, Schmidt-Rutloff) were students of architecture at the Dresden technical college. As readers of modern literature, they were inspired by the poetic and prophetic strain in Nietzsche, the social concerns of Ibsen, and the spiritual concerns of Dostoyevsky. They were profoundly dissatisfied with academic tradition and used the words *Einfühlung* (empathy) and *Durchgeistigung* (impregnated with spirit) to define their expressive aims.

They believed that all art should achieve the immediacy of emotional impact that they attributed to music. Also, art should be accessible to those without money, and so the early expressionists did much of their work in woodcuts, thereby reviving a traditional German craft and making their art available for the price of a magazine. They shared their studios, models, and working-class quarters, and exhibited together several times between 1905 and 1911 under the collective name *Die Brücke* (the bridge)—a name chosen to indicate their openness to different techniques, styles, and subject matter. They were keenly and sympathetically aware of developments in Paris and admired Van Gogh, Gauguin, Matisse, and the anonymous artists of Africa and the Pacific.[3]

German cultural life was much less centralized than that of France, and a group of artists equally as important as the Dresden group flourished in Munich during the years 1909–1913. *Der Blaue Reiter* (the Blue Rider) was also a collective with high ideals and varied philosophical interests. It included two transplanted Russians, the lawyer Wassily Kandinsky and the imperial army officer Alex Jawlensky, and two important women painters, Marianne Werefken (wife of Jawlensky) and Gabriele Münter (companion of Kandinsky). The group was consciously internationalist in spirit and organized Munich exhibits of French and Russian painters; of African, Latin American, and Pacific masks; and (in 1913) the first European exhibition of Islamic tapestry. Largely through the influence of Münter, they also became interested in such local folk-art traditions as the glass painting, furniture making, and doll construction.

Kandinsky was greatly interested as well in novel philosophical concepts: the *élan vital* of Henri Bergson, the educational proposals of Rudolph Steiner, and the mystical ideas of Madame Blavatsky. He shared with Franz Marc a general theory concerning the significance of different colors—blue as masculine, yellow as feminine, and red as violent. At times he proclaimed that art would be the true religion of the future. It would be a mistake to read too much into Kandinsky's ideas and theories and the work of the group as a whole. The evidence of broad intellectual curiosity and an experimental spirit is more important than specific "influences." Indeed, twenty years after the fact, Kandinsky once explained that the name *Blaue Reiter* had been chosen over coffee by Marc, who loved horses, and himself, who was fond of blue.

Considered as a whole, all these factors—the beginnings of fauvism, cubism, and expressionism; the rapidly growing interest in African, Asian, and Pacific arts; the participation of women artists; and the broad intellectual curiosity and the social concerns involved in these movements—indicate how tolerant, nonchauvinist, and inventive was the spirit of the fine arts in the years preceding the First World War. Two other movements deserve mention in this rich panorama: futurism and constructivism, centered in Italy and Russia, respectively (two nations which had arrived late but enthusiastically to the industrial revolution). The several solemn futurist manifestos published between 1909 and the outbreak of the First World War provide an especially vivid illustration of the contradictory cultural

impulses of the era. On the one hand, the manifestos confuse the need for liberation from stuffy academic traditions with a totally ignorant exaltation of war and
sexism, seen as somehow "healthy" for an unquestionably male-dominated culture.
On the other hand, the futurists saw the aesthetic potential of machines, ships, railroads, aircraft, bridges, and urban architecture. They developed the artistic possibilities of metal and glass, of industrial design, of urban apartment blocks, and of
window displays and printed advertising. Their paintings, sculpture, and architectural designs brought elements of cubism and expressionism into the vision of an
industrial future which would (hopefully) one day replace the squalor of contemporary cities.[4]

Somewhat similar in its hopes was the constructivist movement, which was
influenced by Italian futurism and flourished in Russia from approximately
1915–1925. The constructivists were Marxists and ardent partisans of the Bolshevik revolution; they were determined to remove the arts from their limited aristocratic sphere and place them at the service of the proletariat (i.e., of society as a
whole, according to their anticipation of what the future would bring). To achieve
this, they eliminated the distinction between the fine arts and the applied arts.
Their leading members taught the use of metals, wood, and ceramics, and designed
factories, furniture, workers' clothing, theaters and cinemas, posters, and magazine
layouts. In their painting, sculpture, and design, the constructivists used geometrical forms and solid blocks of color and avoided all rococo ornamentation. Two
words recur in their explanations of their work: *tectonic*, meaning that all materials
should be manufactured and used for social purposes; and *factura*, meaning that
all objects should be functional not just in their use but in their creation, and that
the natural properties of all raw materials should be carefully respected.

The more intellectual of the Bolshevik leaders welcomed constructivist art,
but between the ruins of world war and civil war and the relative backwardness of
Russian technology, it was impossible to carry out their architectural designs.
Numerous ironies of the twentieth century entered into the fate of constructivism—
for example, what could be only utopian plans in post-revolutionary Russia became
quite influential in the German, West European, and American architecture of the
1920s. The emphasis on simple lines, replaceable units, the combination of beauty
and utility, and the use of glass, aluminum, and light metal alloys entered the work
of the *Bauhaus* in Weimar Germany, of Le Corbusier and his colleagues in France,
and of numerous industrial architects in New York, Detroit, and Chicago. The constructivists themselves either emigrated to the West or altered their styles to suit
the "socialist realism" of the Stalinist era. Their principal achieved building—
functional, geometric, and free of rococo ornament—was the tomb of the revolutionary leader Lenin in Red Square.

In fact, the years from roughly 1910 to 1930 were among the richest in
Russian art history. Before the revolution, the members of a small but ardent, west-

ward-looking elite were producing their own versions of fauvism, cubism, and expressionism. They celebrated the traditions of the icon and the Byzantine mosaic and gave high value to the rugs and tapestries woven by anonymous artists who might well have been servants on their own families' rural estates. Icon and tapestry forms affected their own painting styles and mingled with the new cubist influence. From the German expressionists, they were quick to pick up the renewed (and socially motivated) interest in woodcuts and pencil and ink drawings. And also like the German expressionists, they were moving towards abstraction, towards the idea that non-representational painting could be just as "expressive" as descriptive painting.

These people were spiritually generous, if politically naive, and welcomed the successive revolutions of 1917 as liberating Russia from an oppressive, antiquated regime. In their initial enthusiasm for change, they saw no contradiction between their interest in the nonpolitical experimental movements in the West and the new Bolshevik demands for proletarian, political art. Between 1917 and the mid-1920s they painted peasants and factory workers with the same warmth and fauvist or expressionist enthusiasm that they had previously shown in painting their families and friends, and their nonobjective canvases.

In the five years from 1925 to 1930, they shifted from the experimental to the conventional and the gigantic. In the later years of the NEP, even the more enlightened Bolsheviks demanded an increasingly utilitarian and political attitude in the arts. With the consolidation of Stalin's dictatorship, the older and wiser artists, if they wished to sell paintings, converted from expressionism or constructivism to massive, conventional oil paintings of party leaders and exemplary workers and peasants.[5]

Futurism, constructivism, and the entire range of Russian painting during the first decade of the revolution, had all looked optimistically towards the future. But in the heartland of developed Europe, among young artists and students of many nationalities, the pointless, bloody stalemate and mass slaughters on the Western Front created a mood of antiwar protest, intellectual nihilism, and a desperate, exhibitionist affirmation of artistic enthusiasm. According to the important dadaist (and later surrealist) painter Hans Arp:

> In Zurich in 1915, losing interest in the slaughterhouses of the world war, we turned to the Fine Arts [his capitals]. While the thunder of the batteries rumbled in the distance, we pasted, we recited, we versified, we sang with all our soul. We searched for an elementary art that would, we thought, save mankind from the madness of these times.[6]

The dada movement was shortlived, depending as it did on the theatrical, musical, and artistic talents of a relatively small group. Since it was not only antiwar and internationalist, but also defied all social conventions (using toilet seats as props, proclaiming that urine made an excellent varnish, etc.), its popularity depended on its capacity to shock, provoke, and entertain all at the same time. But it produced a strong impression on cafe audiences in neutral Zurich during the war, as well as in postwar Berlin and Paris. As for its deliberately childish-sounding name, the then medical student and later successful New York psychiatrist Richard Huelsenbeck explained the coinage in his *Memoirs of a Dada Drummer*: in French, the two syllables meant a "hobby-horse"; in Russian, they said "yes, yes"; in Romanian, they meant "of course"; in Italian, "wet nurse"; in Swahili, "sister"; and in old Swabian argot, they referred to a "sexually obsessed cretin."

This kind of brilliant, thoroughly irreverent word play was typical of dada poetry. It could not have been produced by uneducated or intellectually dull authors. They were also fully aware of the creative movements described in this chapter, and in fact Huelsenbeck coined another phrase which he claimed had occurred to him in the three-language form here quoted: "Art is dead. Viva la Machinenkunst of Tatlin" (one of the principal Russian constructivists).

Finally, to illustrate the imaginative power and the cultural wealth of dada, I quote the English version of a poem which Huelsenbeck recited in German to musical (especially percussive) accompaniment in a noisy, crowded, smoke-filled Zurich cafe:

> The heads of the horses float on the blue prairie
> like huge dark purple flowers
> the bright disk of the moon is surrounded by the shrieks
> of the comets stars and glacier dolls
> schalaben schalamai schalamezomai
> Canaanites and janizaries are fighting a great
> battle on the shores of the Red Sea
> the heavens draw in their flags the heavens
> slide the glass roofs over the battle of the bright armors
> oh you ceremonious shadows terebinth and hogweed
> oh you ceremonious worshippers of the great God
> behind the veils the horses are singing praises to the great God
> schalaben schalamai schalamezomai. . . .[7]

In the long run, the principal significance of dada was its contribution to the more organized and less completely iconoclastic movement known as surrealism. The surrealists flourished between 1922 and c. 1960, first in Paris, then in Europe generally and the United States as well, due to the emigration of important surrealists to America during the Nazi era.

The fundamental concepts of surrealism came from a richly suggestive combination of philosophical, psychological, and anthropological ideas elaborated by André Breton in the early 1920s. Like the dadaists and the futurists, the surrealists rejected academic art and the general "respectable" framework of European bourgeois civilization. They had also been bitterly disillusioned by the recent suicidal world war. They felt that European culture had lost touch with its own mythological and religious roots, that it had become overly rational and heavily repressive of human emotions.

The surrealists were thus attracted by the nonrational, vitalist, beautifully written philosophy of Henri Bergson; by the burgeoning ethnographic and anthropological descriptions of "primitive" societies; by African, Indian, and Eskimo art; and by Freud's beautifully written analyses of dream experience, as well as his insistence that the rational portion of the human mind was but a small proportion of the total.

Out of these readings came the conviction that the full character of human experience could be recaptured by the fusion of reality and dream to form a super-real, or surreal, understanding of the world. Some surrealists practiced "automatic" writing and drawing as a way of exploring beneath the rational academic surface of literature and art. All of them prized their dreams and fantasies as raw material, and all of them felt an affinity for the ritualistic and oniric elements in non-European art. Most of them were not political militants, but the central group around Breton were antifascist during the 1930s and pro-Soviet during the first decade after World War II. All of them prized nature and were concerned with the threat of industrial pollution several decades before Western society in general became environmentally conscious.

In their painting, sculpture, and collage, the surrealists were enthusiastically eclectic. They portrayed their fantasies with all the resources developed by Cézanne, the fauves, the cubists, the expressionists, the futurists, constructivists, and dada. Their most impressive work was done between the mid-1920s and the mid-1950s. Their creative energy was closely bound up with the wider cultural beliefs of their contemporaries.[8]

"Primitive," for example, was a word with many implications. It referred to the technically less developed nature of societies called "primitive," to their relatively lower levels of literacy, scientific knowledge, and economic and military power. It also referred to their apparent closeness to organic nature, to their ability to live without the artificial complexities of European society, and to their apparently less inhibited sexual and emotional lives. It referred to their little understood religions and their greatly admired capacity to combine representational and abstract elements in their art. It referred to their apparently less aggressive, certainly much less massively destructive manner of life, both in terms of one another and the natural world.

Surrealist art was nourished by the positive aspects of this image of "primitive" societies—artistic, imaginative, less aggressive, more closely related to nature. In his 1920s manifestos, Breton saw "primitive" societies as offering a model for the uninhibited expression of feelings long repressed in the West. Nor did he (or Freud, or anthropologists in general) sense anything condescending about the application of the word "primitive" to non-European civilizations.

By the late 1950s, Breton felt that "we remain largely ignorant" of the real nature of those societies, and he counseled artists to return to the study of their early European roots. The decline of the idealized image of African and Pacific Island societies, and the increased contact with their negative political and social aspects, corresponds to the decline of surrealism as a creative movement. Likewise, the relative decline of faith in Freudian and Jungian therapies has undermined the doctrinal bases of surrealism and sapped its creative vigor.

To capture the surrealist faith at its most impressive, including its relationship both to war and to Oceanic totemic faith, I quote an autobiographical statement of Max Ernst from the year 1941, when he had escaped from Nazi-dominated Europe to America:

Max Ernst died on August 1, 1914. He was resuscitated on November 11, 1918 as a young man aspiring to become a magician and to find the myth of his time. Now and then he consulted the eagle who had hatched the egg of his pre-natal life. You may find the bird's advices in his work.

* * *

European music also underwent a technical and conceptual revolution in the decade preceding the Great War. As with painting, music by c. 1900 seemed to have come to a dead end. Wagner and Brahms had pushed to their outer limits the tonality and harmonic resources which were based on the tempered scale of J. S. Bach, and which had been developed by the great classic and romantic composers of the eighteenth and nineteenth centuries. Mahler was expanding the traditional scope of the symphony by adding the human voice and by directly incorporating folk melodies. The French "impressionists" Debussy and Ravel were using Greek pentatonic scales, creating whole tone chords, and rejecting the inherited "rules" of voice-leading and modulation. The work of these three great composers added important nuances to the Bach-to-Brahms-and-Wagner tradition, but they were nuances, not fundamental changes.

Fundamental change began with Arnold Schoenberg—not, indeed, at the beginning of his career, but as a result of his own conviction that the traditional vocabulary had exhausted its creative possibilities. Schoenberg's life involved full exposure to both "civilization and barbarity" and his personal fate was constantly intertwined with the several stages of his creative development.[9] Born in 1875, in what was then the Hungarian city of Pressburg (now Bratislava), he was raised as an orthodox Jew and was largely self-educated as a composer. In turn-of-the-cen-

tury Vienna, he received encouragement from the great composer-conductor
Gustav Mahler, and like Mahler he converted to Christianity—not out of any desire
to hide his Jewish origins, but because he hoped, as did many Jews in Germany
and in the Habsburg Empire, that conversion would eliminate the main obstacle to
his social acceptance in that German cultural world which he ardently admired
(and to whose arts and sciences the Jews had long been major contributors).

Austrian academic anti-Semitism prevented Schoenberg's becoming a professor of composition, though it did not prevent performance and critical recognition of his music. In 1911 he moved to Berlin, where he found important patrons
but still faced anti-Semitic attacks in the press. But it was also in Berlin that he
enjoyed the greatest single public success of his career with the premiere in 1912
of *Pierrot Lunaire*, an atonal dramatic and satirical work for soprano and chamber
orchestra. From 1914 to 1936, his professional life depended crucially on conditions beyond his control. He wished to serve in the Austrian army and performed
a number of nonmilitary duties until asthma led to his discharge in 1917. Well-to-
do patrons subsidized publication and performance of his work from 1917 until the
inflation of 1922–3. Then in Berlin of the Weimar Republic, from 1925 to 1933, he
enjoyed the best working conditions of his entire life: a professorship in the
Prussian Academy, recognition by the finest German conductors, and perfor-
mances for small but educated and appreciative audiences.

In the spring of 1933, when the Nazis announced that they would expel the
Jews from all academic and cultural posts, Schoenberg resigned his professorship
without waiting to be fired. There followed three years of temporary posts as an
emigrant in the United States. Finally, from 1936 until his death in 1951, Schoenberg lived in Los Angeles, where various institutions helped him to make a modest
living, though he never felt culturally at home. During the First World War Schoenberg had begun a steady evolution back towards Judaism, and in the last year of
his life he was named Honorary President of the Israeli Academy of Music.

There is a general chronological correspondence between the biography
sketched above and the stages of Schoenberg's life as a composer. His early works,
before 1907, show a complete mastery of traditional compositional technique and
an emotional spirit very close to those of his acknowledged models—Wagner,
Richard Strauss, and especially Brahms. From 1908 to 1920, he experimented with
atonality (a term he disliked, but which is certainly both accurate and useful, as a
description of the listener's experience): That is to say, while continuing to use traditional dance and sonata forms and employing the greatest contrapuntal ingenuity
since J.S. Bach, he detached music from any tonal center. There was no key, or set
of recognizable modulations, through which the pieces developed and no final
cadence in which the music would "come to rest," but rather a development of the
thematic and rhythmic materials completely independent of any specific key.

Between 1920 and 1936, he developed the "serial" technique for which he is best known. Schoenberg always believed in the need for compositional rules, and he always urged his students to master traditional harmony and counterpoint. But he had also, as a matter of personal experience, become convinced that Wagner and Brahms had exhausted the creative possibilities of existing technique. Why not free music from the tyranny of key centers and the prohibition of strong dissonances? Life was not as transparently ordered as an Italian garden or a Mozart sonata. Why should music not be free to express the confusions, the ambiguities, the fierce and disorderly energies of life itself? Thus in the years 1908–1920, Schoenberg and his Austrian and German disciples, and also the young Russian composers Stravinsky and Prokofiev, had already moved away from tonal centers and employed strong dissonances. The new theoretical order worked out by Schoenberg was called *dodecaphonic*, because it used all twelve tones of the chromatic scale as equals, not as dominant and subordinate members of a major or minor "key."

The composer arranged the twelve tones in a "row" of his choice. Both the horizontal (melodic) and vertical (harmonic) aspects of the composition were to be developed from this initial row. He could vary the rhythm in which the row was sounded, and also invert the intervals and run them backwards, thereby giving himself potentially 48 (4 x 12) different ways to manipulate the series—plus all the variety that could be added by changes of rhythm and the use of different instruments and human voices.

In practice, almost all serial music continues to employ elements of traditional harmony and counterpoint. The purpose was to add resources, not systematically to reject the entire past. Schoenberg sought to free music from the requirement of cadences and the prohibition of strong dissonances, not to advocate that all cadences were forbidden and that dissonance must be universal. And indeed, though Schoenberg felt the need to codify his new concepts, his theories would not have been important in the first place if not for the high quality of his music. The pre-1908 works express the same gamut of emotions as do the works of Wagner, Brahms, Mahler, and Debussy; and in such scores as *Verklärte Nacht, Pelleas und Melisande*, and the impassioned *Gurre-lieder* (settings of a medieval love story by a Danish poet), the convert from Judaism was identifying himself strongly with the spiritual world of the great German and French masters.

From 1908 to the late 1930s, Schoenberg constantly sought to expand the musical vocabulary and simultaneously to express the varied facets of his own complex emotional nature. There are colorful, humorous treatments of conventional dance forms, generally atonal but with chords open enough so that most listeners can hear the intended harmonies. There are both songs and instrumental pieces reflecting the bitter disillusionment of the post-1918 European psyche and dramatizing quasi-Freudian interpretations of individual psychology. There are the indecisive but musically rich struggles back towards the Jewish faith of his childhood (the song cycle *Jacob's Ladder* and the opera *Moses and Aaron*, both unfinished).

There are constant acoustic experiments, particularly with wind instruments and percussion. There are moments of great tenderness, and—in his last years—important choral works on Jewish texts.

It should be noted here that the musical revolution of the twentieth-century does not involve as many separate "movements" as does the history of twentieth century painting and sculpture. In large measure this is due to the fact that the latter arts have been highly developed in all human cultures, starting with the cave-dwellers, and that in Europe itself there have always been more great painters at any given time than great composers. Some forms of both vocal and instrumental music have also existed in all civilizations. But modern opera, ballet, and keyboard and orchestral music (which we call by the adjectives "baroque," "classic," "romantic," and "modern") are far more complex than any other past music of which we have knowledge. There are no equivalents of Bach and Beethoven outside the musical experience of Europe. "Classical" music from the seventeenth century to the present, along with mathematics in the same period, have indeed been the special contribution of Europe to world civilization.

Schoenberg's is the most intellectually worked out—and the most completely revolutionary—of the novel developments in twentieth-century Western music. But his younger contemporary, Igor Stravinsky—perhaps the greatest single composer of the century (and in any case the most versatile)—created his most revolutionary instrumental scores as part of a great renovation in the traditional and highly structured art of ballet. Traditional European ballet, as cultivated by the aristocracy, had restricted itself to a very limited range of subjects—principally variations on the theme of the seduction of working girls by bourgeois or noble gallants. It had employed a refined but also very limited repertoire of steps and had reserved the principal roles for women. Suddenly, between 1909 and 1913, a Russian company recruited by Serge Diaghilev introduced new dramatic and mythological subject matter, included natural bodily movements along with the required formal steps, gave leading roles to men, and sought the collaboration of the greatest composers, painters, set designers, and couturiers available in Paris.

This coincidence of unique circumstances made possible what might be called without exaggeration the Diaghilev terpsichorean revolution. The finest Italian and French ballet masters were already teaching in St. Petersburg and the tsar's official ballet school provided a superb technical education to students who literally became the adopted children of the ballet-loving royal family. The completely pre-democratic conditions of Russian life made possible for the faculty (and acceptable to the pupils) a degree of discipline and single-minded concentration that could not have been imposed in Western Europe. And Russia's finest composers, less attached than their Western colleagues to the sonata form and to absolute music in general, were delighted to give much of their best efforts to composing for ballet.

Serge Diaghilev, son of a tsarist general and nephew of a minister of the interior, began his career with the substantial advantages of belonging to an important family and sharing in the considerable income of that family's distilleries. But he was also a man of great general intelligence and aesthetic perception. He could convince top bankers to lend him large sums. He could supervise the laying of a new parquet floor in the dilapidated Châtelet theater. He could house his company in modest pensions, pay them minimal wages, act as their educated guide in museums and at concerts, make love to the men and send flowers to the women, and generally convince them all that they were serving the cause of a sacred art.

Diaghilev was also determined to see Russian culture recognized in the West. In 1906 he arranged the first large exposition of Russian painting in Paris, and in 1907 he was the impresario for a series of concerts introducing new Russian music. But his most important contribution was undoubtedly his conceptual and executive leadership in the renewal of the art of ballet. His artists took Europe by storm in the years 1909–1913. Nothing since 1913 has had as great an impact as the dancing of Vaslav Nijinsky and the music of Igor Stravinsky, but the entire subsequent twentieth-century development of creative dance in Europe, Soviet Russia, the English-speaking countries, and Latin America owes its original inspiration to the pre–World War Diaghilev company. Rarely has a single businessman been so important in the history of the arts.

Returning to the subject of music, Stravinsky, in his prewar ballet scores, *The Firebird*, *Petrushka*, and especially *Le Sacre du Printemps* (The Rite of Spring) in 1912, brought atonality, heavily dissonant chords, and wild rhythms into orchestral music. Along with Debussy and Ravel, he also introduced African American jazz rhythms and harmonic styles to European music. In the works composed between the two world wars, Stravinsky retreated from the radical rhythms and dissonances of the *Sacre*, but he continued to be a "composer's composer" in his renewal of classical (particularly Italian) forms and in his experiments with both harmony and instrumental coloring. In the 1930s he became increasingly religious, and he also paid closer attention to the work of Arnold Schoenberg and his disciples. This effort at self-renewal (in both the spiritual and the technical spheres) led to a number of great religious works created between the Second World War and his death in 1971.

Stravinsky's spiritual history shows some striking parallels with the major events of his lifetime. The three great pre-1914 ballets partake of the extraordinary novelty, demonic energy, and sensitivity to nontraditional, non-European cultures that were characteristic of the prewar decade. His post-1918 neoclassical music reflects the sudden sobering, the disillusionment of Europe in the wake of the Great War. Light humor, clarity, and moderation (especially in the use of barbaric rhythms and dissonances)—these were the sentiments prized by audiences trying to regain their equilibrium after the suicidal slaughter. Important also was the perceived exhaustion of traditional art forms, which led to cubism and surrealism in painting and to atonality and serialism in music. And like many political pes-

simists (as well as those shocked by the violence of the fascist and Stalinist dictatorships), Stravinsky took increasing refuge in his religious convictions. As a nondogmatic European, he retained the Orthodox faith of his upbringing while with
equal sincerity, he set Latin and Hebrew texts to music.

In the first decades of the twentieth century, cultural nationalism was also an
important influence in the work of many composers. The Hungarians Béla Bartók and
Zoltán Kodály, the Romanian Georges Enesco, the Spaniards Manuel de Falla and
Isaac Manuel Francisco Albéñiz, and the Englishman Ralph Vaughan Williams,
among others, introduced the folk melodies and rhythms of their native lands into
classical contexts, often modifying their scales and harmonic practices in the
process—though not nearly so radically as in the case of atonal and serial music.

Unique is the example of Jean Sibelius, whose music (created almost entirely
between 1892 and 1926) came to be thought of as the quintessential expression of
the Finnish soul. Sibelius did not use folk music. He had perhaps the greatest gift
for pure melody of any composer since Franz Schubert, and he created themes that
flowed so naturally, so expressively, that even music critics thought they must be
derived from folk melodies. Sibelius's orchestral tone poems were inspired by
Finnish mythology and poetry. He limited himself almost entirely to the pre-
Schoenbergian vocabulary and showed that, at least in one important instance, the
creative possibilities of that vocabulary had not been exhausted! His accomplishment was to give convincing, aesthetically satisfying musical expression to the psychology and the emotional atmosphere of Finnish legends; and in his seven sym-
phonies, he fused that poetic spirit with the inherited nineteenth-century European
symphonic form.

Finally, if one were to listen to a half-dozen great nineteenth-century composers and then to the works of Debussy, Schoenberg, Webern, Stravinsky, Bartók,
and Sibelius, one could not fail to note how much more varied is the music created
in the first decades of the twentieth century. At the same time, one would also note
that—with the exceptions of Debussy and Sibelius—most of this music is difficult
to comprehend and requires a degree of attention and effort that the nineteenth-
century music does not ask.

The musical revolution, then, had one important characteristic which later
became notable also in poetry, painting, fiction, and even literary history and criticism. Atonality, dissonance, and serial technique threatened to separate the composer from a large portion of his intended audience. Most listeners to new music
expect to respond emotionally and appreciate aesthetically on first hearing—or if
not on first hearing, at least on second or third. They do not feel satisfied with being
told that they are not expected (nor is it important for them) to hear all the trans-
formations of a twelve-tone row. For these reasons, atonal and serial music have
remained very much a minority taste among the listening public. Similar trends
have prevailed in many of the other arts: poetry with increasingly arcane classical

allusions or metaphors that have to be puzzled over; literary criticism using a highly specialized vocabulary and assuming a background in one or more literary theories; abstract painting and sculpture which have to be carefully explained before viewers feel able to understand what is before their eyes—all these trends have tended to create small specialized audiences and involuntarily to destroy the long held (and once highly valued) idea of a widely shared humanistic culture.

*   *   *

Such problems of comprehensibility did not occur with the one great new art form of the twentieth century, namely motion pictures. The first projection machines that made it possible for a large audience to see film sequences were invented in France in 1895. The Paris Exposition of 1900 included five- to ten-minute sequences on contemporary subjects, explained by commentators and sometimes accompanied by piano music or percussion. Camera and lighting technology were international from the beginning, and between 1900 and 1914 short action films and animated cartoons were produced in the United States, France, Germany, Italy, Belgium, and Scandinavia. Charlie Chaplin, Buster Keaton, Will Rogers, and Lon Chaney were all known to international audiences before the First World War.

Moving pictures, even without sound (which came only in 1928), held out unlimited prospects of entertainment, education, and propaganda. Most of the early actors and directors came from the vaudeville stage or the circus, and most of the two- or three-reel films (each lasting ten or fifteen minutes) specialized in slapstick comedy, domestic crises, and spectacular police and detective chases. But there were also travel films showing the beauties of nature and exotic cultures to audiences who had never traveled more than a few miles from home. And there were a few documentaries, such as *Baby's Toilet* (1905), which showed mothers how to hold, carry, change, and bathe infants.

In the first decade of active filmmaking, dramatists and stage directors were slow to realize the serious theatrical potential of cinema. However, the Italians, with their sense of Roman and recent Italian history, made several historical films between 1905 and 1914: *The Taking of Rome* (1905), glorifying the unification of Italy in 1870; *The Fall of Troy* (1911), with a spiritual bow in the direction of Virgil; *Quo Vadis?* (1913), based on the international Polish bestseller of that title; two versions of *The Last Days of Pompeii* (both also in 1913), based on the Victorian novel by Edward Bulwer-Lytton; and *Cabiria* (1914), concerning the Second Punic War and with explanatory titles by the famous contemporary poet Gabriele D'Annunzio.[10]

Thus by 1914 it was already possible to produce two-hour films, and many playwrights who had thought of movies only as light entertainment for the less-educated population began to think in terms of operatic and theater-like productions. In fact, silent movies could be even more fascinating to their viewers than traditional theater. Closeups and lighting effects brought the actor's expressions much closer to the audience than could be the case for any but the first few rows of theater patrons. Directors inevitably concentrated on facial expression, and the absence of dialogue permitted the viewer to imagine all sorts of possibilities supplementing the titles that were flashed on the screen between episodes and the suggestive atmosphere of the accompanying gramophone or piano music. The fact that nothing on the screen was "real," that there were no flesh-and-blood actors and yet the image was so vivid and all-encompassing in the darkened theater, gave wings to the imagination of audiences of all classes, ages, levels of intelligence, and education.

The First World War temporarily brought to an end the making of films (except for troop training) in France, Germany, and Italy; and the United States established during those years the supremacy which it has enjoyed ever since. Two of the historical films of D. W. Griffith, *Birth of a Nation* (1915) and *Intolerance* (1916), were to be much more widely distributed and much more influential technically than the previously mentioned Italian productions. The war also provided a great opportunity to the Swedish film industry. A number of factors contributed to the high-quality Swedish achievement between 1913 and 1924. The dramatist Gustav Strindberg and the Nobel Prize–winning novelist Selma Lagerlöf had both been quick to recognize cinema a true art form and not just a vehicle for simple entertainment. The Royal Dramatic Theater produced actors and directors as fine as any in neighboring Russia or the European and Anglo-Saxon worlds. It also had a strong tradition of collegiality and an atmosphere much more intellectually serious than the free-for-all exhibitionist rivalries which characterized Hollywood life from the start.

Sweden was going through the political struggles which were soon to lead to the establishment of the welfare state. A great deal of attention was being focused on the problems of the poor. Moreover, the nation was neutral in the war, and its artistic community was, by and large, strongly opposed to the barbarities it saw being practiced on the continent and on the high seas.

Ingeborg Holm (1913) was a realistic and sympathetic portrayal of the trials of a widow who was unable to support her children and lost them to mediocre and heartless municipal employees. It was a movie which directly influenced public opinion in favor of the proposed welfare reform. *Terje Vigen* (1916), based on a poem by Henrik Ibsen, celebrated the heroism of a fisherman running the British blockade during the Napoleonic wars in order to bring food to his starving family and village. This movie, and several others of the decade, included both the artistic sensitivity to natural beauty and the theme of man's struggle against the forces of nature which have ever since been characteristic of Scandinavian films. Swedish comedies were also notable for their emotional and visual frankness regarding sex, and a 1922 film entitled *Witchcraft Through the Ages* gave both serious and comic treatment to the many ways in which sexual prejudices and fears have been the motive force in the persecution of so-called witches.[11]

In the immediate postwar era, the most creative developments in European cinema took place in Germany, France, and Russia. In Germany, defeat had discredited the boastful pretensions of Hohenzollern imperial culture and created an atmosphere which nurtured both experimentation and cynicism. In France, the surrealists were fascinated by all the psychological and technical opportunities offered by the new art. In Russia, the two successive revolutions had simultaneously created utter chaos in daily life and utopian expectations for the future.

The first years of the Weimar Republic witnessed the production of numerous melodramas: richly costumed versions of the *Nibelungenlied* (an epic filled with gloomy violence and numerous personal betrayals) and lurid contemporary tales of sexual obsession like *The Cabinet of Dr. Caligari.* The Germans also produced many "historical" dramas which inaugurated a continuing international tradition of historical movies which tend to be accurate in costumes and (with honorable exceptions) grossly unreliable as history.[12]

In France, the surrealists—many of whom came from other countries such as England, Belgium, Spain, Germany, Russia and Romania—thought of cinema not as narrative, but as pure visual experience. Just as the cubist painters strove to show all aspects of a three-dimensional object simultaneously, surrealist filmmakers employed lighting effects, magnification, quick changes of perspective, and rapidly altering rhythms to intensify visual experience. And like the cubists, they used common household articles rather than art objects so as to highlight the expressive possibilities of film itself.

Important avant-garde artists, notably Kandinsky and Robert Delaunay and—for a short time—the composer Schoenberg (who was also a competent painter), espoused theories relating painting to music. Musical pitch was said to be the equivalent of chromatic vibrations (color). Two- and three-dimensional patterns could be compared with musical forms and the use of color with the use of different instruments (orchestration). These theories were applied experimentally in avant-garde movies, but they had much less influence on the subsequent development of cinema than did cubist and surrealist art on the development of painting and sculpture. Actually, it has never been possible to do away with narrative if a filmmaker wishes to hold his audience for more than a few minutes. Most European cineasts recognized that no matter how visually startling a movie might be, it must also to tell a story. The great French directors of the twenties and thirties frequently used surrealist devices as enrichment of a story, not as the principal material of a movie.[13]

During the 1920s in revolutionary Russia, both the government and the younger generation of intellectuals looked upon the cinema as *the* art of the future. For Lenin and his Commissar of Education Anatoly Lunacharsky, the film would direct the thoughts and create the new morality of the working class. For teenage enthusiasts of all new technology, for young people liberated from their bourgeois heritage and identifying themselves with a variety of collectivist blueprints for the future, the new art of film would embody the hopes of the emerging secular utopia.

The first films with proletarian heroes and heroines, made under the NEP, emphasized past economic and sexual exploitation. They had strong social content but were not heavy-handed propaganda. They were genuinely realistic in the sense that actors and settings were not made "prettier" on the screen than they were in real life. Later, as Stalin consolidated his power in the 1930s, a change of style occurred—not necessarily dictated by him personally, but developed by those who wished to flatter him. Peasant women and factory girls now became well-scrubbed, healthily buxom, with smiles revealing pearly white, and very even, teeth. Workers of both sexes no longer simply walked or ambled; they marched gaily toward the bright future.

Constant political intervention in the making of Soviet films can be illustrated by important milestones in the career of Sergei Eisenstein, internationally famous as an innovator in camera technique and montage. *The Battleship Potemkin* (1925), which glorified the role of "politically correct" sailors in the Bolshevik revolution, was considered by Stalin to be a model of revolutionary filmmaking. On the other hand, Eisenstein's celebration of the Mexican revolution, shot in 1928, was never shown in the Soviet Union because aspects of it appeared too sympathetic to anarchist and rural Church elements.

In 1934, Eisenstein tried twice to make a film biography of Pavlik Morozov, a peasant boy who was being touted as a hero of the collectivization campaign. The regime at this time was publicly encouraging children to report the "opposition" words or deeds of their recalcitrant relatives. Pavlik had bravely reported to the authorities the fact that his parents were opposed to the collectivization, and he subsequently achieved martyrdom when a posse of village kulaks lynched him. Eisenstein did his best to produce a sympathetic version of this heroic snitching, but Stalin was dissatisfied with both his efforts.

Alexander Nevsky (1938), with music by Serge Prokofiev, who had recently returned to Russia after living in the West during the first fifteen years of the revolution, depicted the heroic rescue of thirteenth-century Muscovy from an invasion by the Teutonic Knights. This film, released toward the end of Stalin's first set of blood purges, was awarded the Order of Lenin in 1939, and was withdrawn a few months later when the USSR and Nazi Germany signed a nonaggression pact.

Ivan the Terrible, Part 1 (1944), portrayed the sixteenth-century tsar as a harsh despot, but also as the sovereign who had rescued Russia from its feudal lords, the boyars, and from its external enemies, the Poles. Ivan had created a disciplined, loyal army and expanded Russian sovereignty to the Baltic coast. If *Alexander Nevsky* had deserved the second-highest Soviet award, the Order of Lenin, Part 1 of *Ivan*, released while the remnants of the German army were retreating in defeat, deserved the highest award, a Stalin Prize. However, Part 2, announced for 1946, was never shown. It portrayed the older Ivan as a paranoid tyrant and, according to the condemnatory decree of the Central Committee of the Communist Party, it pictured his glorious soldiers as if they were Ku Klux Klan thugs.

Thus far I have concentrated on the aspects of cinema which were related to contemporary European art, drama, and political events. But the invention of the movies involved two other factors whose importance can hardly be exaggerated. One is the sheer quantitative democratization of the audience. Gauguin and Picasso, Debussy and Stravinsky, reached the entire educated middle class, perhaps ten to fifteen percent of the European, Russian, and American populations. Max Ernst and Arnold Schoenberg reached perhaps one percent, those with active intellectual curiosity and a willingness to work hard in order to appreciate the full value of surrealist art and atonal music. But *everybody* saw Charlie Chaplin and Mary Pickford. This complete democratization of the audience applied as much to revolutionary Russia, and to the poor peasants of the Mediterranean countries, as it did to the established urban centers of culture. And during the second half of the present century, India, China, and Japan developed movie industries with similarly universal audiences within their own culture areas.

The second factor is the powerful domination of Western world cinema by Hollywood from 1914 to the present. Many more Frenchmen and Russians in the 1920s saw the films of Mary Pickford and Douglas Fairbanks than saw the surrealist *Ballet Mechanique* of Fernand Léger or the experimental films made by Soviet directors. Hollywood films drew larger audiences in Sweden and Germany than did the excellent films made by native directors, and Hollywood in the twenties hired a large proportion of the finest German and Scandinavian actors and directors.

The French, Swedish, British, and German film industries had all begun the postwar era with high hopes, and all had lost out to Hollywood by the end of the twenties. For a moment they had also thought that the "talkies," by introducing dialogue, would create a strong demand for movies in the several languages. But the introduction of sound meant a substantial increase in costs just at the beginning of the world economic depression; in addition to which, European audiences were apparently satisfied to listen to English and read subtitles.

The relationship between the intellectual elites and the moviegoing public has always been a tug of war. The taste of intellectuals and artists is different from the taste of the great majority of human beings. There have always been fruitful cross relations between the fine arts and popular culture. In the present century, for example, the expressionist painters, the composers basing their work on national folk music, and many film-makers in both Europe and the United States have been motivated by the desire to reach mass audiences with works of the highest artistic and intellectual caliber, and they have often succeeded in doing so.

But the costs of production and distribution, technical complexities, and the consciousness of an audience seeking relaxation and entertainment rather than

"uplift" has influenced movie production overwhelmingly in the direction of standard themes and simple emotions and ideas. The individual poet, artist, or composer works by himself, with relatively inexpensive materials, at home or in a small
studio or in an open field for which he is not paying rent. He dreams of reaching a
mass audience, but he does not have to do so. The central creative figure in the
film—the director—has to have a producer who will supply, at a minimum, hundreds of thousands of dollars. He has to have enormous supplies of high-quality
film and the technicians to process that film, build sets, and supply the lighting and
sound. He has to pay a handful of "stars" and hundreds of bit players and stage-
hands. And to recover the investment, he has to have wide distribution and a finished product which millions of ordinary souls are willing to pay to see.

Both in their silent form, and with the addition of sound from about 1928; in
the form of drama, and in newsreels, animated cartoons, and documentaries, the
movies became the great new art of the twentieth century. They reached everyone,
not just the educated and prosperous classes. They showed what other continents,
seas, and even universes look like. They provided manifold examples, and therefore standards, of personal beauty, and personal and social behavior, and the
design and furnishing of farms, estates, palaces, city apartments, prisons, and sky-
scrapers. They enabled their viewers to be eyewitnesses of great events. In the lives
of most people, they were far more influential than any other form of art or social
communication.

Finally, it should be noted that between 1914 and 1939 *European* culture,
both artistic and scientific, became *Western* culture. Most of the important scientific theories and artistic movements early in the century were European in origin;
but by 1914 university laboratories and libraries in the United States, Canada, and
Japan were rapidly equaling those of Europe. The first World War brought with it
American supremacy in the new art of film, as well as the rapid introduction and
success of American jazz and popular music into the 1920s.

Talented art students flocked to Paris, medical students to Vienna, and graduate students in the sciences to the great German and English universities. Then
after 1933, thanks to Adolf Hitler, the current reversed. Leading Jewish scientists,
musicians, and doctors were forced out of Germany—and after 1939, out of continental Europe as a whole. Most of the exiles from Nazism (and in smaller numbers
from Italian fascism) were Jews, but a substantial number were simply scientists,
artists, and professional people who refused to live under fascism and could, at
some economic sacrifice, leave their dictatorially governed homelands.

The Spanish Civil War of 1936–1939 caused a diaspora to England and the
Americas of many leading intellectuals and professionals, and in the spring of
1940 a substantial number of Dutch, Belgian, and French intellectuals followed
them. The cultural life of the entire New World was to be immensely enriched by
the contributions of these European exiles. Latin American universities, literary

life, and art galleries; North American university departments of German and Spanish literature, symphony orchestras, science faculties, Broadway and Hollywood acting groups, art galleries and museums—all received a permanent infusion of European talent, courtesy of Hitler, Mussolini, and Franco. Since 1940, in all artistic and scientific matters, European and American cultures have become *Western* culture.

ENDNOTES

1. *"Primitivism" in 20th Century Art*, edited by William Rubin, 2 vol. (New York: The Museum of Modern Art, 1994). Particularly valuable for photos comparing on the same page African or Pacific art objects with European works which show an "affinity" to them. Rubin specifies the choice of the word *affinity* because in many instances the European artist could not have actually seen the object with which his work is compared.

2. For definitions of the several movements, I have depended principally on *Concepts of Modern Art, From Fauvism to Postmodernism*, 3rd ed., edited by Nikos Stangos (London: Thames and Hudson, 1994). On Fauvism, Jean Leymarie, *Fauvism*, Editions d'Art, Albert Skira, 1959.

3. Wolf Dieter-Dube, *The Expressionists* (London: Thames and Hudson, 1933); and George Boudaille, *Expressionists* (New York: Tabard Press, 1976).

4. Caroline Tisdall and Angelo Bozzolla, *Futurism* (London: Thames and Hudson, 1993).

5. *Soviet Art, 1920s–1930s* (Moscow: Sovietsky Khudozhnik, and New York: Harry N. Abrams, 1988). The book has excellent reproductions, with dates that permit the reader to follow the evolution described in the above paragraphs.

6. Quoted in Nikos Stangos, *Concepts of Modern Art*, 3d ed. (London: Thames and Hudson, 1994), 114.

7. Richard Huelsenbeck, *Memoirs of a Dada Drummer* (New York: The Viking Press, 1974), 31–34, for the full text in both German and English.

8. Enrico Crispolti, *Ernst, Miró, and the Surrealists* (London: Bloomsbury Books, 1989).

9. *New Grove Dictionary of Music and Musicians* (London: Macmillan, 1980). See the chapters on the "Second Viennese School" for biographical information and definitions. The evaluations of Schoenberg's spiritual development and of his music are my own as an amateur performer and listener.

10. Robin Buss, *Italian Films* (New York: Holmes and Meier, 1989), *passim*.

11. Peter Cowie, *Scandinavian Cinema* (London: The Tantivy Press, 1992), *passim*.

12. Siegfried Kracauer, *From Caligari to Hitler* (Princeton University Press, 1947), chapters I and II.

13. Standish D. Lawder, *The Cubist Cinema* (New York: New York University Press, 1975), *passim*.

7

The Confrontation of Fascism, Communism, and Democracy

During the 1920s, Europeans were principally concerned with domestic affairs —the recovery of their own country or region from the destruction and economic dislocations of the Great War. The conservative elites in the democratic countries were strongly anticommunist, and the small but militant communist parties looked to the Soviet Union for leadership in a postponed (but still "inevitable") world revolution. However, the general population was not involved in ideological battles and, to the extent that ordinary people concerned themselves with international affairs, it was to hope that the League of Nations would provide a successful forum for mediated solutions to territorial disputes, as well as for the reintegration of Germany and Russia into the concert of nations and for progress towards international disarmament.

But the October 1929 stock-market crash in the United States, followed by the deepest depression of the modern capitalist era and the rise of Nazism in Germany, were to destroy the hopes of international cooperation and polarize the European world around the ideological alternatives of fascism, communism, and democracy. Of course, boom and bust cycles in the stock market, as well as bank failures, business and farm bankruptcies, and consequent large-scale unemployment, were not unfamiliar phenomena. But never had the threat of paralysis been so great, or the leading industrial countries so critically affected. Thus during the worst period of the Great Depression roughly 1931–33, fully one-third of the able-bodied men in Germany, Great Britain, and the United States were unemployed. Moreover, the purely financial aspect of the depression was much exacerbated by the completely unsolved problems of German war reparations to the Allies and Allied war debts to the United States. Largely on American initiative, the German reparations (but not the Allied debts) had been twice scaled down, in 1924 and 1929. But the Depression brought to a complete halt both the reparations and the Allied debt payments.

The capitalist leadership of all three principal industrial countries tried first to solve the crisis by deflation: cutting government expenses, reducing labor and white-collar salaries, and maintaining high interest rates so as to defend at all costs the international exchange value of their currencies. The idea was that investment and consumer buying could not be restored unless people were confident of the value of their money. That was (and always is) quite true for those who have money. But the problem in 1930 was that the circular flow of wages and consumer spending had been drastically reduced; most people had very little money and were afraid to spend the little they had.

Generally speaking, deflation is fine for creditors and hard for those who depend entirely on their monthly wages; and in 1930, all the leading industrial countries had governments that were more responsive to the wishes of the well-to-do than to the problems of wage earners, both employed and unemployed. Moreover, each nation practiced financial orthodoxy, the English and the Americans because they considered their currencies to be the currencies of world trade, the French because they had already suffered severe devaluation in the early 1920s, and the Germans because the experience of the hyperinflation of 1922–23 had inoculated all classes against the use of the printing press as a solution to monetary problems.

Deflation, however, was not the only possible reaction to the frightening decrease of economic activity. There was an alternative policy proposed by the British economist John Maynard Keynes, who had been one of the first persons to criticize the economic insanity of the Versailles treaty. Keynes accepted as normal the sequence of cyclical expansions and contractions in total economic activity. But he advocated government investment in public works as a way of "priming the pump" during the periods of contraction. By this method, the periods of depression could be shortened and—not the least virtue of the policy—the government could improve infrastructure and provide services which the private sector had not developed or did not find sufficiently profitable. All this might well cause mild inflation, but only by putting money into circulation and giving people useful jobs could confidence really be restored—after which general production and consumption would recover. (And mild inflation—a few percentage points per year—actually tends to stimulate investment, because if people know that their interest and mortgage debts will be smaller upon repayment over the years, they will be more ready to risk the original investment in a home or farm or business.)

Keynesian pump-priming was applied as of 1932 by the Social Democratic government of Sweden and in the American "New Deal" as of 1933. Great Britain increased unemployment benefits and increased some social services but did not undertake real Keynesian pump-priming. The Scandinavian countries, Britain, and the United States all left the gold standard and devalued their currencies as a way of increasing their exports by automatically lowering their prices in international trade (what was left of it).

France, which was not as heavily hit by unemployment as the more industrial countries, thought it worthwhile to import gold and enjoy the unusual pleasure (useless vanity, under the circumstances) of possessing one of the world's "strongest" currencies. Deflation meant stagnation domestically and was also harmful to the economies of France's small neighbors, Belgium and Holland, and to her client states, the Little Entente countries and Poland, whose economic health depended upon French loans and French purchases of their exports. Meanwhile, in Germany, the financially orthodox government of Heinrich Brüning maintained its deflationary policies, thereby fostering involuntarily the conditions of heavy unemployment and low consumer spending.

Taken together, German unemployment, French stagnation, British timidity and the necessity of deficit financing in Scandinavia and the United States all tended to undermine the confidence of all classes in the efficacy of capitalism. At the same time, the Soviets, Mussolini, and Hitler a few years later all claimed to have dynamic, successful alternatives.

From the viewpoint of Western ruling classes, the Soviet challenge was the most worrisome. Between 1921 and 1928, the Russian economy had recovered to its pre-1914 levels. Under the New Economic Policy, Russian and Ukrainian agriculture began the process of mechanization. Indeed, in the mid-1920s, more Russian peasants knew the names of Henry Ford and International Harvester than the names of Soviet leaders. The German and Soviet military establishments were cooperating under a treaty signed between the two governments in 1922. European and American engineers were being employed to supervise important infrastructure projects, and the Soviet economic bosses (up to and including Bukharin and Stalin) were all enthusiasts of American technology and efficiency, despite the fact that American diplomatic recognition was not extended to Soviet Russia until 1933.[1]

*   *   *

Indeed, after Lenin's death in January 1924, economic questions were inextricably entwined with the inner party struggle over future leadership. By 1928, Stalin had emerged as the uncontested party chief. He decided to end the NEP and inaugurate a series of "five-year plans" to industrialize Russia and collectivize her agriculture. By 1933, while the capitalist world was mired in its worst depression ever, Stalin announced that the first five-year plan had been completed in four years. He listed tremendous increases in the production of coal and steel, in the extension of railroads and the number of freight cars, in the construction of factories of all sorts, in the production of electricity, and in the harvests of the farms which had been 90 percent collectivized between 1929 and 1933. He also had put a number of foreign engineers on trial for presumed sabotage, and there were numerous unofficial reports concerning mass resistance to collectivization and mass deportations of peasants to Siberia.

To outside observers, the Soviet Union was an almost unimaginable and fascinating mixture of revolutionary enthusiasm, dogmatic politics, experimental culture, inefficient but impressive industrial accomplishments, upward mobility for the intelligent and ambitious, increased opportunity for women and non-Russian nationalities, cruel discipline, and omnipresent police. At the same time, it was a much more closed society than that of the tsarist empire or any contemporary European dictatorship. As of 1930, for example, in Italy, Poland, or the Balkan and Baltic dictatorships, it was dangerous to report unfavorable truths, and foreign correspondents were frequently threatened and occasionally expelled. But it was still possible to travel freely within the country, observe events, and interview personalities of the opposition.

In Soviet Russia, however, correspondents had to ask permission to go anywhere outside Moscow and Leningrad, had to live in special hotels and be accompanied by "interpreters," and were shadowed by plainclothes police (who were also keeping an eye on the interpreters). People outside the ruling circles were afraid to have any kind of personal contact with foreigners lest they be accused of espionage or "slander" against the Soviet state. Reports of the sabotage trials had to be cleared with the censors and had to reflect the official views. Reports of resistance and starvation in the Ukraine were automatically condemned as slander. Since Western journalists were not permitted to travel in the newly collectivized areas, their tales of the Bolshevik war against the "kulaks" (prosperous peasants) had to be based on the stories told by refugees escaping to Romania or Poland.

Nevertheless, with all its contradictory traits, the period from 1928, when Stalin consolidated his control, to 1936, when he staged the first of the "show trials" against the older generation of revolutionary leaders, was a period of great accomplishment in the basic tasks of industrialization. There are numerous concordant testimonies in the memoirs of young leftist (not necessarily communist) workers, students, and professionals who went from Europe and the Americas to help construct socialism under the five-year plans. These foreign volunteers were swept along by the enthusiasm of the local workers for "overfulfilling" the production plans of the "Vanguard Party" and its great leader, Comrade Stalin. Steel mills, apartment buildings, engine-repair shops, locomotives, rolling stock, and dams housing water-driven turbines are all very tangible items, and their production created a sense of very real accomplishment. Those who came from the middle classes in Western societies were deeply impressed by the new schools and hospitals, the high proportion of women doctors (positively rare at that time in the West), and the number of important positions filled by Bashkirs, Tatars, and members of smaller nationalities of which they had never heard.

On construction sites far from Moscow and Leningrad, police and bureaucrats were not quite as omnipresent as in the capital cities, and human contact was more informal. Among the American volunteers at the new steel production center of Magnitogorsk (meaning "the iron mountain") in the Urals was John Scott, leftist son of the American radical economist Scott Nearing. Here is how he first impressed his future wife Masha:

> The first American I had ever seen, he looked like a homeless boy. I saw in him the product of capitalist oppression. I saw in my mind's eye his sad childhood; I imagined the long hours of inhuman labor which he had been forced to perform in some capitalist factory while still a boy; I imagined the shamefully low wages he received, only sufficient to buy enough bread so that he could go to work the next day; I imagined his fear of losing even this pittance and being thrown on the streets unemployed in case he was unable to do his work to the satisfaction and profit of his parasitic bosses.[2]

In the decade after the demise of the Soviet Union such a vision may seem incredible—but at the time, it was by no means far fetched. Germany and the United States were suffering mass unemployment, along with the "overproduction" of goods and services which millions of their citizens could not afford to buy. The Soviet government hardly needed to exaggerate the truth in its incessant propaganda about Western unemployment. Except for a handful of diplomats and trade representatives its own citizens were not allowed to travel abroad, but the presence of the non-Russian volunteer workers seemed to confirm the statements made by the Soviet authorities.

Meanwhile, their own country claimed to be building a better future for all humanity—without unemployment, without sex or national discrimination. Soviet citizens had to carry internal passports and register with the police whenever they moved to a new home or job, but a wise government was presumably doing its best to distribute resources rationally for the benefit of everyone. Aggressive nationalism seemed to be a thing of the past. Ethnologists were collecting the music and dances of the more than one hundred nationalities that comprised the Soviet Union, and linguists were preparing dictionaries of what had been only spoken languages until the 1920s, but there were no pogroms or interethnic wars taking place. West Europeans, Americans, Canadians, Russians, Ukrainians, and Asian peoples were mixing their work, their hopes, and their genes in the Soviet Union.

During these same years of the initial Soviet industrial and agricultural triumphs (c. 1928–1933) the Weimar Republic was proving to be incapable of coping with the depression. The Social Democrats and the Center Party—the only parties truly committed to civilian, democratic government—floundered without strong leadership or clear programs. At the same time, the National Socialist Party of

Adolf Hitler, which in the early twenties had seemed to be only a handful of noisy street-brawlers, suddenly emerged in the elections of September 1930 as the second-largest party in the Reichstag, with 107 deputies (as against 143 Social Democrats).

Public life in Germany at this time was also plagued by numerous private political militias: the *Stahlhelm* ("steel helmets") patronized by reactionary industrialists; the *Saalschutz Abteilung*, Hitler's "Meetings Protection Section" led by one of his earliest and crudest mercenary followers, Ernst Roehm; the *Schutzstaffel*, the Nazi black-shirt-and-death's-head "Protective Squads" led by Heinrich Himmler; the *Rot Kämpferbund*, the "Red Fighters" of the Communist Party; and the *Reichsbanner*, defensive militia consisting mostly of Social Democrats with a sprinkling of Centrists.

The Nazis campaigned without any such rational and revolutionary vision of the human future as that which inspired the communists. Theirs was an openly nationalist and racist vision not of a better future for humanity in general, but of a Europe to be conquered and dominated by a "thousand-year German Reich." Their orators appealed to an extraordinary combination of hatreds and ideals: They were anti-Bolshevik, anticapitalist (in rhetoric at least), anti-French, anti-Jewish, anti-democratic, and determined to avenge the humiliations of the Versailles Treaty. They also promised to overcome economic stagnation and unemployment. But most importantly for his countrymen (and even more for his countrywomen who seemed mesmerized by his oratory), Hitler promised a restoration of German "values," of an earlier, pristine rural and artisan culture which was being destroyed by capitalist industry and urbanization, and which was idealized in memory as superior to the culture of industrial grime.

Hitler was Austrian, a lover of Wagnerian mythology and music drama, a disappointed landscape painter, a man who had witnessed the great advances made by the emancipated Jews of Austria in the early twentieth century, and a fervent admirer of Vienna's popular, able, and anti-Semitic mayor Karl Lueger. Neither his own personal anti-Semitism nor the importance of anti-Semitism to the whole Nazi world view can be understood without reference both to traditional European stereotypes about the Jews, and to the rapidly changing situation of the Jews in the German-speaking world during the approximate period from 1890 to 1930.

To speak first of the general stereotype: the Jews observed a religion that was related to, but different from, that of predominantly Christian Europe. Judaism and Christianity shared monotheism and shared the Old Testament. Jesus himself had been a rabbi; but whereas Christians believed that he was the Son of God—that he had taken human form and allowed himself to be crucified in order to purge the sins of all humankind—the Jews refused to acknowledge him as the Savior and had in fact been responsible, along with the Roman provincial government, for his arrest and crucifixion.

The Jews had different dietary laws, festivals, and family customs from those of their neighbors. During the Middle Ages, it was widely believed—(without a scrap of evidence)—that the Jews killed Christian children in order to use their blood in all kinds of diabolical rites. By the late nineteenth century, almost all literate and urban Europeans had rejected such beliefs, but they remained alive among peasants and villagers and were a factor in the instigation of pogroms in eastern Europe well into the twentieth century. Until the legal emancipation in the half century following the French Revolution, Jews had been forbidden to own land. They were therefore known to most of the population as peddlers and money-lenders, which occupations added to the impression of their being "rootless" and untrustworthy (since the great majority of rural people distrusted money and those who handled it).

Turning to the specific experience of the Germans: until 1871, Germany had been divided into dozens of small but economically and culturally prosperous states ruled by centuries-old royal families. The Jews had not been permitted to attend universities or to belong to the craft and professional guilds which licensed almost all economic activity; hence their concentration in small and itinerant businesses. A small and highly cultured handful of Jewish financiers had served as the treasurers of German princely houses and as the estate managers of rural landlords, for whom business activity was a function to be assigned to their social inferiors. Thus, for all the classes in Germany, the Jews were looked down upon socially but were considered useful as peddlers, small merchants, and financial and business managers.

The nineteenth-century legal emancipation of the Jews coincided with the rapid industrialization and urbanization of Germany. The Jews moved in large numbers to the growing industrial cities, where they exercised their traditional urban occupations with great energy and success. The Jews also had a long tradition of respect for philosophy and scholarship—a respect whose principal outlet had been biblical and talmudic commentaries and linguistic and logical exercises. With emancipation, they crowded into the universities and the liberal professions. Although they constituted less than 1 percent of the population, they suddenly appeared, after c. 1890, to be immensely numerous and influential in medicine, law, big business, journalism, art, music, theater, and the new art of motion pictures.

In addition to the abovementioned religious and economic bases of anti-Semitism, the Nazis skillfully exploited two other factors. They adopted literally the pseudobiology and theory of supposed "Aryan" racial superiority that had been developed in the late nineteenth century, from which they drew the conclusion that Jewish blood (not to speak of Gypsy or Negro blood) would "pollute" the pure healthy blood of the German people. Finally, they exploited a factor which has always been present in anti-Semitic violence, a factor which might be labeled "safe hatred." The Jews were always small in number; very few of them served as career military or police, and of course they had no state—or army—behind them. Hence it was safer to attack Jewish capitalists than German or Anglo-Saxon capitalists. The same held true for Jewish industrialists, Jewish trade unionists, and so on.

From late 1930, while the depression deepened, Hitler moved swiftly and confidently towards power. He made sure the major capitalists and bankers knew that he had no intention of socializing their property. He made an electoral alliance with the Nationalists of Alfred Hugenberg, a wealthy press magnate and film producer. In the presidential elections of April 1932, he polled thirteen million votes against the war hero Marshal Hindenburg, who was nevertheless re-elected by the nineteen million voters who hoped to avoid both Hitler and the communists. During this and other electoral campaigns, Hitler never pretended to avoid violence, but on the contrary used his brownshirted storm troopers to smash the windows of Jewish shops and smash the skulls of socialist and communist workers. When Chancellor Brüning tried to disband the party's armed gangs, Hitler forced the aging Hindenburg to rescind the order.

Brüning in turn resigned rather than yield to the presidential intervention, and in the ensuing parliamentary elections on July 31, 1932, the Nazis became the largest party in the chamber with 37 percent of the vote—the largest percentage they would ever receive in a free election. But Hitler would not accept a coalition government in which he would be named as *vice-chancellor*; and so the parliamentary deadlock continued, necessitating new elections in November, at which time the Nazi vote diminished to 33 percent.

With the support of his Nationalist allies and industrialist backers, Hitler now decided that he must come to power constitutionally before his vote might recede still further. On January 30, 1933, President Hindenburg authorized a Nazi-Nationalist coalition cabinet. The new government began to arrest socialist and communist leaders and stepped up the existing Nazi boycott of Jewish-owned businesses. Hitler also announced new elections for March 5, which he publicly predicted would be the last elections for the foreseeable future. On February 27, the Reichstag went up in flames, a politically convenient act of arson which the Nazis and the Communists blamed on each other, and which was apparently carried out by a lone, feeble-minded Dutchman (though the case has never been completely solved).[3]

With Nazi street terror redoubled, the party managed to win 44 percent of the votes on March 5. Along with their Nationalist allies, they now possessed a bare majority—but Hitler intended to rule as a dictator, not as the prime minister of even a majority coalition. In a dramatic meeting of the parliament on March 23, using the Kroll Opera House in place of the burnt Reichstag building (and lining the aisles of the auditorium with armed stormtroopers), the Nazis introduced an "Enabling Act" which would legalize Hitler's dictatorship. Few communist or socialist deputies were still free—or even dared—to attend the session, but crucial to Hitler's triumph was the favorable vote of the Catholic Center deputies. The Center Party had maintained its voting strength and its opposition to Nazi paganism and violence through all the recent elections. But in the emergency atmosphere following the Reichstag fire and the March 5 election, the party's leaders, in consultation with the Vatican—had decided to vote in favor of the Enabling Act.

During the month of April, the Nazis promulgated a series of decrees eliminating Jews from the officer corps, public hospitals, the civil service, and the teaching profession. Deliberately and effectively, they deprived the patriotic German Jews of any illusion that their services might be acceptable to the "new" Germany. On May 10, the books of Jewish authors—now purged from the university libraries and from all bookstores—were ceremoniously burned in city squares across Germany. On July 30, the Vatican signed a concordat which broke the several-months-long diplomatic boycott of the Nazi regime which had been imposed to protest its violence against the Jews and the entire Left.[4]

In the course of the eighteen months from January 1933 to June 1934, Hitler established his uncontested dictatorship. The party had always accepted the *Führerprinzip*, the dictum that Hitler's decisions in any area were final and to be carried out with blind loyalty by all party members. The Enabling Act granted him the legal power to apply the *Führerprinzip* to the remodeling of the civil service and the judiciary, and a large percentage of Germany's lawyers and judges eagerly supplied the new laws desired by the Führer.

The climactic action in Hitler's gathering of supreme power into his own hands was the blood purge of June 30, 1934. On this occasion, he got rid of Gregor Strasser, the leader of the more left-leaning Nazis for whom the socialism in "national socialism" was important, and of General Kurt von Schleicher, the one high officer whose political skill might have hampered his control of the army. He also personally assassinated Ernst Roehm, whose brownshirted stormtroopers were too rowdy for a government which sought the loyalty of the order-loving Germans. The SA were henceforth subordinated to the more disciplined elite SS troops under the command of Heinrch Himmler.

Because of Hitler's ranting oratory and his open brutality, many people—both Germans and others—underestimated his political ability. Once in power, he showed a great capacity to win the willing cooperation of the German elite and to improve the country's economic situation. Unemployment stood at 44 percent in 1932 and was reduced to 1 percent by 1938. The miracle was produced first by large-scale public-works programs—the construction of a national highway network, the opening of new canals and bridges, the repair and expansion of existing transportation facilities, a reforestation program—and an accelerating program of rearmament.

In economic matters, Hitler was completely pragmatic. He had no qualms about deficits or about private versus public investment; he used both, and he doubled tax revenues between 1933 and 1937. He delegated currency and trade relations to the very able (and initially non-Nazi) banker Hjalmar Schacht, whose father had named him after the nineteenth-century American antislavery editor Horace Greeley. Schacht made numerous bilateral trade agreements with Latin American and Balkan countries, exchanging their raw materials (much needed by German industry) for German manufactured goods and machines. The constant example of Nazi brutality helped in his negotiations, but it is also a fact that the weaker partners were finding markets for their exports, and that both they and the Nazis were finessing currency problems by using barter for the bulk of the exchanges.

Nazi ideology was rhetorically anticapitalist, but Hitler combined a policy of high taxes (including profits taxes) with constant assurances that he would not confiscate any non-Jewish property; he could also bestow the award of long-term favorable contracts in the rearmament program. At the same time, the party and the industrial elite made conscientious efforts to assuage the feelings of those who were still dreaming of a restored rural paradise and who felt that modern industrialism was soulless. They spoke of technology as an expression of German culture, one that was being developed to improve the aesthetic nature of public works and the aesthetic use of forests, waterways, and mountains. They pointed to the healthy, open-air, well-lighted nature of public spaces and buildings, and contrasted this German technical culture with the presumed money-grubbing and urban blight of Anglo-American capitalist technology.[5]

The Nazis were also well aware that the industrial working class, through all the free elections before 1933, had maintained its loyalty to the Marxist parties. They established a national Labor Front, which like many other youth and athletic organizations combined Nazi propaganda and blackmail with a measure of appeal to both the interests and ideals of the working class. The Labor Front conducted productivity competitions and awarded substantial prizes to the winners. Its athletic clubs took over entire hotels and bus companies for the vacations of its members. It greatly expanded an educational program to produce skilled workers, a program which had been launched in the late twenties by conservative industrialists.

By late 1935, the rearmament program was short of skilled metal and construction workers, and the graduates of Labor Front training programs gained in both professional skill and economic security. The "heating up" of the industrial economy from 1935 to 1939 caused a certain amount of inflation, so that real wages were not in fact higher than they had been before the depression, but everyone had work and many people were better fed and better housed than during the Weimar Republic. It thus becomes perfectly understandable that although Hitler never convinced more than one-third of his fellow citizens in free elections, he became an acceptable ruler for a people who remembered the postwar inflation and the terrible unemployment of the depression years.[6]

Among those who had greatly underestimated both Hitler's ability and the extent of his popularity were the Communists. Marxist theoreticians in both

Moscow and the Western democracies believed that fascism (as a generic phenom-enon in Italy, Germany, and Central Europe) represented a last, desperate effort on the part of world capitalism to prevent the inevitable victory of socialism. In Weimar Germany, the Communists remembered with great bitterness that the pro-visional government in 1919 had used the notorious *Freikorps* to suppress the Spar-tacus revolt and other revolutionary demonstrations. In the Communist press, the Social Democrats were referred to as "social fascists" and, on a few occasions, the Communists even voted with the Nazis against them in the belief that the destabi-lization of the Weimar Republic would redound to their benefit after a perhaps short Nazi interval of power.

In the years 1930–33, Nazi street violence was directed especially against the Communists. Upon taking power, they immediately arrested those militants who had not successfully hidden or fled abroad and, after the spring of 1933, the Com-munists were never able to exercise more than symbolic resistance against the Nazi regime. Meanwhile, the Soviet government—which was committed to Stalin's policy of building socialism in one country though it also exercised complete con-trol over the public pronouncements of the world's communist parties—rethought its position in the light of the German disaster. Thus, as of mid-1935 they decided to make a distinction between the capitalist democracies and the fascist powers. In the interest of preventing fascist barbarism from triumphing all over Europe, the Communist parties were urged to seek alliances with the Socialist parties and with all "progressive" elements among the political parties, trade unions, and intellec-tual elites of the democratic capitalist world. This was the policy of the "Popular Front" of liberal, socialist, and communist forces against the threat of fascism. On the internal front it meant supporting reformist programs like those of the Amer-ican New Deal and the Swedish Social Democratic "Middle Way." On the interna-tional front, it meant building "collective security" on the basis of defensive mili-tary alliances between the Soviet Union and the Western democracies.

The ideas of the Popular Front were gratefully welcomed by all those on the democratic Left who felt able to credit the sincerity of the new communist outlook. But significant legislative popular fronts were achieved only in Spain and France, and the years 1936–1938 were to witness the only serious efforts before the inva-sion of Russia in the Second World War to bridge the gap between the democratic Left and the Communists.

Spain had become a republic in 1931, and during the first two years the new government had consisted of a coalition of parliamentary middle-class republicans and democratic Socialists (the Communists being a tiny, internally divided party at this time, while the anarchists were opposed to political participation in any "bour-geois" regime). The coalition had produced a democratic constitution, separated church and state, passed Spain's first divorce law, granted "home rule" to Catalonia and suffrage rights to women, improved rural wages, and initiated land reform and school-building programs. But by the autumn of 1933, the republican-socialist coalition had split apart and, running as separate parties in the elections that November, they were defeated by a coalition of conservative forces which proposed to cancel most of the significant laws passed by the Constituent Cortes. Moreover, rather than accept a regime whose policies amounted simply to a "monarchy without the king," a sizeable proportion of the Left became involved in two simultaneous uprisings against the now-reactionary (in the literal sense of the word) government.

In early October of 1934, the Asturian miners (traditionally the most combative section of the labor movement) declared a "commune" with the support of the local socialist, communist, Trotskyite, and anarcho-syndicalist organizations; one of their slogans was "Better Vienna than Berlin," a clear reference to the fact that the Viennese socialist workers had resisted fascism in February 1934, whereas the German workers had allowed the Nazis to come to power without resistance in January 1933. The second uprising, in Barcelona, lasted only a day but was very symptomatic of the political atmosphere. It proclaimed a "Catalan republic within the Spanish federal republic." In Spanish politics, "federal" was a code word for further decentralization and more leftist social policies than anything which the reactionary republican government would contemplate or the existing unitary constitution could authorize.

Both revolts indicated the extreme fear of fascism on the part of the entire Left and the readiness to revolt against parliamentary government rather than allow it to be captured by fascist politicians, who had, after all, come to power legally in Italy and Germany. The Asturian revolt was suppressed with deliberate cruelty under the overall direction of Spain's youngest general and future dictator, Francisco Franco. In Barcelona, the leaders of the *Generalitat* government were arrested and the autonomy statute suspended.

It thus happened that, as of 1935 and on the basis of their own unhappy experience, the parliamentary socialists and the reformist republicans in Spain were thinking along lines that coincided with the new communist line: that is to say, that only an alliance of the democratic Left, the Communists, and (if possible) the anarchists could prevent republican Spain from evolving towards fascism on the Italian or Austrian model. The elections of February 1936 were hotly contested between the Popular Front coalition and an alliance of conservative parties whose propaganda methods and proposed program clearly reflected those of Mussolini (including huge portraits of the "leader" and mass chanted greetings "Jefe, Jefe, Jefe" in imitation of the Italian "Duce, Duce, Duce").

The Popular Front—with many anarchists deciding to vote this time—won a narrow but legally recognized majority. However, because of incessant "victory" demonstrations featuring revolutionary slogans on the one side and widely rumored military plots on the other, the new Left Republican government was barely able to function. Nevertheless, its clear intent in the spring of 1936 was to resume the reformist program of the years 1931–33. Meanwhile, in May 1936, the French Popular Front won the parliamentary elections and began to legislate such things as paid vacations for industrial workers and a Keynesian-type public-works program.

The domestic reform programs of both the Spanish and the French Popular Front governments were to be overtaken by international events not of their making. Rearmament had placed the initiative in the hands of the fascist governments. In 1935, Hitler began to rebuild the German navy and the English, hoping to limit the damage, signed a naval agreement with him, thereby annulling the principles—as well as the specific provisions—of the 1919 war settlement and sending a shiver down the spines of the French. Also in 1935, Mussolini invaded, fire-bombed, and annexed the only remaining free country in Africa, the kingdom of Ethiopia. In March 1936, Hitler sent his troops into the demilitarized Rhineland. They had secret orders to retreat if they met resistance from the Allied occupation forces, but they met no such resistance.

Up to this point, the Western powers could comfort themselves with the notion that Hitler was only destroying the Versailles treaty and that he would become a good citizen as soon as he had avenged the humiliation of 1919. As for Mussolini, he had created a successful antidote to Bolshevism, and his Mediterranean and North African ambitions could be accommodated. But the outbreak of the Spanish Civil War was to prove decisively that the two fascist powers meant to dominate Europe. On July 18, a major portion of the Spanish army attempted to overthrow the Popular Front government by a *pronunciamiento*, the sort of military revolt which had many times in the past led to relatively bloodless changes of government. But this time a combination of loyal units, together with thousands of socialist and anarchist trade-union members, prevented the success of the revolt in the main cities.

As of July 20, a failed *pronunciamiento* had been converted into a civil war which was to last for two and a half years. On one side were the elite army units, the majority of industrialists and financiers, the Church, the Monarchists, the small fascist party known as the *Falange*, and the conservative peasants of the Castilian meseta. On the other were the parties of the Popular Front, the bulk of the air force and the navy, the autonomous regional governments of Catalonia and the Basque provinces, the majority of the peasants of southern Spain, and the anarchists, who decided that in the present instance political action was necessary to save the country from fascism.

Both sides immediately appealed to their European friends for military aid, and the now-internationalized civil war became the test (in the end a failed test) of the readiness of the democratic powers to resist the aggressions of fascism. The French government, headed by the intellectual socialist Leon Blum, quickly sent a few dozen overage but still usable airplanes and permitted volunteers and trucks loaded with miscellaneous arms to cross the Pyrenees. But these acts led the

British to warn France against any moves that might provoke Germany and Italy, and they also produced a threatening reaction among French conservatives, many of whom were both profascist and anti-Semitic (Blum was Jewish).

Meanwhile, the Spanish military junta had sent emissaries to Italy and Germany, and both Mussolini and Hitler decided to send substantial quantities of artillery, aircraft, tanks, and small arms, together with pilots, communications specialists, and military advisers. Thus by early August, France (timidly) and Italy and Germany (boldly) had begun to send military aid to the Spanish combatants. However, taking fright at the British warning and the threat of civil disturbances at home, France closed its frontier in early August and took the diplomatic initiative to establish a "nonintervention" committee. By early September, Britain, France, Germany, Italy, Portugal, and Soviet Russia had all agreed "in principle" not to send personnel or military supplies to either side.

The agreement was not a resounding success. One of the novel features of diplomacy as practiced by Mussolini and Hitler was to reply to the coded euphemisms of the tradition-minded English with energetic cynicism. It cost them nothing to say that they agreed to something "in principle." Under British chairmanship, moreover, the Non-Intervention Committee obliged them by adopting cumbersome rules by which it would take months even to begin considering the evidence of intervention. When the landing of Italian planes in Morocco and the unloading of German freighters in Lisbon were reliably reported in the world press, the fascist powers declared that the reports were without foundation, so that acceptance of the evidence would have involved branding the accused governments as liars.

Actually, from July 1936 until the assurance of General Franco's complete victory in March 1939, the fascist powers made no effort whatsoever to hide their continued—and decisive—intervention. Part of their original purpose was to bully the Western powers, and this purpose was well served by the policy of open intervention openly boasted about while gleefully tying up the Non-Intervention Committee in procedural knots. The Soviet Union warned in October 1936 that it would not be bound by any restrictions which were being violated by others. In that same month, it began to supply aircraft, tanks, trucks, food, medical supplies, and military advisers to the government of Francisco Largo Caballero (a Socialist, former stucco worker and trade-union official, and the first European prime minister to have come from the industrial working class).

The Spanish Civil War was to be headline news for over thirty months. For almost all politically conscious people in Europe and the western hemisphere, it was seen as the critical battleground between the forces of political liberty and economic progress and the forces of reaction and traditional privilege. The defense of the republic involved nothing less than the defense of the entire emancipatory heritage of both the French and Russian revolutions: individual liberty and constitutional, civilian government; economic reforms in favor of landless peasants and exploited industrial workers; separation of church and state; universal public education and basic medical and social services; linguistic rights and local autonomy for the minority nationalities within Spain; and acceptance of anarchist and socialist collective experiments both in agriculture and factory management. The cause of *los nacionales*,[7] meanwhile, was nothing less than the defense of the entire conservative heritage of Europe: the sanctity of private property and public order; hierarchical social and economic relations between the existing classes (thought of as the God-given nature of human society); centralized, authoritarian political and religious institutions; and the rejection of Marxism, atheism, universal equal suffrage, parliamentary sovereignty, and political parties.

Within Spain itself, it was a war not just of interests but of ideals. The liberal republicans and the parliamentary socialists were fighting to bring Spain into the ranks of twentieth-century democracy, to endow it with institutions like those of France, Scandinavia, and the Anglo-Saxon world. The left socialists, anarchists, and various non-Stalinist Marxist parties were fighting to give Spain the revolutionary institutions which they ardently imagined had been the original intent of the Russian revolution, however much it had been deformed by Stalinist bureaucracy. The Catalan and Basque nationalists were fighting to give Spain not only a civilian democratic regime, but one which would recognize the rights of non-Castilian languages and cultures.

On the side of General Franco, Catholics were fighting to defend their Church against anti-clerical outrages and to maintain Catholic education and morality. Alphonsine monarchists were fighting for the eventual restoration of a parliamentary monarchy under the Bourbons, and Carlists were fighting for a more traditionalist authoritarian monarchy as espoused by the Carlist branch of the royal family. Middle-class conservatives were fighting to preserve the growing secular capitalist society, which they saw as the best means to improve Spain's economy and attenuate the class struggle. The Falange was fighting to establish an Italian-style fascist state, which it saw as the best means to combat the danger of atheist, materialist Marxism. General Franco was fighting to restore traditional authority and order. Also, at a time when churches were being desecrated by the anarchists, Franco felt that he had been destined to save Christian Spain from atheist, masonic, and materialistic hordes.

All wars involve a mixture of ideology and specific power interests. But in the case of Spain, the relative weight of political ideologies and moral ideals was much greater than in most wars. Hence the commitment, the heroism, the sense of universal "destiny," the self-sacrifice, and the cruelty to opponents. The first months of the war in particular were marked by revolutionary and counter-revolutionary terror. In the Popular Front zone, priests and nuns were killed as members of a privileged Church which had dominated the social and cultural life of Spain for centuries and which had almost always taken the side of the wealthy and powerful against the poor and powerless. Landlords and businessmen were killed in vengeance for real or alleged oppressions by persons whose economic possibilities they controlled. Civil Guards and members of the Falange were killed as presumed supporters of the privileged classes.

In the zone dominated by Generals Franco, Mola, and Queipo de Llano, teachers and doctors were automatically suspected of support for the Popular Front and many were shot for no other reason. In southern and western Spain, relatively small numbers of troops invaded large zones whose peasant population was (correctly) assumed to be hostile to the military rising. In Morocco in the 1920s, the army had slaughtered the inhabitants of rebellious moorish villages. Now in Spain, the army had no compunction about machinegunning peasants armed with pitchforks and hunting muskets or executing workmen with bruises on their shoulders—bruises which might have resulted from firing a rifle.

News of the terror was much more harmful internationally to the republican cause than to that of the military. The Popular Front stood for liberty and social justice; its supporters could well understand the confiscation of Church real estate and the closing of Church schools, but not the lynching of priests. In addition, many of the wealthy individual victims were well known in France or England or had family and business connections in those countries, whereas the peasants and school teachers executed by the military were unknown outside their native villages. Foreign newspapermen could report freely what they observed, good or bad, in the republican zone, but tight censorship prevented any such reporting from the nationalist zone. And in fact, the number of victims in the military zone was much larger than in the republican area. The republican government broadcast warnings to people not to open their doors to strangers, allowed refugees into the embassies and consular buildings in Madrid and Barcelona, and even issued passports (and sometimes provided police escorts) to conservative citizens who felt threatened and wished to emigrate. In nationalist Spain, the military leadership considered that they were simply cleansing the nation of vermin. No republicans could take refuge in consulates, and ordinary soldiers were assigned duty with the squads that took batches of republican prisoners from the jails to the execution grounds. On one side, the government was ashamed of irregular terror; on the other, the military junta practiced open terror as a "legitimate" means to establish its control.

The ideological content of the party programs and the personal idealism of the combatants was largely responsible for the terror on both sides in the early months of the war. But in the long run, the political behavior in both zones, and ultimately the results of the war, were determined by international factors. Crucial to developments in the republican zone were the roles of the Soviet Union and the Spanish Communist party. The Spanish Civil War seemed to provide the great opportunity for collective security to stop the march of fascism without the necessity of a second world war.

The Soviets simultaneously joined the Non-Intervention Committee, countered fascist aid to General Franco with their own aid to the Republic, and tried steadily through diplomacy to construct a defensive alliance of antifascist powers. Majority public opinion in all the Western countries was sympathetic to the Republic, especially as the anarchic terror virtually ended by November 1936 and as the defense of Madrid proved the military capacity of the Republic. Between July 1936 and the end of 1938, some forty thousand volunteers from all over Europe and the Americas, with small contingents also from Africa, Asia, and Australia (plus hundreds of doctors and nurses), served in the International Brigades defending the Republic. The role of the Communist parties was critical: Their own younger membership supplied about half the eventual volunteers, and their organizations supplied the passports and transport for all of them, communist and noncommunist. Their fraternal connections with democratic intellectuals gave them favorable treatment in the press and permitted them to organize mass meetings in the name of the Popular Front rather than the Third International.

From September 1936 to the end of the war, the Soviet Union was the one leading power which sent military aid, defended the legal rights of the Republic in international forums, and which called a spade a spade concerning Italian, German, and Portuguese military aid to Franco. Soviet workers melted down candlesticks and threw family jewelry into the collection pots for aid to republican Spain. This was one of the rare instances in which the Soviet government felt able to allow a spontaneous expression of public opinion. But the Soviet Union of the years 1936–38 was also the land of Stalin's blood purges: the show trials in which dozens of lifelong Bolshevik leaders confessed to acts of presumed sabotage and plots to murder Stalin, and in which several million persons signed false confessions and were deported to concentration camps in northern Russia and Siberia.

To Madrid, Valencia, and Barcelona, along with Stalin's military advisers came Stalin's secret police, to purge Spanish and Catalan political life of all non-Stalinist and anti-Stalinist leftists. The successive Popular Front governments and the *Generalitat* had to tolerate this interference which constantly mingled practical military and political advice with sectarian purges. The Spanish Communist party and the International Brigades also were obliged to accept increasing domination by Stalinist agents.

Inside Spain, the growth of communist power was accompanied by the disillusionment and growing defeatism of the noncommunist Left. In London, at the farcical proceedings of the Non-Intervention Committee, the English and French spokesmen bemoaned the excessive influence of the Communists while refusing to call the fascist powers to account for the over one hundred thousand uniformed and fully armed troops which they had sent to fight on the side of General Franco. One-sided "non-intervention" thus made the Republic completely dependent on Soviet material aid and left the Popular Front government with but two choices: to accept Stalinist domination or to surrender for lack of arms.

The Spanish Civil War also showed that, where ideologies were in question, the Right was much more capable of unity than the Left. Many British, French, Belgian, and Swiss bankers and businessmen supported General Franco. A considerable percentage of these persons were neither fascist nor militarist in outlook, but in pragmatic terms they found the nationalists much more able to make viable contracts—and in general, businessmen prefer governments which maintain public order regardless of the barbarities they may commit. In the nationalist camp, there were also bitter internal divisions between monarchist factions, Falange factions, and military officers ambitious to shine on their own. But none of these conflicts was permitted to destroy the unity of the nationalist cause in the way that the internal divisions of the Popular Front helped Franco destroy the Republic.

The "non-intervention" policy confirmed Hitler and Mussolini in their beliefs that, as long as they were not directly attacked, England and France would do everything in their power not to thwart the ambitions of the two dictators. The policy pursued by the western democracies from 1935 to 1939 has ever since been known by the name "appeasement," and their diplomacy during the Spanish Civil War is perhaps the most important single instance of this appeasement. The United States had followed Anglo-French leadership on the Spanish question, but by mid-1938 President Franklin D. Roosevelt, and in England the dissident Tory Winston Churchill, were regretting the non-intervention policy and hoping that the Spanish Republic could continue to resist conquest by the combined forces of General Franco, Italy, and Germany.

One other extended diplomatic crisis was to provide a last opportunity for a policy of collective security to save Europe from a general war. In March 1938, Hitler intimidated the last chancellor of independent Austria into permitting a Nazi takeover of the country without military resistance. He then announced that the terrible oppressions allegedly being suffered by the German minority in Czechoslovakia must be ended by freeing the largely German-populated portion of northern Czechoslovakia (known as the Sudetenland) from the Czechoslovak state. At this time France and Soviet Russia, both of whom had signed treaties of mutual defense with Czechoslovakia, quietly announced that they would honor those treaties if Czechoslovakia were attacked. Speaking in Parliament, however, British Prime Minister Neville Chamberlain explicitly refused to pledge support of France in case of German aggression against Czechoslovakia.

Hitler was not slow to seize the opportunity. Municipal elections were due to be held in the Sudeten provinces on May 22. On April 24, the Sudeten German Party of Konrad Henlein—following a well publicized visit of Henlein to Berlin, opened its campaign with the announcement of the "Karlsbad program," which demanded full self-government for the Sudeten area. Nazi advisers orchestrated the same kind of street demonstrations and blackmail which had characterized the elections of 1932 in Germany itself. And just coincidentally, the German army decided to hold maneuvers close to the Czech border on the day of the elections—maneuvers to which the Czechoslovak army responded with a partial mobilization of its own. At this point, Chamberlain warned Hitler that Britain might become involved if there were a war, and Hitler ordered Henlein temporarily to moderate his tone. Nevertheless Henlein's Party had by now completely replaced the Sudeten German parties, which had represented the German minority in Czechoslovak parliamentary politics since 1919. He won 80 percent of the votes cast on May 22, and that victory became the basis for immediate demands that would in fact have expelled all Czechoslovak civil servants and police from the Sudetenland and dismembered the existing state. Like the ultimatum sent by Austria to Serbia in 1914, the demands were intended to be unacceptable, as Hitler was now looking for an excuse to invade Czechoslovakia.

In this new situation, Chamberlain warned the French that their Czechoslovak ally should make the necessary concessions to satisfy Hitler's demands. He then sent a personal friend of his, Lord Runciman, to act as a mediator, the idea being to avoid war by giving the Sudeten Germans de facto independence from the Czechoslovak state. But Hitler wanted a military victory, and Henlein was under orders not to accept any compromise the Czechs might offer. After three draft offers had been refused, the Czech negotiator, in the presence of Lord Runciman, exposed the Nazi aim by offering a signed blank sheet of paper on which Henlein refused to write anything.

Runciman had to admit the failure of his month-long "mediation." It was the week of the Nazis' annual Party Congress in Nürenberg. On the podium before his massed stormtroopers and SS units, Hitler barked his fiery denunciations of the intolerable provocations of the Czechs. Simultaneously, Henlein's followers rioted in the Sudetenland, Czechoslovakia declared martial law, and Henlein himself fled to Germany. It looked for a few days as though David had successfully defied Goliath. But on September 15, Prime Minister Chamberlain flew to Berchtesgaden to meet the Führer at the latter's convenience and accept a map in which the German-inhabited border areas, together with the best fortification system on the European continent, would be annexed by Germany. On September 22, Chamberlain flew to Godesberg for the signing ceremonies, only to find that Hitler had produced a new map including many indisputably Czech areas. The angry prime minister felt betrayed, and he now let the Czechoslovak government know that he would not be opposed to mobilization—which was ordered the next day.

However, no one except Hitler was eager for war. The equally frightened French and Italian governments now used their good offices to calm the German dictator down to the point where he would accept a four-power conference to be held in Munich on September 28. The Soviets, who had not been consulted, reassured Czechoslovakia that they would honor the mutual-defense treaty, but the value of that pledge for the beleaguered Czechs was doubtful because neither

Poland nor Romania was willing to allow Soviet troops to cross their territory in order to reach Czechoslovakia.

At the Munich conference, from September 28–30, 1938, England and France obliged Czechoslovakia (also not present at the conference table) to cede the entire Sudeten area as defined by Hitler. The one remaining democratic state in Central-Eastern Europe was to be dismembered with the endorsement of the Western democratic powers and in the name of falsely exaggerated ethnic grievances. The morale of the Czechoslovak government and army was broken, and hundreds of anti-Nazi Sudeten Germans fled to Prague. The West had cheered when the Czechoslovak government had stood up to Hitler with the partial mobilizations of May 24 and September 24. Now they sacrificed that same courageous people to appease Hitler rather than achieve collective security against his aggressions by reaching an understanding with Soviet Russia.

Never in history have the intentions of an aggressor and the mistaken calculations of his potential victims been clearer than in the Czechoslovak crisis of 1938. Everyone but Chamberlain realized how carefully (not to say opportunistically) Hitler was able to turn on and off the spigot of his terrifying threats. But Chamberlain was the prime minister of the leading democratic power, and both English and French public opinion were so frightened of the possibility of general war that they cheered the results of his diplomacy. The German people were also frightened, and a portion of the military was thinking about a putsch against Hitler if the West were to stand firm. But Hitler gambled on the internal divisions among his opponents, and he won.

Yet it must be recognized that Nazi propaganda in the years 1935–38 had fallen on fertile soil. Henlein's Nazi-directed party, in free elections, completely replaced the Sudeten German parliamentary parties as the "voice" of the German minority. Every diplomatic and psychological error of the Czech civil service in dealing with the Sudeten population since 1919 was skillfully exaggerated. At the same time, by the mid-thirties, the numerous complaints to the League of Nations on behalf of ethnic minorities all over Central Europe had disposed many Western politicians to believe that multinational states simply could not survive peacefully.

The Munich agreement also broke the morale of the Spanish Republic by making it clear that the democratic powers would not resist even the direct Nazi destruction of a sovereign nation, let alone the kind of limited intervention which had been occurring in Spain since August 1936. The French leaders had had no illusions about Munich even at the moment of signing, and within a matter of weeks Chamberlain also was to be completely disillusioned with Hitler. Great Britain and (to a lesser degree) France stepped up their rearmament programs in late 1938. Then in March 1939, Hitler occupied the entire Czech lands and established a puppet Slovakian state in the Slovak portion. In doing so, he showed his complete contempt for his own signature upon solemn agreements made less than six months earlier. During the same month, General Franco completed his conquest of republican Spain.

Hitler now turned his malevolent oratory against Poland and denounced the intolerable sufferings of the mostly German population of the city of Danzig. Even Chamberlain doubted that appeasement could work again. In the spring and summer months, British, French, and Soviet diplomats carried on conversations aimed at a possible agreement—at long last—on collective security. But Stalin had decided by the time of Munich (and probably earlier) that one of the unacknowledged aims of appeasement was to signal Hitler that he could attack the Soviet Union without unduly disturbing the sleep of Western statesmen. It became a matter of simple common sense to sound out the Germans as to whether the two supposedly irreconcilable ideological enemies might not find it possible to make mutually advantageous agreements with each other.

Within the democracies, especially Great Britain, the governments and the most influential banks and businesses were clearly much more anticommunist than antifascist. In general, the middle classes were deeply divided over fascist and communist propaganda. The working classes and intellectuals were firmly antifascist and inclined to give the Soviet Union the benefit of the doubt in both domestic and international politics; they considered the Nazi regime to be a throwback to the Middle Ages (thereby unintentionally maligning numerous princes whose regimes had not been nearly as brutal as Hitler's).

Stalin's blood purges and the increasing dominance of the Communist Party within republican Spain had created inevitable doubts about the intentions of communists everywhere. At the same time, it was increasingly evident that the fascist powers could only be restrained if there were basic agreement between the Soviets and the West as to the containment of fascist aggression. In general, the democratic Left preferred cooperation with the Soviets and the Right preferred to appease Hitler and hope that he would point his armies eastward. As of late 1938 events in Spain and Czechoslovakia seemed to consecrate the almost bloodless (there were some thousands of Italian and German casualties in Spain) victory of fascism.

Unhappily, it is also true that even if the Western powers had had leaders less willing to appease the fascist dictators, the political tactics of both the fascists and the communists posed a still-unresolved dilemma for democratic polities. How can constitutional, democratic societies protect themselves from political movements which use constitutional techniques to destroy liberty? Democracy is largely a matter of government by discussion. It can tolerate considerable stupidity and corruption, but its survival always depends on the basic honesty and predominantly decent intentions of those in power.

Mussolini established his dictatorship so gradually that the Italian public never had a clear chance to stop him even if it had wished. Hitler announced beforehand that there would be no more elections after those of March 1933, but he had already achieved power legally when he said this. The Communist parties in the Popular Front era knew perfectly well that they were minority parties, but they somehow assured themselves that they were a wise and benevolent vanguard. They may have sincerely hoped to convince their partners, but they often manipulated (or simply overrode) the democratically expressed wishes of the other parties to the Popular Front. And they never acknowledged the obvious fact that their policies were determined by a political "line" established in Moscow.

Thus the failure of the democracies to arrest the international aggressions of fascism was not simply a failure of understanding or a matter of nerve, or of slow economic recovery and slow rearmament. It was also a technical political dilemma, namely how to deal with parties that claim all the rights of democracy for the purpose of destroying democracy. It was a problem in the 1930s and also after the Allied victory in World War II, and it remains a potential problem today.

ENDNOTES

1. Hans Rogger, "Americakanizm and the Development of Russia," and Kendall E. Bailes, "Ideology and American Technology in the USSR, 1917–1941," both in *Comparative Studies in Society and History*, 1981.

2. John Scott, *Behind the Urals*, 119. Long out of print, reissued in 1989 by the Indiana University Press.

3. Hans Mommsen, "Der Reichstagbrand und seine politischen Folgen," *Vierteljahre für Zeitgeschichte*, 1964, 352–413.

4. Karl Otmar Feiherr von Aretin, "Pälat Kass, Franz von Papen, und das Reichskonkordat von 1933," *Vierteljahre für Zeitgeschichte*, 1966, 252–79.

5. Jeffrey Hert, "The Engineer as Ideologue . . . in Weimer and Nazi Germany," and Anson G. Rabinbach, "The Aesthetics of Production in the Third Reich," *Journal of Contemporary History*, October 1984, 631–48.

6. T. W. Mason, "Labor in the Third Reich, 1933–1939," *Past and Present*, April 1966, 112–41.

7. In Spanish usage *nacionalistas* generally refers to the Catalan and Basque autonomist parties and *los nacionales* to the troops under General Franco's command during the civil war. English lacks this distinction, but the reader should know that in the following paragraphs the term "nationalists" without adjective refers to the armed forces of General Franco.

8

The Second World War, 1939–1945

*B*y the end of March 1939, Hitler had completed the destruction of Czecho-slovakia, and his junior ally, General Franco, had completed his victory over the Spanish Republic with the occupation of Madrid. The Italian and German troops could now be repatriated for use in other fascist adventures. Thus on April 7, Mussolini invaded Albania without informing Hitler (who had occupied Prague on March 15 without notifying Mussolini).

One week earlier England had formally offered guarantees to Poland. More-over, in the following weeks the Chamberlain government introduced peacetime conscription for the first time in British history and offered guarantees to Greece and Romania as well. On May 3, Stalin replaced Maxim Litvinov, the foreign min-ister who had been the spokesman of cooperation with the League of Nations and then of collective security. His successor was one of the few really able "Old Bol-sheviks" whom the dictator had spared in the 1936–38 purges, Vyachislav Molotov. In the course of the summer, France and Germany both increased the garrisons manning their lines of defensive forts, the so-called Maginot and Siegfried lines.

Thus it was clear that, while they had not been openly disavowed, both appeasement and collective security were no longer the guiding policies of the Western powers and Russia, respectively. Hitler in turn was quite ready to provoke war with his next aggression, but he wanted to be sure not to provoke a two-front war—the strategic error which had been fatal to Germany's ambitions in 1914. Thus, while he fulminated against the Poles, he welcomed the secret feelers being extended by his long–proclaimed principal enemy, the Soviet Union.

The British and French governments could not conceive of the possibility of an alliance between the world's two greatest ideological enemies. Unhurriedly, they sent a low-level diplomatic mission to Moscow to discuss defensive military arrangements against Hitler. This mission could not seriously consider the Soviet demands for a military protectorate over the Baltic republics and was not disposed to press the Polish government to allow the passage of Russian troops in case of war. Meanwhile, by late July, Herr Hitler—prepared, as always, to make promises and sign agreements which he had no intention of fulfilling—decided to conclude a treaty with Russia in order to free his hands in the rest of Europe.

Thus on August 23, 1939, the pipe-smoking, benign-looking Soviet dictator, the broadly smiling and very Aryan-looking German Foreign Minister Joachim von Ribbentrop, and the dour-faced Molotov announced the completion of a treaty of non-aggression between their two peace-loving governments. Hitler had the guarantee he needed before launching the invasion of Poland, the appeasement governments were now left to face Germany alone, and the world communist parties needed between a week and a month (depending on the flexibility of the personalities involved) to discover that the coming war was purely a war between "imperialists."

World War II thus began with the diplomatic humiliation of the democratic powers, a new masterpiece of calculated hypocrisy by Hitler, the renunciation of collective security by the Soviets, and the confusion and demoralization of the world communist parties, as well as that substantial portion of the democratic Left which had admired the Soviet stances during the Spanish Civil War and the Czechoslovak crisis.

In the first phase of the war, from September 1939 to June 1941, the Germans triumphed spectacularly on the European continent, but failed either to defeat England or to force it to accept peace on German terms. They also attempted to starve Britain through submarine warfare. As in the First World War, they did tremendous damage to the British merchant fleet; but as of the summer of 1940, President Roosevelt (who had been Assistant Secretary of the Navy in World War I) was already cooperating with Prime Minister Churchill (First Lord of the Admiralty during the same war) to supply Britain with overage U.S. destroyers and with state-of-the-art intelligence information on submarine movements, and also to build freighters in American shipyards more rapidly than they were sunk by U-boats.

In the land war, however, it took Germany less than a month to destroy the Polish army (in September 1939), and only a few hours to occupy Denmark and a few weeks to defeat Norway (in April, 1940). A bungled effort by the British navy to come to Norway's defense led to the resignation of Chamberlain and the appointment of Churchill as prime minister on May 10. On that same date, coincidentally, the Germans launched their attack in the West, and in barely five weeks, from May 10 to June 15, they defeated the Netherlands, Belgium, France, and the British expeditionary troops which formed an important part of the Belgian-French defense force.

The Polish victory showed the effectiveness of German tanks and bombing planes operating in open country against an army which consisted of unmechanized infantry and horse cavalry. The Polish ground units were simply encircled and pulverized by mobile troops pouring through the gaps which tanks had punched in the Polish defense lines. With their famous *Stuka* dive bombers, the Germans destroyed the small Polish air force on the ground, broke up the few paved highways, and terrorized the civilian population of the towns. Only in the capital city of Warsaw was it possible for the defending army to conduct a street-by-street, house-by-house resistance which delayed the surrender by about ten days.

The Soviet-German nonaggression pact of August 23 included secret clauses whereby the signatories divided Poland and the Baltic republics between them. On September 17, the Red Army moved into the eastern, largely Ukrainian and Belorussian provinces which had been assigned to Russia. This action confirmed the hopelessness of Polish resistance, but the surprise and speed of the initial German assault from the west would have destroyed Poland in a month even if the Soviets had not participated.

The military victories over Denmark and Norway require little explanation. Both were small neutrals who had done everything to avoid irritating the Nazis and whose populations consisted overwhelmingly of "Aryan" racial elements. After the First World War, many Scandinavians had aided German families to recover from the near-starvation of the blockade years. Now the invading German troops at various points were guided by soldiers who had grown up in Danish and Norwegian foster homes during the early 1920s or had vacationed on Danish beaches or skied in Norwegian mountains, and therefore knew the geography of the areas to be occupied. (With the Führer having shown many times over how betrayal can lead to success, many of these young men seemed to think they would actually be welcomed by their former hosts.) The German navy had been swept from the open seas in the first months of the war. In preparation for the Norwegian landings, it had an opportunity to demonstrate its capacities for deception by docking on "peaceful" missions in Norwegian ports and then, on April 9, disgorging mobile military units. During the brief combat period, it also proved its efficiency at escorting troop ships across the uncontested Baltic.

The five-week *Blitzkrieg* victory in Western Europe employed the same tank and aircraft tactics which had been so successful in Poland. The Dutch had been neutral in the First World War; their small garrisons were overwhelmed in a couple of days, and opening the dikes had only a brief delaying effect on German armor. France had depended strategically and psychologically throughout the interwar years on the construction of the Maginot line. But since Belgium had hoped to maintain its neutrality by not provoking a resurgent Germany, the Maginot line did not extend into Belgium. The Belgians resisted for two weeks, but in the absence of heavy fortifications—and also of any coordinated defense by the allies—German tanks and bombers repeated their Polish successes. By late May, the German army was encircling the British units in western Belgium and northern France. Incredible as it may seem, the British and French general staffs had not made any clear agreements as to war aims or specific defense responsibilities on the ground during the months of the so-called phony war between October 1939 and May 1940.[1] They had apparently counted on the Maginot line to discourage Hitler from attacking, lest he involve himself in a disastrous war of attrition. Whether the French fortifications would have provided an effective defense will never be known because the Germans outflanked them completely by overrunning Holland and Belgium. After the first few days of the German offensive, the rout of the Dutch and Belgian armies was complete. The British and French field commanders began multiplying calls for more troops and supplies, arranging joint strategy meetings at which many of the cited officers could not or did not appear, and preparing to blame one another for the predictable defeat of their own divisions.

The French naval command announced that it was not prepared to evacuate the British; the British wanted the French to attack the Siegfried line so as to reduce the pressure on their troops in Flanders; and both commands found that many of their telephone lines had already been cut. The encircled troops of both nations retreated towards the channel port of Dunkirk. The French resented British destruction of heavy equipment on the beaches and the evacuation of municipal defense posts while they, the French, had orders to fight on. With the help of foggy weather, the British managed to evacuate about 335,000 troops troops with some of their light equipment before the Germans arrived on June 4.

The *Wehrmacht* was now able to move rapidly towards Paris. The highways of northern France were clogged with the automobiles, farm carts, and bicycles of Dutch, Belgian, and French civilians fleeing from the invader. Indeed, this refugee traffic slowed the progress of the motorized columns more than did any resistance by military units. Stuka bombers dropped explosives and machinegunned the fleeing civilians as they had in Spain and in Poland. The French sued for an armistice on June 15, and the Germans delayed granting it for a week in order fully to occupy the northern half of France and collect approximately two million prisoners of war. Hitler demanded that the armistice be signed in the same railroad car in which the Germans had signed their surrender in 1918, and on the present occasion he hopped about like an elated little boy.

The French government had been utterly disorganized and demoralized. The Churchill cabinet had made a desperate last-minute proposal of political union to the government of Paul Reynaud, which had attempted to continue fighting during the first days of June. But on June 16, Reynaud resigned in favor of Marshal Philippe Pétain and the French government, having fled from Paris to Bordeaux, refused the British offer. Germany's conditions included the division of France into a northern zone, plus the Atlantic coast, to be directly occupied by Germany; and a southern, interior rump state to be presided over by Marshal Pétain. On July 12, in Pétain's investiture as head of state at Vichy, the same Chamber of Deputies which had legislated the reforms of the Popular Front program voted full powers to the hero of Verdun by a total of 569 to 80. Of the 80 "no" votes, 73 came from parties of the Popular Front; but of 152 socialist deputies present, 83 voted for Pétain. The overwhelming rapidity of the German victory made it psychologically impossible to conceive of systematic resistance to the conqueror. The communists were of course "neutral" because of the Nazi-Soviet pact, and the democratic Left was as demoralized as the rest of the French population.

Indeed, the speed of victory had surprised the Germans themselves, and they had neither the means nor any detailed plans to invade Great Britain. From late July to mid-September, they tried to destroy British resistance from the air, but their bombers were slow and vulnerable to the British fighter planes which were qualitatively superior (and whose crews were as well trained and more highly motivated than were their enemies). In addition, the Germans could not decide where to concentrate their efforts: on airfields, on shipping, on radar stations, on factories, or on civilian neighborhoods. As of September 15, after losing more than 1,200 planes, Hitler called off the massive air attacks. The British had lost over seven hundred fighter planes; never had so many owed so much to so few, as Prime Minister Churchill said in his tribute to the Royal Air Force.

The Second World War, in its European phases, was decidedly Hitler's war. He had repeatedly told his generals and his closest party comrades that Germany must conquer Europe and that, for demographic and strategic reasons, the optimal time for completion of this task would be the year 1943. Moreover, Hitler was the one who made all the major decisions: to aid General Franco, to occupy Austria, to destroy Czechoslovakia, to make a temporary agreement with Stalin, to attack Poland despite the risk of a general war, and then to occupy Denmark, Norway, and Western Europe. But Hitler was not a systematic ruler. He relied on his intuition, including his intuition as to the abilities and the loyalty of dozens of military and civilian subordinates. He made rearmament the center of his industrial and employment policies from 1934. He favored the development of the air force and the use of tanks as the spearhead for infantry advances, as well as the stockpiling of important metals and oil. But he never centralized procurement, manufacturing, or distribution, and he seemed not to be bothered by the constant rivalry between military and industrial interests. Another of his intuitions was that each of his military campaigns would be brief and decisive. Thus one of the main results of his unsystematic administration was that his armies were excellently prepared for *short* campaigns, and the war between September 1939 and June 1940 seemed fully to vindicate his "genius" as a military planner.

Away from the main theaters of combat, there were several important but not decisive developments between the *Blitzkrieg* of May to June 1940 and the invasion of the Soviet Union in June 1941. Mussolini had told Hitler before the invasion of Poland that Italy was not ready for immediate combat in Europe; however, rather than miss the chance of spoils in the conquest of France, he declared war on June 10. The Soviets, equally surprised and worried by the rapidity of Hitler's victories, occupied the Baltic republics and Bessarabia in the second half of June. On October 7, Hitler occupied the Romanian oil fields, thereby assuring his future supply of petroleum and serving notice to Russia that Romania would remain in the German sphere of influence. On October 28 Mussolini, who had occupied Albania without too much trouble, invaded Greece, where he met stiff resistance and eventually needed German help.

Also in October, the Führer honored Marshal Pétain and General Franco with meetings intended to consolidate their cooperation with the New Order which he was improvising. Franco explained that Spain was much too exhausted from the civil war to offer military cooperation against Gibraltar and other Mediterranean objectives, and Hitler reported to friends that he would rather have a tooth extracted than go through another interview with his Spanish ally. With Marshal Pétain he was circumspect. He had imposed immense daily occupation costs on France, but he wanted to speak in terms of cooperation in the hope that the French navy and French colonial garrisons would not go over to the English.

In 1941, German troops—called to aid their Italian ally—did threaten the North African colonies and the Middle Eastern League of Nations mandates of Britain and France, but they were eventually defeated. Much more important in the decisive European theater of operations was the fact that by early 1941, Hitler was planning a massive surprise attack on Soviet Russia. He was accumulating food and raw materials from the countries he had occupied in 1940 and also from the compliant and frightened governments of Slovakia, Hungary, Romania, and Bulgaria. The memory of the First World War blockade, and the complacent belief in German racial superiority, led Hitler to make every effort to see that his own people were well fed.

He had also secured a treaty of cooperation with Yugoslavia, which included the right to transport troops through that country to Greece. Both the Serbian elite and the general population felt that this treaty made their country a virtual German colony, and a military rising forced the Belgrade cabinet to resign on April 6. The German retaliation was swift and complete: occupation of Yugoslavia by Germany and Italy, expulsion of the British from Greece (where they had landed to aid in the war against Mussolini), and a spectacular occupation of Crete by German airborne troops.

Meanwhile, the Soviets continued punctually to fulfill their trade obligations under the August 1939 pact. For reasons still unknown (but perhaps related to his morbid suspicions of the West), Stalin did not heed the warnings he received of German preparations to invade the Soviet Union. Then on June 22 1941, Hitler launched "operation Barbarossa." Approximately four million men, thirty-three hundred tanks, and five thousand planes attacked along the frontier between

German and Russian-occupied Poland as it had been established in September 1939.[2] Hitler anticipated a two- to three-month campaign and had not supplied his armies with winter clothing. As a matter of fact, by late October the Wehrmacht had occupied all of the Ukraine and Belorussia, was threatening Rostov in the south, and had advanced to within a dozen miles of Moscow and Leningrad. It had taken almost four million prisoners and destroyed approximately two thousand aircraft and fourteen thousand tanks and miscellaneous military vehicles.

Many municipal and collective-farm authorities had welcomed the invaders as potential liberators from the Russian-dominated Soviet system. But the German soldiers could not hide their racist scorn of a population which was indeed used to much lower standards of living than that of the Germans. They alienated the villagers rapidly by their massive confiscation of local food supplies, their cold-blooded reprisal shootings at the slightest sign of noncooperation, and their cruel treatment of prisoners of war. Meanwhile the Moscow authorities had appealed to the patriotism of all Soviet peoples to save the fatherland from the barbarous invader. Soviet defense strategy had always included plans for the evacuation to Siberian cities of the factories located in the Ukraine and the Crimea. Industrial and railroad workers had managed successfully to dismantle and transport a large proportion of this valuable equipment. The populations of Moscow and Leningrad had also eagerly aided the Red Army to dig trenches and tank traps at the outskirts of the urban areas. The Germans were unable to decide whether to give priority to Moscow or Leningrad, with the result that they could not take either city before winter weather forced them to suspend their offensives.

As of March 1942, Hitler was reliably reported (in the diaries of his faithful propaganda minister Josef Goebbels) never to wish to see snow again. The Wehrmacht nevertheless conducted a moderately successful summer offensive which led to the capture of Sebastopol on July 2, and of Rostov on July 28. These were to be the last of its victories, however. Disregarding cautious advice from his generals, Hitler insisted on the capture of Stalingrad as much for symbolic as for strategic reasons. In late November, the Soviet armies achieved an encirclement maneuver of the sort which had previously been a German specialty. Throughout December, the Wehrmacht tried unsuccessfully to break the encirclement; it began also to withdraw from its most advanced positions in the Crimea, and on January 31, 1943, General Friedrich von Paulus, disobeying Hitler's orders, surrendered the remnants of his starving and frostbitten army.

Throughout 1943 the Germans were slowly forced to give up most of their positions in Russia and the Crimea, and in 1944 to retreat steadily from the Ukraine, Belorussia, and Poland. The balance of resources, manpower, leadership, and morale had shifted decisively from the German to the Soviet side. Russian tanks, mortars, and trucks were not quite as technically advanced as those of Germany, but they were sturdy, effective, and produced in increasing quantity from early 1942 onward. Their fighter planes were excellent and their artillery incorporated the use of rockets, which Soviet scientists had worked diligently to develop in the 1930s.

Within days of the German attack, the British government had offered an immediate alliance to the Russians and the promise of a future second front, and the United States—brought into the war by the Japanese attack on Pearl Harbor on December 7, 1941, and by Hitler's subsequent declaration of war—included Russia in the "lend-lease" program. The United States was rapidly to become "the arsenal of democracy," supplying arms in quantities which Germany could never hope to match despite its complete domination of "Fortress Europe." According to *Pravda* for June 11, 1944, the United States had by that point supplied the Soviet Union with 6,430 aircraft, 3,734 tanks, 206,771 motor vehicles, 245,000 telephones, 5,500,000 pairs of boots, 2,000,000 tons of food (mostly canned meats and powdered milk), and unlisted quantities of ammunition and high explosives.

One of the most important aspects of the war in the West was the reliance on strategic bombardment. There were numerous reasons for this emphasis on air power. One was the immense industrial capacity of the United States to produce both the aircraft and fuel. Very significant from a psychological point of view, the role of aircraft restored a degree of individual initiative, and a sense of individual and team heroism, which had almost entirely disappeared from the war experience of combat infantry in the stalemated trench battles of the First World War, and had been totally absent in the disastrous retreats of May and June 1940.

Bombers were manned by a crew of four or five men and their escorting fighter planes by one or two. These crews trained together, ate together, were housed together, and constituted an elite branch of the military separate from the land (army) and sea (navy) forces. The pilots learned not only to control powerful machinery but to understand the use of dozens of subtle, fine-tuned indicators of speed, air pressure, altitude, temperature, fuel pressure, availability of oxygen and fire-fighting chemicals, and so forth. The navigators had to pass detailed courses in astronomy and cartography; the bombardiers were also trained as map readers and as expert handlers of precision controls. Fighter pilots had to be equally adept at controlling their flight paths and defending themselves with machine guns. Thus the air forces gave their men a sense of separate mission, of highly skilled and often heroic action.

In September 1939, the Germans had pitilessly bombed civilians in Poland and recorded the destruction on film, which was then proudly shown to a domestic audience that had been more worried than enthusiastic at their Führer's declaration of war. To similar film sessions in their embassies they invited the representatives of their allies (such as Italy and Slovakia) and future victims (such as Denmark and Norway). In May 1940, they destroyed Rotterdam from the air as part of their swift conquest of the Netherlands. Between August 23 and September 15, 1940, they tried in similar nightly raids to destroy London. On November 14, they flattened the city of Coventry with a combination of explosives and firebombs; and on December 29, they caused huge fires in downtown London. But over the course of 1941, first "lend-lease" shipments and then the entry of the U.S. into the war enabled the Allies to begin giving the Germans a taste of their own medicine.

Then, too, as of early 1942 the Russians were pressing for the opening of the promised second front. The Allies renewed their assurances of a cross-channel invasion to liberate France and the Low Countries, but they could not and did not set a date. England had never had conscription until 1939, and the United States had to start almost from scratch in the creation of a land army. What the Allies could do while forming their armies and building landing craft was to bomb German industries, rail lines, and military bases. Increasingly during the years 1942–45, the Allied air forces carried out massive raids on German cities, with the British flying mostly nighttime missions and the U.S. flying during daytime at heights presumed to be beyond the range of German anti-aircraft batteries.

Strategic bombing sought to achieve two general objectives: the destruction of the enemy's military installations and the undermining of civilian morale. The Allies did not flaunt their capacity to terrorize the civilian population, but there was a widespread sentiment that the Germans had to be taught a lesson and that the destruction of their homes and lives was also a legitimate—indeed, a neces-sary—military objective. From late 1941 to the end of the war, some sixty-one German cities with a population over one hundred thousand were submitted to "saturation" bombing. The estimated results included six hundred thousand civilian deaths and the destruction of about 20 percent of the existing housing. As for the bombing of military installations, factories, roads, and railroads, there are no reliable quantitative results to be listed. Analysis of the damage done depended on photos taken at altitudes of thirty to forty thousand feet, through smoke and flak, of buildings which may or may not have been put out of use, and may or may not have housed military activities, or of transportation and communication lines which clearly were damaged, but were in most cases rapidly repaired to the extent nec-essary for their continued use.

Despite the fact that the German air force was completely outnumbered and outgunned in the last three years of the war, its anti-aircraft artillery forced the Allied planes to fly higher and faster, and thus to drop their bombs with less pre-cision than they wished. German anti-aircraft fire also exacted a heavy toll in planes shot down. According to the estimates of a British economist cited by Ray-mond Aron, Allied bombing reduced German arms production by about 2.5 per-cent in 1942, 9 percent in 1943, and 17 percent in 1944.[3] No precise basis can be offered for these figures (especially for the use of a decimal point), but they are probably indicative in an approximate sense.

From a psychological point of view, the most important things about strategic bombing were the unconfirmable but comforting claims of military effectiveness and the rationalization of civilian destruction on a scale never seen in earlier European wars. Cities like Hamburg and Cologne were blanketed with incendiary bombs which caused tremendous firestorms and inevitably killed tens of thousands of persons not engaged in anything that could be accurately characterized as military action. Dresden was wiped out by firestorm in February 1945, when it was obvious that the war was coming to an end. To justify such gratuitous destruction, the communiques claimed the elimination of railway depots and traffic hubs. Massive bombing also had one advantage for the air crews, that they were not personally present to realize who was being killed and what was being destroyed.

The carpetbombing of German cities did not break the morale of the Germans people. It did indeed hamper their movements, deprive them of sleep, and oblige them to use some four million older civilians to clear the rubble from the streets; and by 1944, it was interfering substantially with war production. But it also created habits of mass destruction without real evaluation of either the economic or human costs, and perhaps prepared the way morally (or rather immorally) for the use of the atom bomb in 1945.

The Allied demand for "unconditional surrender" probably played a considerable role both in the superdestructiveness of the air raids and in the later suicidal resistance of both Germany and, in the Far East, Japan. The demand was intended to forestall any such ending as that of 1918, in which the German military forced the civilian government to sue for peace before the Allies had occupied an inch of German soil and then created the legend that an undefeated army had been "stabbed in the back." This time Germany was to be occupied so that the German people could have no illusions as to whether they had been defeated in battle. And the phrase "unconditional surrender" also created among the victors a sense of clarity and moral virtue: that they were punishing two arrogant governments which had been guilty of blatant aggression and of unspeakable atrocities against their victims. But it also created a sense of desperate determination among the Germans and the Japanese.

Though it was clear by the end of 1943 that Germany had irremediably lost its gamble on the conquest of Europe, the German armed forces—and Himmler's parallel army, the SS—did indeed resist more desperately than had the imperial army of World War I. When the Allies landed in Sicily and southern Italy in July 1943, the King forced Mussolini to resign and Italy hoped either to leave the war entirely or enjoy a benign Allied occupation. But the Germans seized Rome, exacted a heavy toll for all Allied advances, and were still occupying much of northern Italy when the war ended in May 1945. Similarly, when the Allies landed in Normandy on June 6, 1944, they encountered stubborn and effective resistance at every hedgerow and bridgehead. From June to September, Germany rained seven thousand unmanned flying bombs (the so-called V-1 missiles) on England, and from September 1944 to April 1945, one thousand of the much more dangerous V-2 rockets, product of the rocket science and slave labor directed by the young Nazi scientist Wernher von Braun, later to be a key figure in the defense establishment of the United States.

The Germans evacuated Paris in August without destroying the city, perhaps yielding to the mystique of Paris as a world capital rather than as the capital of their hereditary enemy. But they continued mass reprisals against all partisan and civilian resisters falling into their hands, and even after they had been driven back into Germany itself, they launched a briefly successful and very destructive offensive in the Ardennes forest, the so-called Battle of the Bulge in December 1944.

In the East, both the Soviets and the Germans were determined to shape the future while fighting in the present. Stalin was publicly committed to the restoration of an independent Poland and privately determined that Poland should be governed by communists. The Polish Home Army, loyal to the exile government in London, was determined to fight the Germans but not to permit Soviet domination of their homeland. The Wehrmacht and the SS, obeying the personal obsessions of Hitler, were determined to destroy Poland before retreating to Germany.

On July 22, 1944, the Soviets established the Committee of National Liberation in recently recaptured Lublin. That committee—composed mostly of Polish communists who had spent the war in Moscow and were considered as loyal as Stalin could conceive *any* Poles to be—rapidly replaced the London government as the Soviets' interlocutor in liberated Poland. On July 29, Moscow radio urged the citizens of Warsaw to rise. General Bor-Komorowski of the Home Army knew that a few Soviet tanks had appeared in Praga, across the Vistula from the capital, and mistakenly supposed that they heralded the arrival of the main Soviet army. In order to assure the noncommunist underground some role in the liberation of Warsaw, he gave the order to rise against the occupying Germans. In the following two months, the Germans crushed the local resistance and, after the surrender of the Home Army on October 2, drove the bulk of the remaining half million residents of Warsaw into concentration camps and carried off 150,000 able-bodied survivors to work in German factories. While this was occurring, the Red Army fought through southern Poland and entered Hungary. Stalin disclaimed all responsibility for the Warsaw rising, which he characterized as the work of "adventurers" and "criminals."

At the same time, he made one slight concession to the political and humanitarian concerns of his Western allies. On September 18, he authorized American and British planes to land on Soviet airfields after they had dropped several hundred tons of food and arms over Warsaw (most of which material fell into German hands). Meanwhile, the Germans were exterminating a quarter million Warsaw residents along with the Home Army which had hoped to "welcome" the Soviets with a noncommunist municipal government in place. It was not until January 17, 1945, that the Soviets occupied the charred ruins of what had once been a city of 1,300,000 inhabitants.

In the second half of 1944, Stalin was more concerned to occupy as much as possible of Central Europe than to complete the reconquest of Poland (which, along with the Baltic republics, would surely fall to Soviet armies in any event). In Stalin's view, it was essential to forestall any Western military action in Central Europe. Thus when Churchill offered in October to attack Budapest from the south, Stalin decided to push towards the Hungarian capital as rapidly as possible—while Hitler, knowing the Russians were not fully prepared for such action, decided to resist the Soviet siege. It took General Malinowski six weeks (from late December to mid-February 1945) and heavy casualties to conquer the city and its suburbs in street-by-street fighting. He then reported to Stalin that he had knocked out 180,000 German troops and taken 110,000 prisoners. Stalin ordered him to send the 110,000 for labor service in Russia. Malinowski had in fact captured only 40,000 prisoners, and so some 70,000 Hungarian police, firemen, railroad workers, civilians, and Jews were rounded up to produce the necessary labor contingent. The long siege also permitted Hitler to drive thousands more Jews out of the one Central European state which he had not actually occupied until March 1944.

The Battle of the Bulge in the West, and the fierce resistance to the Russians at Budapest, were the last serious delaying actions carried out by the German army. Any sane ruler would long since have sued for peace, but Hitler insisted on contesting every inch of soil. To his immediate entourage he opined bitterly that the German people had not been worthy of their Führer, and he staged the *Götterdämmerung* (The Twilight of the Gods) of that unworthy people by ordering ceaseless resistance to the overwhelming firepower and the crushing quantitative superiority of the converging Soviet and Allied armies. As for the Russians and the Allies, they used the winter months to gather supplies for the final push and to agree on the areas to be occupied by each army.

On March 7, 1945, the Americans captured an important bridge at Remagen before the Germans could blow it up, and American troops quickly poured into the Rhineland. By April 20, the Russians were at the outskirts of Berlin and, on April 26, the Russian and Allied armies met and celebrated at Torgau on the River Elbe. On April 28, Italian partisans hung Mussolini and his mistress in Milan, and on April 30, Hitler and his bride of one day (Eva Braun, a faithful companion for many years) committed suicide in the dictator's Berlin bunker. The following day, his distraught propaganda minister Josef Goebbels—who to the end had believed in the ideological (if not the "factual") content of his own messages—committed suicide with his wife after the latter had arranged the painless murders (by poison) of their six children. Between May 1 and May 8, all the German forces in Italy, Austria, and Germany surrendered, either to the Allies or to the Soviets. Militarily, the European war was over.

*   *   *

The Second World War, like its predecessor, had also been fought, without head-lines, on the scientific front. Teams of highly competent British, German, American, and Soviet physicists served their governments loyally from the start and, in the United States and Canada, a number of exiled anti-Nazi scientists were especially concerned that Germany might produce atomic weapons before the West.

To return for a moment to the pre-war years: despite the extreme political tensions of the 1930s, scientific communication had remained completely open. After the discovery of the neutron by the English physicist James Chadwick, laboratories in Italy, Germany, Denmark, France, and the Anglo-Saxon countries began bombarding some of the heavier atoms with neutrons and exchanging papers on the results. A sometimes friendly, sometimes tense (but always honest) rivalry pitted the French chemist Irene Curie and her physicist husband Frederick Joliot against the Austrian Jewish physicist Lise Meitner and her German chemist partner Otto Hahn (whose Aryan ancestry and personal decency enabled him to protect her against the Nazi anti-Semitic laws until after the Nazi occupation of Austria). The Meitner-Hahn team announced the splitting of the uranium atom in January 1939, and within weeks similar experiments were successfully performed in Paris, Rome, and Copenhagen.

The scientific community knew immediately that atomic energy could eventually be used to generate electricity and to produce unprecedently powerful explosions. However, when the war began in September, no one had yet solved the problem of how to build a uranium pile to achieve *controlled* fission. The most important source of uranium in Europe was the mines of Czechoslovakia. When Germany occupied the whole of that unfortunate country in March 1939, it forbade the export of uranium ore, thereby signaling its interest in the military uses of that element.

During the first year of the war, it appeared that heavy water was the substance necessary to slow down the bombarding neutrons and thus to control the atomic explosions. Norway was the only supplier, and France imported 165 liters in March 1940 (the last month of the so-called phony war or "Sitzkrieg"). A month later, the German invasion of Norway gave Hitler the monopoly of European heavy-water supplies. In the course of the following two years, the factory producing heavy water was several times sabotaged by the Norwegian underground, bombed by British aircraft, and eventually rendered useless to the Germans.[4]

All these activities meant that both Germany and the Western countries were presumably racing to see who could first harness atomic energy. In the United States, the exiled antifascist physicists Enrico Fermi (Italian) and Leo Szilard (Hungarian) found that carbon graphite powder—much more readily available than heavy water—could serve as the retardant regulator in uranium fission. The Berkeley cyclotron inaugurated in 1939 gave the U.S. a tremendous advantage over Germany in the study of atomic particles, leading in 1945 to the successful production of two atom bomb prototypes, one using uranium and the other plutonium, the new man-made element 94 created in the course of cyclotron experiments.[5]

The Germans possessed all the same theoretical knowledge as the West, but they did not make the practical discovery that carbon graphite could be used instead of heavy water. German scientists had been consulted by their government as to whether atomic energy could be used for military purposes; they assumed (incorrectly) that Germany was ahead of the West in theoretical knowledge but that it had less raw materials available, and, therefore, that a crash program to develop rockets would be more useful than a similar effort with atomic energy. They assumed that rockets could be ready by 1944, and that an atomic bomb would take a year or so longer. On these points, as it turned out, they were correct: The V-2 rockets were ready in 1944, and it took the Allies, with their own accelerated program employing American, Canadian, British, and European refugee scientists, until the summer of 1945 to produce the bomb.[6] Indeed, it was in the spring of 1942—at about the same time as the Germans decided to concentrate on rockets (a decision which was not known to the Allies)—that the latter had decided on a crash program to achieve the atom bomb. The top physics departments in U.S. and Canadian universities, with the enthusiastic collaboration of the anti-Nazi European refugees, worked in secret under the command of the U.S. and British military authorities. It was by no means easy for such pacifistically-inclined scientists as Albert Einstein and Neils Bohr to recommend the production of an unimaginably destructive bomb, but the necessity to forestall Hitler overcame their scruples.

It is indeed a sobering thought that if Hitler had not driven all of the German-Jewish and half-Jewish scientists into exile (as well as those married to Jews) the balance of scientific talent and wartime accomplishment might have favored him. He might have had more and better rockets to rain down on England much sooner, and there would have been far less urgency (or even high talent available) for an Anglo-American atom bomb project. History is not a counterfactual narrative, but everything we know about Hitler indicates that he would have used any weapon available to him, and everything we know about his scientists indicates that however unhappy they may have felt about some aspects of Nazi rule, they worked for the regime according to the decisions taken with their participation.

In actual fact, Germany was defeated several months before the first atomic explosion took place at Los Alamos in July 1945. It also became immediately clear when the Allies occupied all of Germany in May that the Nazis had been nowhere near producing an atom bomb of their own. There was now a brief opportunity—albeit of tremendous moral and political significance—not to inflict on humanity this ultimate weapon, the building of which had been justified by the need to forestall a psychopathic dictator.

The United States was still at war with Japan, and the eventual victory was not in doubt. But President Harry Truman (who had taken over the office after Roosevelt's death on April 20, just days before the victory in Europe) had the obvious duty to minimize American casualties and end the war as quickly as possible. After the German surrender, there were clear indications from Japanese diplomatic messages in neutral capitals and from military intelligence that Japan was seeking some way to end the war without "unconditional surrender"—the same demand which had played a part in prolonging Germany's hopeless resistance. Nevertheless, all of Truman's senior advisers (with the exception of Assistant Secretary of Defense John J. McCloy) approved the use of the nearly completed atom bomb to force the Japanese surrender and thereby save the tens of thousands of American lives that would have been lost in an invasion of the home islands of Japan.[7]

But among the scientists who knew the awesome power of the atom, there were strong doubts. The German-Jewish exile physicist James Franck, together with the Hungarian Leo Szilard and the American Eugene Rabinowitsch, recommended in June 1945 that the bomb be demonstrated in an uninhabited area in the presence of representatives of all the Allied countries, and that on the basis of the devastating results an ultimatum be issued to Japan.[8] In that same month, a straw poll of one hundred and fifty scientists working in the Chicago University section of the atomic project indicated that two-thirds of them favored a demonstration over the ocean before its use in inhabited areas. Both these documents were labeled secret so as to prevent their circulation among colleagues.

It is not merely with historian's hindsight that I refer to the moral and political opportunity lost in August 1945. Throughout the three-year development effort in British and American laboratories, it was a well-known (and frequently stated) fact that an atomic bomb would be infinitely more destructive than any previous weapon created by man, its explosive force unimaginably greater than that of even the most powerful artillery shell or aerial bomb. It was because of the absolute certainty of this utterly unprecedented destructiveness that the Allies had felt it imperative to forestall the Germans.

Nevertheless, only a minority among the working scientists (and apparently none of the top military advisers to the President) gave serious consideration to the Franck-Szilard-Rabinowitsch proposal. The bombs were dropped over the centers of two heavily inhabited cities, Hiroshima and Nagasaki, with only a three-day interval—that is to say, without giving the Japanese government the minimum reasonable opportunity to reconsider its position in a uniquely terrifying situation. Nor does the argument for the necessity of "unconditional surrender" hold up as a reason, because the U.S. granted the main condition that the Japanese absolutely insisted upon, namely, that the Emperor would not be forced to abdicate or treated as a war criminal.

To me, an American serving at the time as a military cartographer, it seemed literally a "war crime"—and I have never read, in the half century since, any convincing explanation as to why no demonstration in an uninhabited (or thinly inhabited) area could have been made, with a view to saving *human* lives, not only those of American soldiers. In the specific circumstances of August 1945, the use of the atom bomb showed that a psychologically very normal and democratically elected chief executive could use the weapon just as the Nazi dictator would have used it. In this way, the United States—for anyone concerned with moral distinctions in the conduct of different types of government—blurred the difference between fascism and democracy.

In general terms, World War II, for both Europeans and Asians (but not for Americans), was more devastating to the civilian population than to the military forces. The Germans had forced three million French and Polish civilians and prisoners of war to work in Germany by the summer of 1940. As of late 1944, there were an estimated two and one half million foreign workers in German factories, only a small proportion of whom had volunteered; and among the nonvolunteers were some six hundred thousand Italians, hostages to German bitterness at their country's withdrawal from the war.

Although different sources give widely varying estimates, all of them show that only in Britain and Germany did deaths in military action exceed civilian deaths. In Italy, Greece, France, Belgium, and Holland, the deaths due to air raids and reprisal killings far exceeded those of the combat forces. In Poland, Yugoslavia, and the Soviet Union, the Germans conducted a war against the civilian population, one intended to wipe out the Jews and to reduce the long-term demographic advantage of the Slavic as against the "Aryan" populations.

Altogether, Poland lost about 15 percent of its prewar population (including three million Jews among the five million total Polish loss). Yugoslavia lost about 10 percent of its prewar population, and the Soviet Union suffered anywhere from seventeen to twenty-five million deaths, more than half of them the results of deliberate slaughter, mass starvation, freezing, and disease directly attributable to the German invasion.

The Nazi techniques of terror had loosened the normal inhibitions of German soldiers, and the crimes committed by all branches of the German military and civil services naturally bred a desire for vengeance on the part of those who suffered Nazi barbarism. For the Western Allies, carpetbombing was one form of revenge, though one rationalized with various exaggerated claims as to its military objectives. In the light of known German behavior in the years 1939–42, very few persons in England or the U.S. questioned either the military effectiveness or the human destruction involved in the day and night bombings.

The Soviet army took its revenge in the last months of the war. In Budapest, the largely Siberian infantry sacked the proletarian districts, mistaking workingclass apartments for those of the hated bourgeoisie. In Austria and Germany, they raped the women and stole all the portable household goods that fell into their hands.

"Total war" had started with the German blitzkrieg and continued with massive slaughters by the German military in the East and massive bombings of German cities by the Allies. It had obliterated every trace of restraint, every effort to limit war to the formal combatants, such as had still been practiced by the high commands in the First World War. Even the Geneva convention, observed with the officers of the Western armies, had been egregiously violated in the treatment of noncommissioned prisoners in the West and in the treatment of all prisoners in the East.

Over and above the thirty to forty million death toll and the vast quantities of physical destruction, some 22,930,000 persons had been registered in the new social category known as "displaced persons" (DP's): 830,000 Balts fleeing to Sweden and Germany, and Finns evacuating the territories annexed by Russia; 2,300,000 Soviets (mostly Ukrainians and small nationalities of the Caucasus): 4,500,000 Ukrainians and Belorussians from what had been eastern Poland between 1919 and 1939; 1,950,000 Czechs migrating to Austria or Germany; 12,350,000 *Volksdeutsche* fleeing, or being expelled, from their former homes in Silesia, Pomerania, East Prussia, the Sudetenland, and numerous regions of Yugoslavia, Hungary, and Romania; and 1,000,000 leaving Germany for the Low Countries and France.[9]

Endnotes

1. John C. Cairns, "Great Britain and the Fall of France," *The Journal of Modern History*, December 1955, 365–409.

2. For numbers and statistics I have depended, unless otherwise indicated, on Frank B. Tipton and Robert Aldrich, *An Economic and Social History of Europe from 1939 to the Present* (Baltimore: Johns Hopkins University Press, 1987); and *The Longman Handbook of Modern European History*, 2d ed., 1992.

3. Raymond Aron, *The Century of Total War* (Boston: The Beacon Press, 1995), 40. The present writer's skepticism concerning the results of bombing raids is based in part on his experience as a photo interpreter in World War II.

4. Bertand Goldschmitt, *The Atomic Adventure* (London: Pergamon Press, 1964).

5. Robert Jungk, *Brighter than a Thousand Suns* (New York: Harcourt Brace Jovanovich, 1958).

6. Mark Walker, "Legenden um die Deutsche Atombomb," *Vierteljahrshefte für Zeitgeschichte*, 1990, 45–74; David C. Cassidy, *Uncertainty, the Life and Science of Werner Heisenberg* (New York: W. H. Freeman, 1991); Thomas Powers, *Heisenberg's War* (London: Jonathan Cape, 1993).

7. Ian Buruma, "The War over the Bomb," *The New York Review of Books*, 21 September 1995, discussed six recent books and the internal U.S. debate over the use of the bomb on the fiftieth anniversary.

8. Junk, 348–60.

9. Figures from *The Times Atlas of World History*, revised edition by Geoffrey Barraclough (London, 1984), 175.

9

The German Occupation
of Europe, 1940–1945

While the Second World War was physically far more destructive than the "Great War" had been, it is also true that intelligent policies and abundant resources made for a much healthier economic recovery after 1945. On the other hand, the occupation of the entire continent by the obedient armies of a psycho-pathic dictator was the single most traumatic experience of the European peoples in the twentieth century. The Germans treated their European victims—especially in the East—very much as the Europeans had treated the African peoples during the imperialist conquests of the late nineteenth century. Even the majority of the Russians, Ukrainians, and Belorussians who had been the victims of Stalin's forced collectivizations, deportations, and blood purges of the 1930s preferred the Soviet dictator to Hitler once they had experienced the behavior of the German military and civil authorities. Only the Poles and the Baltic peoples felt equally oppressed and betrayed by both the Germans and the Soviets.

Generally speaking, in the West (and before the assault on Russia), the Germans tried to combine the exploitation of the conquered nations' economies with at least a tender of eventual participation in the New Order which was to follow the German victory. But in the East, their strategy was far different: from the moment that Poland was attacked in September 1939, and on a much larger scale after the invasion of Russia in June 1941, the Germans conscientiously conducted a *Vernichtungskrieg*, a "war of annihilation" intended to destroy the local elites, make semi-slaves of the entire population, and provide land for the settlement of Germans.

Most of the generals and party officials who ruled in the occupied territories had had no previous experience of governing large civilian communities; nor had the countries under their control—with the exception of Poland, Belgium, and northeastern France—experienced military occupation within living memory.

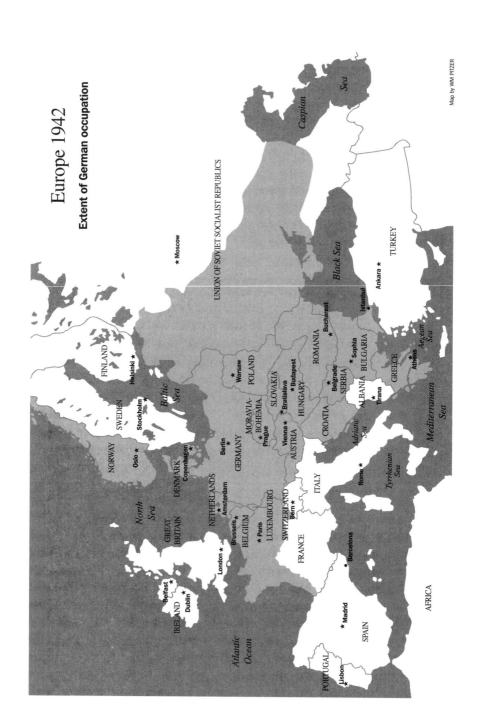

Europe 1942

Extent of German occupation

Map by WM PITZER

Thus, the actual carrying out of occupation policies involved a good deal of improvisation, and the psychological relationship between occupiers and occupied varied substantially according to local circumstances.

Most German officers (whether they were whole-hearted Nazis or not) thought of the Danes, the Norwegians, the Dutch, and the Flemings as potential friends—peoples with cultures, "values," and languages closely related to those of the Germans. For Nazis and other believers in Nordic racial superiority (racism being by no means limited to the Nazis), these peoples were first cousins of the master race. This circumstance led to a curious mix of collaboration and resistance. Danish farmers and merchants, for example, sold their products to the Germans, on German terms (which were not too onerous until the last two years of the war). It was collaboration without love—and with the prospect of devastating punishment if the Aryan cousins did not obey their masters. At the same time, the German Culture Institute tried to carry on its programs as though nothing had changed: the physicist Carl Friedrich von Weizsäcker—son of one of Germany's leading diplomats—gave a series of lectures there in March 1941, to which the Danish intellectual elite were invited. And in September 1941, when the German invasion of Russia still appeared destined for quick victory, the Nobel laureate Werner Heisenberg visited the world-famous, half-Jewish physicist Neils Bohr, with whose institute the occupation authorities had not interfered. Weizsäcker and Heisenberg credited themselves with the best intentions as members of the *world* scientific community, and they seem to have been genuinely surprised and saddened by Bohr's evident distrust of them in the current circumstances. Indeed, there are many evidences, from the wartime cultural efforts made by the Germans in Scandinavia and the West, of their complete inability to imagine the humiliation caused by their efforts to act as "friendly" victors and enlightened representatives of world culture.

The morale of the "silent majority" in both Denmark and Norway was bolstered by the attitude of their sovereigns. When the Danish Jews were ordered to wear the yellow star, King Cristian—and thousands of ordinary citizens—did likewise. In Norway the parliament refused to name the German candidates for civilian rule. King Haakon was able to escape to London, and for the great majority of Norwegians, the exiled king and the closed parliament remained the only legitimate expressions of Norwegian sovereignty.

In the Netherlands, the Germans were courteous at first, and, until the invasion of Russia, they did not need to plunder the Dutch economy. Most of the police, judges, and civil servants cooperated minimally with their unfamiliar masters. In February 1941, there was a spectacular two-day strike to protest the first wave of anti-Jewish violence; but when the Germans arrested hundreds (many of whom were deported to Matthausen) and imposed a curfew, the strikers obeyed in order to avoid a general bloodbath. Indeed, for the ordinary nonpolitical Dutchman, the first year of occupation—from June, 1940 to June 1941—was not so bad. Agricultural exports to Germany increased sixfold in comparison with 1938, and munitions and textile workers could live peacefully at home as long as they produced for Germany. But then winter clothing, automobiles, and bicycles were requisitioned from the fall of 1941 on. Jews were forced to register and sell their property and, in April 1942, to wear the yellow star; soon after, they began to be deported. The Dutch clearly disapproved of the deportation, which took place in stages between June 1942 and September 1943, but there were no mass protests. Culturally the population was divided between Catholics, Protestants, and the secular-minded democratic Left, each with its own social-service and labor organizations; and not since Napoleonic times had they had to cope with foreign occupation. Individuals helped individuals when it came to hiding Jews or anti-Nazi students, and there was limited organized resistance by small groups. When the Germans tried, in March 1943, to impose a "loyalty oath" in the universities, for example, the faculties quietly advised against signing and somehow neglected to distribute the forms.

The doctors also engaged in a moderate degree of non-compliance. As an alternative to accepting a Dutch Nazi doctor as head of their national organization, they established their own informal "Medical Contact" group. In June 1943 (during the later stages of the Jewish deportations and the tightening of the labor draft), they wrote to the Nazi governor that medical and ethical norms might prevent them from obeying unacceptable demands. The governor (an Austrian Nazi lawyer) declared himself personally insulted and ordered the detention of three hundred and sixty doctors as hostages. "Medical Contact" apologized officially, declaring that no personal criticism had been intended, and the hostages were slowly released. As in the university situation, the Dutch doctors manifested (albeit mildly) their rejection of Nazi ideals, the Germans showed the mailed fist beneath the velvet glove, and both groups avoided a head-on clash.[1]

Resistance remained discreet, and the fate of the Christian and secular communities was very different from that of the Jews. Thus, 110,000 of Holland's 140,000 Jews were deported to the death camps, and barely 5,000 of those survived the war. By contrast, forty-three Protestant ministers and forty-nine Catholic priests were executed for opposition activities, and some 5,000 of the three hundred to four hundred thousand Dutch labor draftees died in Germany. Altogether, some 240,000 Dutch died as a result the occupation. But the total population of Holland actually *increased* about 5 percent during the war, in stark contrast to what occurred in Eastern Europe.

In Belgium, both the government and the people were anxious to avoid a repetition of the brutality and famine suffered in World War I. King Leopold III, the business elite, the Church and the civil service, all accommodated themselves to German rule without enthusiasm but without resistance. A significant proportion of the Flemish population were pro-German while Germany was victorious. The occupation authorities never tired of assuring the Flemings that they were Aryans and held out the hope that, after the war, the Walloons might also be designated Aryans who just happened to speak French.

In France, the psychological shock and national humiliation were much greater than in the Low Countries or Scandinavia. France had been *the* major power on the European continent from the early seventeenth to the mid-nineteenth centuries. Then, within a space of barely fifty years, the French were swiftly defeated by Prussia in 1870, barely avoided defeat in 1914, had eventually "won" the Great War only through an alliance with Britain, supplemented by the intervention of the young United States. Now they had been defeated again, as rapidly and decisively as in 1870. The Germans were simply too numerous, too aggressive, and too efficient for civilized but tired old France to cope with.

Thus, in the summer of 1940, the majority of the French undoubtedly agreed with the venerable Marshall Pétain that open resistance was futile. Many of the middle classes and the peasants also shared his view that secularization, especially the dissolution of traditional pieties concerning family and soil, were responsible for the "decline" of France. And many in all classes (including the leading intellectuals) were tempted to a kind of masochistic acceptance of superior German vitality. At the same time, after the failure of Hitler to bring England to its knees, the great majority hoped for an eventual British victory, and many took great risks, for example, to hide British fliers shot down over France.

The domestic political situation of France was unique among the occupied countries. Poland, Norway, and the Netherlands all had governments-in-exile established in London and recognized by the Anglo-Saxon powers, while Denmark and Belgium retained (in form, at least) their traditional monarchies. All five countries were in fact ruled by German satraps counting on a greater or lesser degree of resigned acceptance on the part of the populations. But France had been divided into an occupied and an unoccupied zone, and the latter zone was governed, until late 1942, by a paternalistic dictatorship voted into office by the last freely elected parliament of the defunct Third Republic. In addition, France had always had a very lively intellectual life regardless of the type of government in power. This intellectual life did not disappear under the occupation, nor did the Germans try to suppress those aspects of French culture that did not interfere with their political and military purposes.

Despite the absence of a free press or democratic political life, there were at least three distinct currents competing for influence at the "court" of the old marshall. Pétain's own immediate followers were anxious to create a Catholic, rural-dominated France which would collaborate minimally with Germany in order to be left in peace. Admiral Jean-Louis Darlan, vice-premier between December 1940 and April 1942, was violently anti-British and anticommunist; he hoped to use the navy and the empire as bargaining chips to obtain a recognized role in Hitler's New Order, though after the start of the Russian campaign the Führer was too busy to gratify him. Pierre Laval, who had vigorously lobbied his fellow deputies into voting full powers to Pétain, served as vice-premier from July to December of 1940 and then again after the Darlan era. Laval had been a prominent appeaser of Mussolini at the time of the Ethiopian conquest, and he considered himself the person best qualified to collaborate partially with the Germans and at the same time to protect France from their most draconian demands. A final current—much stronger in the occupied zone than at Vichy—were the followers of the former communist leader Jaques Doriot, secular fascists who favored full collaboration and integration into the Nazi New Order. Each of these groups had its own press, and debated the potential roles of "their" France as a partner in German-organized Europe.

What these political currents all had in common were a sometimes gleeful, sometimes masochistic acceptance of defeat and their own purely opportunistic, self-serving efforts to win favor—and a jackal's portion of power—from the victors. The collaboration of police and functionaries in both zones made it possible for the Germans to save precious manpower of their own for direct military tasks and physical repression of civilian resistance. Even so, Laval justified his actions and statements (such as his expressed hope for a German victory) with the excuse that, by flattering the occupiers, he was able to reduce their demands for French goods, services, and industrial manpower. He let it be known that proportionately fewer French than Belgian and Dutch workers had been required to work in German factories, and he dropped dark hints about "Polandization" as the only alternative to his skillful handling of the Germans. (Though at the same time, those statements must surely have confused his countrymen as to his real intentions.) In any case, the politics of hints, ruses, opportunism, and ambiguity testified to the shame of a highly civilized and formerly very powerful people.

Thus it was of tremendous moral importance that a little-known brigadier general, Charles de Gaulle, raised the banner of "Free France" even before the establishment of the Vichy regime. DeGaulle had flown from Bordeaux to London in a British airplane on June 18, 1940, and had immediately committed himself to persevere in the struggle against Hitler. His action was critical as a counterweight to the surrender/collaboration of the bulk of the French army and civil service. In the first year, while de Gaulle talked of saving France—but not necessarily the parliamentary republic—his political intentions and capacities were not wholly clear. But as his organization grew, he committed himself to the restoration of republican democracy and showed his ability to understand and win the loyalty of men of very different views—from conservative Christian democrats to communists and anarchists. After the German invasion of Russia, the communists supplied the most active elements of the resistance; the total number of such resistance fighters, however, was very small until the German labor draft placed workers in the position of having to choose between deportation to German armament factories and joining the clandestine forces of Free France.

The varying attitudes of the Anglo-Saxon powers did not help to create a unified resistance. Churchill supported DeGaulle from the start, despite the temperamental differences between the two men, each a prickly patriot convinced of his own unique role as the embodiment of his nation in its hour of mortal peril. Franklin Roosevelt maintained a high-level diplomatic mission at Vichy on the theory that his ambassador, Admiral Leahy, could strengthen the backbone of Marshall Pétain, and also because he felt a profound dislike and distrust toward DeGaulle. Even when the Allied landings in North Africa precipitated the German occupation of all France and the end of Pétain's shadowy "independence," the United States preferred to deal with Admiral Darlan and General Giraud—anything not to recognize the political leadership of DeGaulle, a fact which was to cast its shadow over postwar relations between France and the US.

The French resistance was important principally in terms of Allied morale, war aims, and military intelligence. The great intellectuals might be silent, the great painters and musicians might continue their activities with an air of normality, the farmers might produce for export to Germany, and the majority of functionaries might obey the German or Vichy authorities in the divided territory. But a socially conservative French general, uncontaminated by Marxism and committed to political liberty, had raised the banner of "Free France," under the Cross of Lorraine, the symbol of Joan of Arc; and this act had made it possible for Britain, and later the United States, to treat the "real" France as a dependable, democratic ally.

The agents of Free France, dropped by parachute, traveling with false papers, and protected by local partisans, were able to supply important intelligence as to German movements and capabilities, and to indicate the wooded areas where British fliers should drop arms for the growing units of *maquis*. (They also resisted Gestapo torture in order to protect the identities of their comrades.) Under DeGaulle's authority, guerrilla units composed of young Frenchmen and Spanish republican veterans sabotaged German rail shipments and truck convoys during the months of preparation for the Allied landings in June 1944; and after D-Day, they participated actively in the liberation of French territory. By mid-1944, the forces of Free France also included enough militants of the prewar Popular Front parties so that, as the Germans were driven out, a provisional republican administration could take over immediately without the need for an Allied "occupation."

As humiliating and exploitative as were the occupations of Scandinavia and Western Europe, they were mild compared to the occupation of the Slavic lands of Eastern Europe. In the latter area, the Germans were seeking *Lebensraum* for their own imperial future—an aim by no means limited to the Nazis, and one which had been part of German ambition in the First World War and part of pan-German ideology since the late nineteenth century. The example of extreme brutality was the special contribution of the Nazis, but German soldiers in general—and the Wehrmacht as an institution—felt themselves clearly to be a superior, master race in their lightning conquest of Poland, and even more so in their later invasion of the Soviet Union. In the first weeks of the advances into Belorussia and the Ukraine, they were frequently met by town and village authorities who hoped that the Germans might be an improvement on the Soviet rulers—or at the very least, that they could be placated, perhaps even negotiated with. But very few of the invaders spoke Slavic languages. They doubly scorned the population as Slavic and as communist-ruled. They had no plans to cooperate with local functionaries, and the Soviets had themselves destroyed every vestige of the kind of middle class that had collaborated in the Western European occupations.

The German army's main purposes were to inspire sufficient terror so as to be obeyed without question and to send back to Germany all the food and natural resources which they could confiscate. By early December 1941, the Germans had taken close to four million prisoners, for whom they had made no previous feeding or housing plans. For the most part, they simply herded these captives into makeshift camps and left them to die of starvation and exposure. On the other hand, the failure to take Moscow and Leningrad meant that they had lost the gamble for quick victory, and the more foresighted among them realized that they would need the labor of these prisoners during the next year's campaign. To quote an economic report to the Ukrainian armaments administration dated December 2, 1941, by one Herr Peter Heinz Seraphim (sic!):

> If we shoot the Jews, let the prisoners of war die, expose much of the population of the large cities to death by starvation, and lose some of the rural population by famine in the coming year as well, the question remains: who is to do the work here?[2]

Labor shortages were an increasing problem for the Nazis from early 1942 until the collapse in 1945, and there was a nuance of difference within the Nazi hierarchy as to how Slavs and Jews should be treated in the circumstances. Marshall Goering, who had administered the prewar arms buildup, as well as the armaments minister Albert Speer and the industrial managers of I.G. Farben, Daimler-Benz, and the hundreds of small subcontractors involved in arms production, favored providing the Slavic worker-prisoners with the minimal survival requirements of food and housing, and even the use of Jews; whereas the most fanatical ideologues (led by Hitler himself) preferred to work the prisoners to death in a fashion that would make them useful for a time to the Reich but would at the same time eliminate them as mouths to feed in the future. Heinrich Himmler, head of the SS, took a middle position: ideologically, he would of course prefer to see all the Jews and Soviet prisoners die but, as the head of an industrial empire within the occupation zone he was also concerned with regularity of production.

As of February 1942, only 1.1 million of the 3.9 million prisoners taken in the second half of 1941 were deemed available for labor service. Thus, for practical reasons, the Germans were a little more careful in the treatment of human resources when they moved further into the Ukraine and Crimea in the spring and summer of 1942. Instead of breaking up the collective farms (their original intent), they simply named their own Kolhkoz managers—either Germans or Ukrainians and Tatars, nationalities which they favored in comparison with Poles and Russians. They were also willing to conciliate the Orthodox and Islamic religious leaders and allow their schools to remain open, in return for which they expected their to help in reconciling the population to German control. The Red Army had a tradition of partisan warfare dating from the civil war years of 1918–1920; and while the officially listed infantry divisions retreated, they left numerous cadres to organize partisans in the hill country east of Sevastopol. In the spring of 1942, famine was so severe among these guerrilla units that their own chiefs advised them to filter back into the towns and seek whatever food and work they could find, with a view to resuming partisan operations in the fall. The Germans frequently knew who these men were but, instead of executing them, they sent them to work in German factories.

At the same time, of course, the occupied territories were to be made *judenrein*—cleansed of Jews, to use the "neutral" German adjective. In the course of their work sober German functionaries (ever attentive to detail) asked the advice of Berlin as to whether the *Tschaken* and the *Karaites* were to be treated as Jews. The former seemed indistinguishable from the mass of Tatars except for the fact that they wrote the Tatar language in the Hebrew alphabet. The latter were non-Talmudic Jews who had lived in southern Russia for more than a thousand years and had been specifically exempted from tsarist anti-Semitic laws in 1863. The answer from Berlin was to eliminate both groups.[3]

Actually, despite the German sense of superiority in relation to all non-Aryan peoples, wartime circumstances led the Nazi rulers to favor several small nationalities whose cooperation could be militarily and economically useful and whose political attitudes carried no threat of resistance to German hegemony. The Croats, the Slovaks, and the Ukrainians were three such peoples. The Croats had been one of the less dissatisfied nationalities within the Habsburg empire, but their nationalist groups (as always, not to be confused with the people as a whole) felt very resentful of Serbian domination within the post-1918 kingdom of Yugoslavia. After the German invasion in June, 1941, the fascist puppet government of Anton Pavelich (one of the assassins of King Alexander of Yugoslavia, who had been living since the murder in Italy under the protection of his patron Mussolini) willingly cooperated in the slaughter of Jews, anti-Nazi Serbs, and the pro-Soviet partisans of Josep Broz Tito.

Slovak nationalists, in the relatively less developed eastern half of the Czechoslovak Republic, had deeply resented the assumption made in 1918 that they and the Czechs were one nation. The Nazis made a show of granting statehood to Slovakia under the presidency of a pro-Nazi priest, Father Tiso. Slovakia in turn contained a sizable Hungarian minority, the existence of which gave Hitler and his Slovak puppets the opportunity quietly to blackmail the Hungarian government of Admiral Horthy, which was not as completely docile as the Nazis would have liked. The Slovak government was particularly cooperative in handing over Jews for deportation to the Polish death camps. Finally, the Ukrainian nationalists had looked to imperial Germany during the First World War and had resisted incorporation into the Soviet Union during the revolution and civil war years. Their ambitions and enmities could now be used against both the Poles and the Russians. In addition, the occupation authorities sometimes favored the Tatars as a way of reining in the non-docile Ukrainians and opening diplomatic channels to the warlike and potentially rebellious Islamic populations of the Caucasus.[4]

In all three instances, the Nazis worked with a combination of the local religious authorities and their own secular fascist allies. At times, both Catholic priests in Croatia and Slovakia and Orthodox priests in the Ukraine were troubled by Nazi brutality. Thus, the Metropolitan of the Uniate Church in the western Ukraine (Ruthenia) had welcomed the Germans in 1941, but in August 1942 he wrote to the Pope saying that the Germans were worse than the Bolsheviks. Croatia was theoretically under Italian occupation, and many thousands of Jews and Serbs escaped murder at the hands of Pavelich's *Ustachi* militias through the clandestine help of Italian officers and functionaries.

In the end, of course, Germany was defeated by the revived Red Army and by the overwhelming logistic superiority of the Allies. But Nazi brutality and the cynical playing off of one small nationality against another played a role in the collapse of Hitler's empire and, more significantly, in the post-war expulsion from Central-Eastern Europe of between twelve and fifteen million ethnic Germans whose forebears had lived in those countries for centuries. Ultimately, then, the Nazi era, instead of producing *Lebensraum*, led to the forced repatriation of millions of *Volksdeutsche* after the defeat.

To turn from the Ukraine to Belorussia, the Nazi conquest was never as complete as it appeared in radio reports and contemporary newspaper maps. The White Russians had been treated as second-class citizens by the Polish republic of 1918–1939. They were aware of the schools and medical services which the communist regime had established in the Soviet-held portions of Belorussia, and for various reasons they were neither as nationalist nor as anticommunist as the Ukrainians. On September 17, 1939, they tentatively welcomed the Red Army, which (by previous agreement with Germany) was annexing the Belorussian portion of interwar Poland. The Soviets proceeded to deport Polish landlords and "kulaks," to treat the "middle farmers" well, to build schools and dispensaries, and to establish collective farms which gave the local peasants their first experience of machine aids to plowing and harvesting.

The Soviets also began to organize popular militias in the revolutionary partisan tradition, but when the Germans launched their attack in June 1941, the swift triumph completely disorganized the militias and sent the Red Army into retreat. However, the Germans were too busy rushing towards Moscow and Leningrad to consolidate a local administration in Belorussia; but they shot enough Jews and Soviet functionaries so that no one had any doubt as to the eventual fate of the country if the Germans were to win.

White Russia is a land of forests and marshes, with a comparatively low population density and, like Poland, a relatively high percentage of Jews. Thousands of young men (and some young women) of both Slavic and Jewish families took to the forests. The Germans established control of the roads, the railroads, the radio, and the towns and began herding the Jews into ghettos. They shot anyone they caught listening to Soviet radio, but the news spread anyway that Stalin was now calling the struggle the "Great Patriotic War" and that clandestine communist officials and partisan leaders were suggesting that after the war, the Soviet regime would be more flexible and more attentive to local needs than it had been during the first brutal decade of industrialization.

By mid-1942, while the Germans were still advancing towards the Caucasus, half of White Russia was controlled by the partisans, who were supplied with arms coming from Russia and who observed a certain pluralism of leadership: Soviet communists, Belorussian communists and nationalists, socialists of several varieties, and Left Zionists all headed up the partisan units. In the towns, the Germans found they needed skilled Jewish labor and so established the *Judenräte* (Jewish councils), to whom they gave governing responsibility in the ghettos. The presumed advantage for the Germans was to free up scarce German personnel for military tasks; the presumed advantage for the *Judenräte* was to allow them to become so important to the Germans that the latter would decide to treat the Jews better than in the first days of the invasion. Jewish workmen also acted as liaisons between opposition groups in different towns, but both the communist and nationalist partisans were hostile to Zionism and were often infected by the traditional anti-Semitism of Poland and Russia. In the light of the brutal German reprisal (i.e., mass executions) for partisan activity—and especially when escapees from the ghettos described the sheer obsession of the Nazis with killing Jews—the non-Jewish partisans would accept only those persons whose physical appearance was not too obviously Jewish. Regardless of their internal political differences, the main triumphs of the Belorussian guerrillas were to divert about half of collective-farm production to the uses of the local population and to blow up numerous German troop trains during the months of steady German retreat, from September 1943 to January 1944.[5]

Descending further into the circles of Hell, we come to the ghastly phenomenon known to the Jews and to the majority of decent humankind as "the Holocaust," and to the Nazi elite as "The Final Solution." The complete physical destruction of European Jewry was a mania of Hitler's during the war, an obsession he had arrived at by stages. As a young man, he had not been particularly anti-Semitic and had, in fact, spoken affectionately of the Jewish doctor who treated his widowed mother in her last years. An admirer of Karl Lueger, Vienna's able and popular mayor between 1897 and 1910, Hitler seems to have imbibed the former's anti-Semitism, which warned against the supposed evils of Jewish cultural and eco-nomic influence (although Lueger did not remotely advocate or suggest physical destruction). He was also influenced by the well-known anti-Semitism of his musical idol, Richard Wagner, and by the late-nineteenth century pseudobiology which classified the human species into superior and inferior races. More specifi-cally, Hitler was one of that large percentage of Germans who believed in 1919 that the German army (in which he had served) had not been defeated but rather "stabbed in the back" by its civilian enemies, principally the Jews. Anti-Semitism became a major plank in the Nazi political program, and the brown-shirted stormtroopers beat up Jewish workmen and smashed Jewish store windows in the years before their Fuhrer came to power. Between 1933 and 1939, the Nazis passed a the series of anti-Jewish laws that also permitted the Jews to emigrate—provided they left all their money and property behind. And they noted with pleasure the reluctance of Western Europe and the United States to accept more than a small proportion of the Jewish refugees.

In January 1939, after the Munich Pact—and when it was obvious that Eng-land and France were stepping up their own rearmament—Hitler stated in a Reich-stag speech that if "international Jewish financiers" were to cause another war, it would result in "the annihilation of the Jewish race in Europe."[6] His speeches and writings of the prewar decade show that he had convinced himself that the Jews were the principal leaders of both world capitalism and world communism. (Indeed, the Nazi press referred to President Franklin Roosevelt as "Rosenfeld" and alleged repeatedly during the war that he, Winston Churchill, and the Pope were all "in the pay of the Jews.") This double allegation,—Jewish-controlled capitalism and com-munism—was also believed by non-Nazi Germans and reflects the fact that many Germans and Austrians thought of their society as representing a purer, peasant- and artisan-based culture (idealized in Wagner's Die Meistersänger von Nürnberg, in much German fiction of the imperial era, and in many movies made under the aegis of Josef Goebbels during the Nazi era) as against the exploitative industrial cultures of both modern capitalism and Soviet communism.

After the conquest of France in 1940, the Nazis talked of resettling the Jews on the island of Madagascar, at that time part of the French empire. This talk enabled them to offer "cooperation" with the French and also the English, if the latter would accept peace on Nazi terms; it also allowed them to continue to highlight the West's refusal to undertake any large-scale rescue of the German Jews. And as discussed earlier, the invasion of Russia, begun on June 22, 1941, was conceived as a war of *Vernichtung*, of annihilation. The "Final Solution," discussed in the summer of 1941 and implemented from that time until within a few weeks of the total collapse in May 1945, meant the physical elimination primarily of the Jews, but also of the gypsies and the mentally and physically handicapped of all "races." Commandos of both the Wehrmacht and the SS shot captured Jews in batches as they entered the villages of White Russia and the Ukraine. They also experimented with carbon-monoxide poisoning and with machine-gunning groups of Jews in front of the graves which, moments before, they had been forced to dig at gunpoint.

These methods were too slow, however, as well as too obvious to the shocked local populations. The more discreet, methodical solution was the building of specific death-factory camps (complete with ovens) in Poland and the use of zyklon B, a gas which had been developed as an insecticide. This method was implemented early in 1942. The railway systems of all the occupied countries supplied the freight cars, the coal, and the train crews. German chemical firms supplied the gas, the high-temperature ovens, and the means to convert to industrial uses the tooth fillings, jewelry, leather goods, and clothing systematically confiscated from the victims.[7] Himmler's SS was charged with administering the camp system. Depending somewhat on the whims, the degree of humanity (or inhumanity), and the pragmatic intelligence of the SS officers in charge, some of the camps used able-bodied prisoners as industrial laborers before consigning them to the gas chambers. Something like 2 percent of German arms production in the years 1943–44 occurred in camp factories. The SS administration received daily "wages" for the use of prisoner-laborers and also collected bribes from German businessmen—a few of whom, like the now-famous Oscar Schindler, used the bribes to save a pitifully small percentage of the total camp population.[8] A few of the camps conducted medical-biological "research," on prisoners to test the human resistance to cold, hunger, and various chemical substances, and the Berlin-Dahlem Institut für Rassenbiologie also recorded information on the comparative morphology and metabolism of twins, mailed regularly by Dr. Josef Mengele, who also supervised the twins' deaths and the preparation of the resulting autopsies.

What can possibly account for the fact that thousands of Germans and other Europeans willingly took part, over a period of four years, in this process of mass annihilation? The principal impulse came from Hitler himself, the charismatic leader of first the Nazi party and then the German nation-in-arms. Although many of his lieutenants, like Goering, Speer, and Admiral Doenitz, did not share his insane obsession, they were of course completely indifferent (not to say morally challenged), otherwise they would never have risen to leadership positions in Nazi Germany. As for those who did share the racial obsession, like Goebbels, Reinhard Heydrich, Ernst Kaltenbrunner, and the sadistic, buffoonish governor of occupied Poland (and patron of the arts), Hans Frank; these men never possessed the per-

sonal authority to have imposed the policy on the entire civilian and military establishment. Hence the decisions, and the authority to implement them, came from
Hitler personally.[9]

Perhaps the most impressive single example of what one might call "rational
insanity" in implementing the Holocaust was the career of the abovementioned Dr.
Mengele. His father was the owner of a successful military supply business; his
family were conventional Catholics and had a number of Jewish friends during
Josef's boyhood in the pre-Hitler years. Mengele himself took degrees in both medicine and anthropology and became a disciple of the internationally famous anthro-
pologist-eugenicist Otmar Freiherr von Verscheur, who believed that the Jews
should emigrate, that intermarriage should be avoided, and that the feebleminded
should be sterilized (but not murdered).

Mengele was ambitious to make a name for himself through his research, and
saw his opportunity as an SS doctor during the war. At Auschwitz he met the
arriving trains and supervised the selection process on the platform, separating
those people who would be used as workers from those who would be immediately
gassed, and seeing to it that the occasional set of twins was set aside for his
research. Neither a fanatical Nazi nor a rabid anti-Semite, Mengele employed the
services of three able subordinates: Dr. Ella Lingens, an Aryan Viennese prison
physician who had been assigned to Auschwitz as punishment for helping Jews to
escape; another SS Doctor, Hans Münch, who was to be acquitted in a postwar trial
because he had refused to take part in the selection process; and Dr. Miklos
Nyiszli, a Hungarian-Jewish pathologist who had been "selected" by Mengele as a
research assistant.

According to the postwar testimony of these three professionals, Mengele was
truly enthusiastic about the scientific possibilities of his research. He was also a
stickler for cleanliness and discipline, was completely rational and impersonal in
conversation, and respected the competence of his research team, even if they
included anti-Nazis and Jews. After the German defeat, Mengele escaped to
Paraguay, from whence he wrote numerous letters feeling sorry for himself as an
exile but never mentioning Auschwitz (he referred instead to his research and
administrative responsibilities in "the second half of the war"). His personality
epitomizes the ability of top Nazi officials to suppress all normal emotional and ethical impulses in the name of their duty to the Führer, whose own wishes relieved
them of all personal responsibility.[10]

As for the systematic collaboration of those directly involved in the Holocaust,
they could claim (and did) that they were obeying orders, something both soldiers
and civil employees are expected to do. In addition, many of them—not only Germans but also the Slavic and Baltic police and prison guards—shared the racial
concepts of the Nazis: They considered the Jews a "problem," looked askance at
mixed marriages, thought the Jews has achieved too much prominence in business

and the professions, and so on. These views did not mean that they would have advocated mass murder, but they certainly undermined in advance any systematic resistance to the persecution of the Jews. Indeed, those who were assigned to military duty in the camps had already seen, before the war, how neighbors stood by passively—or sometimes even approved—while Jewish businesses were confiscated, Jewish children removed from school, Jewish families expelled from apartment blocks, and so on. There was also, of course, an underworld of habitual criminals and sadists who were pleased to exceed official orders in their behavior, but these were a very small minority and could never have carried out the "final solution" without the "normal" functionaries and soldiers who composed the majority of the camp staffs.

It is also true that the "normal" majority were themselves aware of doing something utterly shameful. Revealingly, the Nazis were careful to employ euphemisms in all their administrative documents and took some pains to hide the process—especially the killing of the feebleminded—from the general public. The camp guards and Nazi doctors did not boast of their activities, either at the time or in the postwar era. They drowned their doubts in increasing quantities of alcohol, though it is impossible to know how much this occurred because they were sick of killing innocent people and how much because they were losing the war and feared the eventual revenge of the victors.

As for the European population, nominal Christians and Jews alike, the news of the genocide was met by varying degrees of incredulity, denial, and horror. By the spring of 1942, the Polish exile government in London and several embassies in Hungary and Switzerland possessed convincing eyewitness reports—but not official documents—of the genocide occurring in Poland under Nazi auspices. Many of the English and Americans to whom they passed on the information literally could not believe that such things were happening in the twentieth century. This is in itself not surprising: Most people, most of the time, make intuitive credibility judgments about all kinds of things of which they do not have direct personal experience. But it is also possible, if one does not wish to believe, to insist on greater and greater quantities of detailed confirmation before admitting the truth of distant events. In short, the majority of the Germans, the peoples of occupied Europe, and the Allied political and military leaders, did their very best *not* to believe the reports. In the case of the civilians, there was a desperate desire to deny the genocide because so many of them had been indifferent or hostile whenever they had directly witnessed acts of persecution—and very few there were who could honestly claim never to have witnessed an attack on a Jew or an act of vandalism against Jewish property. In the case of the Allied military leaders, there was the reluctance to divert airplanes to other targets (such as bombing the rail lines leading to Auschwitz and other camps), as well as a concern that their own soldiers and governments might accuse them of fighting the war in order to save the Jews.[11]

As for the Jews themselves, they reacted in a variety of ways. In occupied Norway, France, Yugoslavia, and Eastern Europe, the young took to the forests and mountains when the Nazi orders came to register in person and move into ghettos. In the small, densely populated countries—Denmark, Holland, and Belgium— they changed names, produced false identity papers, and were often hidden (or vouched for in the false identity) by their Christian neighbors. In the Slavic territories, it was harder to hide because of more widespread local anti-Semitism, greater differences in appearance and culture between the Jews and Christians, and greater ferocity on the part of the Nazis. Even so, considerable numbers of courageous Poles forged registration papers, work permits, travel documents, and gasoline and ration coupons for the people they considered as fellow Poles after five hundred years of fruitful coexistence in the same territory.[12]

Nothing in the entire war showed more clearly the psychological sadism of the Nazis than their insistence that the ghettos be "governed" by councils of Jewish notables, the so-called *Judenräte*. Using the Jews in this way of course saved German manpower for other tasks, but the principal aim was to break the morale of their victims. The council would be made responsible for the distribution of rations, for communal medical care, and for reuniting members of separated families that often ran to three generations. In this fashion, the councils were forced to do much of the Nazis' dirty work. If the Germans gave three ration books for a family of five or one pair of shoes for a couple, for example, it was up to the council to decide how to divide the inadequate supplies. If the Germans needed a dozen workmen to build a barracks or repair a shed, it was up to the council to choose the work detail. If the Germans demanded a dozen hostages to guarantee the peaceful behavior of a ghetto street, it was up to the council to choose the hostages. If the Germans gave them the choice between choosing a number of persons to be deported and seeing the same number shot as punishment for the community's refusal to "cooperate," the council chose the group to be deported. And if a member of the council decided that he could no longer serve, he would first have the choice of changing his mind or being placed in the next train to Auschwitz.[13]

There is by now a large literature—produced mainly by emigres living in reasonable comfort in the United States—which castigates the ghettoized Jews for cooperating in their own destruction. It is of course true that some council members were simply opportunists trying to save their own skins by currying favor with the Nazis, and also that many younger, secularized Jews thought of the councils as collaborators or dupes. But any blanket condemnation of the *Judenräte* indicates an utterly inadequate appreciation of the actual situation of the persons involved. In late 1941, no one absolutely *knew* that *all* the Jews would be systematically exterminated. The Germans needed labor, and the Jews had all kinds of skills to offer. The ghetto councils in Poland and Belorussia hoped they could make Jewish labor so indispensable to the Germans that the inhabitants would survive the war.

If in fact the Hitlerite leadership had been at all rational, they would indeed have provided minimal survival conditions for useful workers, just as they would have ended the war before their own country was completely destroyed. Who could have predicted their suicidal behavior? And who are the great moral philosophers who would automatically condemn the *Judenräte* for that forlorn hope of at least minimal rationality on the part of the Nazis, or for the terrible decisions they often were forced to make in trying to maintain that hope?

The apparent compliance, the alleged passivity, of the Jews has also given rise to a large literature. But that passivity was by no means unique or complete. It has often been observed that defenseless human beings do not resist in a completely hopeless predicament, where all the food, economic resources, and weapons are on the other side. The semi-starving gypsies and the Soviet war prisoners did not resist their deaths any more than did the deported Jews—or, in the sixteenth century, than did the demoralized Indians imprisoned and slaughtered by the Spanish conquistadors, or their nineteenth-century descendants when treated similarly by the self-appointed agents of United States "Manifest Destiny."

It is also an ironic fact of political loyalties in the twentieth century that many Jewish resisters did not identify themselves as Jews in their struggle against Nazism. With few exceptions, those Jews who fought on the Republican side in the Spanish Civil War identified themselves as workers, students, trade unionists, socialists, and communists. In the French and Italian *maquis* during the years 1943–45, they also identified themselves solely with those resistance groups. In Eastern Europe, they usually had to hide their Jewishness as the price of participating in the national resistance movements. Thus, it was only in the 1980s, with the new emphasis on ethnic identities, that Jewish scholars sought to establish the Jewish identity of thousands of Jewish International Brigadiers and World War II resistance fighters. If their numbers and deeds are added to those of the Warsaw ghetto uprising in April 1943 and Jewish partisan bands in Poland and the Soviet Union, the myth of generalized Jewish passivity fades away.

One of the most difficult questions regarding the Holocaust has been the attitude of the Catholic Church as an international institution governed from the small sovereign territory of Vatican City. There can be no doubt that both Pope Pius XI and Pius XII, who succeeded him in 1939, took it as axiomatic that communism was their greatest enemy and that fascist governments (whatever their shortcomings from a Catholic point of view) were necessary allies in the fight against communism. Pius XI negotiated the Concordat of 1929 with Mussolini, often praised the Italian dictator publicly, and also supported the dictatorships of Dollfuss in Austria, Salazar in Portugal, and the cause of General Franco in the Spanish Civil War. And as Vatican secretary for foreign affairs in 1933, Cardinal Pacelli (the future Pope Pius XII) advised the Catholic Center Party and the Catholic bishops not to oppose Hitler. In the crucial Reichstag session which voted the Enabling Act in

March 1933, Pacelli urged the Center deputies to vote for the act which legalized the Nazi dictatorship, and he negotiated the July 1933 Concordat, by which agreement the Center Party dissolved itself and Catholic priests promised not to engage in political activity. Various priests and nuns were to experience Nazi brutality directly in the ensuing years, to the point that, in 1937, Pius XI issued the encyclical *Mit Brenneder Sorge* (With Burning Anguish), which finally condemned the paganism and violence of the Nazis. But the fact remains that, throughout the Nazi era from 1933 to 1945, the Vatican treated Hitler's regime as a lesser evil than communism and never endorsed the Allied cause in World War II.

The official attitude of the Church during the war rested on a combination of the pope's natural conservatism and cautious temperament, caution, his concern for the Catholic population in nations at war with each other, his profound anticommunism, and his readiness to save persecuted individuals if it could be done quietly. Pius XII privately encouraged the few German bishops who protested Nazi policies, but he did not back them with public statements. For example, in March 1943 the strongly anti-Nazi Bishop Preysing wanted him to react to a new wave of deportations in Germany. On April 30, the pontiff answered that he could only pray for the persecuted non-Aryan and half-Aryan Catholics.[14] Pius XII undoubtedly agreed with the increasingly anti-Nazi postures of Cardinal Gerlier of Lyon, Archbishop Salièges of Toulouse, Bishop Théas of Montauban, and the Belgian Cardinal van Roey, but he did not add his voice to their protests. He knew of the hierarchy's cooperation with the openly anti-Semitic Croatian and Slovakian puppet regimes, but he voiced disapproval only in a few of the most flagrant cases. In 1942, he was as well informed as either the Swiss or the Hungarians concerning the mass murder taking place at Auschwitz, but he took the position that publicity would only make matters worse.

A particularly agonizing incident in Holland surely reaffirmed Pius XII in his determination to keep silent. In a gesture towards the Dutch as fellow "Aryans," the Germans at first refrained from deporting converted Jews. However, as of July 1942 the Catholic and Dutch Reformed Church leaders had agreed to protest together publicly against the deportation of the Jewish community. In the face of threats of German reprisal, the Protestants refrained from reading the protest in their churches, whereas the Catholics acted on the original agreement. In a classic "divide and conquer" response, the Germans deported the Catholic converts but not the Protestant ones.[15] And in October 1943, when the Germans occupied Rome and began arresting Jews within sight of the Vatican, the pope authorized the use of some 155 church buildings to shelter about five thousand Jews. He also gladly cooperated with the German ambassador to the Vatican, the conservative anti-Nazi Ernst von Weizsäcker, in facilitating Vatican City protection for Jewish refugees and in communicating to German bishops his horror at the Nazi deportations.[16] Thus, the Pope saved Jews from deportation and indicated his moral condemnation to the German hierarchy whenever he could do so without publicly defying the Nazis.

To turn from the behavior of the Vatican to that of the many peoples of Europe, a few of the smaller governments were particularly vehement in their anti-Semitism. The Slovak regime deported three-quarters of its Jewish population by October 1942, after which quiet Church intervention and generous bribery of the police stopped further action until the SS occupation of Slovakia in late 1944. The Romanian government in late 1941 supplied cattle cars in its eagerness to cooperate not only in the deportation of its own Jews but those of the Ukraine and Bessarabia.[17]

On the other hand, it is a most striking fact that where public opinion really opposed the persecutions, the Nazis found it impossible to carry out their plans for mass deportations. The great weakness of the occupiers was their lack of numbers—especially when, after the Battle of Stalingrad at the end of 1942, they had to commit all able-bodied German males to direct military service. In Norway, for example, the collaborationist government of Vidkun Quisling obeyed German orders to intern the very small Jewish community in late 1942; but it refused to deport them, and the majority eventually escaped, with Norwegian help, to Sweden. In Denmark, much of the civilian population wore the yellow star and—as it happened—the German military authorities decided to drop intentional hints concerning the imminence of a general roundup in September 1943. As a result of this forewarning, about half the nation's Jews escaped to Sweden in small boats which were silently observed by the Germans, and most of the other half survived the war with the clandestine aid of neighbors. In Belgium also, the police and the railroad administration did not collaborate in round ups, with the result that approximately half of the Jewish community survived.

In France, the Vichy functionaries and the police in the occupied zone cooperated in rounding up non-French Jews, including the children of those families— thereby exceeding the actual orders issued by the Germans. But the general population, and the functionaries who shared the general opinion, were opposed to the deportation of *French* Jews, and so well over half of the highly assimilated French Jewish community survived the war.

A similar situation existed with Germany's European allies. While the fascist government of Mussolini was still an honored partner of Nazi Germany, the Italian authorities published various anti-Semitic decrees but did not intern or deport Jews. After Italy tried to pull out of the war in mid-1943, the Germans occupied Rome, and in October they raided the traditional Jewish quarter (which was not a walled ghetto). Italian people, however, helped the entire community, so that some seven thousand of Rome's eight thousand Jews escaped capture at that time. Several months later, however—in the spring of 1944, when they knew they would very soon lose the war—the Germans took more drastic measures and themselves deported the great majority of Italian urban Jews whom they could identify as such.

Bulgaria was another German ally, though for reasons of historic friendship it did not declare war on Russia. Under German pressure, the Bulgarian government passed anti-Semitic laws in 1941 but exempted baptized Jews, which led to a rush of conversions. It was public knowledge that both the king and the Metropolitan of Sofia were opposed to the persecution of the Jews, an attitude which was reflected throughout much of the population. Thus, due to the state of governmental and public opinion, (and to the shortage of German manpower), the majority of Bulgarian Jews survived the war.

In Hungary, as in Italy, there was a spiritual gulf between the Nazi gangsters and the reactionary, proto-fascist (but not racist), government of Admiral Horthy. By early 1944, Hitler had succeeded in destroying about five million Central and Eastern European Jews, but his armies were in full retreat from Russia and his Magyar ally was sheltering approximately half a million Jews. In March, Hitler ordered the occupation of Hungary and put Eichmann in charge of the Hungarian Security Services. Between April and December, more than 400,000 Jews were deported to Auschwitz. Moreover, it was thoroughly obvious to the diplomatic corps in Budapest that the Germans had occupied Hungary solely for the purpose of completing the massacre of the Jews. In the circumstances, the Spanish and Swedish embassies issued visas to thousands of Jews who would otherwise have been deported. During the same months, Eichmann and Himmler—conscious that the war was lost and not sharing Hitler's suicidal, all-or-nothing frame of mind, negotiated with the world Jewish community to ransom Hungarian Jews for hard currency and military trucks. Some 2,700 persons had been saved in this way by December, at which time Hitler got wind of the negotiations and explicitly ordered that no Jews were to survive the war.[18]

And what of the general civilian population in the areas where no local authority evaded the Nazi demands? Here, a tiny minority of decent human beings redeemed the indifference—and fear—of the great majority. They were not the sort of people to draw attention to themselves, especially when their own neighbors might have reported their deeds to the authorities. And so their acts are known principally through the later researches of historians and social scientists of the *Yad Vashem*, the Israeli Holocaust Remembrance Authority.

Relevant to those researches is an understanding of the figure known in Jewish folklore as "the just man" (or woman). He (or she) is not necessarily a highly educated or philosophically inclined, individual, but rather a person who loves life, who has many good qualities and many weaknesses. The essential point is that, at the moment of crisis, the just person spontaneously does the decent thing—takes the necessary risks to show solidarity with the persecuted and to resist cruelty and injustice. The Israeli Holocaust Remembrance Authority researchers found them by the thousands: men and women alike, heterosexuals and homosexuals, of all ages and social backgrounds. In a population of millions, they constituted approximately one-tenth of one percent who raised Jewish children as their own, hid partisans in the barn or the attic, forged passports for colleagues and strangers, misled the police as they attempted to round up Jews, or passed themselves off as representatives of the appointed authorities.

In a text that has insufficient space for purely individual sagas, let the story of one such person stand for all those thousands. Giorgio Perlasca was a young businessman, a sales representative in Budapest of an Italian meat company. After the Italian surrender to the Allies, Perlasca was interned by the Hungarian authorities as the subject of a now-enemy government. But he was also a veteran of the Italian expeditionary force which had helped Franco win the Spanish Civil War and, as such, the Spaniards had told him to come to their embassy if he ever needed help. Escaping from Hungarian custody, he sought documentary protection for himself and, at the same time, volunteered his services to assist in the housing and feeding of the thousands of Jews being placed under protection of the Spanish Legation.

In this capacity, Perlasca carried a letter from the chargé d'affaires, Angel Sanz-Briz (whose memory was honored by the Hungarian government in 1994), identifying him as an employee of the Spanish Legation and responsible for the Jews under its protection. But in late November, just before the final Russian siege and desperate Nazi defense, Sanz-Briz was recalled to Madrid and the Germans began to empty the apartments containing the protected Jews. At this point, Perlasca (who spoke fluent Spanish) passed himself off to the Germans as the new Spanish chargé and was thereby able—at substantial risk to his own life—to save some five to six thousand others.[19]

A final subject to be considered in this chapter is the attitude of the German and Austrian peoples, in whose name the Nazis were conquering and exploiting the entire continent (with the exception of the Iberian peninsula). The German resistance, like the Holocaust, has inspired an immense literature. In the immediate aftermath of the war, very few Germans were willing to discuss the subject. But pre-1933 Germany had been one of the world's most highly cultured and admired nations, and the postwar generations—citizens of a now prosperous, peaceful, and democratic Germany—wanted to know how their forebears had reacted at the time.

In the late 1930s, there was strong, intuitive popular protest when the "euthanasia" of the handicapped and the feebleminded became known. Both the Catholic and Protestant churches and their lay organizations condemned the policy and were able to restrain it, to some extent, before the war. But the Nazis continued the killings secretly, and the process was merged with the genocide of the Jews during the war years.

Unfortunately, the often unconscious racism of the Germans prevented any widespread protest against the anti-Jewish laws before the war. Although some Protestant churches criticized the anti-Semitic laws, a high proportion of them echoed the Nazi propaganda portraying the Jews as too prominent, too economically and politically powerful; and when baptized Jews were forced to wear the yellow star, the evangelical churches in seven different *Länder* expelled their converts.[20] The anti-Nazi mayor of Leipzig, Carl Goerdeler (who was to become one of the most honored of the resistance martyrs) spoke of the Jews before the war as belonging to a separate race, one alien to the Germans. He favored limiting their activities and supported the idea of a Jewish "homeland" elsewhere. Similar sentiments were expressed by many of those who risked their lives in the plot to assassinate Hitler in July 1944, so that one must recognize a degree of anti-Semitic feeling as endemic to many of the best brains in Germany.[21]

Additionally there were many liberal, religious, and ethically sensitive Germans who made a distinction between the war in the East and the war in the West. Especially among university-educated scientists, professionals, and civil servants, the war in the West was seen as regrettable. Some thought that the Allies bore part of the responsibility by not standing up to Hitler at the time of the Czechoslovak crisis. Thus, a number of authors have made much of the fact that a handful of German diplomats and army officers in the late 1930s tried to warn the West, and they claim that these officials would have gladly overthrown Hitler if they could have counted on Western aid. Another line of discussion has been the argument that Germany was caught between the "civilized" West and "barbarous" East, the latter image combining rejection of communism with long-held prejudices about the inferiority of the Slavic peoples. Even as fine a human being as the great physicist Werner Heisenberg hoped that Germany would defeat Russia, and he tried to convince himself that, given the passage of time as well as the responsibilities of governing, the Nazis themselves would behave less barbarously.

The tremendous number of memorials and publications concerned with the small student, aristocratic, and military opposition groups serve also to highlight the sad fact that very little active resistance occurred among the general German and Austrian populations. These opposition groups felt completely isolated from all but occasional Catholic and Protestant church supporters. On the other hand, it should never be forgotten that approximately one million Germans (about 1.4 percent of the population) spent time in concentration camps between 1933 and 1939, that some twelve thousand political executions of Germans and Austrians occurred between 1933 and 1938, and that more than 32,000 political executions took place between 1938 and 1945.[22] But these people—mostly socialists, communists, and pacifists—were easily neutralized by the Nazis because no widespread opinion came to their defense. The Nazi-sponsored economic recovery, combined with the citizenry's readiness to attribute all responsibility for good and evil to the Führer, seems effectively to have blunted the moral sensibilities of the general public.

To sum up: where traditional anti-Semitism remained strong (i.e., among much of the Germanic and Slavic populations), the Nazis enjoyed the support of the military and civil service elites and met little resistance to their criminal policies, which were unprecedented in such highly cultured and technically advanced countries as Germany and Austria. In Scandinavia, Switzerland, and Western Europe, where the anti-Semitism was much less virulent, the Nazis encountered a mixture of incredulity and mostly cautious, inconspicuous resistance. Then, too, when respected public figures like the kings of Denmark and Bulgaria, or the bishops of southern France provided a measure of moral resistance, much of the public followed their example. And the Nazis themselves were sufficiently aware of their own criminality that they made considerable efforts to hide the genocide from the people of both their own and the occupied nations. Nevertheless, for all Europe north of the Mediterranean, the Holocaust of Jews, Slavs, and gypsies remains a part of what the Germans call *die unbewältigte Vergangenheit*—"unmastered past."

ENDNOTES

1. Werner Warmbrunn, *The Dutch under the German Occupation, 1940–1945* (Stanford, CA: Stanford University Press, 1963), pp. 107–11, 146–60, and *passim*.

2. Quoted in Ulrich Herbert, "Labor and Extermination . . . in National Socialism," *Past and Present*, February 1993, 144–95.

3. Michel Luther, "Die Krim unter deutscher Besatzung," *Forschungen zur Österreuropäischen Geschichte*, 1956, 28–29.

4. John A. Armstrong, Collaboration in World War II: the Integral Nationalist Variant in Eastern Europe," *The Journal of Modern History*, September 1968, 396–410.

5. Witalij Wilenchik, "Die Partisanbewegung in Weissrussland, 1941–1944," *Forschungen zur Östereuropäischen Geschichte*, 1984, 129–251; and Harold Werner, *Fighting Back* (New York: Columbia University Press, 1992). Werner's book is careful memoir of Jewish resistance in Poland and White Russia.

6. Quoted in Michael Marrus, "History of the Holocaust," *The Journal of Modern History*, March 1987, 121. I have depended on this excellent bibliographical and interpretive analysis for many of my general statements about the Holocaust.

7. Jean-Claude Pressac, *Les crématoires d'Auschwitz* (Paris: CNRS, 1993) (the work of a French pharmacist originally skeptical about the truth of genocide).

8. Thomas Keneally, *Schindler's List* (Serpentine Publishing Co. Pty. Ltd., 1982), later reprinted by Simon and Schuster. Used as the basis for the Stephen Spielberg movie, Keneally's book contains much more conclusive evidence than the film as to Schindler's serious commitment to the Jewish community.

9. On Frank, see Christoph Klessman, "Gouverneur General Hans Frank," *Vierteljahrshefte für Zeitgeschichte*, 1971, 245–60; and Wolfgang Jacobmayer, "Die polnische Widerstandsbewegung in Generalgouvernement," in the same journal, 1977. The use of the French spelling was an affectation of Frank's, intended to relate his regime to that of the eighteenth-century enlightened despots and sometime-sovereigns of Poland, Stanislas I and II, both of whom were patrons of the arts and of French culture.

10. Zdenek Sofka, "Josef Mengele zur Typologie eines NS-Verbrecher," *Viertel-jahrshefte für Zeitgeschichte*, 1986, 245–67; Dr. Miklos Nyiszli, *Auschwitz* (Greenwich, Conn.: Fawcett Publications, 1960).

11. Concerning Allied disbelief, two articles by Walter Laqueur in *Encounter*: "Hitler's Holocaust," July 1980, and "How Not to Break the Silence," April, 1987.

12. Stanislawa Lewandowska, "Authentication Activities of the Polish Resistance," *Acta Poloniae Historica*, 1984, 181–218.

13. Lucy Davidowicz, The War Against The Jews, New York: Holt, Rinehart, and Winston, 1975, chapter 11, and *passim*; Reuben Ainsztein, *Jewish Resistance in Nazi-Occupied Eastern Europe* (London: Paul Elek, 1974).

14. Wolfgang Schieder, "Pius XII im II Weltkrieg," *Historische Zeitschrift*, 207, 1986, 346–56.

15. Leon Polikov, "The Vatican and the Jewish Question," *Commentary*, November, 1950; Anthony Rhodes, *The Vatican in the Age of the Dictators* (New York: Holt, Reinhart, and Winston, 1973), pp. 342–46.

16. Leonidas E. Hill, III, "The Vatican Embassy of Ernst von Weizsäcker," *The Journal of Modern History*, June 1967, 138–59.

17. Davidowicz, pp. 510–22.

18. César Vidal, El Holocausto, Madrid: Alianza Editorial, 1995, pp. 120–45.

19. Judith Weinraub, "Common Man, Uncommon Decency," International Heral Tribune, September 12, 1990; and Juan Arias, "El italiano que salvó a miles de judios . . ." *El Pais*, August 17, 1989.

20. Raul Hilberg, *Perpetrators, Victims, Bystanders* (New York: Harper Collins, 1992), 261.

21. In my general statements concerning Germany and the Jews, I have relied heavily on the writings of Raul Hilberg, Leon Polikov, and Walter Laqueur; and on the many interviews, opinion polls in both Germany and Poland, and investigate articles published in *Die Zeit* concerning German reactions to the Stephen Spielberg movie *Schindler's List*.

22. Hans Rothfels, *The German Opposition to Hitler* (London: O. Wolff, 1961), 13–14; and J. Nobecourt, *Le Monde*, July 21, 1964, commemorating the twentieth anniversary of the unsuccessful attempt by anti-Nazi army officers to assassinate Hitler.

10

The Welfare State, 1945–1990

*T*he most destructive of European wars was succeeded, in the West and in Scandinavia, by the development of a society which offered greater personal liberty, economic security, and opportunity in matters of education and leisure time than any previous society. The rise of the welfare state also coincided with the Cold War, the division of Europe between the American-dominated North Atlantic Treaty Organization (NATO) and the Soviet-dominated Warsaw Pact, the retreat from old forms of imperialism and the elaboration of new ones, and the emergent "balance of terror" between the nuclear arsenals of the United States and the Soviet Union.

It would require far more than a single chapter to elucidate all these interconnections, and the news of diplomatic and military threats is in itself more attention-getting than a steady, sober improvement of the human condition. But in the interest of evaluating one of the most hopeful features of "civilization" rather than "barbarity," I shall concentrate in this chapter on the positive aspects of European development in the four decades following the Second World War and devote only the minimum necessary attention to the negative aspects.

In the spring of 1945, the European populations were utterly exhausted after five years of military occupation, aerial bombardments, food and material shortages of all kinds, and the destruction of much of the infrastructure roads, railroads, bridges, public buildings, family housing, and merchant shipping. The people were physically undernourished and—with the exception of the numerically small resistance cadres—spiritually undernourished as well. Most civic and religious leaders had set the example of extreme prudence in the occupied countries, and of course there had been no freedom of the press and political discussion.

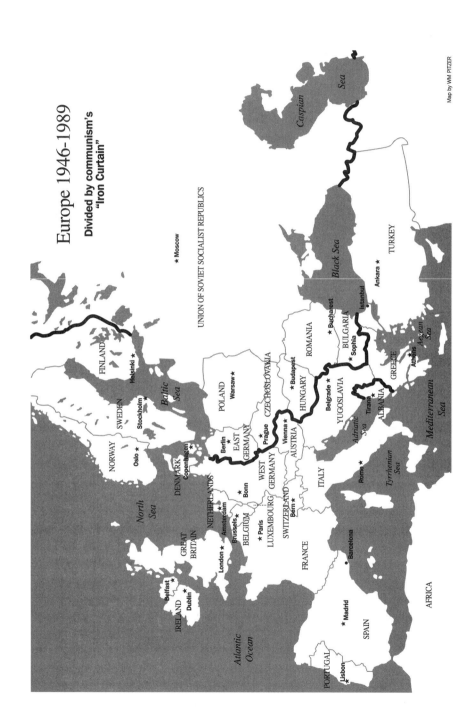

Europe 1946-1989

Divided by communism's "Iron Curtain"

Map by WM PITZER

But after the German defeat, there was also a certain consensus of hope. Four years of military cooperation with the Soviets had given rise to a very general feeling of admiration and gratitude toward the Red Army. Only a minority of Western Europeans remembered the Stalinist show trials and blood purges of 1936–38, and only a minority thought that a future armed conflict between the capitalist and Soviet worlds was inevitable—especially as the Soviets themselves spoke of continuing cooperation between themselves and the "progressive" forces in the bourgeois West. Fascism had been the great enemy of both the USSR and the democratic capitalist states. Now, with the exception of the Iberian dictatorships of General Franco in Spain and the former professor of economics Antonio Salazar in Portugal, fascism and fascist-supported regimes had been eliminated.

In two summit conferences, at Yalta in February 1945 and at Potsdam in July of the same year, the "Big Three" (as represented by Roosevelt, Churchill, and Stalin) had forged their agreements concerning the fates of Germany and Eastern Europe. They had agreed upon the military border between the territories to be occupied by the Western and Soviet armies, respectively. Also, as the aggressor, Germany was to pay heavy reparations in kind and, as the main victim of Nazi destruction, Russia would receive the bulk of those reparations. Germany, however, was to be treated as a single economic unit. This meant that approximately one-quarter of the industrial production of the zones occupied by the United States, Britain, and France—and much of the coal and iron of the Ruhr—would be delivered to the Soviets. In return, much of the agricultural produce of the Soviet-occupied eastern zone would be sent to help feed the much more populous western areas.

England and the United States also agreed to Soviet annexation of the eastern provinces of Poland and to Polish annexation of Silesia, Posen, and West Prussia. In short, Poland was displaced bodily westward, and in the process acquired industrial provinces in exchange for its eastern forests and fields. The Western powers also confirmed (unhappily but silently) the Soviet annexation of the Baltic republics, which had taken place in June 1940 during the era of the Nazi-Soviet Pact. The Poles and the Russians spoke of the Oder-Neisse line as the new, permanent "frontier" between Poland and Germany, and the Western powers accepted it as a temporary "administrative" border.

Besides these specific terms for Germany and Poland, the Big Three also signed at Yalta a Declaration on Liberated Europe which committed the victors to "form interim governmental authorities broadly representative of all the democratic elements in the population and pledged to the earliest possible establishment, through free elections, of governments responsive to the will of the people." But except for the territorial division of Germany and the new Polish frontiers, none of these agreements was fulfilled. The Soviets, besides receiving one-fourth of the industrial production of the occupied zones, carted whole factories off from their own zone, together with large quantities of railroad track and rolling stock. The

Western powers felt that they were being obliged to subsidize the minimum needs of German reconstruction in order to compensate for the Russian dismantling of whatever was left of Germany's industry and infrastructure. The Soviets felt that the West was stalling on its delivery of industrial products, and by mid-1946 deliveries of reparations from the West and food from the East both had been suspended.

An ugly conflict (hidden from public opinion at the time) was also taking place regarding the repatriation of prisoners of war. As allies, the Big Three had agreed to send home all Allied personnel in their own zones. In the Western camps (mostly under British control), thousands of Poles and hundreds of thousands of Soviets refused to be repatriated, alleging that they would be politically persecuted in their homelands. The Soviets insisted that the resisters were "White Guard," counterrevolutionary elements and made the repatriation a question of honor between allies. The British military authorities, worried about possible Soviet delays in the return of English and French prisoners, ultimately complied with the demand. As a result, unspecified numbers of families fled the camps and a number of suicides occurred.[1]

As for the agreement on free elections, noncommunist parties were only acceptable if they were "friendly" (i.e., completely subservient) to the Stalinist bureaucrats who had accompanied the "liberating" forces of the Red Army. Without going into detail about the takeover of each national government, suffice it to say that by 1948 all the Eastern European governments had been purged not only of "petty bourgeois" peasant party leaders (those who had in fact received the most votes in the elections of 1946), but also of communists whom Stalin had decided were not completely loyal to him personally.

Within three years, then, of the Yalta and Potsdam accords, the wartime alliance of the Big Three had been transformed into the Cold War that would condition all European developments from 1948 to the late 1980s. The military frontier traced in February 1945 in anticipation of the German defeat, had become the "Iron Curtain," and for the next four decades an American-sponsored Europe would coexist uneasily side by side with a Soviet-sponsored Europe. In the present chapter, I will discuss the democratic-capitalist welfare state as it developed in Western Europe and Scandinavia.

In point of fact, the basic economic and human conditions in the West were not anywhere near as calamitous as they had appeared to be in the news photos of May 1945. The Allied and German bombing campaigns had failed to destroy as much of either German or British industry as had been assumed in the military communiqués of the respective air forces. Food supplies from the United States and the British Commonwealth flowed in after the end of the naval blockade and the ground fighting, and domestic agricultural and industrial production resumed rapidly once peace had been restored. There were also numerous long-term factors which made the development of the welfare state possible. For one thing, the fabric of civil society had not been destroyed. There were brief, sanguinary purges of about ten thousand collaborators each in France and Italy (countries with populations of more than forty million) but, on the whole, national loyalties and national cohesion were quickly restored. Political and economic liberty had been stable conditions of life in England, France, the Low Countries, and Scandinavia, and they had been powerful aspirations—interrupted by fascism and war, but not destroyed—in Germany, Italy, and the Iberian peninsula.

Then, too, women had entered the work force in large numbers during the war, and they were not disposed to return solely to *Kirche, Küche, und Kinder* (church, cooking, and children) as had recently been urged by such conservative political philosophers as Hitler, Mussolini, Marshall Pétain, and General Franco. All classes and political parties agreed that the sacrifices of the war years should be rewarded by a more just distribution of wealth than had existed during the 1920s and the Great Depression. And even the most conservative capitalists were aware (indeed, more so than ever) of the example of a socialist society being built, albeit crudely and dictatorially, in the Soviet Union.

What was lacking in 1945 was ready capital, and this was supplied by one of the more farsighted and generous international actions of the United States. In June 1947, General George Marshall, who had been chief of staff during the war and now was serving as President Truman's secretary of state, announced the readiness of the United States to fund an Economic Recovery Plan (ERC). All European governments, including the Soviets, were invited to submit specific proposals regarding infrastructure, industrial reconstruction and new investment. The East European countries, in particular Czechoslovakia, were anxious to participate, but Stalin obliged them to refuse.

American example and advice led to the substantial reduction of inter-European tariffs and internal quotas. Altogether, in the decade 1947–56, about twenty-five billion dollars were injected into the economy, mostly for infrastructure and investment in new technology. There is no way of knowing how much economic suffering and military tension might have been avoided if the Soviets had participated, but in fact the ERC, together with its rejection by the Soviets, sealed the economic and political division of Europe as of late 1947.

The Marshall Plan was followed quite naturally in 1957 by the formation of the Common Market, consisting at first of the core nations of continental Europe— France, West Germany, Italy, and the Benelux nations. These countries were more psychologically prepared, than England or Scandinavia to accept supranational economic controls. Indeed, political motives were probably more important to them than economic ones: The customs union, together with greatly increased trade among "the six," meant that war would become unthinkable between Germany and France, that the Low Countries would be freed of similar nightmares, and that Italy would become an integral part of democratic capitalist Europe.

Three years later, in 1960, Great Britain, Norway, Sweden, Denmark, Austria,

Switzerland, and Portugal—appropriately known as "the outer seven," formed their own, more loosely organized European Free Trade Association (EFTA). Both the Common Market and EFTA accepted only democratic governments as members, which led to some curious distinctions: for example, England's virtual protectorate Portugal was somehow considered democratic despite the iron rule of Antonio Salazar, whereas General Franco's Spain was ineligible as a dictatorship. The co-existence of the two organizations illustrated the difficulties of fully uniting the prosperous capitalist democracies, but those difficulties were overcome in the ensuing decades.

England, Ireland, and Denmark joined the Common Market in 1973, and by the late 1980s Spain (which became a democratic monarchy after the death of Franco in 1976), Portugal, Greece, Sweden, and Norway had also joined, and EFTA was quietly dissolved. At the same time, the recognition of the great mutual benefits to be gained from lowering trade barriers did not alter the fact that the European countries varied greatly in national outlook, and that each sovereign nation retained its domestic powers and pursued its traditional interests within the Common Market.

There were three important models of economic development. The Keynesian model, put forth by the great British economist John Maynard Keynes, was applied principally in Britain and Scandinavia. Keynes had emphasized that prosperity depended upon an equilibrium in the production and consumption of goods and services, and also upon liquidity, the constant flow of money within the economy. In times of recession, therefore, it was not only permissible but necessary to "prime the pump," which could take two forms—government investment in public works and unemployment benefits (to put cash in everybody's pocket). If priming the pump created deficits, the ensuing prosperity would make it possible for a government to recover, through tax revenues, the money it had used to prime the pump. If the system showed a general tendency toward mild inflation (no more than a few points annually) such inflation was an acceptable price to pay for social peace and the provision of educational and social services to the general population.

Postwar Germany had developed its own model, however, the so-called "social market" economy. Bismarck's rule in the 1870s and 1880s, nostalgically remembered by the Germans after two lost wars, had shown that conservative governments, in a society with marked class divisions, could nevertheless offer basic social security to the entire population. In addition to this historic example, the traumatic experience of hyperinflation after the First World War had made it absolutely necessary, in terms of public confidence, for any German government to avoid even the mild inflation characteristic of the Keynesian approach. Thus, the social-market economy was to be based, first and foremost, on a strong currency. Germany in the immediate postwar years had a largely barter economy, with food, cigarettes, gasoline coupons, and sex having a more dependable value than currency. In the 1948 currency reform, the economics minister, Ludwig Erhard, carefully restricted the issuance of new marks so that cash would be scarcer than saleable goods. This policy brought onto the market the valuable merchandise that people had been hoarding—or at any rate, that they had refused to sell for inflation-endangered marks. This new, strong mark was the first element in the "economic miracle" of West German recovery.

German social-market policy also left investment decisions in the hands of the traditional business classes and banks, but it did not leave the mass of citizens to sink or swim in a purely market economy. Most of the nation's urban housing had been destroyed during the war, and in the late 1940s the federal government and the *Länder* provided approximately 50 percent each of the capital necessary to build several million housing units. In line with German tradition, the state provided minimal unemployment, health, and old-age benefits, and it also established a tradition of wage-and-hour negotiations with the mostly Social Democratic labor unions. And in recognition of the permanent presence of women in the work force, the West German republic offered six weeks' pregnancy leave at full pay (before and after the date of birth) and made it illegal to fire a woman for becoming pregnant. Thus, the postwar prosperity in Germany depended on the continuing work ethic and self-discipline of the German people and, in the early years, on their willingness to accept personal austerity for the sake of maintaining a strong, stable currency.

The third model was the prosperous small-scale capitalism of France, combined with what might be dubbed the "eternal Colbertism" of the descendants of the Sun King. France was a nation of individual entrepreneurs and family businesses, large and small. There were steel and armaments barons comparable in power to the more publicized corporate nabobs of Germany, England, and the United States. There were also prosperous specialized industries, capitalizing themselves from their commercial revenues and maintaining high qualitative standards, as well as thousands of small family businesses and self-financing farmers.

Tax evasion was an honored tradition in France, in the wider interest of permitting small enterprises to stay afloat in a competitive environment, and large enterprises to take care of executives and their families in the style to which they were accustomed. The French distrusted banks and governments even more intensely than did other European peoples. They had lost a great deal of money when their generous investments in imperial Russia had been liquidated by war and revolution, and they were also philosophically tolerant of considerable inflation.

The Marshall Plan, with its from-the-top-down largesse to those with intelligent investment ideas, enabled the nation to hark back to the days of Louis XIV and his great economic minister, Jean-Baptiste Colbert. This meant a program of generous state investment combined with frequent nationalization of key industries, protection of the domestic market from outside competition, taxes on consumption rather than on business enterprise, excellent education of an economic-political elite in the *grandes écoles*, and not too much fuss over discreet, unofficial bribes and perks. France managed for several decades to combine this Colbertism with membership in the Common Market, substituting national pride for the tariffs which were necessarily being lowered and turning a blind eye when its farmers destroyed Spanish trucks bringing fruits and vegetables across the Pyrenees.

Nationalized industries have been a particular bête noir of the United States, and also of the conservative economists who have set the tone of discussion in recent years. It is therefore important to realize that England, the Scandinavian nations, Germany, and France all combined essentially a private-enterprise system with considerable elements of national participation. English broadcasting and public utilities, and German and French state railways have been administered by their governments with an efficiency comparable to the best of private-sector management, and without being labeled as Bolshevism in their own media.

The British Labor Party until the 1970s did cling to the Marxist (and Fabian socialist) belief that the main natural resources, as well as the industries that affected the lives of the whole population, should be nationalized. In the years from 1945 to 1951, Labor governments nationalized the Bank of England, the coal industry, most forms of transport and public utilities, and the steel industry. The Conservatives denationalized steel in 1953, but Labor, during its later years in office (1964–70 and 1974–78), renationalized steel, freight and bus transport, Rolls Royce Aviation, and various gas, oil, aerospace, and shipbuilding firms.

Some of these nationalizations had to do not so much with the essential nature of the industry as with rescuing firms from bankruptcy and workers from prospective unemployment. In the course of the postwar decades, democratic socialist thought shifted from an emphasis on "ownership of the means of production" to regulation of private enterprise as a way of protecting the working classes from the impersonal brutality of the market. At the same time, in Britain and similarly in Sweden, the socialism of public ownership came to be thought of as inefficient— or, cynically, as a means of dumping on the public finances those industries which were no longer profitable for private enterprise. In the eighties, the Conservative government of Margaret Thatcher reprivatized the great bulk of industry and let market forces determine the survival of specific firms. Socialism lost its ethical hold on educated opinion, because of both poor management in democratic England (where there were no *grandes écoles* but rather an amateur tradition of "muddling through") and gross economic failure in the Soviet world.

But the examples of France, Germany, and Italy show that nationalization need not be connected with socialist doctrine. After the war, the very bourgeois French governments also nationalized coal, most banking and insurance, the Renault automobile works and the Berliet truck factories, the important arms factories, and most of the railroads. Management was put in the hands of well-trained technocrats, the same elite which ran the private sector. In Germany, where both the federal government and most of the *Länder* were dominated by the Christian Democrats, public transport and public utilities were financed principally by public investment at municipal, state, and federal levels. In postwar Italy, the recently discovered gas and oil reserves were exploited by a government corporation set up for that purpose.

When Italian industry boomed in the 1960s, it largely followed the French model, producing even higher percentages of inflation and tax evasion (and with substantial bribery of both politicians and professional intermediaries). During the same decade, Spain, Portugal, and Greece, all still under authoritarian rule, initiated economic booms in the Italian style. It would be difficult to say whether corruption was more prevalent in the public or private sector. Regarding efficiency of management and quality of products, the training, morale, and salary levels of workers and managers—and the freedom of the investigative press—were all more important in their effects than technical ownership of the means of production.

Political and diplomatic traditions also created quite different national styles among the members of the new Common Market (the European Economic Community, or EEC). The English continued to hold the continent at arm's length and vice versa most notably when President DeGaulle twice vetoed an invitation from the rest of the EEC for England to join). The English themselves remained largely ignorant of the continent: Conservatives leaders sometimes took vacations in southern France or Italy, as the upper classes had done in the nineteenth century and between the two world wars; but Labor leaders vacationed in the British Isles, and very few of them spoke a continental language or read continental literature. The English relied instead upon their "special relationship" with the United States and the Commonwealth. As Churchill had courted Franklin Roosevelt, so Prime Minister Harold Macmillan cultivated his personal relationships with Presidents Dwight D. Eisenhower and John F. Kennedy and Margaret Thatcher her spiritual kinship with Ronald Reagan and George Bush. The common language, similar legal systems, multiple intellectual and academic exchanges, and basing of American armed forces in England during World War II each contributed its share to the sense of a special relationship between the two nations. Similarly, Queen Elizabeth II's frequent visits to her English-speaking dominions and to former colonies which were now independent members of the Commonwealth helped to maintain the notion that Britain had more world interests and more significant relations with the English-speaking countries than with continental Europe.

Germany had never had independent, truly sovereign parliaments like those of England, and the nation also had to overcome its terrible legacy of Nazi depredations both at home and abroad. The denazification conducted by the Allies had been quite superficial (notwithstanding the Nüremberg trials of the top surviving leaders). So many civil servants and functionaries had been party members that it would have been impossible to find Germans to govern the country if all ex-Nazis were automatically eliminated. In addition, both political and cultural factors disposed the Anglo-Saxons (if only unconsciously) to be lenient with even very obviously authoritarian German mayors, judges, and civil servants. The Iron Curtain and the Cold War inevitably motivated the occupation authorities to think of the Germans as potential allies against a hostile Russia. Probably more important at the intuitive level, Americans and Britons admired the efficiency and the work ethic of the Germans and thus shared with them a certain general feeling of superiority over less disciplined "Latin" and "Mediterranean" peoples.

In these circumstances, it was most fortunate that an experienced republican politician from the Weimar era, clearly pro-Western and anti-Nazi throughout his career, emerged as the head of the majority Christian Democratic coalition and as the prime minister of the newly self-governing West German Republic. Konrad Adenauer, "der Alte" or "the Old Man" (seventy-three when he became prime minister and eighty-six when he retired), had been repeatedly elected as mayor of Cologne during the interwar years. Adenauer was socially and politically very conservative, and his personality imposed itself on his colleagues in a way that has been much more frequent in Germany than in England or America. But he knew and respected the rules of parliamentary democracy and, for fourteen years (1949–1962), he made it possible for Germany to recover its self-respect and end the Western military occupation. With the complicity of most Allied officials, Adenauer avoided any general purge of Nazi-era civil servants. The French were happy because he had strongly favored Franco-German reconciliation in the 1920s and, during his years at the head of the Bonn government, he steadily promoted all moves toward Franco-German cooperation and the formation of the Common Market. The Anglo-Americans were happy because Adenauer was an able *civilian* anticommunist leader, and one who favored the establishment of the North Atlantic Treaty Organization (NATO).

The formation of the welfare states and the creation of the Common Market also benefited from the liquidation of European territorial imperialism. Italy lost her relatively small African empire as a result of having fought in the war on Hitler's side. England, France, and Holland had seen their Asian colonies occupied by Japan and, in any case, had become too weak financially and militarily to maintain their empires after the war. Churchill said belligerently that he had not become prime minister in order to preside over the demise of the British Empire, but in fact, the British in the Middle East, Burma, and India, like the Dutch in Indonesia, had no practical alternative to giving up their colonies.

Perhaps to their surprise, however, these pragmatic peoples discovered by the early fifties that they were better off without the burden of governing unwilling subjects. Once the Europeans had relinquished their imperial hold, the new independent governments were quick to direct the bulk of their trade toward the former "mother" country. They also used the English and Dutch languages for communication among their multilingual populations, sent their elites to English and Dutch universities, and retained much of the European institutional structures in the construction of their own regimes. At home, there were more mixed marriages and more social acceptance of interracial couples. I do not mean to suggest that racism miraculously disappeared at this time from northern Europe, but, more modestly, that the end of the imperial era brought with it a small dividend in civilized behavior toward Asians.

France was much more reluctant than England or Holland to relinquish control of its empire. For a decade (until the disaster of Dien Bien Phu in 1954) the French struggled to reestablish their rule in Vietnam. In North Africa, they recognized the independence of Tunisia and Morocco and were rewarded by trade and diplomatic friendship. But until 1961, they insisted that Algeria was an integral part of France itself. It was indeed true that Algeria had not been merely an exploited colony; French immigration to the very sparsely populated territory had begun in 1830 and, 120 years later, there were over a million Frenchmen cultivating the land, running small businesses very much as in metropolitan France, and considering themselves every bit as Algerian as the Muslim majority. However, the muslims had been second-class citizens in French Algeria and, as part of the whole decolonization movement after World War II, they not only demanded independence but fought for it when it was not granted.

On the one hand, the French in 1945–46 had chosen to establish a Fourth Republic which, like its predecessor, was characterized by shifting coalitions in the legislature and relatively weak cabinets. But on the other hand, the French greatly cherished the memory of having been the leading continental power for several centuries prior to the Franco-Prussian war in 1870; they were also proud of having remained the principal European center of the fine arts between 1870 and 1940 despite their loss of political and military superiority. Thus, while recognizing the need to liquidate nineteenth-century imperialism, France was determined to establish some equivalent of its former power. When legal independence was finally granted in the years 1960–62, the enfranchised colonies—now theoretically sovereign nations— included Mauretania, the Sudanese Republic, Niger, Chad, the Central African Republic, Gabon, the Voltaic Republic, Senegal, French Guinea, the French Cameroons, and the Ivory Coast. These "new" nations, without either economic or political infrastructure, were tied to their former "mother country" by a number of bonds, including French training of their armies and police, the discreet maintenance of elite French troop units, the ceremonious exchange of gifts between French and African presidents, and the education of their small family elites in France.

Portugal, now the weakest (but also the oldest) of the European imperialist powers, tried the longest to hold on to its colonies in Goa, Angola, and Mozambique. The maintenance of "historic ties," as well as the mythology of a civilizing mission since the mid-fifteenth century and a presumed readiness to offer economic and civil-service training to the natives without racial discrimination, motivated the conservative Salazar dictatorship to sacrifice the prosperity of Portugal itself to the retention of the colonies. Their liberation, in 1975–76, coincided with "the revolution of the carnations," the bloodless military revolt in which Portugal recovered its political liberties and began a rapid process of modernization within the EEC.

Italy also had special traits which influenced its behavior in the new democratic Europe. Both as a parliamentary monarchy (1871–1922) and as a fascist dictatorship (1922–1943), the nation had been a Great Power "also ran" in comparison with Great Britain, Germany, and France. Then, too, the contrast in living standards, health, and literacy between the industrial north and the agricultural south were much greater in Italy than similar regional contrasts within the above-named powers. Finally, Italy's position after 1943 as an ex-fascist country with the most dynamic Communist Party outside the Soviet Union was an especially sensitive situation from the Anglo-American point of view. Liberation had not come in a matter of months, as with France and the Low Countries; on the contrary, the Allied expeditionary force and the slowly retreating Germans had fought many long and bitter battles between the first Allied landings in July 1943 and the final withdrawal of the Germans in April 1945. The king and his generals were not sorry to get rid of Mussolini, but they had no stomach for fighting the Germans and were hardly the persons to lead in the democratic transformation of the peninsula.

The Anglo-Americans worked with the small anti-fascist intellectual and political elites and (as in defeated Germany) with the mass of functionaries who had loyally served Mussolini but were now ready to serve any paymaster who would keep them in office. During the twenty-two month military campaign, there was mutually respectful cooperation between the Allied armies and the partisans, though on terms decided almost entirely by the military and without economic or social commitments for the future. Indeed, both Britain and the United States were ready to accept either a monarchy or a republic in postwar Italy, just so long as minimum political liberties were guaranteed and the Communist Party was not allowed to participate in national (as against municipal) governments. The result was a parliamentary republic—decided by plebiscite in 1946—and a series of governments dominated by the Christian Democratic Party until 1992. The Christian Democrats' repeated majorities were obtained in relatively honest elections, but the fact that their local organizations depended heavily on clientelism and bribery—and that the United States indicated whenever necessary (mostly in the 1950s) that economic aid would cease if the Communists won—meant that Italy was not a democracy in the same sense as England or the north European countries. There was no alternation in power between different parties, but only shifting coalitions in which the Christian Democrats remained the dominant partners.[2]

Perhaps the most spectacular "good luck" story in the postwar formation of the European welfare state was that of Austria. The country's fate between the two world wars had indeed been difficult; the 1919 settlements had reduced Vienna from the principal city of a prosperous multinational empire to an oversized capital containing one-third the total population of a small, ethnically homogeneous state.

In addition, the new republic was expressly forbidden to unite itself to the also defeated (but much more economically viable) Germany.

During the decade after the first World War, political power in Austria was almost equally divided between the urban-based Social Democrats and the rural-based, Church-dominated Christian Social Party. The country suffered heavy unemployment and intense social strife from the start. Between 1927 and 1938, the Austrian government looked to Mussolini's fascism as its political model and—after Hitler's rise to power in 1933—it also hoped for Mussolini's protection against the more brutal German version of fascism. But while clerical conservatives increasingly dominated the national government, the Social Democrats continued to hold majority power in the Viennese municipal government. Among other social-welfare projects, the municipality had erected blocks of worker housing, including playgrounds, gardens, and part-time care centers for pre–school age children. For both architectural and political reasons, these apartments had great symbolic value for the Left all over the world. In February 1934, the conservative national government used fascist militias to repress a Viennese general strike which had been called to resist a series of decrees curbing democratic liberties. The socialist workers fought back, and in the course of their resistance many of these buildings—bearing the names of Marx, Goethe, and Beethoven—were damaged by heavy artillery fire.

The tragedy was not soon forgotten. At the beginning of the Spanish Civil War, the leftist militias in Madrid and Barcelona coined the slogan "Better Vienna than Berlin"—better the doomed resistance of the Viennese workers to fascism than the demoralized passivity of Berlin's workers during the Nazi takeover of their capital. The apartments were repaired and improved after World War II and remain one of the first examples of the aesthetically pleasing public housing that became characteristic of the North European welfare states.

To return to the fate of Austria: in March 1938, Hitler carried out the *Anschluss* (annexation) which had been forbidden by the 1919 peace treaties and Austria disappeared as a sovereign state. But after World War II, this very fact redounded to the country's advantage. Austria was officially reconstituted and considered an innocent victim of Nazism although, as a matter of fact, anti-Semitism was relatively stronger among the Austrians (and Bavarians) than among the northern Germans. After the war, Austria, like Germany, was occupied by the four victorious powers, but neither the Russians nor the Western allies felt as vindictively toward it as they did toward the former Third Reich. In contrast to the situation of Germany, Austria was treated as an economic unit and allowed to govern itself within fairly generous parameters. Moreover, after Stalin's death, his heirs wished to counter the growing strength of West Germany and its incorporation into NATO. They offered to end the military occupations of both Germany and Austria in return for the strict neutrality of both countries. The negotiations never got beyond the propaganda stage in the case of Germany, but both the Soviets and the West took the opportunity to reduce Cold War tensions by signing a peace treaty with Austria.

Thus, in 1955—seventeen years after having been wiped off the map—Austria was reborn as a sovereign parliamentary (second) republic. Both the West and Russia accepted the presidency of Karl Renner, one of the more prestigious Socialist politicians from the time of the first republic. The urban-rural split was again mirrored in the near-equal strength of the Socialists and the (Catholic) People's Party. But ideology was not as important after the war as it had been in the twenties and thirties; the Socialists had abandoned revolutionary Marxist rhetoric and the Vatican was now the partner of a democratic rather than a fascist Italy.

Most Austrian governments in the half-century following the second World War have been coalition cabinets; neutrality has been readily accepted by all political parties, and economic policies have been largely consensual. As in the Scandinavian countries—and to a considerable extent also in Germany and the Benelux countries—economic consensus was achieved not only by legislation but (perhaps even more) by regularly scheduled meetings of sectorial governing boards that included representatives of the trade unions, the chambers of commerce, the chambers of agriculture, and the relevant regional and municipal authorities. Marshall Plan money was used wisely to modernize Austria's obsolete state-owned steel, chemical, coal, and iron-mining industries, and also its excellent railways, postal service, and road network. As with the Scandinavians and the French, the question of private versus public ownership was not a passionate political question in Austria. Approximately 20 percent of industry remained state-owned and was, in general, as well-administered as were the privately owned enterprises.

The almost even division of political power between the Socialist and People's parties has meant that the Austrian consensus took elements from both the Swedish Keynesian model and the German social-market economy. The Socialist Prime Minister Bruno Kreisky used countercyclical "pump priming" to mitigate the effects of the oil shocks in the 1970s. At the same time, Kreisky maintained a strong schilling tied to the German mark at the insistence of his conservative partners. During the seventies and eighties, the Austrian government also increased the educational budget at all levels. A final significant element of Austrian luck was the absence of a large military establishment, a condition of sovereignty imposed by the victorious powers and gladly accepted by the population.[3]

To turn from the various national idiosyncrasies mentioned above to a comprehensive picture of postwar Europe west of the Iron Curtain, all the nations moved steadily toward increased economic unity from the time of the Marshall Plan to the early 1990s. The years from 1950 to 1973 (when the first sudden rise in oil prices took place) were years of sustained economic growth all over the world, but the greatest benefits to the general population occurred in the United States and non-Soviet Europe. After 1973, energy costs—and also a growing realization of the ecological damage being done by worldwide economic growth—reduced both the rate of growth and the general optimism concerning the long-term future. But the main features of the welfare state were not seriously questioned until the collapse of the Soviet Union in 1991. (Since then, the failure of authoritarian socialism has been increasingly used as an argument to discredit the Western forms of state responsibility for the minimum security of all citizens.)

Ideologies aside, however, the indisputable fact is that the postwar prosperity of Western Europe and Scandinavia as a whole has been based on high rates of both public and private investment. First came the rebuilding of the infrastructure and the provision of housing to a steadily growing population. Next came continual investment in new electronic and chemical technologies, the development of national-health services, and the mass production and sale of automobiles, television sets, washing machines, refrigerators, and all kinds of labor-saving devices. There was also the constant defense umbrella of American power as exercised through NATO, making it unnecessary for the European states to support large military budgets unless they chose (as in the case of Britain and France) to maintain strong national military forces.

Unemployment ran at average of 3 percent during the fifties and at only 1.5 percent in the sixties, thereby giving labor an unprecedented degree of bargaining power. High employment enabled Germany by 1960 to absorb the millions of *Volksdeutsche* (ethnic Germans) who had been expelled from Eastern Europe. During the sixties, some five to seven percent of the total work force of northern Europe consisted of immigrants from the Mediterranean countries. These people lived in poorer housing than the local citizens and suffered many forms of ethnic prejudice; but they also learned the use of modern machinery, were able to send part of their wages to their relatives, had their children educated in the public schools of the host country, and received basic health services.

In the development of the Common Market, it is necessary to recognize simultaneously the growth of ethnic tensions in working-class neighborhoods and the extension of unprecedented opportunities even to the poorer classes and historically poorer peoples. As the distinguished Swiss writer Max Frisch once stated succinctly: "We asked for workers, but human beings came." And, indeed, although Turks, Greeks, Spaniards, Portuguese, and North Africans all suffered from the prejudices and stereotypes of northern Europe, they also found life better in those countries than at home. They were not deported slave labor as in World War II, but voluntary immigrants. Many became the proprietors of small retail businesses in the countries to which they had emigrated, and many others used their savings to buy homes and businesses in their countries of origin.[4]

Thus, in the forty years following the Second World War the European peoples (along with those of the United States and the British dominions) acquired a higher standard of living than they had enjoyed in any past era. The benefits arrived earlier, and in greater measure, to the northern countries, but by the late 1980s, the Spanish, Portuguese, and Greek peoples were sharing in this rising standard of living and also had achieved a level of political liberty comparable to the historically democratic nations.

People who had lived in hovels, without electricity, and drew their water manually from wells were now living in apartment blocks with running water, electricity, and gas. People who had never been able to afford doctors or dentists were now receiving minimal health care—perhaps waiting hours for a visit or months for nonemergency surgery, but still receiving a basic level of care that had never been available to them in the past. They also had a few weeks of annual paid vacation, and many who had never left home before World War II were flying to Mediterranean beaches in July and August. People who had always either walked or propelled a bicycle with their own leg power were now riding motorcycles and driving their own small automobiles. In villages where people had had to use the same homely utensils for generations, there were now brightly colored plastic buckets, kitchen and tableware, and curtains, as well as an abundance of inexpensive plastic toys to keep the infants busy under the supervision of their grandmothers while their mothers worked in stores or local factories. And those mothers were wearing a variety of patterns, colors, and fabrics that in the past had been the privilege only of a handful of village gentry.

Free public education was now available up to the age of fourteen or sixteen, in accordance with the legislation of the individual nations, and while the quality varied considerably from country to country and even from district to district, total illiteracy was virtually eliminated. University systems were greatly expanded as higher education became a normal ambition for modest families and a necessity for well-paid employment in both the industrial and the service economies. The rapid expansion caused very real problems of "massification" and shortages of laboratory equipment and libraries. But such problems can be solved with time, and it is important to recognize that massification has become a problem precisely because so much larger a proportion of the population reaches the university now than in any past epoch.

Athletics has become a major leisure-time activity for all classes of the population. Every school (and many businesses and factories) have its own soccer and basketball teams. Tennis, golf, sailing, and mountain-climbing—once activities only of the wealthy—are becoming increasingly available in municipal parks and through organized excursions. Light-weight sleeping bags, tents, butane stoves, and canoes have led to a great increase in hiking and camping and incidentally, to both a greater appreciation of the natural environment and a need to protect that environment against thoughtless damage. Similarly, although the movies have of course been a mass entertainment since the first half of the century, the years since 1950 have witnessed an explosion of new technologies. All but the poorest families have had televisions in their homes since the 1960s and videocassette equipment since the 1980s. Long-playing records, cassette tapes, and CDs—along with increasingly high-quality equipment both for recording music and reproducing it—have enormously increased the audiences for all types of music, classic and popular alike, listened to at home, at work, in bars and restaurants, and in auditoriums and athletic stadiums, over very high-fidelity speakers.

Another important qualitative factor in the development of the democratic welfare states has been the admirable human qualities of a number of their main leaders. The mass sufferings and massive crimes committed under the fascist, Nazi, and Stalinist regimes, and during the Second World War, created an ethical sensibility which has not normally been a significant factor in European (or any other) politics. In peaceful times Konrad Adenauer would probably have been quite satisfied to retire after a few terms as mayor of Cologne. Two world wars made him the principal conservative German architect of Franco-German reconciliation. In peaceful times, Charles DeGaulle would doubtless have had a brilliant technical career as a theorist of tank warfare. The defeat of France in 1940 made him the spokesman of a nation which, though physically conquered, refused to accept Hitler's European order. Later, for all his personal haughtiness, DeGaulle understood the need to withdraw from Algeria, as well as the need for both a presidential–type republican constitution and a reconciliation with Germany. What these two men might have been like if they had been servants of the Hohenzollern or Bonaparte dynasties is anyone's guess (or nightmare). But in Europe after the Hitler era, they contributed mightily—by personal example and by policy—to the recovery of civilized political standards.

And there were other distinguished statesmen (and at least one stateswoman) who presided over the governments of Europe in the postwar era: the British prime ministers Clement Attlee, Harold Macmillan, and James Harold Wilson; the Swedish prime ministers Tage Erlander and Olaf Palme; the Germans Willy Brandt, Helmut Schmidt, and Helmut Kohl; the Austrians Bruno Kreisky and Franz Vranitsky; the Portuguese prime minister (and later president) Mario Soares; the Spaniards Adolfo Suarez and Felipe González; the Norwegian (female) prime minister Gro Harlem Brant; and the Italian president Sandro Pertini. The importance of the examples set by such public figures—even in democratic societies where the notion of one's "betters" has disappeared—should not be underestimated. Despite major differences in policy and personal style, these leaders were all united in their attachment to democracy, their commitment to civilian supremacy in government, their modesty of appetite and ambition, their scrupulous personal integrity, and their intelligent concern for the needs of all people without regard to ideological, national, or racial criteria. One final development, little mentioned but also very important in creating a new internationalist atmosphere, was the pairings of "sister cities" under their auspices, as well as the various fraternal ceremonies and student and professional exchanges growing out of that movement.[5]

Despite the enormous success and prosperity of these welfare states, however, all of them—whether their economies were modeled upon the Keynesianism of Britain and Sweden, the social market of Germany, of the Colbertism of France— ran into financial difficulties following the first wave of development and prosperity in the 1950s and 1960s. Those difficulties, moreover, applied to all the Western countries. Tax receipts were increasingly unable to cover the costs of pensions and health services. The market for large machines and household goods became saturated, and at the same time labor-saving devices began replacing workers in large numbers. Increased industrial activity was polluting the air and water that everyone had long taken for granted, and the necessary measures to control that pollution added to the overall costs of production and distribution.

Agricultural costs also added to the growing annual deficits. In all the highly industrialized countries (including, notably, the United States and Japan), governments have found it necessary to subsidize their national agriculture. Early in the twentieth century, farming still occupied about half the population; but by 1990, mechanized agriculture was producing record crops while only 5 to 10 percent of the population still lived on farms. Aesthetic and moral questions were involved as well. Wherever the soil was arable and rainfall sufficient, European fields and forests had been carefully maintained for their beauty as well as their productivity. Hunting rabbits or partridges on the weekends, hiking in forests where the underbrush had been carefully cleared, and gathering edible mushrooms and strawberries were not unpopular pastimes, and governments could not permit the landscape to be neglected simply because salaries were higher in the city. This is why all governments have continued to subsidize their agriculture, exempting it from the effects of uncontrolled market forces.

For all these reasons, therefore, at the end of the period covered in this book (c. 1990) the welfare states are producing deficits which they cannot allow to accumulate indefinitely. As in the case of university massification, much of the problem in fact reflects the great success of the welfare state. Pension plans are in trouble because normal life expectancy has increased much more rapidly than anyone could have predicted in 1945. Problems of psychological stress and depression, high blood pressure, and various allergies and chemical imbalances are increasingly treated with a sophisticated array of synthetic drugs; but these drugs are the result of expensive research and experiment and are therefore priced accordingly. Surgery is also able to treat many organs and extremely delicate nerve and brain areas that were formerly untouchable; but once again, the equipment and procedures are very expensive.

Welfare-state economics has also been harmed by three other problems which indeed were partly anticipated but could not have been quantified in advance of the facts. One is that people are having fewer children, so that the number of active wage-earners contributing to pension funds in the future will be much smaller than the number of people living to a ripe old age and receiving those pensions. The second is the rapid industrialization of China and Southeast Asia, which means that many products which used to be manufactured only in the West and Japan are now being manufactured in countries with much lower labor costs and much less social protection. And the third is the growth of automatization, which drastically and permanently reduces the number of industrial jobs, and the computerization of paperwork, which drastically reduces the number of white-collar jobs.

Finally, there has been an important psychological factor aggravating the sense of crisis concerning the welfare state. The competition of newly industrialized Asia and the structural unemployment due to automatization and computerization has coincided with the collapse of the one major noncapitalist power, the Soviet Union. The Western victory in the Cold War and the repudiation of communism by all the populations living under Soviet domination until 1989 has directly discredited the authoritarian versions of Marxism, and it has indirectly but powerfully tended to discredit (by association) democratic socialism and social democracy as well. The West's economic and political victory, moreover, has also naturally increased the prestige of monetarism and the demand for complete deregulation of capitalism worldwide.

It will most certainly require great changes of attitude, much reallocation of resources, and some fairly large-scale changes in methods of public financing to solve the financial problems of the existing welfare state. I return in the final chapter to a consideration of what those changes might be. But simply in terms of factual history, it is important to note that, between 1950 and 1990, the now-threatened welfare state offered the best conditions of life for the highest proportion of people, and broke through more barriers of class and social rigidity, than has any other society created by human ingenuity up to now. Such a historic achievement is not something to be relinquished casually because of red ink.

ENDNOTES

1. Nikolai Tolstoy, "Victims of Yalta—an Inquiry?" *Encounter*, June 1980, based on documents released after thirty years by the Foreign Office concerning the repatriation of 2,000,000 Soviet and Polish prisoners and their families.

2. For the complexities of Italian politics and economics, I have depended heavily on Paul Ginsberg, *A History of Contemporary Italy* (Penguin Books, 1990); and Linda Weiss, *Creating Capitalism* (Basil Blackwell, 1988), which deals primarily (though not exclusively) with the state role in the Italian postwar economy.

3. John Fitzmaurice, *Austrian Politics and Society Today* (New York: Macmillan Press, 1991).

4. Ray C. Rist, "Guest Workers in Germany and France," *Daedalus*, spring 1979, 95–108.

5. Edwina S. Campbell, "The Ideals and Origins of the Franco-German Sister Cities Movement," *History of European Ideas*, v. 8, 1987, pp. 77–95.

11

The Soviet Empire, 1940–1991

*B*ecause communism has been the most controversial ideology of the twentieth century, all the terms used in reference to Soviet history inevitably carry strong political connotations. For reasons given below, I think of "Soviet Union" as the least inaccurate name for the years 1917–1939, and I prefer "Soviet empire" for the years after 1940.

As a result of revolution and civil war (1917–1920), the Communist Party had established its rule over the great bulk of the European and Asian territories that constituted the Romanov empire. In both the economic and political spheres, Great Russians were the principal administrators of the territory inherited from the tsars and reconquered in the civil war. Ukrainians, Georgians, and Armenians were strongly represented in the Moscow government, but the Soviet regime—like that of the tsars—claimed legitimacy as a federation of many nationalities, religions, and linguistic cultures. Since Soviet power was exercised only in lands which had been part of the tsarist empire, and since the early Soviet regime was internationalist and non-racist in ideology, it is reasonable to use the term "Soviet Union" for the years from 1917 to 1939.

But in 1940, Stalin's government annexed the Baltic republics. During the later stages of World War II, the Red Army occupied Poland, Czechoslovakia, Hungary, Romania, and Bulgaria. According to the Yalta agreements of February 1945, these countries were to choose their own governments through free elections with all "antifascist" parties having the right to participate. But then, between 1945 and 1950, Stalin did to the East European governments and communist parties what he had done to the Soviet government and Communist Party between 1936 and 1939.

The brutal political and military takeover of these countries amply justifies the term "Soviet empire" for the present chapter. It is also one of the great ironies of Soviet history that a regime which was supposed to be fulfilling objective laws of history was far more subject to the control of individual rulers than were any of the capitalist democracies, or even the fascist and right-wing dictatorships of the interwar period (with the exception of Hitler's dictatorship). During the revolution and civil war, Lenin's word had been law. After 1928, the same thing was virtually true for Stalin—and became explicitly, murderously true from the time of the Great Purge of 1936–1939.

For their massive character (and the paranoid reasoning behind them), Stalin's purges are unique in the history of civilized nations. Prior to this time, Roman emperors had exiled or killed numerous individual rivals; polygamous dynastic rulers had in many instances killed off the potential male rivals within their own families; while in the civil wars of late medieval England and France, members of royal families and their principal supporters were often executed in the name of national unity. In the twentieth century, Mussolini fed castor oil to selected members of the opposition, and Hitler purged several hundred followers of whose personal loyalty he was uncertain. But Stalin's methods were both quantitatively and qualitatively unique. He was not, like Hitler or Mussolini, the charismatic leader of a mass movement; rather, he was the successor of a charismatic leader, Lenin, who in the last months of his mortal illness was looking for ways to prevent the future domination of the party by Stalin. The latter was aware, of course, of Lenin's doubts. He had also long resented the roles of the Europeanized intellectuals who had shared Lenin's Austrian and Swiss exiles and on whom Lenin relied for the principal administrative posts in the first years of the revolution.

In his rise to supreme power during the decade from 1924 to 1934, Stalin pursued twin aims. One was the normal political tactic of naming his own protegés as the secretaries of local party branches throughout the Soviet Union, a process which enabled him to command a voting majority in party congresses. The other was to discredit the entire generation of Lenin's collaborators—and eventually, to destroy them physically. Most of these men either despised or completely underestimated the importance of organizational and administrative tasks. Their prestige was based on their closeness to Lenin and on the ability with which they carried out the tasks he assigned to them; but after Lenin's death, that prestige rapidly lost its value.

By the late 1920s, Stalin's control of the party apparatus meant that his policies won the inner-party debates over the ending of the NEP and the adoption of the first five-year plan. He was able to exile Trotsky, the creator of the victorious Red Army, and repeatedly to humiliate such prestigious revolutionaries as Zinoviev, Kamenev, and Bukharin. They were not only outvoted but obliged to confess their mistakes, acknowledge the wisdom of "the party" (that is, of Stalin), and recant in order to be appointed to posts of lesser authority. Slowly but steadily, Stalin identified himself personally with the mantle of Lenin and with the only permissible interpretations of historical materialism, the history of the revolution and civil war, and the correct methods and tempos by which to achieve industrialization and collectivize agriculture.

No one can say exactly when Stalin decided not merely to humiliate and demote but to kill the older generation of Bolshevik leaders. What can be stated with certainty is that the assassination in December 1934 of Sergei Kirov, the party boss in Leningrad (and one of the few Bolshevik leaders to enjoy genuine popularity with those in whose name he ruled), gave Stalin the opportunity for legalized murder on a grand scale. It is still an open question whether Stalin was personally frightened by the Kirov murder or whether he actually arranged it as a way to rid himself of a potential rival. But the investigation of Kirov's murder led to hundreds of deportations and executions.

Thus far, of course, Stalin's tactics are not exactly unfamiliar to students of history; after all, had not Lenin done the same in 1921 after the attempt on his own life? The unique Stalinist touch was not the death penalties but rather the elaborately staged show trials of 1936–38, in which prominent defendants reviled themselves and confessed to a variety of charges, including espionage on behalf of Nazi Germany and Japan, plots to assassinate Stalin, sabotaging mine machinery and other industrial facilities, and deliberately placing factories so that their poisonous fumes would be blown toward the housing compounds of the workers. The defendants in these successive trials were divided into "left Trotskyite" vermin and "rightist Bukharinite" saboteurs. In the overcrowded prisons, hundreds of potential defendants rewrote their confessions in 1937 to bring those confessions into line with the shift from Trotskyism to Bukharinism as the main ideological sin. And the trials would invariably end with paeans of praise to the wisdom of Stalin and a readiness by the defendants to accept the verdict of "History," which now replaced the inquisitions of the sixteenth and seventeenth centuries as the great arbiter of "Truth" and "Justice."

In this incredible atmosphere of false confessions, it is not difficult to understand why thousands of small fry would sign anything in the hopes of slightly better prison conditions or simply ensuring their survival. It is not as easy to explain why revolutionary leaders who had suffered in tsarist prisons would not only sign false confessions, but repeat them word for word in court and glorify their murderer into the bargain. Some were perhaps promised mercy for their families in return for collaboration in the show trials. Others may have felt remorse for real or imagined revolutionary violence in which they had taken part and later regretted. Still others may have been destroyed morally by the memory of having opposed some Stalinist policy which they now acknowledged to have been necessary, however crude or cruel. These were men, moreover, who had staked their whole lives on the cause of revolution. They had approved exile and death for counter-revolutionaries. Under the pressure of unending police questioning and ideological sermons, many broke down and considered themselves in some sense guilty; what was the difference, really, between having *wished* that Stalin would fail and having plotted to murder him? The trials thus offered them a last opportunity to serve the party by their confessions and their deaths.

On the other hand, during World War II—known in the Soviet press as the

"Great Patriotic War" and as the "War to Defend the Fatherland" (not communism)—Stalin seemed more flexible. He not only appealed to the historic sentiments of the Russian people but also allowed the Orthodox Church to function publicly. Poets and novelists felt safe to express their personal sentiments, especially as the sentiments of patriotism and antifascism were indeed a common denominator for the rulers and the ruled. Dmitri Shostakovich's seventh symphony, dedicated to the besieged city of Leningrad, could be performed all over the world as a great antifascist work of Soviet art. No one could know at the time that, for the composer, it was a symphony that mourned the fate of his native city, devastated *twice* over—first by Stalin's prewar purges and then by the Nazi siege.[1]

Despite this wartime "thaw," however, in 1945 Stalin immediately restored the strictest ideological and police control. Demobilized soldiers could be sent off to prison labor camps—the "Gulag"—for nothing more than having made admiring remarks about the things they had seen in "liberated" Europe. Stalin's cultural watchdog, Andrei Zdhanov, warned writers to avoid the sins of "rootless cosmopolitanism" (an all-encompassing term that included Jewish origins and an attachment to such Western intellectual currents as surrealism and psychoanalysis). Zdhanov was not at all amused when the famous satirist Soshchenko published the story of a monkey who escaped from the Leningrad zoo. At first, the happy simian was delighted with the chance to inspect all aspects of Soviet life, but after a while he found living conditions so bad that he voluntarily returned to the zoo. Zdhanov also rebuked the leading composers Prokofiev and Shostakovich for producing unmelodious music that could not be whistled by Soviet citizens, and he ridiculed the poetess Akhmatova for writing purely subjective verses which were utterly silent on the triumphs of Soviet socialism. None of these artists was imprisoned, but they all had to wait until several years after Stalin's death before they felt free to write or compose as they truly wished.

Then in 1948, Zdhanov—whose political base was also the unreliable (from Stalin's point of view) city of Leningrad—died unexpectedly. The aging dictator promptly conducted a massive blood purge of the Leningrad district, the details of which are still not known and which was referred to in the brief press notices simply as "the Leningrad case." Then, in late 1952, Stalin announced the discovery of a mysterious "doctors' plot" in the Kremlin—an alleged conspiracy by physicians, most of whom turned out to have recognizably Jewish names.

On March 4, 1953, while the doctors' confessions for a new show trial were still being prepared in a central Moscow prison, Stalin died. He was seventy-three years of age and had been suffering common forms of arteriosclerosis for some years, so his death was, in all likelihood, perfectly natural. But it may have been slightly hastened by the fact that the colleagues who found him lying partially paralyzed on the floor were afraid to touch him lest they later be accused of having murdered the Father of Soviet Peoples.

But to return to 1945, Stalin was determined not only to restore Stalinist ortho-doxy in the Soviet Union but also to impose it upon the occupied states of Central and Eastern Europe. All of these countries—except for the western (Czech) portion of Czechoslovakia—were predominantly peasant societies. They had small com-munist parties and large peasant parties, and the latter parties won the largest per-centage of votes in the first postwar elections with programs that emphasized nationalism, the defense of peasant property, and the local forms of Christianity.

The leaders of these peasant parties were permitted to form governments, but the ministers of interior and defense were always communists. Within three years, the several important peasant leaders were forced into exile by means of various false accusations of "corruption," beatings of family members, and other such stron-garm tactics. As for the communist parties themselves, Stalin divided their leader-ship according to whether the individuals had spent the war years in Moscow or in the West, whether they had served in the International Brigades during the Spanish Civil War, and whether they were unconditionally loyal to him or suspect of various "bourgeois deviations." In general (though not without exceptions), Stalin promoted those who had spent the war in Moscow and had not been contaminated either by the non-Stalinist Left in Spain or by wartime experience in Western Europe or Eng-land. Between 1948 and 1952, he repeated in Eastern Europe the style of purges he had conducted in Moscow before the war. In Romania, Bulgaria, Hungary, and Czechoslovakia, the secret police obtained "confessions" of sabotage, plots to assas-sinate the leaders chosen by Stalin, and so on. The defendants confessed their sins and were promptly hanged. The one exception was Poland, where the presumably deviant nationalist Gomulka was imprisoned but not executed.

Turning to the consideration of Soviet postwar history as a whole—that is, the history of the "Soviet empire"—we may divide it into four periods, each associated with the supreme leader who placed his personal seal on the direction and style of development. From 1945 to 1953, Stalin restored the ideological, paranoid, purge-ridden police state he had created before the Great Patriotic War. The first thing his heirs did upon his death was to release the supposedly treasonous doctors and drop all charges against them. They had probably agreed before Stalin's demise to reduce the power of the secret police, and a few months later they arrested and shot Lavrenti Beria, Stalin's last minister of the interior, who had been the executive agent of all purges since 1939 (though, ironically, not the creator of the "doctors' plot," of which he had been slated to become one of the victims!).

The atmosphere of massive terror was lifted by Nikita Khrushchev, the former Ukrainian miner and party boss who dominated the regime from 1955 to 1964. In 1956, in a carefully leaked "secret" speech to the party congress, Khrushchev revealed many (but by no means all) of the crimes of the late J. V. Stalin. He also greatly reduced the number and population of the gulag work camps. In 1957, he demoted several of his inner-party rivals but, in sharp contrast to Stalin, he did not shoot them, rather assigning them to minor administrative and diplomatic posts. This in itself was a momentous change: Without in any sense democratizing the regime, Khrushchev showed that it was possible to adjudicate political conflicts without killing people. Moreover, when the party majority under the leadership of Leonid Brezhnev decided to remove Khrushchev from office in 1964, they adopted his bloodless tactics. The old gentleman became an official "nonperson," but was permitted to live his last years in peace (and on a generous pension).

After Khrushchev's ouster, Brezhnev dominated the regime from 1964 until his lingering death in 1982. The Khrushchev era had been replete with various economic and administrative experiments—some successful, some not. The Brezhnev era emphasized stability and slowly declined into a stagnant gerontocracy. During the last three years of his reign, Brezhnev had to be physically assisted by two strapping bodyguards every time he sat down, stood up, descended a staircase, or entered an automobile. His condition aptly foreshadowed the last years of the communist regime. After another three-year interim, the relatively young and vigorous Mikhail Gorbachev was chosen as First Secretary of the Communist Party. Between 1985 and 1991, Gorbachev made worthy but totally unsuccessful efforts to modernize and democratize the collapsing empire.

It is worth remembering, however, that the disappearance of the Soviet regime was by no means a foregone conclusion; in fact, it took most Western political commentators (and diplomatic and espionage services) by surprise. Until at least the mid-1960s, the Soviet Union remained a model for Third World countries seeking to overcome the heritage of European and Japanese colonialism. In Western Europe and the Americas, many respected historians and social scientists thought they saw a certain convergence occurring between the democratic and capitalist welfare states and a highly industrialized communist power which seemed to offer basic security, education, and medical care to a population that no longer needed to be visibly dragooned by secret police or aggressive party cadres. It is therefore important both to assess the successes of the post-1945 regime and to inquire into the causes of its ultimate, spectacular failure.

Common to all the successive Soviet governments until the last years of Gorbachev was a centrally planned command economy, in which economic decisions were made on a political basis and market relationships played virtually no role. At no time did Soviet officials question the correctness of their traditional interpretation of historical materialism; at no time did they question the dominant role of a single political party and the celebration of "elections" with only a single slate of candidates. At no time, moreover, did they question the right of Moscow to direct the foreign and military affairs of the empire. From 1945 on, the Soviet leadership dictated the economic planning and foreign trade of the East European satellite nations. They did not hesitate to threaten Poland in 1956 and 1981 when it appeared that government would adopt policies of which the Soviets disapproved. They did not hesitate to invade Hungary in 1956, Czechoslovakia in 1968, and Afghanistan in 1979 in order to insure that "friendly" governments controlled those countries.

In the late 1940s, heavy industry, oil and other mineral extractions, cement production, and the rebuilt railroad and electricity networks all recovered to productive levels above those of 1940. East German coal and chemicals, Polish coal and a newly expanded steel industry, Czech heavy industry, and Romanian oil also contributed significantly to Soviet recovery. Women—one-third of whom would never have an opportunity to marry—performed almost as much hard physical labor as did men. Some 10 to 20 percent of the surviving males spent several months or years in the gulag on their way home from the victory over Nazi Germany and contributed their forced labor to the postwar recovery. The triumphs of Soviet production occurred in the same aspects of the economy (mainly heavy industry and mining) in which the prewar five-year plans had been most successful. At the same time, Soviet scientists—in a crash program administered by the ruthless Beria and employing a combination of free and prisoner scientists and labor—produced an atom bomb in 1949.

As in the 1930s, however, consumer goods lagged in both quantity and quality, and agricultural production remained below the levels of 1940 until after Stalin's death. Before the war, Stalin had mollified the disaffected peasants by permitting them to use 1 to 2 percent of the collectivized land as private family plots. These plots, not surprisingly, had immediately become far more productive than the collectively cultivated hectares. In the face of dire war needs after the Nazi invasion, Stalin permitted a dozen or so peasants (friends or members of the same extended family) to assume responsibility for a specific portion of the Kolkhoz lands. This was the so-called link system, and it brought a much higher proportion of the total land under the careful management of peasants who had something to gain for their hard work. Provided they met their assigned quantities of grain or dairy produce, the peasants could raise and sell whatever they wished on the open market. Under these conditions, Soviet agriculture became far more productive, but as in the 1920s with the New Economic Policy, the communist government was loath to let the peasants become "rich." After the war, the party not only abolished the link system but consolidated many small and middle-size collective farms into state farms on which the peasants were paid hourly wages, as in any industrial establishment. Productivity lagged on the collective hectares and soared on the tiny private plots which were not abolished—so much so that, as of 1950, half the vegetables, two-thirds of the milk and meat, and almost 90 percent of Soviet eggs were produced on the 1 to 2 percent of the land which the peasants could cultivate on their own.[2]

During these same years, the East European economies were forcibly integrated with the Soviet economy. The Soviets set production targets for each nation's industry and agriculture; they were careful to go slow on agricultural collectivization and offered social-security pensions to industrial workers who met the norms and maintained discipline on their jobs. But these decisions were made on the basis of Soviet interests, as the Soviet leaders defined those interests. Indeed, from 1955 on, Nikita Khrushchev and his colleagues—after lifting the worst of the Stalinist terror, were anxious to improve the living standards of the long-suffering Soviet peoples. They improved the pension system for war widows and the disabled, and revised work norms and piece wage rates at least slightly in favor of the less specialized workers and of the many single-parent families. They also increased the number of clinics and child-care centers staffed mostly by well-trained, morally committed women doctors and teachers. And they doubled the amount of available housing between 1955 and 1964.

Khrushchev was an earthy, ebullient personality, the only Soviet leader whose public behavior showed the kind of voluntarist enthusiasm that had characterized the first generation of believing communists. He urged the predominantly skeptical peasants to volunteer a higher proportion of their time to work the collective lands with the same efficiency that they devoted to their family plots. He called for improved public transport and pooh-poohed the idea of private automobiles as an individualistic Western fetish unworthy of a socialist society. Khrushchev also shook up the party cadres and hectored the local apparatchiks to earn their salaries by giving a better example of socialist commitment. He called for more local initiative in both factories and farms. However, the Stalinist era had taught administrators not to take responsibility for any innovations, and Khrushchev was often frustrated by some of the forms taken by "plan fulfillment." For example, since the plan for sheet metal was given in tons, the factories produced sheets whose sheer tonnage fulfilled the requirement more easily but which were far too heavy to be used properly. Quantitative norms also led to the production of oversize furniture, ridiculously heavy lamps and chandeliers, too many large-size shoes and boots, and so forth.

As always, agriculture lagged behind industry and mining. As of 1955, grain production was still below 1940 levels and livestock herds were smaller than those of 1928 (the end of the NEP) and 1916 (the last year before the revolution). Khrushchev called for increased production of chemical fertilizers and machinery and gave the collective farms greater control of their tractors and harvesters. But the centerpiece of his policy was the opening of millions of hectares of "virgin lands" in Kazakhstan. In this campaign, Khrushchev appealed to the idealism of students, thousands of whom went out to help in the first ploughings, seedings, and harvests. The 1955–56 harvests were a resounding success, but in the course of the following decade a combination of drought and wind storms virtually ruined a high proportion of this new grain belt.

In October 1957, the Soviet Union achieved perhaps the most prestigious scientific accomplishment of its seven-decade history—the launching of "Sputnik," the first man-made satellite, which inaugurated the era of space exploration. Taken together with the opening of the virgin lands and the substantial recent improvement in standards of living, these were probably the proudest and happiest moments in

Soviet history. Two years later, Khrushchev, who had expressed admiration for American agricultural productivity—visited the United States. Among his other whirlwind activities, he toured an Iowa maize farm, inspected prize beef cattle, and (along with his appreciative remarks) cheerfully announced that, within a few decades, "We will bury you." By this earthy metaphor he did not mean another world war but rather that Soviet industry and agriculture would "overtake and surpass" (as Stalin used to put it in his economic pronouncements) the capitalist West.

At home again, Khrushchev preached the planting of maize on the virgin lands without seeming to realize that the climate involved was much colder and drier than that of Iowa. In general, one of the great failures of the Soviet economy was its lack of attention to environmental problems. Not that the record of the West has been ideal in this matter, but there has been a significant difference of scale in the mistreatment of the planet. From the beginning of the revolution, the Bolsheviks liked to think in gigantic terms about the conquest of nature. One of Stalin's strongest arguments for the decision to establish socialism in one country rather than concentrate on "world revolution" was the immensity and natural wealth of the Soviet Union—one-seventh of the land surface of the planet Earth and stretching across eleven time zones from Brest-Litovsk to Vladivostok.

Even more than the Americans in the late nineteenth century, the Soviets literally raped their land. Thousands of square miles were chemically poisoned by the experiments leading to the creation of the atom bomb. Thousands more were exploited with brief success in the virgin-lands campaign, only to be turned into desert within a decade. The digging of canals and the redirecting of rivers was intended to improve the economic conditions of the immense central Asian and Siberian territories, as well as to improve the moral fiber of the prisoners doing the main labor. But in many cases, the unintended results were disastrous to the ecology of the areas and to the health of the people living in them. Since many of these problems were never publicly acknowledged, it is impossible to quantify the losses.

Khrushchev's impulsiveness and his plebeian manners eventually led to his undoing. In 1960, he expressed his anger at the downing of an American spy plane over Russia by taking off his shoe and banging it on the desk while he spoke at a meeting of the United Nations General Assembly. A year later, he tried unsuccessfully to intimidate John F. Kennedy in his first meeting with the new American president, whom he took to be young and insecure. In 1962, he planned to establish ballistic missile bases in Cuba at the request of Fidel Castro and was forced to back down when Kennedy's administration indicated it would use force to prevent such an eventuality. In 1964, thanks to his swiftly accumulating agricultural problems and the lowered international prestige, Khrushchev was peacefully deposed. In the long historical perspective, he will probably be remembered gratefully by the Russian people as the leader who put an end to the the terrible tradition of government by paranoia and blood purge.

The next supreme leader, Leonid Brezhnev, inherited what he and his colleagues considered to be a functioning multinational socialist society, second only to the United States in military, diplomatic, and industrial power. Brezhnev had the instincts of a big-city political boss such as those who had run the machine politics of New York, Boston, and Chicago in the first half of the twentieth century. He remembered names, threatened people when he felt it necessary, and could deal with underworld types, though he preferred to govern through stable, civilian, reasonably able cadres. Under his rule, the nomenklatura—the millions of party functionaries—came into its own. The members of this bureaucratic class had been recruited and promoted by Stalin (with the accompanying risk of purge) and criticized and arbitrarily moved around by Khrushchev; but under Brezhnev, they enjoyed security of employment as long as they obeyed orders and maintained appearances. The social structure of the Soviet Union was also stabilized under Brezhnev. Special housing facilities, schools, and stores selling imported consumer goods were available for the upper class of functionaries. All urban dwellers had internal passports and residence permits and, according to the data in those papers, citizens knew what sort of housing they could claim and which cities they could move to (Moscow being the most coveted and most difficult destination). The collective farm peasants were the one category who had no passports: As in tsarist times, they could leave the village only if they had special industrial skills to offer or had received scholarships for higher education.

In the 1960s, the regime was confident enough of its power, and was earning enough foreign exchange from its mineral and lumber exports, that it could improve the supply of consumer goods by making contracts with foreign industries. FIAT established an automobile factory in southern Russia at Stavrapol (conveniently close to the Black Sea resorts frequented by the *nomenklatura*). The Brezhnev government also bought mining, chemical, and food-processing machinery from the West. The Soviet peoples could now relieve the winter diet of potatoes and cabbage with occasional cans of vegetables and fruits. It became customary for traveling diplomats, scientists, and academicians to bring back Japanese cameras, French perfumes, name-brand American jeans, German hi-fis and automobiles, and Scotch whiskey for their families and friends. There was also a thriving underground economy in spare parts and repair services for all types of vehicles and domestic appliances.

At the same time, it was clear by the late sixties that economic growth was slowing—and by the end of the Brezhnev era, it had fallen to practically zero. It was also clear that, except in military technology, the relation of the Soviet economy to that of the West was virtually the same as that of underdeveloped supplier nations to the capitalist powers. Neither the Soviets nor their satellites had finished products to sell in Japanese or Western markets; they earned foreign exchange for their lumber, minerals, caviar, and sturgeon. The oil crisis of 1973 enabled them for approximately the following decade to earn bonanza prices for their oil and natural-gas exports. But they had to spend precious foreign exchange on the import of grain, and neither in agriculture nor in civilian industry did productivity and quality improve as they had—slightly—during the first two decades of the postwar era.

At least three important causes for the stagnation of the Soviet economy can be named. One was the general unsolved problem of motivation in the peacetime economy: Why work hard when individual initiative reaps no rewards and there are no quality goods to be bought with one's savings? Another was the fact that, even more than in the United States, a disproportionate share of the gross national product went into arms production, both to maintain superpower status and to compete with the US and Europe in the sale of arms to underdeveloped states—(most of which tried to maintain overdeveloped military establishments). Indeed, throughout the 1970s and 1980s, between 30 and 40 percent of the industrial working class was employed in military production.

But the most important single factor affecting the Soviet economy was the government's fear of the computer. Soviet mathematicians, physicists, and engineers were every bit as capable as their Western colleagues and had stayed fully abreast of developments in the computer revolution beyond their borders; the Soviets themselves, moreover, used computers in their military industry and in calculating the production quotas of the command economy. But their authoritarian, highly centralized state did not dare to permit the kind of freewheeling amateur experimentation that constantly produced novelties and improvements in Western computer frames and software. Creative science and technology require personal liberty in investigation, especially freedom from politically or metaphysically motivated prohibitions. Such research is also greatly aided by the right to seek patents, to establish one's own enterprise and market one's own products. In Russia, a handful of privileged physicists could work in relative freedom, but the vast majority of applied scientists were required simply to follow orders, to apply known and officially approved scientific formulae. "Hackers" of the Western variety were rare and likely to be treated as subversives. For this reason, even if there had been less emphasis on military production, the Soviets would still have fallen far behind the West and Japan.

In 1985, the gerontocracy itself chose the relatively young, very intelligent and energetic Mikhail Gorbachev as the new first secretary of the party. Gorbachev called for *glasnost* (candor in the publication of information) and *perestroika* (the restructuring of the economy and the political system). Like the "enlightened despots" of the eighteenth century, he meant well, and he imagined that a complex society could be rapidly and peacefully reformed from the top down. Gorbachev intended to square the circle by introducing some market elements, and some freedom of speech and publication, though without permitting Western-style political parties and free elections. At the same time, however, he was unsure of exactly how much de facto liberty and economic restructuring he could permit without destroying "existing socialism."

Gorbachev reduced the power of the *nomenklatura* so that it would not be able to sabotage his reforms. But he also gave vacillating, contradictory answers to key questions about flexibility in planning, allocations, prices, and local versus national powers of decision. He had neither personal knowledge of market economics nor trained personnel with which to replace the conservative bureaucrats. Like Khrushchev, he exhorted his countrymen to make voluntary efforts on behalf of a renewed "socialism," but few citizens of any class still believed in the system.

Several unanticipated situations destroyed whatever possibility Gorbachev might have had to reinvigorate the Soviet system. In 1979, the Soviets had invaded Afghanistan, thinking to rule it through a malleable satellite regime like those of the East European countries. But by the mid-1980s, they were hopelessly bogged down in a costly colonial war such as the Americans had recently lost in Vietnam. At the same time, the United States was proposing to build a space shield to protect itself against Soviet missiles. The so-called "Star Wars" program threatened to end the balance of terror which had existed between the Soviet empire and the US since the 1950s, and competing with the US in a new technological arms race would have crippled the Soviet economy. Then, in 1986, there occurred the worst single ecological disaster of the postwar era—the meltdown of the nuclear power plant at Chernobyl. Despite *glasnost*, Moscow did not publish the truth until forced to do so by Swedish and German reports of intense radioactivity that could not possibly be explained without acknowledging the accident. Taken together, Afghanistan, the "Star Wars" programs, Chernobyl, and the utter confusions of *perestroika* led to the rapid decomposition of the Soviet Union in the late 1980s. At the same time, Gorbachev was loath to use force to hold on to the restive East European satellites, so that the rapid decline of Soviet authority at home was accompanied by the breakup of the Soviet empire.

Nevertheless, no consideration of twentieth-century European civilization can be complete without discussing those aspects of Soviet life that were felt to be an improvement by a large proportion of the population. If the reader can put to one side for a moment the ingrained Western conceptions of individual liberty and constitutional guarantees, and if he or she can imagine the state of near serfdom in which 90 percent of the imperial population had lived before 1917, it should be possible to appreciate the relative successes of the Soviet Union.

Soviet citizens in the mid-twentieth century lived in a society which had pulled itself up by the bootstraps, a society which had industrialized itself without becoming politically or economically subordinated to the advanced capitalist powers. It was a society that had survived Stalin's purges and the onslaught of the Nazi military machine. And it had become a much more stable and less terror-ridden society after the death of the paranoid dictator. Stalin himself had not discouraged comparisons between his rule and that of Peter the Great or Ivan the Terrible, and many of his more sophisticated defenders (in both the Soviet Union and the West) referred to him variously as the Cromwell, the Robespierre, or the Napoleon of the Russian Revolution.

In some ways, the Soviet Union was a *socially* democratic society. The *nomenklatura* of the fifties and sixties were largely of worker and peasant origin. They had sought higher education and deservedly enjoyed the upward mobility of those who had worked hard to advance themselves and their class brothers and sisters. As for the purges of the 1930s which had given them their opportunity, it is an old saying (but a true one) that "you cannot make an omelette without breaking the eggs." Indeed, under Stalin's aegis—forgetting for a moment the brutal methods—literacy, basic medical care, and old-age pensions had become nearly universal. Approximately 140 different ethnic peoples had received alphabets and dictionaries for their hitherto spoken-only languages. The likes of Shostakovich and Kabalevsky delighted in their folk music; their dances and costumes were celebrated in Moscow and Leningrad theaters, and their traditional poetry was printed in large, inexpensive editions. Moreover, when party officials visited the villages and collective farms, they were no longer greeted by serfs who bowed obsequiously and dared not to look directly in the eyes of their superiors, but by locally chosen delegates shaking hands with the representatives of party authority.

Then, too, in the old days, women had worked without wages at the unquestioned orders of their husbands and employers. Now, 80 to 90 percent of women were salaried workers and practically the entire corps of school teachers and doctors were women. The male-dominated society got a bargain, in that women's wages still averaged only about 65 percent of those of men doing equivalent work. But Rome (as another old saying reminds us) was not built in a day; equalization of salaries was a legitimate and theoretically acknowledged aim in the Soviet Union, and not even in the capitalist nations were women paid as well as men. Meanwhile, quite a few Russian husbands stopped beating their wives and even began helping with the children.

Of course, the Soviets never permitted political parties or competing lists of candidates; but at the local level, at least, they made a continuous effort to involve all kinds of persons and viewpoints in day-to-day administration. Promotion into and then within the *nomenklatura* was a process of cooptation. Candidates were proposed and advanced by their hierarchical superiors, in a form of clientelism not too different from much local government in the West or in the governance of business corporations. It is sometimes forgotten that a relatively small proportion of Western governance actually results from political campaigns and multi-party elections. And the Soviet Union—in marked contrast with most of Asia, Africa, and Latin America—kept its government firmly in civilian hands. The great majority of the ruling Central Committee members were graduates of the administrative and party hierarchies. As of 1981, only 7 percent were military men and only 3 percent—reflecting a marked distrust of intellectuals—were scientists or artists.

From the 1960s onward, academic exchanges and scientific and cultural conferences of all kinds became more frequent, thus leading to increasing intellectual contact between the Soviet and Western elites. Sophisticated professionals from both worlds knew perfectly well that they were not being (and could not be) completely frank with one another. But the generally positive features outlined above made it possible for persons of goodwill on both sides to hypothesize an eventual convergence between Western social democracy and a scientifically and educationally progressive Soviet society. The Soviet government was indeed a dictatorship, but it was not a racist dictatorship proposing to subjugate the world as the Nazis had sought, and after Stalin's death the principal leaders had been the powerful chairmen of a collective leadership rather than arbitrary, murderous dictators.

Why, then, did this society—apparently strong, stable, and sanely governed after Stalin's demise—collapse three and one half decades later, despite the earnest efforts of Gorbachev and the goodwill of the conservative Western governments of the late 1980s? The principal answer, I believe, is the sheer accumulated weight of many practical errors due to dogmatic ideology, as well as the censorship which made it impossible to recognize and correct those errors in timely fashion.

No better single example of this phenomenon can be given than the sad fate of Soviet genetics between the mid-1920s and the mid-1960s. Charles Darwin had taught that biological evolution occurred as a series of minute, incremental changes in which species either succeeded or failed to adapt themselves to their environment in a wholly natural, undetermined unintentional process. Evolutionary theory was materialist and so it undermined all religious—specifically biblical—explanations of how life had appeared and developed on earth. Not surprisingly, the clearly materialist implications of Darwinism were thoroughly endorsed by Marx, Engels, and all later generations of Marxists, both in Soviet Russia and the West. But Darwin had not been able to explain the mechanisms of evolutionary change. There was a very real and unanswered question as to whether traits acquired by environmental adaptation in the lifetime of a given organism might be heritable, or only those which occurred as a result of accidental changes in the reproductive tissue—the chromosomes, or genes, whose exact mechanisms were still unknown. It was only after Darwin's death that Mendel's studies of inheritance patterns were rediscovered, and that T. H. Morgan's experiments proved that only genetic mutations were heritable.

Genetics, like Darwinian evolution, offered materialist explanations. However, Marxism was not only materialist but also "environmentalist" in its beliefs—that is to say, in the longstanding educational controversy over whether heredity or environment—"nature" or "nurture"—is more important in the formation of human beings, the Soviets stood squarely in the environmental camp. They shared with a high proportion of Western educators the belief that improved infant care and nutrition, improved instructional methods, and new social attitudes acquired through education would combine to produce an improved human race—more skillful, more cooperative, more peaceful than the existing species and motivated by concepts of the general welfare rather than by private profit.

In the 1920s, Soviet geneticists were divided between the "Mendelians" (those who believed only in the heritability of genetic mutations) and the "Lamarckians" (those who believed that acquired traits were also heritable, a hypothesis associated with the late-eighteenth-century French naturalist Jean Baptiste Lamarck). Obviously, the Lamarckian viewpoint was more congenial to environmentalists, and had an urgent appeal for those like the Soviet rulers who were anxious, in the late 1920s and ever after, to improve plant and animal food yields as rapidly as possible.

All scientific controversies include personal affections and antagonisms as well as scientific evidence (or alleged evidence). In 1928, when the first five-year plan was being launched, the young geneticist Trofim D. Lysenko criticized Western geneticists for paying "undue attention to hereditary factors as expressions of abstract mathematical probability laws." In general terms, the Mendelians were seen as older scientists of bourgeois origin, whereas Lysenko and his lieutenants belonged to the new generation of scientists coming from less privileged class backgrounds. Lysenko advocated what he called "vernalization" of seeds: prolonged exposure to cold and moisture before they were sown in the fields, a process which would allegedly strengthen them against the cold climate and potential drought. Lysenko claimed also that the new seed would have inherited the improved traits of its vernalized ancestors. Three of the features of Lysenkoism which appealed to Stalin were the anti-bourgeois-intellectual stance which he shared with the young scientist, the unambiguous claims for the inheritance of environmentally produced traits, and the notion that the peasants themselves could be actively involved in the vernalization of the seeds.

But Lysenko's procedures also meant that no real laboratory controls could be established by which to judge the results. Laboratory assistants and collectivized peasants exposed the seeds in trays or on the ground. They soaked them for varying lengths of time at varying temperatures, in water containing varying chemical substances in solution. They then planted the treated seeds, but without simultaneously planting untreated seeds as controls in the same fields.

If yields improved—as in some cases they did—the improvement might be due as much to the enthusiastic care given by the peasant experimenters to particular plantings, or to the new and intensive use of chemical fertilizers, as to the virtues of vernalization. Soviet statistics were always doctored in the interest of producing the desired results and, in the absence of laboratory controls, no one could judge whether the seeds of the next harvest had inherited the vernalized qualities of their predecessors.[3]

Yet this amateurish, politically motivated practice of "genetics" went by the name of science for almost forty years. When attempts to duplicate Lysenko's results failed in the West, the Soviet press claimed that the Western experimenters were either incompetent or anti-Soviet. Given the political risks, neither Lamarckians nor Mendelians were anxious to commit themselves; for that matter, neither Stalin in the 1930s nor his cultural spokesman Zdhanov the following decade had committed himself unequivocally to Lysenko. But the latter was aggressive and assured in his claims and egregiously flattered Stalin, then Zdhanov, then Malenkov, and finally Khrushchev when these leaders were concentrating their attention on agricultural production. Meanwhile, numerous Mendelians ended in the gulag or lost their teaching posts and laboratory privileges after Mendelianism had been condemned for its "bourgeois" insistence on the key role of heredity.[4]

In the late fifties, Khrushchev was impressed by Lysenko's claim that his hybrid seeds had been an important factor in the early success of the virgin-lands campaign. In 1960, Khrushchev provided Lysenko with expensive herds of Jersey cattle (high in butterfat, low in quantity of milk) to be crossed with Holstein cattle (low in fat, high in quantity). When the first generation of hybrids showed no discernible advantage, either in butterfat or total milk yield, Lysenko's star (and Khrushchev's) finally sank.

None of the above facts prove that Soviet experiments with hybrid seeds and cattle were useless. Quite the contrary, substantial practical results were achieved over the decades. But the politicization of scientific discussion, the lack of laboratory controls, and the puerile desire to discredit "Western," "bourgeois" genetics means that no adequate scientific judgment can be made of the activities that went under the name of genetics between 1928 and 1965. Other sciences likewise suffered from Soviet ideological dogma—in particular, psychology. Freud was widely read and Freudian analysis practiced during the NEP, but when the combination of dogma and patriotism settled over Soviet Russia with the five year plans, not only psychoanalysis but all forms of Western depth psychology were condemned as "bourgeois idealism." More official interest was shown in behavioral psychology, which was regarded as both materialist and environmentalist. But most important: Soviet Russia itself could endorse the accomplishments of a truly world-class Russian physiologist and experimental psychologist, Ivan Pavlov, who had been awarded a Nobel Prize in 1904 for his work in animal physiology.

In the 1920s, Pavlov established the presence in higher animals (principally dogs) of a phenomenon known as the conditioned reflex. If, over a period of time, a dog heard a bell sounding at the same moment that his master put a plate of food in front of him, the dog would soon begin to salivate when he heard the bell, regardless of whether food was present. Pavlov's experiments were carefully constructed and confirmed by identical results on the part of foreign experimenters. The Soviet authorities were especially delighted to have this completely materialist theory developed by a prerevolutionary, bourgeois scientist who was working happily with the revolutionary government.

The conditioned reflex also contributed to the notion of changing human nature through nurture rather than the accidental play of chromosomes. It occurred to Stalin and his secret police that political prisoners might be "conditioned" to learn and repeat, word for word, the "confessions" which had been drummed into them by endless hours of interrogation. They also used the conditioned reflex to exact obedience—and even verbal conformity—in the prison camps, whose function, they always claimed, was not punishment but "re-education." In this sense, they were much subtler than the Nazis and the general run of right-wing dictatorships, which depended on the use of truncheons and sheer terror to obtain confessions. The monstrous misuse of Pavlovian technology in prison interrogations extended to Eastern Europe and to North Korea and China—so much so that, by the 1950s, serious Western studies were speculating about the potential for creating the "New Soviet Man" by Pavlovian methods. (Pavlov died in 1936 and, needless to say, he bears no responsibility for the misuse of his work.)

After Stalin's death, the techniques were not so crude. But in the 1960s and 1970s, political dissidents were often interned in psychiatric hospitals with the idea that, through a combination of interviews and drug treatments, they could be "conditioned" to take a more positive attitude toward Soviet socialism. To cite one dramatic instance: in 1978, the USSR deprived a war hero named General Grigorenko of his citizenship. The general had been confined as "criminally insane" when he failed to respond to pseudo-Pavlovian conditioning, but also—in the much less cruel conditions obtaining after Stalin's death—he had been permitted to leave the USSR. Grigorenko then came to the United States to undergo psychological examination. According to the report of a Yale University psychiatrist who was also a student of Soviet psychiatry, Grigorenko "reminded us in some ways of the patients in Soviet descriptions. . . . Where they claimed obsessions, we found perseverance; where they cited delusions, we found rationality; where they identified psychotic recklessness, we found committed devotion. . . ."[5] In 1983, the association of Soviet psychiatrists withdrew from the World Psychiatric Association rather than be publicly questioned by their foreign colleagues about this and hundreds of similar cases.

To end this discussion of ideology and Soviet science on a less lugubrious note, the Soviet government did not normally interfere in the discussions of its physicists, men who were the acknowledged peers of their Western and Asian colleagues. In the interwar years, many Soviet physicists (much like Einstein and many world-famous non-Soviet physicists) did not accept such phenomena as "quantum randomness," and its implications of indeterminism as final truths. Some of them regarded probability waves as a form of philosophical idealism; others objected to the fact that the "Copenhagen interpretation" seemed to deny the validity of causality in the subatomic world. Occasionally in the thirties, some Soviet physicists were accused of "groveling" to the West and defending nonmaterialist interpretations. But Stalin—always the decisive person in matters of Marxist interpretation—did not make any official pronouncements as he had concerning biology, psychology, or linguistics.

Whether in the development of aerodynamics and rocketry before World War II, or the crash program to create nuclear weapons after the war, or the development of space and missile programs throughout the postwar era, the Soviet leadership did not interfere with physicists as long as their loyalty to the USSR was assured. Indeed, a leading Soviet physicist, Lev Landau (who had been briefly imprisoned in 1938), once said that the survival of Soviet physics had been the first successful example of nuclear deterrence.[6]

The argument has often been made concerning the failure of Soviet socialism that the nature of socialism as such should not be judged solely by the record of Stalin and his successors. It is therefore of considerable interest to examine the experience of Yugoslavia. The war had ended in Yugoslavia with the triumph of Marshal Tito's partisans, the majority of whom were committed communists. The Tito regime initially modeled itself on that of Stalin, but the Red Army had never occupied Yugoslavia and, as of 1948, Stalin himself refused to allow the Tito regime to partake of the enlightened graces of the Soviet empire. As a result, the development of Yugoslavian communism took place under different auspices than those which prevailed in the Soviet-occupied countries. Tito was a dictator committed to Marxist-Leninist principles; he governed through a single party and had no inhibitions about imprisoning his personal and political opponents. At the same time, however, Tito was not nearly so paranoid as Stalin. He also enjoyed considerable personal popularity as the architect of liberation from the Nazi occupation and he received important support from the West after his break with Stalin. Thus the experience of Yugoslavia under Tito, from 1945 to his death in 1980, constitutes a separate experience from that of the Soviets in "building socialism." Tito permitted the nation's constituent republics (Serbia, Croatia, Slovenia, Bosnia-Herzegovina, Macedonia, and Montenegro) to exercise considerably more local autonomy than did the constituent republics of the Soviet Union. Tito launched no campaigns of militant atheism, no efforts to destroy the Orthodox, Roman Catholic, or Islamic religions; even the initial bouts of forced collectivization were reversed in the 1950s and most Yugoslav agriculture remained in the peasants' hands.

Yugoslavia's economic independence was bolstered by frequent loans from the International Monetary Fund and from Western banks. The average growth rate in the 1950s was a substantial 8 percent, but the country also developed enormous, ultimately unpayable debts for imported machinery and technology. In the 1960s, several hundred thousand Yugoslav *Gastarbeiter* worked in Austrian, German, and Swiss factories. Large numbers of European tourists brought foreign exchange to Yugoslavia, as they did in those same years to the conservative dictatorships in Spain, Portugal, and Greece. There was thus far more contact—and for less tension—between Yugoslavia and the West than between the West and the Soviet empire.

The most radical departure from the Stalinist model was the experimentation with forms of "co-gestion" in Yugoslav industry. The worker-management law of

1950 was explicitly designed to avoid the development of a Soviet-style bureaucracy. Factory worker councils were elected by workers with an actual choice of candidates, and at least one-quarter of the industrial working class served on such councils at some time in the fifties or sixties. They made decisions in the use of social, educational, and welfare funds, though the allocation of raw materials and the technical control of production remained with the engineers and governing officials.[7]

These councils were good for worker morale (at least in the early years), but the fact remains that Yugoslav industry suffered the same problems of low productivity and low quality that dogged the economies of the USSR and its satellites. In 1965, price controls were lifted on everything except food and raw materials. As consumer prices rose, the worker councils understandably voted for compensatory wage increases, regardless of the need for technological investment and improved discipline in their factories. The government in turn related its own investment policies to the profitability—in effect, the market success—of each industry. But as "market socialism" failed to satisfy either local markets or the wider European market, socialist convictions declined and nationalist sentiments rose. In the seventies, Tito's personal prestige—and the devolution of increasing autonomy to the republics—kept Yugoslavia from falling apart. But the gap between the prosperous and the poorer republics continued to widen. By 1983, per capita income in Slovenia was between seven and eight times greater than per capita income in Kosovo. Thus, despite Western economic aid and a less harsh and dogmatic dictatorship than those of the Soviet Empire, communist Yugoslavia was no more an economic success than were the Stalinist regimes.

There is one more grave shortcoming in the communist dictatorships of the years 1945–1991 which remains to be discussed: All of them suffered ecological disasters which they tried to hide (and which they sometimes literally did not understand). In 1957, for example, at the secret nuclear base in Chelyabinsk, an explosion of nuclear wastes caused an unknown number of deaths among the slave laborers and applied scientists and the evacuation of thousands of hectares. The occurrence of the disaster was not officially admitted by the Soviet Union until 1989. Similarly, in 1977 an epidemic of anthrax occurred in the agricultural area south of Sverdlovsk. The human casualties at the time were officially attributed to "spoiled meat," but the post-Soviet Russian government has admitted that the outbreak was caused by a biological warfare experiment which got out of hand. The post-Soviet government has also acknowledged that the Soviet navy dumped nuclear wastes into the Arctic Ocean, in quantities and at locations that are not completely identifiable.

After the rapid recovery from World War II, the Soviets planned to rechannel a number of the largest Central Asian and Siberian rivers for purposes of irrigation, transport, and water supply. If they had been carefully executed with due attention to the likely effects on climate and vegetation, these projects might indeed have offered a better life to millions of Soviet citizens. But scientific criteria frequently yielded to political considerations; in hallowed Soviet tradition, mechanical failures and engineering errors could not be discussed in the press or by technicians for fear of losing their jobs or their personal liberty. Thus, instead of contributing to the overall economy, these projects led to the silting up of rivers, the drying of the Aral Sea, and the loss of millions of hectares of arable soil in dust storms. Similar disasters could be cited for many rivers and industrial areas of Poland, Czechoslovakia, Hungary, and Romania; the Soviet empire paid a tremendous price for its obsessive secrecy and its giantism in industrial planning.

A final reason for the collapse of the Soviet empire was the rational and materialistic nature of its promises. Traditional religions assure their devotees that they will be saved if they observe an abstract set of moral principles and accept certain metaphysical principles on faith. Christians, Muslims, and Jews cannot call God to account for their failures in this world; but under Soviet rule, the peoples were told that they were creating a better life for their children according to "scientific" principles. For the first thirty years or so, many of them believed (or at least hoped) that this might be true. But when, after sixty years, it was plainly evident that "real socialism" was not offering a better life than Western capitalism, the secular faith melted away.

ENDNOTES

1. G. Jackson, "Política y Música en la vida de Dmitry Shostakóvich" and "El significado de las sinfonías de Shostakóvich," *Claves de la Razón Práctica*, Madrid, spring 1993 and winter 1994, respectively.

2. For the political and economic information in my general description of the postwar Soviet Union, I have depended principally on Alec Nove, *An Economic History of the USSR*, new and final edition (Penguin Books, 1992); and Geoffrey Hosking, *The First Socialist Society*, enlarged edition (Harvard University Press, 1990).

3. Loren R. Graham, *Science, Philosophy, and Human Behavior in the Soviet Union*, New York: Columbia University Press, 1987, 105–128; Maxim W. Mikulak, "Darwinism, Soviet Genetics, and Marxism-Leninism," *Journal of the History of Ideas*, 1970, no. 3, 359–76; and Gustav Wetter, "Ideology and Science in the USSR," *Daedalus*, summer 1960.

4. Raissa L. Berg, *Acquired Traits* (New York: Viking Press, 1988) (the sarcastically titled autobiography of a Soviet geneticist).

5. Walter Reich, "The Case of General Grigorenko," *Encounter*, April 1980, 9–24.

6. David Holloway, *Stalin and the Bomb* (New York: Yale University Press, 1994), 209–213.

7. Fred Singleton, *A Short History of the Yugoslav Peoples*, Cambridge University Press, 1985, 216–48; James Simmie and Joze Dekleva, editors, *Yugoslavia in Turmoil: After Self-Management?* (London and New York: Printer Publishers, 1991); Barbara Jelavich, *History of the Balkans, Volume Two: The Twentieth Century* (Cambridge University Press, 1983), 384–92.

12

Science and the *Zeitgeist,* 1940–1990

*H*arold Urey, discoverer of heavy hydrogen and Nobel laureate in chemistry for the year 1934, spent his last active years at the University of California at San Diego advising a team of younger chemists in the search for the origins of life. Something of a father figure to the faculty in the 1970s, he used to say with a twinkle in his eye: "ninety percent of all the scientists who have ever lived are now alive and well in their laboratories." It was a graphic way of illustrating the phenomenal (and constantly accelerating) expansion that had taken place in all the sciences during the twentieth century.

In discussing the second half of that century, there are three general differences to note between the pre- and post-1940 decades. One is the shift in revolutionary discoveries from physics to biology. Before 1940, quantum physics, relativity, and the application of quantum physics to chemistry were the most extraordinary and successful new developments. Since 1940, genetics, molecular and evolutionary biology, neurosciences, and the numerous medical and economic applications of those sciences have been the most extraordinary developments.

Not that the pace of development in physics and chemistry has slowed, but the new advances in those areas—the elaboration of the "standard model" in quantum mechanics and electrodynamics; the "Big Bang" theory of the origins of the universe; the discovery of black holes, of antimatter, and of millions of previously unknown galaxies—are all extensions and applications of the quantum and relativity revolutions. Also, in terms of the purposes of the present book, these discoveries and their effects are increasingly remote from the lives and culture of most human beings. The major new conceptual developments strongly affecting human life took place in what are collectively known as the "life sciences."

A second difference is the shift in balance between Europe and the rest of the world. Up to c. 1940, the great theoretical advances almost all occurred in Europe (including the British Isles) with substantial contributions from the Western hemisphere and Japan. Since 1940, the bulk of new work—both theoretical and applied—has taken place in the English-speaking countries, with substantial contributions from continental Europe, Japan, China, and India. The shift toward the English-speaking world was largely due to the triumph of fascism and to the occupation of all Europe by the Nazi armies. Thousands of the most qualified German scientists, and hundreds of the most qualified Scandinavian, Italian, French, Central European, and Iberian scientists, emigrated to England, the United States, Canada, and Latin America between 1933 and 1945.

In addition, the pioneers of genetics and evolutionary biology were mostly English and American, and America emerged from World War II as the most powerful and wealthy nation on the face of the earth. It is thus easy to understand how *European* science became *Western* science. At the same time, the great increase in the number of Asian graduate students in British and American universities, along with the recovery of Japan, led rapidly to the development of a completely modern Asian scientific community. Thus in the twentieth century, science has first been European, then Western, then global.

The third major difference is the sheer size of the world scientific community, a result largely of the rapid postwar expansion first of American and, soon thereafter, of European universities, laboratories, and research foundations. Before 1914, the world's leading scientists would meet informally in Cambridge or Copenhagen or Paris, in Göttingen or Munich or at the Kaiser Wilhelm Institute in Berlin. After the First World War, they met by the hundreds rather than by the dozens. Since World War II, they have met by the thousands and tens of thousands at mammoth international conferences, and personal contact has been largely replaced by professional magazines, draft papers, faxes, and sandwich boards mounted in the conference rooms of the four- and five-star hotels housing the conferences.

To turn now to the science of genetics: as of the first decade of the century, several German, Swiss, and Dutch chemists had not only rediscovered Mendel's laws of inheritance, but they had begun the analysis of proteins; they had discovered nucleic acid; they had seen chromosomes under the compound microscope; and they had become convinced that some chemical substance in the chromosomes was responsible for the inheritance patterns they had observed. Between 1905 and 1915, the fruit fly experiments of T. H. Morgan and his colleagues confirmed and extended the Mendelian laws of genetic variation and inheritance over thousands of insect generations. Still, no one knew exactly the way in which genes (so named by the Danish biologist Wilhelm Johannsen in 1909) performed their functions. As of 1920, genes were defined specifically as biochemical units controlling heredity and possessing the ability to replicate themselves accurately. Although they were too small to be seen by the microscopes of that era, their practical effects could be fully described.

The increasingly accurate and detailed analysis of organic compounds became possible as a result of new laboratory methods. X-ray crystallography, developed at the Cavendish laboratories in the 1920s, enabled chemists to deduce the structure of complex molecules in their solid state by the manner in which their crystals refracted X-rays. An Indian physicist, Chandrasekara Venkata Ranman, discovered that liquid solutions of proteins and nucleic acids altered the wavelength of light passing through them and, from these changes of wavelength, deductions could be made concerning the molecular structure. Chromatography, developed in Germany in the 1930s (and itself made possible by the earlier development of aniline dyes), provided a means to separate plant pigments of very similar chemical composition. Then, in the 1940s, the spectrophotometer was invented; it measured tiny differences in the intensity of light as reflected by different amino acids. Chemists also developed the process of paper chromatography, whereby amino acids could be separated by the different rates of speed at which, through capillary action, they crept along a sheet of paper that had been dipped in a suitable solvent. And in the same era, the rapid perfection of the electron microscope made it possible to observe not just the cells (which had long been visible to the compound optical microscope), but the larger molecules as well. All these new experimental techniques and laboratory instruments made it possible to study delicate organic molecules without altering or destroying them.

Still, as of the early 1920s, chemists were unable to account in detail for the forces holding complex molecules together. The previously known universal forces of gravitation and electromagnetism could not account for the forces being studied at the molecular level—for example, the way in which a number of positively charged protons held together in the atomic nucleus instead of repelling one another. But the application of quantum mechanics to chemical analysis in the years 1927–1933 defined the nature of the "strong" and "weak" forces which act within the molecules, as well as the nature of covalent bonds (i.e., the complex ways in which molecules can share the electrons of each other's outermost rings). These advances led to the first detailed descriptions of molecular structure.[1]

With the new laboratory methods and the quantum-mechanical understanding of chemical bonds, the study of the biochemistry of life moved into high gear. By 1938, the twenty amino acids of which all proteins are composed had been identified. By 1939—just before outbreak of World War II, which of course greatly reduced both actual experimentation and international communication among experimenters—all chemists knew that chromosomes included both proteins and nucleic acid, but they assumed that the proteins carried the hereditary material. In 1944, at the Rockefeller Institute in New York, a research chemist, Oswald T. Avery, announced that the hereditary material in the pneumonia bacteria he was studying was composed exclusively of nucleic acid (in fact the deoxyribonucleic acid now universally known as DNA). As of 1952, numerous other experiments with bacteriophages (i.e., viruses parasitic on what are—for them—gigantic hosts in the form of bacteria) had repeatedly proved that DNA was the sole and exclusive hereditary material. As of 1951, Linus Pauling at the California Institute of Technology published proof of the helical structure of proteins, and the X-ray crystallography photos of Maurice Wilkins and Rosalind Franklin at King's College, London University, made it possible to study closely the molecular structure of nucleic acids.

As of 1952, the English physicist-turned-biologist Francis Crick and a much younger American biochemist, James D. Watson, together concluded that the structure of DNA would provide the key to the entire mechanism of heredity in all organic life, from viruses to humans. The "private international bush telegraph"[2] was alive with conjectures about the molecular structure of the nucleic acids, and the race to discover that structure was won in April 1953 by Crick and Watson. Using the helical concept and the model-building techniques of Pauling and the excellent crystallography of Wilkins and Franklin, they created the double-helix model of the DNA molecule. In the words of the French molecular biologist and Nobel laureate André Lwoff:

> DNA is two complementary chains, one being the template for the other. It is a unique and hitherto unknown type of structure, able to replicate by separation of the two complementary chains and copying each. It is a unique type of molecule, able to divide into two different, albeit complementary, molecules and to reproduce two identical molecules. The laws of stereochemistry, the crystallographic data, and the chemical data are satisfied by the model, as are the biological requirements for the genetic material.

Rarely indeed in scientific history has the critical importance of a new discovery been so widely and immediately recognized. And rarely has a great scientist been so human (all too human) or so candid as James D. Watson concerning his personal ambitions, his emotions, and not his always admirable treatment of colleagues. Thus the autobiographical memoir of his collaboration with Francis Crick, *The Double Helix* (which he submitted in draft form to a number of the colleagues mentioned in the text) is a uniquely valuable historical document. It offers to anyone moderately interested in how science is actually practiced a highly readable explanation of the research, together with one man's frank, vivid, and humorous account of human relationships within the scientific community—at least in its Anglo-Saxon form in the mid-twentieth century.[3]

The four decades since Crick and Watson's discovery have witnessed continuous further triumphs in molecular biology. In the year of the double helix, Frederick Sanger worked out the exact structure of insulin, essential for the digestion of sugars and the treatment of diabetes. In 1957, it was the turn of myoglobin, which supplies oxygen to the muscles; and in 1959, of haemoglobin, the giant molecule which consists of some 550 amino acids, has a molecular weight of 67,000, and carries oxygen in the blood. Between 1961 and 1967, biologists worked out the genetic code, the chemical signaling system by which the genes direct the creation of the thousands of proteins of which all living matter is composed. As of 1970, it was also possible to isolate specific genes in the laboratory and then place them inside bacterial hosts. By this technique, known as "recombinant DNA," scientists were able to produce, in quantity and in pure form, various enzymes and hormones needed for medical and experimental use.

In the 1980s, an even more powerful, truly mass production technique was developed. The polymerase chain reaction (PCR) enabled scientists to make millions of copies of single bits of DNA in test tubes *without* the necessity of a bacterial host. This tremendous amplification of quantity has numerous applications in forensic medicine, crime investigation, and the identification and dating of bits of organic matter which have been accidentally protected from decay for thousands (or millions) of years. Since the 1980s, scientists have also been collaborating on the so-called human genome project, which seeks to map and sequence the five to ten thousand gene families which are collectively responsible for the individual genetic heritage of every living human being. Since there are also a million or more "inactive" genes (at least as far as protein production is concerned), and since individual genes exercise different specific influences in widely separated aspects of our heredity, the human genome project is extremely complex.

These breathtaking advances in genetics research have raised a host of economic and ethical problems. Laboratory equipment and chemical supplies have become increasingly complex and expensive. Who is to pay the costs of research and development? Such expenses have long since outrun the capacity of the university budgets that covered such costs a half-century ago; what proportions should now be paid by the drug companies or by governments from tax revenues? And who should own the patents on new drugs and diagnostic tests—the university or private labs? The scientist-inventors? The commercial drug companies? By the 1990s, several gigantic legal battles have produced ad hoc solutions, but there is no general consensus looking to the future.

Along with the human genome project, geneticists have also undertaken the complex and expensive work of identifying the genetic cause of diseases such as sickle-cell anemia, Huntington's chorea, Duchenne muscular dystrophy, and cystic fibrosis. No less than seven major-university biomedical-research teams were seeking the cystic fibrosis gene between 1981 and 1989. At one point in 1987, researchers at St. Mary's Hospital at London University thought they had found it. The claim turned out to be mistaken; in the words of the great British molecular biologist Walter Bodmer: "St. Mary's had missed by a couple of thousand DNA base pairs—a hair's breadth in genetic terms."[4]

Everyone wants genetically caused diseases to be identified and drugs made available for their treatment. Most people also support the new techniques for identifying serious defects in the fetus and treating them with drugs, as well as preparing the parents for special challenges in caring for of their baby. But serious ethical concerns arise at the imminent prospect of positive genetic changes—not the treatment of defects, but the choice of sex, the addition of genes for height or intelligence, and so on. Up to now, the action of genes has been too complex and interdependent to allow for our direct manipulation; but the time is certainly coming when such manipulation will be possible. Then, too, serious questions have already emerged about the collection and control of genetic data. Do employers and insurance companies have a right to know that a given individual shows a genetic predisposition to a specific disease? Should the person himself be told—especially when the disease may in fact never manifest itself? Along with their immense triumphs, the past thirty years have forced molecular biologists to become entrepreneurs (constantly seeking funding for their researches, consulting with drug companies, or making their own personal investments in the production of drugs) and, have also obliged them to begin thinking about the ethical norms that will govern their use of the genetic code and the developing human genome.

The second revolutionary scientific development of the past half-century has been the study of the brain in the more complex birds and animals—and in particular in our species, flatteringly labeled *homo sapiens*. This has been a complex, interdisciplinary study involving, at the very least, molecular biology, evolutionary biology (combining Darwinian natural selection with the new genetics), computer sciences and artificial intelligence, cognitive science, and linguistics (since the capacity for spoken language and abstract thought is a uniquely human capacity). This combination of sciences, moreover, involves two very different overall attitudes. On the one side, there is the outlook of the physico- mathematical scientists, whose founding fathers were Galileo and Descartes. Their triumphs have come from complete third-person objectivity; from the removal of the emotional, subjective aspect of thought; from emphasis on measurement and calculation; and from their insistence on a rigorously logical, deductive reasoning about the meaning of the experimental and empirical evidence available. On the other side, there is the attitude of the biological scientists, who emphasize morphology and evolutionary history and are constantly aware of the uniqueness of each individual organism (at least among multicelled creatures). Unlike either math or physics, the solutions of the biological sciences are often "messy," "mindless," and utterly lacking in the "elegance" which physicists and mathematicians consider to be an integral part of "truth."

It may seem presumptuous for a historian (i.e., a scientific layman) to say this, but it frequently seems to me that the conflicting interpretations in the field of brain research depend as much or more on these broad attitudes as on the empirical evidence. The human brain is by far the most complex single organ subject to our observation; it contains something like ten billion neurons and about a million billion synapses. We know these neurons communicate chemically and electrically with each other in multiple ways via these contact points, but we are only at the beginning of a full, detailed knowledge of all the functions possible for the human brain.

Let us consider the brain first in terms of the evolutionary-biological outlook.[5] This most complex of organs has developed out of the increasingly complex nervous systems of the mammals which are our immediate ancestors and cousins. All animals have a primary consciousness which distinguishes them from nonliving matter. They perceive the outside world, react to stimuli, and make decisions about eating, fighting, hiding, etc.—all in the present tense. But they have no past, no future, no capacity to "think" about anything not immediately present, and no language in the human sense of that word. In other words, the sense of time and the capacity for abstract thought are features of the specifically higher consciousness of the human brain. Its chemical composition and its electrochemical forms of internal communication are now known in principle as a result of molecular biology and quantum electrodynamics. But the real mystery is how that brain self-organizes, how the multiple interconnected "mappings" of layers of neurons acquire their morphology and their functions (which, for the biologist, are dependent on that morphology).

According to the Nobel Prize-winning biologist Gerald Edelman, shape is critical, and combinations of genes act to give each organ its heritable shape. The developmental situation of the organism is thus both dynamic and unique, "depending on signals, genes, proteins, cell movement, division, and death, all interacting at many levels"(E64) and varying "as a function of time and place" (E60). The uniqueness of each individual results from the fact that the brain is a self-organizing system—one whose "most microscopic ramifications after development indicate that precise point-to-point wiring cannot occur. The variation is too great" (E25).

The approach of computer scientists is less morphological and historical. They hypothesize that the brain functions very much as a computer does, that among those ten billion neurons there are many complex modules with programs capable of performing all of the brain's reasoning functions. And they have sought (with great success) to simulate many of the reasoning, calculating, and two- and three-dimensional-modeling functions of the brain. Indeed, there are computers now which make reasoned decisions among complex alternatives, such as in the highly intellectual game of chess. However, there are no computers which have intentions, which feel pain or joy when you pinch or kiss them. Then, too, a computer has to be programmed to play chess; it does not make an independent, "self-organizing" decision to play and—insofar as we know—it experiences no emotions. Thus, the computational view of the brain does not account for that individual consciousness and the intentionality we see in all higher animals, including ourselves, however difficult it may be to explain that consciousness.[6] Nor indeed does the biological view account satisfactorily for consciousness—except to insist that morphology, history, and the interaction of numerous neural mappings somehow give rise to emotions and intentions.

Perhaps the most interesting single field in which these two contrasting theses concerning the brain lock horns is the study of linguistics. The ability to speak and write natural languages with detailed grammars and vocabularies of one hundred thousand words or more is a uniquely human capacity, and it depends on a number of morphological factors. One is the large portion of the cortex known as the Broca and Wernicke areas, which coordinate relations between the acoustic, motor, and conceptual activities of the brain. Another factor is the presence in humans of the supralaryngeal tract. As Edelman notes, "This tract becomes mature in human infants when the larynx descends. . . . As part of this evolutionary development, the vocal folds emerged and the tongue, palate, and teeth were selected to allow fuller control of the flow of air over the vocal cords, which in turn allowed the production of coarticulated sounds" (E126).

As for the semantic and syntactical aspects of language, the infant brain, as a result of biological evolution, has the necessary conceptual categories before the infant tries to speak. He or she connects various words with objects and concepts by social communication with the mother, the father and other adults, thereby rapidly accumulating a lexicon. Syntax then emerges "by connecting pre-existing conceptual learning to lexical learning" (E129). As speech practice and lexicon increase, "the brain recursively relates semantic to phonological sequences and then generates syntactic correspondences, not from pre-existing rules, but by rules *developing in memory* [Edelman's italics] as objects for conceptual manipulation" (E130). The biological view thus insists on evolutionary morphology and the life experience of the infant and rejects any "pre-existing rules"—that is, any computer-like module which would act as "software" to the human brain's "hardware."

Contrary to this biological view is the revolutionary thesis of linguist Noam Chomsky that underlying all natural languages (and hence, the language-using capacity of all human beings) is a universal grammar. According to Chomsky, the thousands of natural languages that have been created by humankind all follow certain basic rules: for example, the functions of noun phrases, verbs and prepositions, and all other modifiers are the same in all languages. The word order, on the other hand, can vary immensely because the construction of sentences—like computer operations—involves the infinite use of finite means in the form of "discrete combinatorial devices" whose elements can be arranged in an infinite variety of patterns.

As a lay historian, I shall once again stick close to the phraseology of a recognized expert—in this case, the Chomskyan linguist and cognitive scientist, Steven Pinker.[7] Pinker expounds the copious experimental evidence showing that very young children speak in complete grammatical sentences which are not simply copies or slight modifications of sentences they have heard, but sentences which they have created according to the rules of the underlying universal grammar. For Pinker, the speech organ is "a Darwinian organ of extreme perfection and complication" (P124). He thus accepts the importance of evolutionary morphology and not only agrees but emphasizes that the infant has thoughts and concepts before he or she engages in speech. "Knowing a language is knowing how to translate mentalese. . . . If babies did not have a mentalese . . . it is not clear how learning English could take place" (P82). Grammar is a software "to interconnect the ear, the mouth, and the mind." In other words, the complexity of the mind is not caused by learning; rather, learning becomes possible because of the complexity of the mind (P125).

To return to my earlier point: to the present curious layman, the real differences between the physics and biology-oriented approaches are not as fundamental as they seem in the professional-journal debates. Is it not perfectly possible to conceive of language as having evolved out of the morphology of the brain, ear, mouth, and laryngial tract—and, at the same time, to think of the language-creating ability in terms of a "module" with the universal grammar? If the capacity of birds and whales to navigate thousands of miles, or the myriad skills and sensitivities of the elephant's trunk, have been the products of biological evolution, why should not the same be true for the fundamental rules of human speech?

The fascinating—and agonizing, issues behind the physics-biology controversies, go much deeper, however, than the question of whether there is a universal grammar or rather a historical process of matching life experience with heard speech. The entire tendency of modern science is to eliminate all teleology and all specifically human value from our understanding of the universe. The great Charles Darwin, a deeply emotional man as well as a brilliant scientist, hesitated for years to publish his theses on evolution because he knew that they would destroy the religion in which he had been educated and in which his wife and most of the persons whom he loved still earnestly believed.

Indeed, biological evolution in the form of natural selection is an absolutely mindless, purposeless process. We may talk, as a convenient shorthand, about the "purposes" served by wings, sexual reproduction, lungs, or whatever; but in terms of evolution, all living things are the totally unplanned result of the relative adaptive capacity of accidental mutations over the course of millions of years. In that evolutionary process, moreover, there is no role for God and no inherent principle of "progress" such as constituted the post-Christian faith of many nineteenth- and twentieth-century agnostics and atheists. During the Newtonian era, it was possible to believe in a great clockmaker God who had set everything in motion according to benign and immutable laws (though the first of those two adjectives was always open to question). No less a thinker than Albert Einstein hoped until his death in 1955 to discover a grand unified theory that would penetrate the intellectual secrets of "The Old One," and he never accepted as final the indeterminate aspects of quantum theory.

But the laws of quantum physics and evolutionary biology, as well as the recently developed science of "chaos," have undermined all teleology and left us stranded in a universe without any discernible purpose or morality, other than what we create for ourselves. As for the hardnosed cognitive scientists who do not choose to study anything which cannot be observed in the external world or produced in the laboratory, they can proclaim that the brain is a computer and leave to vague humanists such subjective matters as emotion and intention.

Turning from the life sciences to the *Zeitgeist*—the general spirit of the times in Europe after the Second World War—there was a considerable difference of outlook between the professional and intellectual classes and the students, on the one hand, and the business and salaried working classes on the other. The first group has been confused and alienated—at some times protesting on behalf of important political and moral causes, and at other times passive and pessimistic. The second group, although perhaps no less confused and alienated, has been quick to enjoy the greatly improved material life which began to be available to its members in the 1950s—paid vacations, cars, health insurance, travel, movies and TV, football, rock and folk music—all of which also helped them to escape from the tensions of the Cold War, uneasy race relations between prosperous local populations and immigrant workers, and the always-present potential of nuclear doom. Indeed, as many observers have noted, the exceptional prosperity of the past four decades has been underlain with a haunting sense of persistent malaise, and the causes of the malaise are not hard to find: the horrors of the Nazi occupation, the invention and use of the atom bomb, the revelations concerning the gulag, and the development of the Cold War. And besides these political circumstances, there has been the overwhelming scientific evidence of cosmic processes which cannot in any way be related to traditional religious or humanistic beliefs. Not surprisingly, however, the second half of the twentieth century has also witnessed several dignified (albeit at times desperate) attempts to relocate humanity in a universe without inherent intellectual or ethical meaning, and it is to those efforts that I now turn.

Some of the most exciting of these efforts occurred in France, whose humiliating defeat in 1940 inspired a number of brilliant young intellectuals to devote their lives, while still under Nazi occupation, to creating works that would restore their nation's intellectual leadership once the Nazis had been defeated. Jean-Paul Sartre, Raymond Aron, Albert Camus, Maurice Merleau-Ponty, Fernand Braudel, and Claude Lévi-Strauss (partly in American exile) are but the most famous names among a generation who energetically combined resistance with the launching of their own humanist and social-science contributions to the postwar world.

Among the most influential was the philosophical-political career of Jean-Paul Sartre. As a young man in the 1930s, Sartre had paid very little attention either to the French Popular Front or the Spanish Civil War, but the collapse of France in 1940 had shocked him (as it had almost all his fellow soldiers). At the same time, he had had the good fortune not to be either Jewish, Slavic, or militantly leftist, so that he was not treated by the Germans as an *Untermensch* (subhuman). As a prisoner of war, Sartre had the leisure to study Heidegger's massive *Sein und Zeit* (*Being and Time*) and, by means of a somewhat exaggerated diagnosis of his eye problems, he was able to return to France and civilian life in early 1941. During the ensuing four years of the German occupation, Sartre was an active leader of the underground intellectual opposition and also found time to produce two plays and write his own principal philosophical work, *L'Etre et le Néant* (*Being and Nothingness*).

Without entering into technical considerations of Sartre's philosophical debts to Husserl, Heidegger, Bergson, and Descartes, it is possible to summarize the significance of his "existentialism" in the context of Europe from the 1940s to the 1970s. Sartre starts from an atheistic, "phenomenological" position. There is a real world, known to us through our senses, and the job of philosophy is to study phenomena (which includes both the real objects and our perception of those objects) without any metaphysical baggage. There is no God, no Platonic Ideas, no essences, no Kantian "thing-in-itself" lying unknown and unknowable beneath the immediate experience. Phenomena—all things outside us—have what he calls "being-in-themselves"; and we humans, though we are "objects" to other humans and to the material world, also have "being-for-ourselves." This latter fact means that human beings—although largely constrained by their economic circumstances, their genetic inheritance, and their national and family cultures—nevertheless have choices, make judgments and decisions, and therefore are, in an important sense, freely creating themselves.

This philosophy of free will and individual responsibility was expounded by a man who had suffered the German defeat, who shared and expressed the common French intellectual scorn for the bourgeoisie, who looked back critically at his own prewar insouciance (politically speaking) and became increasingly committed to political action during and after World War II. Sartre was also a writer capable of combining the highest philosophical abstraction with very down-to-earth discussions of human conduct. He used examples of the most ordinary daily situations to illustrate the concepts of "authenticity," (the fulfillment of one's own nature) and "bad faith" (the refusal to make the choices offered by life).

In the constant, lively debate that is the glory of French intellectual life, Sartre eventually became dissatisfied with the excessively individualistic character of his existentialism. Strictly interpreted, even other human beings seemed only "objects" for the lone, autonomous individual making his authentic (or inauthentic) choices. Thus in the late 1940s and throughout the rest of his life, Sartre added Marxist elements to his philosophy. The idea of class struggle, of solidarity with the working classes who were the great majority of of humankind, added a substantial "we-ness" to what had once been an extremely individualistic posture. At the same time, Sartre saw his existentialist humanism as enriching Marxist thought and distinguishing it from the impersonal, bureaucratic psychology of the Soviet and East European regimes. In addition, Marxist existentialism militated against racism and in favor of the liberation of women and of the African and Asian colonies.

In the 1960s, Sartre—like many other left-leaning intellectuals—transferred to Maoist China his lost illusions concerning Soviet communism. But more important than his visceral anti-Americanism and his naive ignorance of much of world politics was Sartre's predominantly positive emphasis on human responsibility and solidarity, his insistence that regardless of the "absurdity" (the absence of rational meaning or predictability) of the material world, human beings can and should create their own values, their own morality.

Sartre was a great editor and polemicist, alternately able to inspire, work with, and break relations with other great intellects of differing viewpoints. The collaboration with Albert Camus foundered on the latter's rejection of Stalinism and his reluctance to condemn as purely imperialist the long French record in Algeria. Sartre's collaboration with Maurice Merleau-Ponty likewise foundered when Merleau-Ponty refused to accept the Soviet explanation of the Korean War as an American-inspired imperialist invasion from the south. And his friendship with Raymond Aron, dating from their student days, foundered on Aron's complete skepticism toward Marxism in all its forms and his view that the United States was clearly less threatening to the future of Europe than the Stalinist empire.

As the above indicates, postwar French intellectual life was highly politicized. During the *Résistance*, men and women of very different political and religious opinions had shared hopes for a thoroughly democratic—and to a large degree, socialist—future. Much of the best French thought between 1945 and 1955 was devoted to the debate over that future in light of the disillusioning events occurring in Russia, the Americas, North Africa, Palestine, and Southeast Asia. From the mid-fifties, there was in French intellectual life a noticeable turning away from active political commitment, and the most significant cluster of new ideas after existentialism had to do with language.

In particular, the multifaceted movement known as structuralism had an immense impact in two social disciplines—linguistics and anthropology—as well as the humanistic discipline of literary criticism and interpretation. Traditionally philologists had studied European languages in historical terms, concentrating on the derivation of words in the living languages from their Latin, Greek, Semitic, and Sanskrit roots, on the family relationships among the Romance and Germanic languages, and on the way different uses of the same words evolved over the centuries. Structural linguistics, on the other hand, set out to study language in general, "synchronically," in a timeless present. Each separate language constitutes a set of sounds which its speakers use to communicate their thoughts and wishes.

Language is thus a social instrument, reasonably stable in form; but within each language, the relation between a given combination of sounds and its meaning is wholly arbitrary. That is to say, there is no logical reason (save constant usage) why a certain domestic canine is called "dog" in English, "perro" in Spanish, "Hund" in German, and so on. Then, too, the full meaning of any given word depends on its relation to the meaning of other words, and hence on its place in the structure of the language as a whole. By far the greatest single triumph of structural linguistics thus far has been the Chomskyan universal grammar, discussed in connection with cognitive science.

Structural anthropology was largely the invention of Claude Lévi-Strauss (who, like a great many thinkers known in the general literature as structuralists, rejected the label). Lévi-Strauss had personal experience with several Latin American Indian cultures and was a voracious reader of the ethnographic literature on numerous Asian tribal societies. To quote his own words for the overall concept of structural anthropology:

> If, as we believe to be the case, the unconscious activity of the mind consists in imposing form upon content, and if these forms are fundamentally the same for all minds—ancient and modern, primitive and civilized . . . it is necessary and sufficient to grasp the unconscious structure underlying each institution and each custom, in order to obtain a principle of interpretation valid for others. . . .[8]

Another definition is provided by J. J. Honigmann in his *Handbook of Social and Cultural Anthropology* in which he states that "conscious, empirical, ethnographic phenomena, are assumed to be concrete realizations of unconscious, structural, and ethnographic systems. These, in turn, are said to be the results of neurological, cibernetic, and physico-chemical universals." The paradigm of structuralism is thus "an encompassing movement from the empirical description of ethnographic models on to their final reduction to unconscious, comparable, and universal structures."

The third area in which structuralism has been important is in the study of literature. Here the emphasis is on the structure of the different literary genres: epic and lyric poetry, narrative prose, drama, expository prose, epistolary prose, political speeches, treaties, satire, detective stories, advertising—any and every organized form in which words are used. Prior to the advent of structuralism, traditional literary critics and historians concentrated on the individual author's intent and meaning; they assumed that the creation of such intent and meaning was the principal objective of the author, and that he or she truly determines the style and content of their chosen phrases. Structuralist critics, however, set out to show (as Jerry Eagleton expresses it in *Literary Theory, An Introduction*) that "meaning was neither a private expression nor a divinely ordained occurrence: it was the product of certain shared systems of signification." As a presumably scientific method, structuralism "bracketed off the real object, it bracketed off the human subject. It is indeed this double movement which defines the structuralist project. The work neither refers to an object, nor is the expression of an individual subject; both of these are blocked out, and what is left hanging in the air between them is a system of rules."[9] Literary images are thus said to have principally relational rather than inherent meanings. The structure of the relations is in any case more significant than the apparent meaning (as in psychoanalysis, where the significance of dreams is their unconscious rather than manifest content). Structuralism aims to be more analytical than evaluative and assumes that, in any narrative or myth, there is always a structural meaning deeper than the surface story.

Whether or not acknowledged such by its practitioners, structuralism advanced its strongest claims in the 1960s. It also met great resistance in all three fields—linguistics, anthropology, and literature—and, in literary studies since the 1970s, it has coexisted with post-structuralism. The dividing line between the two schools of thought is by no means clear; but in general, post-structuralism reduces even further the importance of authors, intentions, and meanings as subjectively expressed. For the post-structuralist critic, literature does not consist of "works" by individuals but of "texts" which speak through their authors. The thinking here is analogous to Lévi-Strauss's interpretation of totemic and kinship systems as social codes permitting the transmission of messages. As Eagleton explains it:

> The mind which does all this thinking is not that of the individual subject: myths think themselves through people, rather than vice versa. They have no origin in a particular consciousness, and no particular end in view. One result of structuralism, then, is the 'decentring' of the individual subject, who is no longer to be regarded as the source or end of meaning.[10]

The literary post-structuralist then "deconstructs" the subjective intentions and unwitting meanings of those who consider themselves to be the "authors." A given text, in this view, has no definitive meaning but is subject to different, non-authorial interpretations according to the principles elucidated by the trained structuralist or post-structuralist critic. On the other hand, if only to judge from their own continued output of books and articles, structuralist and post-structuralist critics alike seem to be fully confident of the meaning of their own assertions.

In terms of my own very conscious authorial intentions, structuralism and its sequels are more important as symptoms of late-twentieth-century culture than as a set of scientific propositions (exception made for the universal grammar of Chomsky and his colleagues). Linguistics and anthropology bear witness to the greatly expanded world-consciousness of European culture, including within their purview all languages, not just those relevant to our linguistic background, and all peoples, religions, myths, and social codes, not just those of the West (together with an effort, wherever practicable, to save small primitive cultures from extinction). It is also certainly healthy to consider not just the role of individual creators, but the ways in which linguistic and ethnological structures constrain speakers and writers without their necessarily being aware of that fact.

On the other hand, two aspects of the structuralist project seem to me rather questionable. One is the sometimes coy, sometimes deliberately mystifying way that its leading theorists speak about their work. This trait can be well illustrated from two interviews with Lévi-Strauss by the cultural critics George Steiner and John Weightman. With Steiner, Lévi-Strauss nonchalantly compares the study of Western and non-European societies with the invention of non-Euclidean geometries and refers in that context to Albert Einstein. At another point, he states that "we cannot at the same time study 'structure' and 'process.' . . . This would be the true uncertainty principle of anthropology." These invocations of Einstein and Heisenberg testify to great thirst to give "social science" the full status of the exact sciences. On the other hand, when Weightman pointed out the lack of scientific verification of his theories, Lévi-Strauss replied that he had repeatedly said that he was not a scientist and that all social science was "pre-scientific." Weightman also asked about the obscurity of much of his prose, to which Lévi-Strauss responded that he had "made free, and perhaps impudent, use of the sort of philosophical language which is common to all members of the Paris intelligentsia," but that he did not attach any great importance to it. At which point, the impudent reader might well ask: Then why should we take seriously either the pseudoscientific claims or the frivolously supplied disclaimers? Without offering similar illustrations from the essays and interviews of Roland Barthes, Michel Foucault, Jacques Derrida, et al., suffice it to say that, for whatever combination of personal and professional motives, many of the leading structuralists and post-structuralists have delighted in their purposeful inconsistency and obscurity. Their behavior is a symptom of the spiritual desperation and even moral nihilism underlying much writing in the humanities and social sciences in the late twentieth century.[11]

The second questionable aspect of literary structuralism is the substitution of critics and theorists for authors as the main spokespersons concerning what litera- ture is all about. It is one thing to point out ways in which an author is strongly con- ditioned by linguistic and anthropological structures; it is something entirely dif- ferent to write as though there were only "texts" and not individual creative works. The matter is not merely one of academic fashion, but has direct economic and pro- fessional implications as well. Novelists and poets may struggle to sell a few hun- dred copies of original works which do not set out to please a large audience. But structuralist critics, meanwhile, can speak arcane jargon to one another while holding well-paid university positions and jetting about in the manner described in David Lodge's wonderful novel *Changing Places*. The complex verbiage of structuralist theory also solves the problem of finding Ph.D. thesis topics for legions of students who have much greater analytic than creative or interpretive abilities.

In the whole new emphasis on language, no single figure has been more important (or symptomatic) than the German philosopher Martin Heidegger (1889–1976). Heidegger was born and educated in the Catholic south of Germany, always idealized rural life, did much of his thinking and writing in a small cabin in the Black Forest, and spent his most important professorial years at Freiburg. Heidegger was a German patriot, deeply discouraged by the loss of the First World War; he shared the philosophical gloom of Oswald Spengler, whose *Decline of the West* was published in 1918, and he was completely indifferent (if not hostile) to the Weimar Republic. He was by many reports a spellbinding teacher and, from the moment he published the first volume of *Sein und Zeit* (*Being and Time*, 1927), Heidegger became an immensely influential figure not only in Germany and France but in the English-speaking world as well.

Sein und Zeit is the single most important of Heidegger's books, the fruit of his decade-long determination to root out the metaphysical underbrush from Western philosophy. His prose style is extremely obscure and there can be no clear, agreed upon interpretation of his (presumably nonmetaphysical) results. But as with the structuralists, I am not so much concerned with Heidegger's doctrines as with his symptomatic importance. Despite the obscurity of his prose, Heidegger makes a very serious, anguished effort to create a nonmetaphysical foundation for philosophy, and there is an ultimate pathos in his own inability to face "authentically" the key historical events of his lifetime.

In *Sein und Zeit*, Heidegger insists that *"Alles Seiende ist im Sein; das Sein ist das Seiende"*—everything which exists is in Being, and the total of Being is equivalent to everything which exists. There are no essences, no Platonic Ideas, no Cartesian split between matter and spirit, no Christian split between body and soul. Of course, this determination to overcome the dualism in both theology and secular philosophy is common to all the agnostic and atheist phenomenologists of the present century; but Heidegger treats its implications in a highly suggestive, poetic manner. Though most of his discussion of Being emphasizes the impersonal, the absence of the divine and the intellectual, it is nevertheless true that Man, with his special self-consciousness, is characterized by *"Da-sein,"* by "being there" consciously, not merely with the presentness of a rock. Man has not volunteered to be born, but instead has been "thrown" into existence.[12] As George Steiner explains it:

> This characteristic of *Dasein*'s being—this that it is—is veiled in its "whence" and "whither," yet is disclosed in itself the more unveiledly. We call it the *"thrownness"* of this entity in its "there." Indeed, it is thrown in such a way that, as being-in-the-world, it is "there." The expression "thrownness" is meant to suggest the *facticity of its being delivered over.*[13]

Self-disclosure and unveiling are two of the most frequent images used by Heidegger to characterize Being. As for the "whence" and "whither," *Dasein* is characterized by an "at handness," a facticity of experience analogous to the experience of an artisan, a tool user, a manual examiner of phenomena rather than a disembodied intellect. And the authentic experience of Being leads to moments of understanding which Heidegger compares to the entrance to a clearing (*Lichtung*) within a forest where the woodsman has emerged into the light.

But most important for human experience is that Being also includes temporality, is Being-toward-Death, a death which explicitly excludes any sort of afterlife. Each human life is unique and includes the unique death of which no outside power can deprive it. This existential sense of untransferrable experience and movement toward death is a basic condition of the dignity and the freedom of human beings—a concept which greatly influenced all the French existentialists who studied Heidegger's work in the 1930s. Taken as a whole, Heidegger's literary climate includes the anti-intellectual, antiscientific, and antimetaphysical; the anguish of St. Augustine and Kierkegaard; and the rural and artisanal sentiments that have entered into many twentieth-century movements of both the Right and the Left.

But if Being is also Being-toward-Death and if Man, in contrast to nonliving objects, is somehow "thrown" into life, then his form of being must be different from that of a rock, and the philosopher cannot avoid the metaphysical problems that have preoccupied all philosophers: how to define the relationship between Being (or God, or the Prime Mover) and beings (the unique, mortal existents). Here is one of Heidegger's first wrestlings with the question, from the introduction to *Being and Time*:

> Being cannot be defined by attributing beings to it. Being cannot be derived from higher concepts by way of definition and cannot be represented by lower ones. But does it follow from this that 'Being can no longer constitute a problem? By no means. We can conclude only that 'Being' is not something like a being. Thus the manner of definition of beings which has its justification within limits—the 'definition' of traditional logic which is itself rooted in ancient ontology—cannot be applied to Being. The undefinability of Being does not dispense with the question of its meaning but compels that question.[14]

Thus ontology from Plato to the present-day is rejected. Indeed, in numerous passages Heidegger refers to metaphysics as a "forgetting of Being," meaning that the whole fraternity of European philosophers have argued about verbal definitions while "forgetting" the sense of life itself. At the same time, Heidegger found himself unable to define Being and gave this as the reason why he had never written the second volume of *Sein und Zeit*. He stated that the existing vocabulary could not express his convictions and that he had been unable to create an adequate vocabulary (though his neologisms and etymological discussions are among those proportions of his work which most influenced later structuralist and post-structuralist theorists).

Meanwhile, the Nazis rose to power in Germany. Heidegger shared their explicit revolt against the Versailles Treaty and expressed his own idiosyncratic form of philosophical racism by asserting that great philosophy could only be created in Greek or German. He shared the romantic vision of the more idealistic left-wing Nazis, who claimed that they would restore the rural and artisanal values of pre-industrial Germany. Heidegger was very sensitive to the degradation of the physical environment by the expansion of the coal, steel, and chemical industries—in this sense, he was a forerunner of the ecology movement. He hoped for a kind of "third way" between Western industrial capitalism, with its rape of natural resources and the environment and Soviet communism, which deliberately destroyed its prosperous peasants and all forms of traditional property, religion, and "bourgeois" culture.

The Nazis appointed Heidegger as the rector of Freiburg university. He had no problems with the removal of his Jewish colleagues, enjoyed wearing the uniform, and demanded that his students use the "Heil Hitler" greeting. According to his longtime colleague Karl Löwith, his audience was "never quite sure whether they should take up the study of the pre-Socratics or join the storm troopers."[15] Like many completely narcissistic intellectuals (one cannot have been a university professor without having known quite a few such persons), Heidegger was in most circumstances incapable of imagining the feelings of others and he was also ludicrously clumsy in academic politics. During de-Nazification proceedings in 1946, he claimed that, after his first few months in the rectorship, the Nazis had begun to persecute him. While it is indeed true that several lesser philosophers outmaneuvered him in the university intrigues of the Nazi era, Heidegger paid his party dues until the end and was in no way persecuted.[16]

During the war itself, Heidegger developed the aesthetic side of his wide philosophical interests, publishing profound interpretive essays on the the poet Hölderlin and the painter Van Gogh. In these essays, it is notable that, as in later structuralist writings, the conscious role of the artists is played down. He wrote now that Being—which had been an essentially impersonal concept in *Being and Time*—was created by language and art, which phenomena expressed themselves through the work of the great artists. In proportion as the actual course of events disappointed him, Heidegger came to think of Being as a creation of poetry and art—a subjective, aestheticist position far removed from his 1920s efforts to define the existing universe as nonmetaphysical Being.

Despite his known Nazi sympathies, Heidegger's French admirers, with Sartre in the lead, hoped to re-establish intellectual contact with him and perhaps also overcome the terrible psychological wounds of Hitler's war. In 1946, Sartre published an essay entitled *Existentialism Is a Humanism*, in which he expounded his ideas of atheistic, existentialist moral responsibility and solidarity—ideas which had been decisively influenced by the Heidegger of *Being and Time* (even though Heidegger had explicitly stated that his book was not about ethics). Also at this time, while the Allied authorities were refusing to allow Heidegger to teach in the university, another young French philosopher addressed a set of questions to him, hoping to provoke a dialogue concerning, among other things, Sartre's views.

In 1947, Heidegger answered these initiatives in his *Letter on Humanism*. In it, he concentrates on summarizing his own ideas concerning Being, aesthetics, and language, but at one point he comments directly on Sartre's essay, proclaiming that "thinking" (no persons indicated) tries to deal with the relationships among Being, Time, authenticity, language, morals, and so on:

> It tries to find the right word for them within the long-traditional language and grammar of metaphysics. But does such thinking—granted that there is something in a name—still allow itself to be described as humanism? Certainly not so far as humanism thinks metaphysically. Certainly not if humanism is existentialism and is represented by what Sartre expresses: "We are precisely in a situation where there are only human beings." Thought from *Being and Time*, this should say instead: "We are precisely in a situation where principally there is Being."[17]

He then goes on to emphasize the highly impersonal nature of Being.

Such is the tone of Heidegger's reply to his young French admirers trying to make human contact with the Great Man. I have quoted him at some length so that the reader may judge for himself the suggestive yet obscure remarks. Exiled former students of his (notably Herbert Marcuse) tried politely but insistently to elicit Heidegger's reaction to the mass murder of Jews, Gypsies, and Slavs by the Germans and their collaborators. But to the day of his death, Heidegger never spoke of the Holocaust, though he found much to criticize in both American and Soviet policies and considered the postwar expulsion of the Germans from Eastern Europe to have been a noteworthy injustice. Clearly devastated by the Nazi debacle and feeling humiliated and unjustly punished by the Allies, Heidegger shared the widespread German refusal in the early postwar era to recognize any moral responsibility for the atrocities committed during the lost war. In September 1966, he granted an interview to the editors of the German weekly *Der Spiegel*, on condition that his words would only be published after his death (a condition which was duly honored). In that interview, full of negative statements about science and technology, the philosopher of Being who had banished metaphysics opined that only a God could save humanity now.

There has been an unmistakably tortured, self-destructive character to much of European intellectual life since World War II. The great language philosopher Ludwig Wittgenstein died in 1951, but his influence was greatest in the decades after his death. As an individual Wittgenstein was full of self-loathing for his wealthy family background and was unable to form stable human relationships with any except a few of his worshipping students. Sometime in 1937, when he was teaching at Cambridge University, Wittgenstein made the following tense, two-point confession to a Ukrainian Jewess from whom he was learning Russian: First, that as an elementary school teacher in rural Austria, he had once slapped a girl and later denied the fact; and second, that people thought he was only one-quarter Jewish when he was actually three-quarters Jewish, but that he never rectified their error. Other interesting observations of Wittgenstein's Russian teacher included her certainty that he had absolutely no idea how uncomfortable he made people in social situations, that he seemed to be completely asexual, and that when she was eight months pregnant he was apparently unaware of the fact.[18]

Like his predecessor Nietzsche and his contemporary Heidegger, Wittgenstein was determined to expose the multiple errors of the Western metaphysical tradition. In his first book, the *Tractatus* (1921), he analyzed the errors due to ambiguities of language but still considered that, at least in nonreligious and nonesthetic statements, it was possible to compose sentences which expressed the truth of a corresponding reality. But in his second major book, *Philosophical Investigations*, published posthumously in 1953, he emphasized the unreliability of all sentences, arguing that their meanings must be ambiguous because of what he called "the language game," the extralinguistic circumstances in which the phrases were uttered. In all his writing Wittgenstein emphasized the difference between what is sayable and what is only demonstrable. All moral and religious values were unsayable— for which reason, after publishing the *Tractatus,* he went off to teach elementary school in an Austrian village and carried in his heart for decades the sense of guilt for having once struck a pupil.[19]

Similarly, Michel Foucault, one of the most brilliant polymaths to teach in both European and American universities in the 1960s and 1970s, was an internally tortured human being. His writings are notable for the vehemence of their attacks on "mainstream" science, history, and the social sciences. He felt deep sympathy for maladjusted, unconventional personalities, and made his most valuable contributions by focusing scholarly attention for the first time on the treatment of the ill, the insane, and the criminal, as well as on the hypocritical ways in which "enlightened" society defines "normality" and then marginalizes its nonconformist members.

Like many recent essayists, Foucault deliberately eschews the *clarté* (clarity) which used to characterize the best French prose. His style combines brilliant insights with a conscientious scorn of mere facts; he uses strings of partially synonymous adjectives and nouns placed within quotation marks so that even the attentive reader does not know which meaning or pseudomeaning of both adjective and noun to apply. With admiring students, he was most supportive and helpful, he also enjoyed treating with egregious scorn those colleagues and administrators whom he thought of as mediocre. His biographers are unable to decide whether Foucault deliberately exposed himself to AIDS, thereby courting the early death which in fact resulted from his "limiting experiences," as he called them, in San Francisco bath houses.[20]

One other crucial aspect of the *Zeitgeist* in the second half of the twentieth century has been the greatly expanded role of youth. The birth rates of the fifties and sixties created a proportionately much younger population. At the same time, families in which both parents worked outside the home, and the increase in class sizes at all levels of education, meant that children received much less adult supervision—or simply adult company, adult example, and adult repression—than in past eras. Two salaries and a welfare state that made it less important than in the past to save money for medical expenses, old age, and so on, also meant that children had more pocket money as well as more unsupervised free time.

New customs and institutions—good and bad—developed rapidly to replace the older family and immediate neighborhood influences: athletic clubs, gymnasia and swimming pools, rock concerts, piano bars, cinema clubs, communes of middle-class youth able to pay the rent, squatter communities of their peers unable to pay the rent, and inner-city gangs. The young were also particularly targeted as the market for CDs, videos, novel clothing, and drugs. The availability of both employment opportunities and the birth-control pill meant that young women could control their own lives much more completely than in the past.

The most spectacular single manifestation of the youth culture in European society was the Parisian student uprising of May 1968. It was sparked by an unprecedented police occupation of the inner court of the Sorbonne, which for centuries had enjoyed a kind of extraterritorial status; but underlying the student unrest was an accumulation of motives that were themselves symptomatic of postwar social trends. In the university itself, the students demanded increased classroom and laboratory facilities commensurate with the increased size of the student body, as well as a student voice in the selection and promotion of faculty. Regarding the world beyond the campus, their slogans concerned personal and sexual liberation, anti-imperialism, and the exaltation of Fidel Castro and Mao Zedong—the Marxist dictators who were thought to be leading genuinely popular revolutions and overcoming the stagnation and bureaucratization of the Soviet Union and the French Communist Party. Indeed, where the leading intellectuals of the late 1940s had idealized the USSR, their counterparts in the late 1960s were doing the same with Castro and Mao.

For almost three weeks, normal Parisian life was replaced by a continuous spectacle of graffiti, processions, the suspension (partly voluntary and partly involuntary) of various public services such as transport and garbage collection, and debate and fraternization with workers who were not sure whether the student demands were really useful to them or not. For perhaps a majority of Parisians and readers of the progressive press all over Europe, it was a genuine festival of intellectual and popular liberation from bourgeois stodginess. For a minority, it was sheer fantasy madness, fortunately involving very little real violence.

On May 30, President DeGaulle, having strategically placed a number of tanks on the outskirts of Paris in case of trouble, dissolved the parliament and called new elections for late June. The government raised minimum wages 35 percent and promised new investments to meet the problems of massification and to give the students some role in university affairs. Normality returned to the streets of the capital and in the subsequent election, the Gaullists won a substantial majority while the communist and socialist parties lost more than half their seats. Indeed, although French public opinion had sympathized with the economic problems of the students, shared their protest at the police occupation of the Sorbonne, and enjoyed such slogans as "The imagination in power," French voters had clearly shown a preference for the restoration of stability and the general conservative continuity represented by the Gaullists. Fairly similar results occurred in West Germany in response to its own radical student protests. And when, during the 1970s, fringe groups of revolutionary students challenged the "repressive" bourgeois state with kidnappings and bombings in Germany and Italy, public opinion approved the severe punishments meted out to the few perpetrators who were caught and convicted.

At first sight, it may not seem that there is a great deal in common among existentialist, structuralist, and post-structuralist ideas, the intellectual profundities and tortured emotions of such thinkers as Heidegger, Wittgenstein, and Foucault, the student revolts of the late 1960s, and the spectacular fringe violence of the Baader-Meinhof gang and the Italian Red Brigades. But all of them share a surprising number of important traits: impassioned intellectual and moral criticism of the existing world systems, American-led capitalism and Soviet-led communism; a reluctant atheism, based on the conviction that God is indeed dead, as proclaimed by Nietzsche, but with this death felt as an emotional loss, not as the triumph of rational thought; the search for a new survival ethic independent of any religious base; the liberation of women, youth, and all racial minorities from "white male" and "bourgeois" domination (exception made for the Germanic chauvinism of Heidegger); an unprecedented cultural variety in "lifestyles" more often implying escapism (that is to say, a concern with more amusing ways to pass the time rather than a strong commitment to any particular aims in life); a feeling of intense alienation from the practical demands and schedules which had been accepted by their forebears; the absence of clear alternatives to existing capitalism and communism; and a combination of hedonism, stoicism, and occasional violence in the face of life's "absurdity."

For thinking, sensitive people, the prosperity and the secular variety of the welfare state in the late twentieth century did not offer enough spiritual sustenance. A positive factor in their alienation, however, was the new attention paid to non-Western cultures, the acceptance of Europe as one civilization among others, increased economic aid to "developing" nations, and the growth of the human-rights and ecology movements. For the less politically concerned majority, there was the enjoyment of a prosperity which contrasted happily with the memory of two world wars and the Great Depression, as well as an extraordinary new variety of leisure-time activities, from the "boob tube" to the finest of art exhibits, concerts, and cinema.

ENDNOTES

1. Linus Pauling, "Fifty Years of Progress in Structural Chemistry and Molecular Biology," *Daedalus*, fall 1970, 988–1014. Pauling himself was probably the greatest single chemist contributing to the precise knowledge of chemical composition and molecular structure.

2. This genial phase and the general account of the background come from Gunther Stent, "DNA," *Daedalus*, fall 1970; and in the same issue, Robert Olby, "Francis Crick, DNA and the Central Dogma."

3. James D. Watson, *The Double Helix*, a Norton Critical Edition edited by Gunther S. Stent, W. W. Norton Co., 1980. I specify this edition because Stent is himself an internationally respected professor of molecular biology, and because the book includes numerous professional evaluations of Watson's text and several key scientific papers involved in the discovery of the double helix. The previously cited definition by André Lwoff appears on p. 229.

4. Walter Bodmer and Robin McKie, *The Book of Man* (Little, Brown & Co., 1994), p. 86.

5. My discussion is based principally on Gerald Edelman, *Bright Air, Brilliant Fire (On the matter of the mind)* (Basic Books, 1992). The paging of the direct quotes is given in parenthesis in the text, preceded by an "E".

6. The most convincing discussions I have read of the problems of consciousness and intention appear in John R. Searle, *The Rediscovery of the Mind* (Cambridge: The MIT Press, 1992).

7. Steven Pinker, *The Language Instinct* (William Morrow and Co., 1994). Citation pages given in parenthesis in the text, preceded by a "P".

8. Claude Lévi-Strauss, *Structural* Anthropology, 2 volumes (New York: Basic Books, 1976), v.1, p. 21.

9. Terry Eagleton, *Literary Theory, an Introduction*, University of Minnesota Press, 1983, quotations from pp. 107 and 112. Since the book had gone through eleven printings by 1991, I assumed it gave acceptable general definitions from the point of view of professors teaching literary theory.

10. Eagleton, p. 104.

11. George Steiner, "A Conversation with Claude Lévi-Strauss," *Encounter*, April, 1966; John Weightman, "A Visit to Lévi-Strauss," *Encounter*, February 1971.

12. My reading of Heidegger is based on the selections in English given in Martin Heidegger, *Basic Writings*, edited by David F. Krell (HarperCollins, 1977); and on George Steiner, *Heidegger*, 2d ed. (Fontana Press, 1992). Though I read normal German prose quite fluently, I am absolutely dependent on translation where Heidegger is concerned.

13. Steiner, p. 87.

14. *Basic Writings*, p. 44.

15. Quoted in Allan Megill, *Prophets of Extremity* (Berkeley and Los Angeles: University of California Press, 1985), p. 130.

16. For Heidegger's academic career and his relations with the Nazis, I have depended principally on Vícto Farías, *Heidegger y el nazismo* (Barcelona: Muchnik Editores, 1989). The original French publication of this book caused furor among Heidegger's admirers, but the scorn which they heaped on Farías did not expunge the facts of Heidegger's long collaboration, as fully documented in Farías' book.

17. *Basic Writings*, p. 237.

18. Fania Pascal, "Wittgenstein, a Personal Memoir," *Encounter*, August 1973.

19. Besides my own nonprofessional reading of his work, I have depended on Erich Heller, "Ludwig Wittgenstein," *Encounter*, September 1959, an essay responding to the statement of Bertrand Russell that *Philosophical Investigations* meant nothing to him; and Stephen Toulmin, "Ludwig Wittgenstein," *Encounter*, January 1969. For a full and admiring biography, see Ray Monk, *Ludwig Wittgenstein: The Duty of Genius* (New York: The Free Press, 1990).

20. The biographical information comes principally from James Miller, *The Passion of Michel Foucault* (Anchor Doubleday, 1993).

13

Excursus on Creative Literature

I n view of the immensity of the field of creative literature, which comprises fiction, drama, and poetry and includes important special genres such as espionage thrillers, mysteries, and science fiction, I shall say at the outset that in the present chapter I will be dealing only with the traditional novel—a form of literature of which I have read a great deal, and which in many instances contributes substantially to an understanding of European history and culture.

Indeed, prior to 1914 novels were overwhelmingly the most important single source of vicarious experience of European life, past and present, and also the principal source of information about distant lands and cultures. In the course of the twentieth century, however, the novel rapidly lost its near-monopoly as the purveyor of vicarious experience. Silent movies, made for both entertainment and documentary purposes and reaching the working classes as well as the middle classes (who were and remain the principal readers of novels), developed rapidly in the first three decades of the century. After 1930, silent movies were replaced by "talkies" and by 1960, movies, radio, and TV serials combined all performed the same entertainment and information functions as had the nineteenth-century novel. By the 1980s, videocassettes came onto the scene and made movies and TV series available to the individual viewer's home "library." Quite literally, in the past decade, video rental stores have become far more numerous than bookstores.

In view of the successful competition offered to the novel by these new forms of fictional entertainment, contemporary literary critics have regularly predicted—and sometimes confidently announced—the "death of the novel." But in fact, although the novel has indeed lost its dominant position, it has remained very much alive for a number of good reasons. One is that a substantial percentage of intellectually curious human beings still prefer to form their own images on the basis of their reading rather than accept a fixed commercial version of a given story. Thus thousands of copies of novels are sold *after* the making of the movies on which they were based. To take a specific example, readers of crime and espionage fiction are frequently people who enjoy testing their wits against those of the author; they want to examine every verbal clue, not simply see the action racing across a screen.

At the same time, as the novel has faced increasing competition from other "media," its greatest creators have stressed the value of what the intellectually lively Prince Hamlet told Polonius that he was reading: "words, words, words." The exquisite descriptions and dialogues of Marcel Proust, the neologisms and language games of James Joyce, the concentration on the problems of intellectuals and artists in Robert Musil, the understated passion and humor of Franz Kafka: all testify to the determination of twentieth-century writers to create novels which cannot be bodily transferred to, or made superfluous by, the radio play or the movie. But more important than questions of form, serious novelists in all the European languages have constantly aspired to deal with the important spiritual problems of their epoch. The greatest of them—such as Jane Austen, the Brontë sisters, George Eliot, and Thomas Hardy in England; Stendhal and Flaubert in France; Galdos and Emilia Pardo Bazán in Spain; Manzoni in Italy; Storm and Fontane in Germany; Tolstoy, Dostoyevsky, and Gogol in Russia—offered, both explicitly and implicitly, a philosophical criticism of human life as reflected in their fictions. Even the finest cinematic and televised versions of these novels cannot substitute for a reflective reading that brings the individual into direct contact with the mental world of the writer. This function remains as important today as in the past.

In the present chapter, without any desire to propound a hierarchy of canonical creative giants (something which, in any case, I am utterly unqualified to do), I will discuss a number of important novels, chosen more for their relevance to the historic experience of the European peoples in the twentieth century than for their formal originality or their aesthetic excellence.

In *The Magic Mountain*, published in 1924—six years after the end of the First World War and midway through the unstable, constantly troubled life of the Weimar Republic—Thomas Mann surveyed the entire spiritual landscape of early twentieth-century Europe. *The Magic Mountain* is a stellar example of the *Bildungsroman*, a type of novel cultivated particularly by the Germans and concentrating on how life educates the story's central figure.

Young Hans Castorp is the scion of a Hanseatic merchant family destined, with his own passive consent, to become an engineer and administrator in the family business. This conventional preparation for a predictable career is interrupted by what is supposed to be a three-week visit to his cousin at a tuberculosis sanatorium in the Swiss Alps. As things turn out, however, it becomes a seven-year educational residence for Hans in the Berghof—not as demanding as an Erasmus or a Fulbright fellowship today, but rather a period of indefinite intellectual rummaging, without responsibilities and paid for by his well-to-do family. Young Hans's return to the "flatland" occurs only with his decision to volunteer in the service of the fatherland in August 1914.

The reader learns in copious detail about the routines, the medical and social life of the Berghof. He is offered encyclopedic information about the history and treatment of tuberculosis, the disease which most preoccupied pre-1914 Europe. Observation and conversation inform him concerning the precise economic and social circumstances of dozens of patients and show him how disease, the threat of death, and the actual experience of intense suffering affect the outlook and behavior of numerous individuals.

Young Hans also falls hopelessly (but silently) in love with a seductive Russian lady who arrives late at meals and allows the dining-room door to slam behind her. Her "Kirghiz" eyes remind him of a school fellow whom he had worshiped from a distance and from whom he had once, memorably, borrowed a pencil. The obsession with Madame Chauchat leads Hans to deep reflexions on the ambiguity and extreme inhibition of his sexual impulses, on the relationship between disease and love, and on the cultural differences between disciplined, orderly Germany and "wild, primitive" Russia. But in relation to the subject of the present book, the most extraordinary portions of *The Magic Mountain* are the political debates in which the Italian anticlerical Liberal Settembrini and the fanatical Jesuit Naphta compete for domination of Hans, their intelligent and willing (but also sturdily independent) pupil.

Settembrini is a republican, an admirer of the French Enlightenment and of the Jacobin traditions of the French Revolution. He is a combative advocate of secular democracy, full intellectual liberty, and constitutional government. He scorns the irrational, including the more dubious aspects of the local medical treatment, the vaguely defined (and at worst pretentious) psychiatric and psychological ideas being propounded in the lectures of the Berghof director, and the "suspect" emotions induced by both Kirghiz eyes and music. For Settembrini, ignorance and injustice are typified by the Austro-Hungarian and Russian empires. The hope of humanity lies in the traditions of Locke and Voltaire, in the presumed rational clarity of the Latin peoples (the French and Italian in particular), in the development of technology and commerce as handmaidens of freedom, and in the internationalist, republican activities of the Freemasons and other secular democratic organizations.[1]

Naphta, by contrast, feels nothing but scorn for the whole secular Enlightenment. Men, he argues, are by nature weak and ignorant; they need authority and hierarchy, and faith must always dominate the intellect. Naphta's ideals are those which he attributes to St. Bernard: "the mill" and "the ploughed field" of earthly labor for the majority, the contemplative life of devotional prayer and penitential discipline for the intellectual elite. He argues vehemently that excommunication and even burning at the stake in the Middle Ages, and the use of torture and capital punishment in the modern age, are in fact pursued for the benefit of men's sinful souls. Moreover, the unchallenged rule of the medieval Church over a predominantly rural society is his idealized past. This ideal was destroyed by the rise of the bourgeoisie, and Naphta identifies all the sins of money-grubbing capitalism with the triumph of secular democracy. He predicts that this bourgeois era will soon be destroyed by a revolution which will combine economic communism with political terror.[2]

This learned, highly intellectual novel was created at intervals between 1914 and 1924. The figure of Settembrini owes much to the personality of Mann's older brother Heinrich, who dared to be pro-French during the war and with whom Thomas himself had quarreled bitterly while adhering to a conservative patriotic position. The figure of Naphta owes much to Mann's acquaintance with George Lukács, a leading Hungarian Marxist and a man of encyclopedic knowledge and dialectical skill who in the early twenties was enthusiastically pro-Bolshevik. Mann himself, after the German defeat in 1918, steadily evolved toward pro-democratic and anti-Nazi political positions.

It is crucial to remember that Settembrini and Naphta are fictional creations, however much they were based on the author's impressions of his brother and Lukács. Yet the power of Mann's creative imagination gave to *The Magic Mountain* the force of an involuntary prophecy. As of 1924, Hitler was a little-known ranting orator, and Stalin was a leading but by no means supremely powerful figure in the new Soviet Union. But all the horrors of the later Nazi and Stalinist dictatorships, the murderous hatred of the bourgeoisie and intellectuals, the "rational" justification of forced confessions and death penalties, the "saving" of souls by inquisitional tortures, the insistence on hierarchy and blind faith, and the treatment of human beings as disposable chattels—all these common traits of Nazism and Stalinism were imagined and dramatized in advance in the figure of Naphta. At the same time, his rival Settembrini displays many of the weaknesses of the typical liberal intellectual—an underestimation of the irrational elements in human nature, a tendency to assume that virtuous proclamations will be followed by virtuous behavior, and a belief that all the problems of a complex society can be solved by rational legislation carried out by (mostly peaceful) Jacobin persuasion.

As for Hans Castorp, the "delicate child of life" (as his creator repeatedly calls him), the young man is happy to learn from everything he experiences: from the debates of his rival tutors; from his own passion for Madame Chauchat; from the honorable and idealistic Prussianism of the military cousin he came to visit; from the sometimes learned, sometimes empty and pretentious, rhetoric of the medical directors of the Berghof sanatorium; from listening to recordings of classical music; from the company of Mynheer Peeperkorn, a retired Dutch colonial planter with a "larger-than-life" personality; and even from an occult session complete with levitating chairs.

The Magic Mountain can hardly be said to offer an optimistic view of European (or human) destiny. Two of the principal characters commit suicide. Despite his immense vitality, his wealth and sociability, and the ease with which he dominates all conversation and enjoys the protective love of Madame Chauchat, the Dutch plantation owner Mynheer Peeperkorn chooses to die by rapid poison rather than bear the slow decline of old age. And despite the apparent certainty of his political convictions and the many material comforts paid for by his Order, the Jesuit Naphta also takes his own life. The occasion is the duel which, in a moment of uncontrollable political passion, Settembrini has provoked with him. Naphta refuses all the efforts of their mutual friends to avoid a fatal outcome. When the two men face each at only three paces, Settembrini—refusing on principle to kill—fires into the air. Naphta, shouting "coward" at his enemy, then fires into his own forehead.

It is the temporal conclusion of all this intellectual and emotional experience that strikingly prefigures the unresolved spiritual purposes of European life in the twentieth century. The First World War breaks out, as unanticipated at the Berghof as among the majority of European citizens, and the intellectually independent but ultimately obedient Hans Castorp returns to the "flatland" to join the German army. He is last seen slogging forward in one of those ghastly infantry battles which characterized the Western Front; Thomas Mann does not tell us whether or not Hans survives the war, nor does he seem to think it an important question.

However, it would not be entirely accurate to say that the seven years of Hans's *Bildung* result in nothing but dire political forecasts and a marvelously rich education wasted in military slaughter. Two things make bearable what would otherwise be heavy, pessimistic reading. One is Mann's ear for speech and his ironic, at times literally fantastic sense of humor. Coupled with his capacity to portray the innermost workings of personality, Mann's wit suggests that life is worth living, and studying, precisely because of its infinite variety—because it is *funny*, and vital. But there is also one significant incident in which Mann raises the possibility of a positive ideal. Young Hans goes skiing, gets lost, and—while in danger of freezing to death—has a series of vivid dreams. In these dreams, he sees images both of the rational, sun-drenched beauty of Greek sculpture and dance, and horrible images of witchcraft, torture, and human sacrifice. At the end of this series of half-waking dreams, after he has recovered the strength to ski back to the hotel, Hans says to himself (in words which are italicized by the author): "For the sake of goodness and love, man shall let death have no sovereignty over his thoughts."[3]

And yet, if this was the priceless lesson learned by Hans Castorp in his seven years at the Berghof, was there no better outcome to be achieved than service in one of the armies which came close to destroying European civilization in the Great War? The question, alas, remains valid seventy years later. Permanent peace has probably been made between the principal antagonists of the First World War— England, Germany, and France—but the existing advanced cultures all over the globe still offer high educational opportunities and economic status to those persons who devote their professional lives to the "improvement" of nuclear, chemical, and biological weapons.

At the beginning of this chapter, I indicated that, in the twentieth century, the novel as portrayer of life has yielded much ground to other sources of entertainment and information: fictional and documentary movies, radio and TV serials, detective and espionage novels. This has indeed been true in the West, and it was also true in the early years of the Russian Revolution. Thus the Bolsheviks at first welcomed all the *avant garde* tendencies in European art and literature; they took great pride in protecting artistic liberty and thought of radio and cinema as excellent means both to entertain and to educate the entire population of the future polyglot, multinational, Soviet classless society. But when it rapidly became evident that their ideals and slogans did not correspond to the real experience of the peoples under their rule, the Bolsheviks sought instead to establish strong ideological controls on publishing, theater, and cinema. The dogmatic tendencies were already clear during the 1920s and became firmly codified under Stalin's dictatorship. Published fiction in the 1930s had to conform to the "proletarian" and "socialist" ideals expounded by the Party. Although these strictures seemed to be somewhat loosened during the war against the Nazis, immediately after the war's end Stalin reimposed tight ideological controls.

Boris Pasternak was already a recognized poetic talent at the time of the Russian revolution. Between 1917 and 1929, he published several volumes of poetry and a lesser quantity of fictional and autobiographical prose. His was a nonpolitical temperament; Pasternak accepted rather than approved the revolution, and although his technique and aesthetics related him closely to the Western *avant garde*, he loved Russia as his homeland and the Russian language as his means of expression. During the purge era, 1936–1939, Pasternak somehow miraculously escaped arrest and—perhaps due to his high poetic prestige and to his firm avoidance of both party and literary politics—he also managed not to denounce (or be fatally denounced by) any of his colleagues.

During the thirties and the war years, Pasternak did not try to publish fiction. Instead, he made his living by translating the great European classics, Shakespeare and Goethe in particular. During the wartime relaxation of ideology, he began to plan a major novel concerning the revolution. He worked on it more or less clandestinely during the decade from 1946 to 1956. During the "thaw" following Khrushchev's de-Stalinization speech, there were announcements that Pasternak's novel would soon be published, but in fact its publication was never authorized in Moscow. The work appeared in 1957, first in Italian and then in many other European languages, on the basis of a copy which Pasternak had permitted his Italian editor to take home with him. Pasternak was awarded the Nobel Prize for literature in 1958, but he refused the honor in order not to be imprisoned or expelled from his beloved Russia. *Dr. Zhivago* was to appear legally in Russia only in 1988, during the brief liberalization of the Soviet Union under its last leader, Mikhail Gorbachev.

The central figure, Yuri Zhivago, is a practicing physician and a poet. Like his creator, he is a deeply reflective man of broad social sympathies and a strong political intelligence, but one who prefers the role of observer to that of protagonist. Though Pasternak himself was a child of the urban bourgeoisie, his characters are by no means limited to the educated middle class. As a device for maintaining some degree of narrative unity over a period of fifteen years (and in dozens of locations across European Russia and Western Siberia), Pasternak has many of his novel's main characters grow up together as children in the same working-class quarter of Moscow. They share school, vacation, trade-union, or strike experiences as youngsters, and meet again years later in their roles as revolutionaries, counter-revolutionaries, or refugees simply trying to survive the catastrophe. Although the device is artificial, it enables the author to portray the interactions and development of the same individuals throughout the range of chaotic and unpredictable situations in which they find themselves. It also permits him to show, without the necessity of theoretical explanations, how persons of very similar backgrounds and characters nevertheless ended up on opposite sides during the civil war. At the same time, Pasternak's love of nature, his sensitivity to the peculiarities of individual speech, and his talent as a sympathetic listener produced a novel in which the rural is as vividly portrayed as any urban or domestic incident. At the same time, persons of many different social classes and nationalities come alive through their individual histories and their roles—voluntary or involuntary—in the revolutions of 1905 and 1917, and the civil war of 1918–1920.

In terms of my theme, "civilization" and "barbarity," there are at least three important reasons to read *Dr. Zhivago* carefully. One is for its richness of biographical detail about dozens of intimately portrayed individuals. Because of the rigid censorship imposed by Stalin (and only slightly loosened by Khrushchev), official Soviet literature could not treat honestly the extraordinary variety of human thoughts, and thus we are virtually dependent for a truthful portrayal of this time on the clandestine writings of a handful of courageous poets, philosophers, and fiction writers.

The second reason is to consider Pasternak's interpretation of the Russian revolution as an ongoing phenomenon. He views the overthrow of the imperial government as having been inevitable, both because of the long history of tsarist oppression and because of its failure to fulfill the promises of reform dating from the late nineteenth century. (Nor is this just one man's opinion. Indeed, despite the tremendous differences in standard of living between the vast peasant majority and the small aristocracy and urban bourgeoisie, Pasternak found that individual Russian workers—servants, small shopkeepers, and functionaries—often expressed themselves very frankly and intelligently, and he had the ear—and the personal sympathies—to bring these people alive on the printed page.) Pasternak was also clearly exhilarated by the first stages of the revolution in 1917. Liberty had appeared (according to Dr. Zhivago) as an accidental, sudden gift of the gods: It had occurred half as a result of the war and half as a result of the vast, oppressed majority's revolutionary self-liberation. At several points in the novel, both Dr. Zhivago and other characters whose views reflect those of Pasternak himself praise the re-distribution of land, the initiatives of village Soviets in education and sanitation, the new laws protecting industrial workers and mothers, the condemnation of speculative finance, and the presumed redirection of national wealth toward the material needs of the long-suffering populace.

In this sense, the revolutions (both the parliamentary revolution of March and the Bolshevik revolution of November) were absolutely unique in human history. Later, during the civil war, Dr. Zhivago—even though he has been kidnapped into service by a detachment of Bolshevik partisans, and even though he sympathizes with specific individuals serving under General Kolchak—considers that, on balance, the Bolsheviks have been less destructive and less arbitrarily cruel than have the opposing White Guards. But at the same time, the revolution offers no worthy long-term solutions to the question of ideals and purpose in life. Slogans of hate, the unification of classes or nations under military banners, the exercise of arbitrary power of life and death, all remind Dr. Zhivago of Old Testament tribal wars, not of revolutionary hopes. This brings me in turn to the third important reason for reading this novel: an interpretation of Christianity that is quietly interwoven with the violent events of the revolution, and which is quite clearly Pasternak's personal message to his present and future readers.

These reflective passages about Christianity often occur as reactions to an anti-Semitic incident interpreted among the troops or villagers. Pasternak himself was a convert to the Orthodox Church, one who at the same time admired the large Jewish contribution to the professions, the arts, and the sciences in Russia and considered anti-Semitic propaganda and violence to be one of the most shameful aspects of Russian popular culture. Several of his main characters (and therefore, we may suppose, Pasternak himself) also wonder why more Jews did not convert. Why, his characters ask, did those who developed the great doctrines of Christianity and, who made outstanding contributions to the emancipation movements in the modern world, still insist on maintaining their own separate religious and national identity?

Scattered throughout the novel are other brief discussions of religious topics. Some of these revolve around theological details which probably do not interest most contemporary readers, but some of them imply a profoundly beautiful world view. For Pasternak, there are three great monotheistic religions. The Jews, escaping from Egyptian slavery, were led by a prince (hidden in the bulrushes as an infant, but still a prince)—that same Moses who was never himself to reach the Promised Land, but who gave national unity and pride of purpose to his people. The Jews were to spread to all humanity the knowledge of a single, supreme, and just God; at the same time, however, they were to remain a separate people in the Greco-Roman world.

The founder of Islam was a merchant and practiced the polygamy which was a normal part of Arab culture. Membership in Islam was open to all individuals without national or tribal distinctions, but its universalism was limited—at least in symbol and image—by the polygamy, the relative wealth of the Prophet, and the obvious subordination of women implied by polygamy. The founder of the third great monotheistic religion (though actually the second, chronologically speaking) was neither prince nor merchant but instead was born in a manger, the child of powerless refugees. His Church was open to all nations and classes, and the circumstances of his birth symbolized not only the inclusion but the emphasis on the salvation of the most poor and exploited.

For Pasternak, the world needed the early, generous, liberating, non-nationalist phases of the revolution and the internationalist, classless universalism of the Christian Gospel. Where the revolution went wrong was in its growing rigidity, its insistence on manipulating human beings for purposes understood only by the top leadership, and its substitution of raw coercion for the economic exploitation it had overthrown.

Integral to Pasternak's religious ideal is a perhaps "old-fashioned" view of the role of women. When Dr. Zhivago observes the look of inward concentration on the face of his pregnant wife, when he observes the total attention and cheerful willingness to sacrifice in the behavior of even the simplest and least educated mother toward her children, he thinks to himself: *This* is the real meaning of the "immaculate conception"—that the birth and early nurture of children is the sacred function of women, to such an extent that the father feels almost like an outsider (like the puzzled and loving Joseph as he appears in many a medieval sculpture). In any case, what every society needs, no matter what its practical material arrangements, is an atmosphere of love in day-to-day human relations. For Pasternak, that love is provided principally (though not exclusively) by women, and the greatest of human principles is the sacred quality of human life.

The third creative writer I wish to discuss, Louis-Ferdinand Céline, was the author of a number of vivid, controversial novels and memoirs, in particular his uniquely moving novel *Voyage au bout de la nuit*, published in 1932. The novel begins with the World War I experiences of its central character and "anti-hero," Bardamu, a reconnaissance cavalry sergeant. Bardamu does not pretend to any patriotic virtues; he is afraid of the Germans and hates the French generals whose tactics are decimating thousands of infantrymen in senseless assaults on German artillery and machine-gun positions. He dreams of getting himself taken prisoner, but instead is wounded in action. The novel continues with Bardamu's convalescence, including love affairs with an American volunteer nurse and a Parisian night-club entertainer, then with his brief stint serving a commercial company in the African colonies. This is followed by a few adventurous months in the United States and a few frustrating years as a not particularly successful doctor with a mostly working-class and shopkeeper clientele, some of whom pay their bills and some of whom do not.

The power of Céline's novel comes from the authenticity and power of its many short character sketches and dialogues. In counterpoint with his extremely negative feelings toward authority, Céline possessed a genuine sympathy toward ordinary, uneducated, and unpretentious working people, a sympathy which has been claimed by many writers but truly felt and demonstrated by very few. Even so, this gifted man was at the same time an anti-Semite and a literary collaborator during the Nazi occupation, a man who fled to Germany with the retreating Nazi army and who, to avoid probable imprisonment and possible death, lived in Denmark until he was officially amnestied in 1951. It also seems to be true that Céline's wartime sins were literary. Prolonged investigation of his conduct has never produced any evidence that he betrayed anyone to the Gestapo. But his writings were full of Nazi venom and he consorted openly with the occupying forces. An indulgent interpretation of Céline's outrageous behavior in the years 1941–1945 might be that he thought of himself as a court jester, immune from political responsibility through his function as jester. The interesting task, in terms of "civilization and barbarity," is to understand the enigma Céline as both a great writer and a Nazi literary collaborator.

Turning to the biographical facts (for which I am principally indebted to Frédéric Vitoux's *La vie de Céline*, Bernard Grasset, 1988) Céline was not, like Mann or Pasternak, a conscientious and successful "man of letters," celebrated as such throughout his career. He entered adult life as a highly intelligent, attractive, and fairly well-educated member of the pre-1914 middle class. He was to become both a doctor and a writer, but he never felt himself secure as a member of the "establishment" in either phase of his career.

Céline's fiction is completely autobiographical. It is, of course, necessarily true that all novelists use their personal experience, but they generally do so in a somewhat more disguised form than Céline. All the events in *Voyage* are directly related to the facts and the fantasies of his own life; some names and sequences have been changed, but there is never the slightest doubt that he is presenting a "novelized" autobiography, a condensation and intensification of the actual truth. Like his fictional hero Bardamu, Céline was a cavalry sergeant serving in the reconnaissance forces. In October 1914, he was wounded in the arm and the head. The arm wound required a long and painful convalescence; the extent of the head wound was never fully clarified, but for the rest of his life Céline suffered from insomnia, heard noises inside his skull, and endured extended periods of extreme nervous sensibility.

Toward the end of his medical studies in 1923, Céline wrote a thesis concerning the Hungarian Jewish doctor, Ignaz Semmelweis, who discovered the cause of the puerperal fever which had been killing so many women in childbirth. Semmelweis's admonition to disinfect all instruments and wash one's hands before delivering babies was not appreciated at the time by the Vienna medical establishment; he lost his hospital post and died soon thereafter, mentally alienated. Céline obviously empathized with Semmelweis as an unappreciated genius mistreated by his colleagues.

Céline himself was interested in public health, and for four years served in the League of Nations World Health Organization. He liked the salary and the frequent travel connected with the job, but he was not so fond of writing reports on such topics as the exchange of health-service personnel among the British, French, and Portuguese colonies in Africa, or the visits of Latin American doctors to various municipal hospitals in the United States. In 1928, he resigned his post and hung out his shingle in Clichy, the district of Paris where he had grown up. His income was not sufficient to cover both his living expenses and his considerable debts from his Geneva period, so in 1931 Céline took two part-time jobs, one as a writer-assessor for a pharmaceutical company and the other as a general practitioner in the municipal-health clinic in Clichy. The tragicomic experiences of "the doctor" in the novel (told in an often-lengthy first person) are those of Céline himself—with a touch here and there of poetic license, perhaps, but still essentially true.

From his career problems, his letters, and his published writings, it is clear that Céline always felt uncomfortable with (if not directly hostile to) political and professional authority. His immediate superior in the League of Nations was a Polish Jewish doctor with whom he had normal, even cordial, personal relations and from whom he received both professional and financial aid. But in his writings, he savagely caricatured this Dr. Rajchman as an official skilled at "wheeling and dealing," abusing his professional travel perks, and turning on the charm as necessary in order to make the most advantageous use of the bureaucracy and the rules.

A few years later, Céline's superiors in the pharmaceutical firm were also Jewish. Thus, to some extent, his anti-Semitism may be explained by the frequent European middle-class stereotype of the Jew as "pushy," as having too much influence in business and the professions, arousing the jealousy of less energetic or less clever colleagues, and so on. Nor do I think Céline's collaboration can be explained principally as a sharing of Nazi racial anti-Semitism. For one thing, many of the references in his books to the black natives of the French colonies are sympathetic to those natives. For another, his caricatures of French military, colonial, and scientific mandarins are as savage as anything he wrote about Dr. Rajchman. There is in Céline a constant tendency to attribute the worst motives to those in authority. They must be cheats and hypocrites, he alleges, otherwise they would never have achieved their success.

Leaving aside for the moment the individual case of Céline, fascist and Nazi intellectuals frequently combined a general resentment against successful business and professional people with a desire to be associated with the kind of authoritarian, violent "masculinity" preached by Mussolini. The Spanish *Falange*, the French *Croix de Feu* and the *Cagoulards*, the Belgian Rexists, the British Mosleyites, and many German lawyers and professors who volunteered as *Gauleiter*, all shared this "with fists and rolled-up sleeves" attitude. Céline does not sound like a bully, but he fully shared the tendency of fascist intellectuals to feel extremely insecure about their own value. Many of them owed their professional advancement in the 1930s to the proscription of men who were their intellectual and ethical superiors—the exiled artists, scientists, and intellectuals of Italy, Germany, and Spain.

If the Céline of the 1920s was insecure in his relation to professional authority, the Céline of 1933 and after felt a bitter hatred toward the French literary establishment. He had worked intensively in the years 1928–1932 on *Voyage au bout de la nuit*. The manuscript had been highly praised by important editors and publishers. As of October 1932, Céline and his publisher both believed that he was sure to win the prestigious Goncourt Prize. But when the vote was taken in December, his several months' illusion was destroyed. Many intellectuals have had to adjust to the fact of not winning a prize they thought was surely theirs, but with Céline it became an obsession which must have been exacerbated by his insecure feelings toward all authority and by the long-term physical effects of his wartime head wound, plus the recurring malaria attacks dating from his period in Africa. During and after World War II, he apparently believed that all his troubles were due to the literary jealousy of anti-Vichy and *Résistance* writers. Because of his overwhelming personal egoism and paranoia, he may well have sincerely failed to realize the political implications of his literary fulminations, most of which do not compare in worth with his first and greatest novel.

Voyage is a sterling example of the ways in which personal misfortune can be transmuted into great art. The invalidated Sergeant Bardamu defends himself as best he can and takes his pleasure where he can find it. Hospitalized, he makes love to an American nurse whose ideas seem positively ridiculous to him, but whose physique and manners delight him. Shipped to Africa in the company of military men who plan to victimize him as a cowardly "civilian," he spouts patriotic drivel which completely disarms their hostility. Having established his medical practice, he is unable to press his patients for payment and often multiplies his verbal recommendations while backing his way out of the patient's apartment, too embarrassed to raise the question of fees. When he goes to a famous research institute in the hope of obtaining information about an atypical form of typhoid which is destroying a little boy of whom he is especially fond, the specialist whom he consults turns out to be utterly useless. To add insult to injury, the doctor is treated to a completely egotistical lecture about the venomous internal politics of the institute and about his interlocutor's plan to "study the comparative influence of central heating on the incidence of hemorrhoids in the northern and southern countries." The great man thinks that this topic will be most likely to interest the mostly older men who will be judging his work. When he briefly refers to the subject of typhoid, it is only to say observe that there are many conflicting opinions, and the doctor should use his intuition. At which point, the academician is in an inexplicable hurry to reach a certain cafe, and the two men arrive just after the teenage girls have gone home from the lycée across the street. "Too late," says the great man. "I know their legs by heart."[4] (Perhaps needless to add, the little boy dies.)

Such was Céline's experience as a poor people's general practitioner. As a writer, he combined a clear, rhythmic expository prose with a fine ear for popular speech, a fantastic imagination, and a Rabelaisian sense of humor. His capacity for affection was channeled into the love of cats and of heterosexual partners, valued as much or more for their companionship as for physical sex. He suffered in the presence of his patients' suffering and he continued to hope for improvements in the system of public health, and bitterly resented the success of powerful people, especially if they were Jews. It is a syndrome of qualities that occurs frequently in all European countries; indeed, Céline expressed all the resentments, the crude humor, and the solidarity of the underdogs, many of whom—if they had not been won over to Marxism—became fascists.

The Russian novelist and historian Aleksandr Solzhenitsyn was another great writer who transmuted his personal suffering into high-quality fiction and tended to resist all political and professional authority (though without the paranoia of Céline). Born in 1918 and educated in the south Russian city of Rostov, Solzhenitsyn was a polymath who successfully finished university degrees in math and physics and also made time for literary studies. He was looking forward to a career of teaching and writing at the time of the German invasion in June 1941.

During the war, Solzhenitsyn was twice decorated for service in the field artillery on the long march from the suburbs of Moscow to Berlin. Although, like any soldier, he must have known that censors read all his letters, he apparently made some uncomplimentary references to Marshall Stalin, for which crime he was courtmartialed and sentenced to eight years of forced labor, to be followed by permanent exile in Central Asia. He spent four years as an applied mathematician in one of the scientific institutes inhabited by prisoner scientists near Moscow (*The First Circle* of a Dantesque Hell) and another four years in a Siberian concentration camp. Released from the camp in early 1953, he expected to spend the rest of his "free" but exiled life as a teacher in a small city in Kazakhstan.

Khrushchev's "thaw" in the years 1955–1964 enabled him to return to Russia and begin publishing fiction, and to conduct the lengthy interviews necessary to prepare an oral history of the Soviet concentration camps, the so-called gulag. In 1962, Solzhenitsyn's first novel, *One Day in the Life of Ivan Denisovitch*, was approved for publication by none less than Nikita Khrushchev himself. In the partial Stalinist restoration after the forcible retirement of Khrushchev (1964), Solzhenitsyn found it impossible to publish his next two novels, but as of 1968 *The First Circle* and *The Cancer Ward* were circulating clandestinely in Russia and appearing in translation in Western Europe and the United States.

A stubborn and courageous man (having survived both the gulag and a bout of cancer), Solzhenitsyn continued to work defiantly on his documentary historical novel, *August, 1914*, and on the oral history, *The Gulag Archipelago*. Neither of these could be published in the Soviet Union, but they were widely read in mimeographed copies. Meanwhile, he was awarded the Nobel Prize in 1970 and, like Pasternak before him, had to refuse it as the price of continued residence in Russia. In 1974 the Western publication of the *Gulag* led to his expulsion from Russia, after which he lived in the USA (in relative self-imposed isolation on a Vermont farm) and returned in triumph to Moscow shortly before the dissolution of the Soviet Union.

For purposes of the present chapter, I will concentrate on *The Cancer Ward*. Both *August, 1914* and *The Gulag Archipelago* are immensely valuable for their information and interpretation, and *The First Circle* is as fascinating a novel as is *The Cancer Ward*. But there are quite a number of memoirs by scientists and intellectuals who survived to describe life in the scientific institutes manned by prisoners, whereas *The Cancer Ward* (like *Dr. Zhivago*) constitutes a unique look at aspects of Soviet society that were completely hidden by seven decades of censorship. (Indeed, not until the development of international scientific exchanges in the 1970s was it possible for Westerners to travel anywhere in the Soviet Union except to Moscow and Leningrad—cities in which they were subject at all times to close supervision by the police.)

Like Céline's *Voyage*, *The Cancer Ward* is based on personal experience: In February 1955, the ex-prisoner and internal exile Aleksandr Solzhenitsyn arrived for treatment at the cancer hospital in Tashkent, capital city of Uzbekistan. In the person of his fictional counterpart, Sergeant Oleg Kostoglotov, we learn in rich detail about the life of the hospital and, in some measure, about life in a provincial Soviet capital inhabited largely by Muslim Uzbeks.

As to the quality of Soviet medicine, Kostoglotov—an eternal doubter-questioner and permanent exile—is grudgingly satisfied. The doctors guard carefully against the dangerous side effects of their X-ray and radiation treatments. There are not enough beds, but the sanitation is excellent, the food is tolerable, and the blood transfusions and chemical injections are competently administered. The internal (therefore reasonably accurate) statistics of the hospital show very few cures but also very few deaths—partly due to the fact that, out of sheer humanity as well as to control the workload, the truly hopeless cases are given as much pain relief as possible and allowed to go home. Despite being constantly overworked, the doctors and nurses are mostly courteous with their polyglot set of patients, and show no political prejudice in their dealings with Kostoglotov and other less-than-honored Soviet citizens. They train Uzbek and other Asian nurses and orderlies without the slightest ethnic condescension. They read the latest medical journal articles, regularly consult their top colleagues in Moscow, and spare no expense or personal effort to secure considerable relief of suffering and a considerable proportion of remissions.

Kostoglotov's conversations with Zoya, a flirtatious, intelligent medical student and nurse, indicate the lamentable ignorance of "free" Soviet citizens about the gulag. Zoya asks Kostoglotov why he didn't come for treatment before he was near death. She is surprised to learn that there is no transport: No planes? No trucks? Why all those copies of different permissions to leave the village? By the way, weren't there doctors in the village? Yes, says Kostoglotov, two of them, both obstetricians—"surplus" in a society that had lost an entire generation of potential fathers. On another occasion, Zoya wants to know why he must return to the unattractive-sounding village from which he came. No, he explains patiently, he is not a Chechen, not a gang member either. As a matter of fact, if he were a common criminal, he would already have benefited from one of the many amnesties. Well, she asks, was he tried and sentenced? No, Kostoglotov replies, he "received eternal exile by consignment . . . something like an invoice." The naive and archly feminine aspiring doctor still cannot understand what he means, and keeps asking Kostoglotov what he actually *did* to be exiled.[5]

There is less humor and more bite in his portrayal of a successful Soviet bureaucrat and cancer patient who insists he does not have cancer. Pavel Rusanov demands (but does not receive) preferential treatment as a Soviet official; he expects Moscow "pull" at any moment to whisk him off to a special hospital for officials only; and he speaks mainly in Soviet slogans whenever he does condescend to take part in the ward conversations. Rusanov's condition improves noticeably after a few weeks, but then he is taken aback by news of the ouster of Stalin's first successor, Georgi Malenkov, as well as of several Stalinist supreme court justices (February 1955). Shortly thereafter, his wife brings him more devastating news: A colleague whom Rusanov had secretly denounced in the 1937 purges has been freed and will likely return to the city where both men were important officials. The pompous and self-pitying Rusanov then shouts: "What right have they to free them now? How can they traumatize people so heartlessly?"[6]

But Kostoglotov's deepest concern (other than for his own recovery) is the situation of Soviet women. He is half in love with both Zoya, the twenty-three-year-old nurse and medical student who cannot understand his exile, and with Dr. Vera Gangart, nearly ten years older than Zoya and a very reserved and sensitive human being. Due to her German ancestry, Vera was not allowed to serve at the front in World War II. After her fiancé was killed in battle, Vera had one unsatisfactory romantic relationship, and since then she has retreated emotionally—and, the novel implies, permanently—into her memories.

Solzhenitsyn's attitude (like that of Pasternak) is quite "old-fashioned": He obviously assumes that all women, despite their numerical importance in Soviet professional life, wish primarily to marry, have children, and rely on a husband for emotional security. Whether or not he is correct on this point, the reader cannot help feeling his immense tenderness and pity toward these millions of still young women who work for a living, take care of their aging parents and their fatherless children, do virtually all the marketing and the housework wherever they live, and are condemned to a lifetime of widowhood (or "old maidhood").

In describing the histories of the many patients, the personal lives of Zoya and Vera in the city of Tashkent, and Kostoglotov's journeys down from his Kazakh village and back to it after his cure, Solzhenitsyn offers what great novelists do best: a sympathetic, factually true, and philosophically critical examination of a given place and time, a panoramic view of an entire society with life portrayed as it is *felt* by those who live it. Even if *The Cancer Ward* had been written in a nation with a free press, uncensored documentary films, and sociological theses prepared in an atmosphere of genuine academic freedom, Solzhenitsyn's novel would be worth reading. But in the case of the officially proscribed Soviet world, the knowledge available in *The Cancer Ward* (like *Dr. Zhivago* before it) is unique.

The novel as a literary form has also held its own in conditions of Western liberty. As one excellent example (among many such possible examples), I will discuss the work of the well-known English novelist Iris Murdoch. She comes of Anglo-Irish background, studied classics and philosophy at Oxford, and worked in the United Nations Relief and Rehabilitation Administration after World War II. Murdoch married a literary critic and specialist in Russian literature, and between 1954 and 1983 published some twenty novels, plus a number of poems and philosophical essays. Thus Murdoch has been an amazingly productive woman of letters, well-established and highly regarded within the academic and intellectual elite of the United Kingdom in the second half of the twentieth century.

Murdoch's novels have mostly to do with the British middle class, whose members range from the well-off to the modest, from the university-educated to the barely literate, and from the conventional to the eccentric. Her characters (of both sexes) are not fantasized or idealized as in much of Pasternak and Céline—and, to some extent, in Mann and Solzhenitsyn as well. Murdoch is very skeptical and observant, anxious to do justice to people's motives, interested above all in the details of personal behavior within a social context, and without any passionate political agenda. She appears to assume, for herself and her public, the sort of reasonableness and tolerance which is indeed more characteristic of British culture than of most.

The particular wisdom that one gets from Murdoch's work is a sense of the complexity and ambiguity of human motives in "ordinary" life. Her novels are not tales of war, apocalypse, revolution, and mass suffering, but rather dramas of civilian life and the important crises that human beings experience in relation to their neighbors and their private emotions. I will draw my examples from one of the more complex of these narratives, *The Philosopher's Pupil*. The philosopher of the title is Rozanov, a native son of the spa town of Enniston, who retires from a successful professorial career in the United States and returns to Enniston intending to write the "great book" he has not previously had time for. Rozanov is anxious to reintegrate himself into a community where he has never been fully appreciated, but his new situation is complicated by the strange outbursts partly love and partly hate, of a former graduate student, and by the very conflicting emotions he himself feels toward the granddaughter whom he has neglected in the past.

Private passions—and their ambiguity in action—particularly characterize this novel. It begins with an automobile accident on a rainy night: Did Rozanov's former student George McCaffrey deliberately push his car into a canal in an effort to kill his wife Stella, or was it truly an accident? We never are certain of the facts, but then Murdoch is not writing a whodunit—in the course of the novel, she shows us that George and Stella themselves cannot really be sure what happened, and why, on the night in question. This profound ambiguity, moreover, touches every character in *The Philosopher's Pupil*. When Rozanov and the homosexual priest Father Bernard meet, the philosopher asks him bluntly: "Do you believe in God?" Father Bernard responds, "No." "Come," Rozanov urges him, "anything counts as belief these days." But again the priest responds, "No." As the dialogue continues, we learn that both men "abominate" the concept of a personal God, but that Father Bernard still insists on a "spiritual reality," though this would hardly seem enough to fulfill his duties as a Catholic priest. Similarly, when George McCaffrey finally corners Rozanov in the sitting room of the local inn and tries to get some kind of human reaction from him, the disappointed former student finds himself rebuffed. Will the professor talk to him? No. What does the professor think about him? He doesn't think anything; he just wishes to be let alone. George asks desperately whether Rozanov realizes how he has destroyed George's "life illusions," his "self-love." Well, says Rozanov, if he destroyed his self-love, so much the better. But doesn't the pitiless professor realize that "without self-love there is nothing but evil"? Rozanov coldly replies that "what you call evil is simply vanity. . . ." And so the tense conversation continues between them. In the course of the novel, we learn a great deal about the various meanings of belief, hope, evil, self-love, vanity, and so forth, but we never arrive at any completely secure, safe, and comfortable definitions.

The other novels I have discussed in this chapter can help us understand the major upheavals of the twentieth century. Iris Murdoch helps us understand what life is like for the contemporary middle class. It is perhaps what life would be like for human beings in general if we could arrive at a world without deep poverty, major wars, and ecological suicide. It would certainly not be a world without conflict—but the conflicts, with a minimum of effort at mutual tolerance, would be contained within the peaceful boundaries of civilian life.

Murdoch's novels also illustrate the great variety of beliefs and skepticisms which can co-exist within European culture. On the one hand, they are not fueled by the intellectual and political passions that bulk so large in authors as different as Mann, Pasternak, Céline, and Solzhenitsyn. On the other hand, a peaceful world requires the kind of skeptical and tolerant understanding that Murdoch herself exhibits. And since human beings will never settle for boredom, for a species of bovine existence, it is important to read a novelist who illuminates the workings of human passions in conditions of relative peace and the absence of ideological oppression.

One could also choose to illustrate these aspects of European civilization through the works of such great dramatists as Bertolt Brecht and Harold Pinter, such philosophical poets as T. S. Eliot and Antonio Machado, such philosophical film directors as Ingmar Bergman and Rainer Werner Fassbinder. The great wealth of European creative literature, theater, poetry, and film is a testament to the continuing spiritual vitality of Europe itself.

ENDNOTES

1. For the principal passages in which Settembrini expounds his beliefs, see Thomas Mann, *Der Zauberberg* (Fischer Taschenbuch Verlag), pp. 161–70, 259–66; and in English, *The Magic Mountain* (A. A. Knopf Vintage), pp. 156–64, 244–50.

2. For Naphta's ideology, see the Fischer ed., pp. 393–409, 414–28, 474–86; or the Vintage ed., pp. 372–86, 393–405, 450–62.

3. Fischer ed., pp. 516–25; Vintage ed., pp. 490–98.

4. For the doctor's problems, *Voyage au bout de la nuit* (Collection Folio, Gallimard), pp. 315–49; for his fruitless visit to the Institute, pp. 354–64.

5. Aleksandr I. Solzhenitsyn, *The Cancer Ward* (New York: Dell Publishers, 1968). For the two conversations explaining internal exile to Zoya, see pp. 39–44 and 190–96.

6. For Rusanov and the Great Purge, see Solzhenitsyn, pp. 202–28.

14

The Cold War in Germany
and Central-Eastern Europe

he Cold War is an apt name for the years from 1947 to 1989, in which the most important single factor in international diplomacy was the hostile but carefully controlled relationship between the United States, the Soviet Union, and their respective military allies and satellites. The Cold War conditioned the development of all the countries of Europe on both sides of the Iron Curtain, albeit with considerable differences of intensity which depended largely on geography.

Except at moments of crisis, Western Europe, the British Isles, Scandinavia (with the exception of Finland), and the Iberian peninsula could all pursue their national policies under the American nuclear umbrella without feeling threatened militarily and with little interference in their internal affairs. The Soviet Union could also freely pursue its own national and international policies. But the areas bordering directly on the USSR—from Finland in the north to Greece and Turkey on the Mediterranean—were never able to forget for a moment their dependence on the superpowers and their frontline exposure in any possible war between them. These areas had long been cultural as well as political borderlands between historic Europe and the "East." As a result, for these nations the Cold War had high religious and cultural stakes as well as the obvious political-economic-military costs.

At the Yalta conference in February 1945, the Soviet Union committed itself to free elections in the countries liberated by the Red Army. At first the Soviets did indeed accept, in Poland, Hungary, Romania, and Bulgaria, the electoral victories of peasant parties which defended private property and the Catholic or Orthodox religious establishments. But since these countries had not had truly democratic governments in the years prior to the war, it was not difficult for the Soviets to discover small electoral irregularities and to invent larger ones. Through control of the police (the communists demanded control of the Ministry of the Interior in any coalition government), the establishment of Leninist "fractions" in the small industrial areas, the provocation of "incidents" at political rallies, and the blackmail and occasional kidnappings of political leaders or their relatives, the Soviets had successfully hounded all the noncommunists out of office by 1948.

Nineteen forty-eight was also significant as the year in which East and West buried any hopes of continued postwar cooperation. Czechoslovakia was the one state liberated by the Red Army which had enjoyed honest elections and full civil liberties in the interwar years. Moreover, Czechoslovakia and the Soviet Union had signed an alliance in 1943, and the Soviets had accepted the return of Czech President Edvard Benes from London exile, together with the restoration of the republic which Hitler and Chamberlain had destroyed at Munich.

But in February 1948, a coalition of communists and the fellow-traveling fraction of the socialist party achieved a parliamentary majority of 51 percent, at which point the communists executed a coup that destroyed the democratic republic and converted Czechoslovakia into one more Soviet satellite. On March 10, the Czech foreign minister, Jan Masaryk, either committed suicide or was pushed from his office window. On June 7, President Benes, who had long been plagued with heart trouble aggravated by heartbreak, resigned. He was succeeded by the communist chief Klement Gottwald, who also suffered from heart disease (aggravated by bootlicking) and who survived as a part-time, ceremonial head of state until March 1953 (the same month in which Stalin died).

In March 1948, the United States launched the Marshall Plan and at Stalin's behest, all the East European governments refused to join. The combination of the Czech coup and the rejection of the Marshall Plan convinced the Western leaders that Stalin was determined to exercise exclusive political and economic control of the lands behind the Iron Curtain. They therefore hastened the integration of the three Western-occupied zones of Germany and, on March 30, the Russians reacted by imposing traffic restrictions between the new "trizonia" and Berlin. On June 24, they imposed a complete land blockade, by means of which they expected to take over the entire city.

In the euphoria of victory in the spring of 1945, the Western Allies had not thought to negotiate specific land-transit rights between their occupation zones and Berlin, though for technical reasons they had made written agreements about the use of airports. This lucky accident now enabled the West legally to mount an airlift and furnish their portions of Berlin with all necessary outside supplies. Eleven months later, in May 1949, the Soviets lifted the blockade. Also in 1949, two German states were created, the *Bundesrepublik* in what had been the Western "trizonia" and the German Democratic Republic in the Soviet zone. The NATO alliance and Comecom, the Soviet-dominated trade alliance for all of Eastern Europe (except for dissident Yugoslavia), completed the picture of a now officially divided Europe.

The accumulating evidence of growing hostility between the recent World War II allies naturally produced powerful effects on Western foreign policy, in particular that of the United States—the only nation not primarily preoccupied with physical recovery from the war. Franklin Roosevelt, who died in April 1945 just before the end of the European war, had dreamed of cooperating with "Uncle Joe" Stalin in a postwar nonimperialist *pax mundi*. But the rapid transformation of the East European coalition governments into naked Stalinist dictatorships produced an equally rapid disillusionment as to the "democratic" intentions of the USSR. Indeed, by 1947 an important analysis published in *Foreign Affairs* outlined the policy of "containment" which was to become the basis of American policy during the four decades of the Cold War. Its anonymous author (later identified as the outstanding Russian specialist George Kennan) argued that the Soviets, as "scientific" Marxists, believed that "History" was on their side, and that world capitalism would inevitably give way to world communism. But, on the other hand, the Soviets had a healthy respect for American power and did not wish to take risks which might unleash a third world war. (And, in any case, Stalin had always been more cautious and rational than Hitler and Mussolini.) Kennan therefore recommended a policy of "containment," with the West ready to apply economic or military force where necessary to prevent further expansion of the Soviet empire. In the short run, Kennan argued, such a policy would serve to restrict Soviet aggression; in the long run, he suggested, the USSR might even lose its present messianic faith and simply break up—a final reflection which turned out to be an extraordinary anticipation of what actually occurred in 1991.

Without going into details, it may be said that the United States—in its diplomacy and its military actions alike—steadily applied economic pressure and resolutely developed its nuclear arsenal with a view to preventing the expansion of the Soviet empire beyond its 1950 borders. At the same time, however—and despite occasional belligerent rhetoric—the US never threatened the existing Soviet empire.

The British and (with various reservations) the West German, French, and Italian governments approved the containment policy, but the majority of active public opinion, in that part of Europe where it could be expressed (i.e., west of the Iron Curtain), did not accept American policy at anything like face value. Many French intellectuals, though they had no direct knowledge of Russia other than for carefully chaperoned visits in Moscow and Leningrad hotels, were convinced that communism was morally and economically superior to capitalism. Indeed, they argued, Russia might be less technologically advanced than the US, and Stalin might have used crude methods with his opposition, but the USSR had saved Europe from Hitler; it was a truly multinational society, and it had industrialized itself without becoming enslaved to Western banks. If its definitions of democracy and its form of elections were different from those of the West, we should recall the many shortcomings of "bourgeois" democracy and realize that the elimination of the former ruling classes was in itself a form of liberation for the citizens of Eastern Europe. The existence of the gulag was also flatly denied by many of these writers.[1]

Thus, the same persons who gave the benefit of the doubt to all Soviet claims were deeply anti-American. For them, the United States was a completely materialistic, uncultured society. Its foreign policy, backed by its nuclear superiority, was intended to frighten the rest of the world into accepting American economic dominance and the culture of Hollywood plus Coca-Cola. And, in sober truth, the very limited denazification of Germany, the U.S. complicity in the escape of ex-Nazis to Franco's Spain and Latin America, and the employment of former Nazi nuclear and rocket scientists in the American military establishment were stark facts which made the fear and dislike of the U.S. comprehensible. But very few "America-bashers" seemed to be concerned about the number of German nuclear scientists employed in Russia, or about the number of ex-Nazis and fascists in the communist parties and governing apparatus of the so-called "people's democracies."

The USSR made very skillful use of these pro-Soviet and anti-American sentiments. They established Stalin Peace Prizes and funded numerous fraternal meetings at which thoroughly frightened Soviet writers and artists would spout Stalinist dogma to fellow-traveling European intellectuals who were convinced in advance of Soviet virtue and American evil. The utter naivete of such spectacles angered those other European and American intellectuals who believed that such things as Stalin's blood purges, his alliance with Hitler until the Nazis invaded Russia, and his destruction of all the noncommunist political parties in Eastern Europe deprived the USSR of any great claim to political virtue relative to the United States. In West Berlin, in 1950 (the year after the unsuccessful Berlin blockade), these intellectuals founded the Congress for Cultural Freedom. In frank competition with the Soviet-sponsored conferences and publications, such remarkable thinkers as Arthur Koestler, Raymond Aron, and Sidney Hook published exposés of the crimes being committed throughout the Soviet empire.

Unfortunately, these anticommunist intellectuals somehow never connected with nearly as wide an audience as that enjoyed by the pro-Soviet groups. For one thing, they were split between hardliners who portrayed the USSR as indistinguishable from the worst fascist regimes and moderates who insisted on telling the truth about the gulag and the secret police, but who still allowed for the Soviet Union's positive accomplishments since 1917. More importantly, there were rumors from the start—later confirmed—that the CIA was funding the Congress. Objectively speaking, there is no reason why the CIA should not have helped anti-Stalinist writers to publicize their work, just as the USSR quietly subsidized pro-Soviet publications. But in the actual state of both West European and American public opinion, the stigma of CIA money was enough to discredit the Congress with most of the democratic as well as the pro-Soviet Left.[2]

In Eastern Europe, freedom of expression had been effectively suppressed by

1948 and was to remain suppressed, with the exception of a few brief moments, until the breakup of the Soviet empire in 1989. In all these countries prior to the war, the majority of intellectuals and university students had admired German science, literature, and musical culture and had, for this very reason, been shocked by the barbarism of the Nazis. Most had also been influenced by Marxism, and a considerable proportion had actively opposed the quasifascist governments which (with the exception of Czechoslovakia) had been so prevalent in the years leading up to World War II. Moreover, very few of these Eastern European students and intellectuals belonged to the Communist Party, and the majority of them felt a kind of cultural scorn for the USSR comparable to the Western European attitude toward the United States. The Nazi-Soviet pact had created utter despair as to any future restoration of liberty in their beloved homelands. But whatever their political opinions of the Soviet Union, after the German invasion of Russia in June 1941, they prayed for Soviet victory as against a Europe completely at the mercy of Nazi Germany.

After the war, these intellectual and students saw an opportunity to help rebuild their countries. The Soviets had promised free elections, were distributing land to the peasants, and were even permitting all antifascist parties—including the traditional peasant and Church-affiliated parties—to participate in the coalition governments. But by 1948, the multiparty governments had been replaced by Communist Party dictatorships and the choices became narrow and clear: to cooperate with the victors, to remain silent (since there no longer was a legitimate opposition), or to go into exile.

Unfortunately, no statistics exist which could tell us what percentage of the small intellectual classes in East Germany and in Central and Eastern Europe decided to cooperate with the communist dictatorships; but it is undeniably true that a sizeable proportion became writers, civil servants, diplomats, and teachers at all levels of the Soviet system. Their motives for cooperation were inevitably varied. If they believed that class privileges should be abolished and that social justice was worth struggling for even under a dictatorship, they could accept a role in the much-less-than-ideal conditions obtaining. To be a doctor or educator was still to contribute to a better future, regardless of present political oppressions. Likewise, if they believed that capitalism was an unjust, exploitative economic system, they could at least give a few decades' credit to the socialist effort being led by a technically backward neighbor. If they believed that internationalist, nonracist motives were more worthy than those of ethnic patriotism or traditional religion, they could cherish the hope that the genuinely internationalist, universalist component of the Soviet revolution would eventually prove stronger than the Great Russian, covertly anti-Semitic tendencies now dominant. And if they had lost all personal faith either in religion, nationalism, or Marxism, there was still the sense of accomplishment gained by serving the practical needs of one's fellow human beings.

Also not to be underestimated, however, is the elixir of power—or, in some cases, the illusion of power. The government could reward its faithful servants with publication, political or diplomatic office, travel and foreign residence, and access to special stores for scarce consumer goods. Finally, as described in that masterly work by Czeslaw Milosz, *The Captive Mind* (New York: A. A. Knopf, 1953), there are a multiplicity of ways in which an intelligent human being can fool himself (and his masters) as to his real motives. In conditions of oppression, the slave's first duty is to survive; if he can also create a better material life for himself and do educational or scientific work that will benefit his fellow countrymen, so much the better.

Turning from these individual matters to larger political circumstances: from 1947 onward, Germany, Poland, Czechoslovakia, Hungary, and Yugoslavia—the key borderlands between West and East—were to be the principal areas of constant tension and occasional physical conflict marking the Cold War within Europe. In the construction of the *Bundesrepublik*, which was to endure from 1949 to 1990, the West counted on both the visceral German hatred of communism and Stalinist Russia and on the truly extraordinary political talents of Konrad Adenauer (already discussed in chapter 10). In East Germany, the principal figure in the new regime was Walter Ulbricht, who bore a striking psychological resemblance to his master in the Kremlin: secretive, conspiratorial, suspicious of intellectuals, and without personal friends or affections. Ulbricht was blessed with a strong memory for names and organizational charts and a shrewd instinct for persons who might make trouble if not first terrorized into obedience.

Like the Soviet constitution, the 1949 constitution of the "democratic" East German republic guaranteed on paper all individual liberties, plus the rights to emigrate, and the right to vote, and to own small private property. In reality, however, party agents and secret police controlled all expressions of opinion, emigrants lost their property (as in Nazi times), authority flowed from the top down, and votes were taken by a show of hands. In the years 1948–1950, while Stalin was once again thinning the ranks of the Soviet Party, Ulbricht purged some 250,000 "unreliable" members from the "Socialist Unity Party" (which had been created by fusing the Communist Party with the more docile remnants of the Social Democratic Party). In the USSR the regimented population could at least take pride in the victory over the Nazis and in the creation of the basis for a modern industrial economy. But in East Germany, the regimented population remembered the raping and looting by Soviet troops (while eagerly forgetting the aggressions and atrocities of the German army). They had passed, they felt, from life in the Nazi dictatorship to life in a satellite Soviet dictatorship and saw themselves as the blameless victims of a malignant fate.

Nevertheless, life goes on, and the Germans are efficient, disciplined workers. Once the end of four-power cooperation deprived the Soviets of West German industry, they strove, with considerable success, to establish steel, energy, and chemical industries in their zone of occupation. They imposed high work norms and low salaries and exported some 25 percent of total production to the USSR as reparations. In 1948, they abolished the factory councils which had been elected by the workers in 1946 and replaced them with Soviet puppets. Materially, they favored the workers over the middle class by abolishing ration cards for the latter, thereby obliging them to buy food at higher prices on the free (or black) market. On the other hand, recalling their own terrible experience with forced collectivization in the 1930s, they treated the East German peasants more leniently. When they broke up the Junker estates, they distributed two-thirds of the land to peasant families and formed Soviet-style collectives on only the remaining one-third. Even so, some 3 to 4 percent of the total population, both urban and rural, fled to the West in the years 1949–1952.

Nineteen fifty-two was the last working year of Stalin's life, and the aging dictator apparently still hoped to neutralize Germany rather than see two hostile states consolidated and rearmed. Stalin's proposed deal offered reunification of Germany on the condition that the reunited country be diplomatically and militarily neutral and that East Germany (with a population of seventeen million, a weak economy, and a puppet communist regime) would be equal to West Germany (with a population of forty-nine million, a strong economy, and a multiparty federal government) in the drafting of the new constitution. Needless to say, Stalin's proposal never got off the ground, and by the time of his death (on March 4, 1953), Stalin's heirs were deeply concerned about the evident hostility of the East German population. They advised the Ulbricht government to offer concessions and, on June 11, an unwilling Ulbricht formally announced a "New Course" (in imitation of Malenkov's "New Course" in Moscow). The government would cancel the recently imposed more stringent work norms and admit to "errors" in its past relations with the working class. It also promised to stop the foreclosure proceedings on the farms of families that had either fled west or were accused of not paying their taxes. But on June 15, another governmental spokesman confused the situation by saying only that the increased work norms would be "reconsidered."

In the tense, hostile, and completely suspicious atmosphere of the moment, the difference between "cancellation" and "reconsideration" led to spontaneous demonstrations during the afternoon of June 16 and the morning of June 17. Some 12,000 steel workers, 16,000 railway workers, and 20,000 construction workers took part in the demonstrations in Berlin, and there were small sympathy demonstrations in as many as 250 other towns and separate factories. There was no sabotage or verbal attacks on the Soviet occupying forces, but an effort was made to fraternize with and win over the police of the puppet regime.

The principal slogans and printed demands of the demonstrators were for German reunification and free elections in the Western sense of that word, including a choice of parties and a secret ballot. The East Berlin government panicked and called in Soviet tanks. According to official reports, twenty-one people died. Unofficial reports put the deaths at two hundred demonstrators and one hundred police. The principal immediate result was the strengthening of Ulbricht's position, since his reluctance to initiate the "New Course" had been confirmed. In the longer term, June 17 led to minor improvements in the East German standard of living, but also exposed completely the myth of harmony between the working class and the regime.[3]

The most spectacular and tragic effort to break free of Soviet domination occurred in Hungary in October and November of 1956. The first (and relatively honest) postwar elections had been conducted in November 1945. At that time, the population was feeling considerable gratitude to the Red Army for the liberation from the Nazis, as well as for its help in sowing and harvesting the year's crops, and for Soviet aid in the massive land distribution of that year. Allied officers were also on hand as election observers, and the Soviets were still hoping for postwar cooperation with the Allies. In these circumstances, the conservative Peasant Smallholders Party won 57 percent of the votes and the Communists garnered 17 percent. For the next two years—until the summer of 1947, the chairman of the Smallholders Party, Ferenc Nagy, served as Hungary's prime minister. But the country was really governed by the vice-premier, Matias Rákosi, the chairman of the Communist Party by personal designation of Stalin, who also controlled all police forces and an increasing proportion of the communications media. After the chairman of the National Peasant Party, Bela Kóvacs, had been kidnapped and deported to Siberia, Prime Minister Nagy was told by his family and friends that it would be better if he converted his short Swiss vacation into permanent exile. Nagy agreed, and Rákosi emerged as the undisguised dictator.

For the next several years, Rákosi sponsored the rapid industrialization and reorientation of the entire Hungarian economy in the interests of the Soviet Union. He pushed through the confiscation of the Church's property and, more important both politically and socially, he nationalized and secularized its large school system. Unfortunately for the Church, the Hungarian primate, Josef Cardinal Mindzenty, was a narrow- minded pillar of the Old Regime who had no more understanding or sympathy for democratic reforms than he had for communism. His attitude fanned the considerable anticlerical sentiments of much of the population and weakened the moral resistance of both Catholics and Protestants.

Throughout the final years of Stalin's reign, Rákosi faithfully served his political patron. When Stalin expelled Yugoslavia from the circle of friendly "socialist" nations, Rákosi outdid the other satellite dictators in propaganda against Tito's heresy. In September 1949, he hanged the former interior minister, Laszlo Rajk, on trumped-up charges of being an "imperialist" and "Zionist" agent. In general he faithfully imposed on Hungary all of the Soviet dictator's exploitative norms. He also purged all slightly independent members from trade union and local party cells—actions which were characteristic of the entire Eastern bloc from 1948 to March 1953.

As mentioned earlier, after Stalin's death his successors quickly adopted the "New Course"—less obvious police brutality, the promise of consumer goods, and a relaxation of the pace of both collectivization and industrialization. In Hungary the new prime minister, Imre Nagy, had not been implicated in the Rajk trial and was known for his mild reservations concerning some of the Stalinist policies. But in the background, Matias Rákosi still wielded decisive power as party chairman. When economic failures increased social tensions again, Nagy was removed as prime minister, expelled from the party (April 1955), and generally blamed for all the failures of the period since Stalin's death.

In May 1955, Khrushchev visited Yugoslavia and publicly apologized for Stalin's attempts to overthrow Tito; and in August of the same year, the Allies and the USSR signed a peace treaty which ended the occupation of Austria in return for strict Austrian neutrality. These two events aroused many hopes in Hungary for a relaxing of the ideological pressure and even for the possibility of a neutral status comparable to that of Austria. Indeed, in March 1956—the month after Khrushchev's "secret" speech about the crimes of Stalin—Rákosi found it advisable to rehabilitate posthumously the reputation of Laszlo Rajk, whose execution on trumped-up charges he himself (as Stalin's lackey) had engineered.

During the months between March and October, there was a "thaw" in Hungary (as in the USSR). "Petofi" clubs—named for one of the intellectual heroes of the revolution of 1848 and consisting of university students and politically conscious industrial and government workers—openly discussed the need for a nondogmatic, truly democratic socialism. They also revived the 1848 manifesto, which had demanded personal liberty, free elections, and the end of the Habsburg military occupation. No one with an ounce of intelligence could miss the analogy to the current situation. The government tried to appease these demands for more freedom without losing control. Some 12,000 political prisoners were amnestied, and several thousand "class enemies" who had been forced to leave Budapest for the countryside were permitted to return to the capital.

But Rákosi was unable to recognize the need for real change. On June 30, he announced that Imre Nagy and the "intellectuals" were leading a conspiracy against socialism. The Soviet government, already dealing with a difficult "thaw" in Poland, decided that Rákosi's rigidity might cause an explosion in Budapest. On July 17, Yuri Andropov (future head of the Soviet secret police) and Anastas Mikoyan (trade minister and frequent troubleshooter from Stalinist times) arrived in Budapest to lend a fraternal hand to their troubled Hungarian comrades. They removed Rákosi and sent him "home" to the USSR, where he lived on quietly until 1971. (The "golden parachute" was not invented by American capitalism in the Reagan era, but by Khrushchev, who wished to remove ossified apparatchiks without shooting them.)

In quieter times, Rákosi's successor, Ernö Gerö, might have been a shrewd choice. Although he had been a loyal Stalinist, he had also served the party in Barcelona during the Spanish Civil War and in France during World War II, and had been interned by the Horthy government upon his return to Hungary. Thus Gerö enjoyed the prestige of having worked in the West, while at the same time avoiding the stigma of those who had spent the war in Moscow and returned as mere functionaries of Stalin. However, his efforts to address the widespread discontent were contradictory in themselves. On the one hand, Gerö proposed to accelerate the collectivization and industrialization programs; on the other, he proposed economic concessions to the industrial workers and the naming to high party posts of comrades who had been victims of Rákosi. Meanwhile, the agitation of the Petofi clubs continued unabated, and the public noticed that, in Poland, the "national" communists who had been imprisoned as "Titoists" were being released from house arrest.

In early October, Gerö and Kádár (one of the purge victims who had been given high party office) traveled to Moscow to inform Khrushchev that only the restoration of his party card to Imre Nagy could keep the lid on the agitation among students and Budapest workers. Khrushchev agreed, and also used his recently restored friendship with Tito to have the Yugoslav dictator invite Gerö to Belgrade for a state visit (presumably to offer the new prime minister a bit of much-needed prestige in the eyes of the Hungarian public). But Gerö's return to Budapest on October 23 coincided with a demonstration of some 100,000 persons celebrating solidarity with the developments in Poland. Somehow the secret police fired into the crowd, and the neighboring Russian tank crews—thinking that the fire was directed at them—also used their own guns, clearing the streets of marchers. Completely surprised and helpless, the party now asked for Soviet military support against what they began to call an imperialist-inspired revolt, and they also asked permission to appoint the newly rehabilitated Imre Nagy as prime minister. Mikoyan flew in from Moscow, accompanied this time by Mikhail Suslov, the hardline Stalinist who remained the ideological watchdog of the party despite the numerous changes of personnel since Stalin's death. On October 24, they confirmed Nagy as prime minister, removed Gerö, and named Janos Kádár as first secretary of the party.

The following week combined moments of hope with sporadic street warfare and treachery. Nagy disappointed his followers by refusing to endorse their republication of the 1848 manifesto and their maximalist demands for Soviet withdrawal. Young groups of "freedom fighters" manufactured Molotov cocktails (something they had learned during their compulsory military training under Soviet instructors) and destroyed a number of Soviet tanks. They were able to bring some of the municipal police over to their side and treated as enemies and traitors those who cooperated with the Soviet forces. Uncoordinated strikes broke out in many industries and transport facilities, especially those identified as serving the Soviets. But there were also all kinds of proposals for substantial economic reform and for Austrian-style neutrality discussed in the press, at public meetings, and (by October 31) at the UN General Assembly. There was even some fraternizing between Soviet soldiers and the younger intellectuals and workers. It was said that Nagy and the Soviets, in a completely friendly spirit, were negotiating the withdrawal of Soviet troops and tanks from the city itself, and eventually from the whole country.

On October 31, Soviet spokesmen told the press that they were planning greatly to reduce their military presence in *all* the Warsaw Pact countries. Simultaneously, however, the Soviets brought eight new divisions across the northern border while ignoring the verbal protests of the new prime minister. In these circumstances—caught between an ever-rising tide of public demand for Soviet withdrawal and the evidence of Soviet deception—Nagy announced that Hungary would withdraw from the Warsaw Pact but remain militarily neutral.

These words were absolutely unacceptable to Moscow. On November 2, Soviet military units took control of all airports and railroads, and surrounded Greater Budapest with tanks. Sometime on November 3 or 4, Kádár and several high military officers left Budapest for Soviet headquarters, and on November 4 Nagy took refuge in the Yugoslav embassy. Moscow announced that the new government would prepare economic reforms, grant more local autonomy in industrial management, cut down on bureaucracy, and scrupulously defend Hungary's sovereignty in international relations. Nothing was said, however, about free elections or a multiparty political system. Soviet tanks occupied the capital, strikes spread through all of national industry and transport, and Workers' Councils were elected in many factories. The freedom fighters continued hopeless, if heroic, operations in the suburbs, and occasional Soviet units were confused by the fact that they did not see any of the American and "Nazi" troops they had been told were the reason for their armed intervention.

Between November 10 and 20, the Soviet army restored order throughout the country. Some 20,000 persons had died in street battles. Despite the barbed wire of the Iron Curtain, well over 100,000 had crossed the Austrian border, to be followed by another 100,000 during the month of December. Soviet trains rolled eastward carrying 10,000 to 15,000 young revolutionaries to Siberian exile. On November 22, Nagy left the Yugoslav embassy with a supposed safe conduct given by the Soviet authorities to the Yugoslav legation. Instead, he was kidnapped and taken to Romania, where, in the summer of 1958, he was shot after a secret trial.

The Kádár government tried—at first, with scant success—to get the Workers Councils to cooperate with its reform plans. Slowly, however—and despite his complete dependence on Soviet armed power—Kádár gave clear evidence of his intention to improve working conditions and to restrict the secret police and its terroristic methods. He launched a slogan which at first was thought to be an exercise in cynicism but which, over the course of time, brought a genuine measure of peace to the martyred nation: "He who is not against us is with us."[4]

I have treated this brief, unsuccessful revolution in some detail because the issues and the persons involved typify clearly the contradictions in the Soviet effort to establish "socialism" in Central and Eastern Europe. In terms of economics, the contradiction was between a politicized command economy, run harshly on behalf of the USSR, and the hope of a voluntary socialism with elements of worker self-management. In terms of foreign policy, it was the contradiction between absolute subordination to Soviet military plans during the Cold War and neutrality along the lines granted to Austria and to Finland. Virtually all interpreters and Hungarian political figures interviewed in the months following the tragedy agreed it was Nagy's announcement that Hungary would leave the Warsaw Pact that precipitated the crushing, completely unilateral Soviet intervention in the first week of November. In terms of internal politics, the contradiction was between rule by a clique of "Muscovite" party stalwarts, many of whom were Jewish (a fact which fanned the latent anti-Semitism of the population and made the rulers all the more dependent on their Soviet masters), and rule by "national" communists willing to cooperate with other Left forces and committed to ending the multiple abuses of the secret police.

The leading Hungarian political leaders themselves clearly personified the alternatives. Matias Rákosi represented the quintessence of Stalinist dictatorship transferred to Hungary with all its brutality and secrecy. Ernö Gerö represented the vain hope of loyal Stalinism modified by experience in the West and nonresidence in Moscow. Laszlo Rajk, on the other hand, was an anticlerical Stalinist intellectual, a secular Jew, the party secretary of the Hungarian battalion in the International Brigades in Spain, and a political prisoner in Hungary during World War II. On all of these counts, Rajk was automatically suspect of disloyalty to Stalin and his Hungarian "Muscovite" sycophants and thus the natural candidate for a false confession of "Zionist imperialism" and a "traitor's" execution.

Under other circumstances, Imre Nagy might have been a good "Muscovite." He spent the war years in Moscow as director of "Radio Kossuth," but as Minister of the Interior in 1946 he resisted the use of torture and had been replaced by Rajk. After Stalin's death, he had been used as a front man for the "New Course" advocated by Malenkov and then was blamed by the party hardliners for the failures of that policy. Once the unrest started, the Soviet "advisers" and the demoralized party named him prime minister because he was the only top communist personality who possessed any credibility with the Hungarian people. They then abused his good faith by talking Soviet withdrawal while the military reinforcements were actually entering the country, and they ousted (and ultimately executed) him for the crime of saying that Hungary had a right to be neutral, and for appealing to the UN to protect his country against Soviet military reprisals. Finally, Janos Kádár represented the small stratum of party functionaries who tried to be sensitive to worker needs while towing the Soviet line in both national and international affairs. He had been tortured and imprisoned by Rákosi, which gave him some personal credibility among Hungarians generally; the experience also led him to prefer massive deportations of the captured freedom fighters as an alternative to their local torture and execution.

A final factor to be considered regarding the Hungarian revolution is the wide-spread unpopularity of all the communist leaders. Among the freedom fighters, there were many who were opposed to any form of socialism (and to most kinds of Western democracy). They represented national patriotic tradition, with all sorts of anti-Slavic and Old Regime connotations. Among the striking workers, there were many who had voted for any party other than the Communists as long as voting was pos-sible. What the Andropovs and Mikoyans and Gerös knew from the first moment (and the well-meaning Nagy and Kádár learned during October), was that the vast majority of Hungarians hated communism and had come to hate the USSR after the brief honeymoon of liberation in 1945. The practical question for all of them to answer—each in his own manner—was how to cope with the fact of that hatred.

The international situation also affected the behavior of both the Hungarians and the Soviets. The Hungarian revolution coincided with the Anglo-French effort to reverse the Egyptian president Gamal Abdel Nasser's nationalization of the Suez Canal. The United States was opposed to that effort, and the diplomatic conflict within the West effectively prevented any possible reaction to Soviet intervention in Hungary. Wild rumors and irresponsible broadcasts from Radio Free Europe encouraged the Hungarian freedom fighters to believe that the West might send them aid, but in reality the Western powers had no plans to intervene in Soviet-dom-inated Europe once the division of the continent had become permanent in 1948.

Almost as dramatic—and more significant strategically than events in Hun-gary—was the successful revolution in Poland against the worst aspects of Soviet domination. Stalin had treated Poland with a combination of brutality and caution. On the one hand, he had literally destroyed the small Polish Communist Party in the purges of 1937–38, and he had slaughtered over 4,000 Polish officers in the Katyn Forest in the spring of 1940. In the immediate postwar era, while Stalin still hoped to maintain cooperation with the Western Allies, he permitted the majority Peasant Party to head the coalition government. At the same, time two survivors of the 1937 purge, Bislaw Bierut and Jakob Berman (both of whom had spent the war years being trained in Moscow), undermined the coalition government and dominated the Stalinist regime from 1947 on; and from 1947 to 1956, a Polish-born Soviet Mar-shall, Konstantin Rokossovsky, was "lent" to Poland as its minister of defense.

But Russian demands at Yalta and in the decisions of the four-power occupa-tion of Germany had been highly beneficial to Poland as well as to the USSR. The Silesian and Poznan territories transferred from Germany to Poland were much richer in both industrial and agricultural potential than the eastern territories annexed by Russia. The communists distributed land to thousands of peasant fam-ilies but moved slowly, and emphasized the voluntary element, in collectivizing a small percentage of the land. In fact, the landless peasants had a choice between entering real collectives (which few did) and working as wage laborers on state farms (which many did). This form of wage labor in farming could also be frequently combined with part-time industrial or service jobs.[5]

The Russians developed a steel industry in Poland and greatly expanded the port of Gdansk. As with all the satellites, they reoriented Polish trade toward the Soviet Union and used the new industries to help in Soviet reconstruction, as well as to aid North Korea and China at the time of the Korean War (1950–1953). They also purged the rebuilt communist party, and kept the principal "national" leader who had not resided in Moscow during the war, Wladislaw Gomulka, under house arrest from 1949 to late 1954.

The East Berlin revolt of June 1953 prevented the post-Stalin "New Course" from being adopted quickly in Poland. But by late 1954, the new flexibility had reached this largest and most anti-Russian of Soviet neighbors. The secret police were completely reorganized and their powers reduced. Gomulka was released and allowed to publish his criticisms of Stalinist economic policies—criticisms, ironically, which echoed those made by Nikolai Bukharin in the 1920s and had been a principal factor in his 1938 trial and execution.

At the time of Khrushchev's "secret" speech (February 1956), the Polish party boss Bieslaw Bierut suddenly died—perhaps as the result of chronic illness, though it was widely believed that he had committed suicide. The Poles openly discussed the crimes of Stalin, with ample evidence being offered by the return of thousands of their countrymen from the gulag in the spring and summer of 1956. The number two Stalinist boss, Jacob Berman, was removed from office; but in the inner-party discussions he stoutly defended his own record, pointing out that in Czechoslovakia, Hungary, Romania, and Bulgaria, "Titoists" and "national communists" had been hung, whereas in Poland they had been held in house arrest. How much credit should go to Berman, however, and how much to Stalin's caution where Poland was concerned, cannot be determined.

Bierut and Berman were replaced by Edward Ochab, a moderate party official (designated by Khrushchev) who mediated between the Stalinist and "national" wings of the party. Ochab officially terminated what was already a moribund voluntary effort to collectivize agriculture; on the other hand, he had neither the knowledge nor the prestige necessary to remedy the disastrous economic errors of the past decade. In the last week of June 1956, matters came to a head in the industrial city of Poznan, where locomotives were manufactured for Russian, Chinese, and Polish use. A high proportion of these Zispo railway engines had been rejected by Soviet and Chinese authorities, and the Polish government found it necessary to pay attention to the complaints of the nation's most powerful "fraternal" customers. On June 20, the government summoned a delegation of workers and management to Warsaw to discuss the quality complaints. The workers, however, had a few complaints of their own: declining real wages, poor factory lighting and sanitation, the failure to pay promised overtime, and the low quality (or simple absence) of essential consumer goods.

In the course of the discussion, the government threatened wage cuts—a threat that was later withdrawn. However, when the majority returned to Poznan, the authorities held as hostages a number of the more outspoken delegates. The news of the hostage-taking spread rapidly and, on June 28, the 50,000 locomotive and associated industrial workers (in a total urban population of 450,000) went out on strike. The city was swiftly paralyzed. While peaceful demonstrators carried signs demanding free elections, religious instruction in the schools, and "Russians Go Home," small militant groups stormed and burned Communist Party headquarters and several police stations (though not before they won over a certain number of policemen and secured small arms). The militants were received with sympathy by much of the public and fraternized with the municipal police, but they were fired on by Soviet security police and a number were arrested.

The Polish government panicked and quickly sent two divisions and some three hundred tanks into Poznan to restore order. By sundown of June 29, the city was quiet; some one hundred persons had died and about three hundred more had been wounded. The Soviet press explained the revolt as a "capitalist plot" financed and armed by the West. The Polish government, however, and all factions of the party rejected this conspiratorial explanation and instead recognized the existence of legitimate grievances. In addition, the news from Hungary—along with the evident popular hope that a similar liberalization would be possible in Poland—influenced the Polish government to be lenient with the arrested strikers. Particularly important was the public sympathy expressed by the prestigious veterans of the Dombrowski Brigade, the Polish volunteers to the International Brigades in the Spanish Civil War. The ensuing trial was brief and the sentences received by the strikers were light.

But the Poznan strike and the resulting violence increased demands that the "national communist" leader, Wladislaw Gomulka, be not merely reinstated in the party but become its first secretary. The Soviets continued to insist on their conspiracy theory of the uprising, and no lesser personages than Prime Minister Bulganin and Marshall Zhukov visited Warsaw in late July to inform their Polish comrades that they would prefer to see someone other than Gomulka as the new party secretary. However, without saying yes or no to the Soviets, the central committee scheduled its meeting for October 20 and, during the interim, negotiated its own consensus on the necessity of choosing Gomulka, acknowledging among themselves that he was the only communist leader who inspired any degree of respect among noncommunists. On October 19, the Soviet ambassador in Warsaw requested a delay in the central committee meeting and, on that same day, a delegation consisting of Khrushchev, Mikoyan, Molotov (most dependable and poker-faced of Stalin's hatchet men), and Kaganovich (Stalin's brother-in-law and one of the more ruthless commissars in the industrialization and collectivization campaigns in Russia itself) arrived at the Warsaw airport, where they were met by a high-level Polish group that included Gomulka himself.

After Khrushchev vented his fury, the Poles agreed to a face-saving postponement of the central committee election, but they ratified their decision to elect Gomulka as first secretary. In actual fact, Khrushchev could recognize Gomulka as an acceptable choice; the Soviet chief, after all, had publicized some of Stalin's crimes and had deliberately sought reconciliation with no less than the original "Titoist," Marshal Tito himself, president of the fraternal "socialist commonwealth" of Yugoslavia (though still not a member of the Warsaw Pact). The real Soviet grievance was that they had not been told by the Poles of their deliberations after the Bulganin-Zhukov visit.

On October 24, Gomulka addressed 500,000 people in an open-air meeting in Warsaw. He could not have been unaware that his own prestige lay in the fact that he had been a victim of the Stalinist regime. He promised economic reforms and an end to police abuses, but he reaffirmed his country's commitment to "socialism" and its membership in the Warsaw Pact. During the following week, his government sent several fraternal greetings to the Nagy cabinet, which had been installed in Budapest on October 23, the day before Gomulka's own return to power. And, indeed, it was Gomulka's affirmation of the Warsaw Pact—and his clear commitment to a more just, but still communist, system—that saved Poland from the fate which overtook Hungary during the first days of November. Gomulka's political instincts served him (and his country) well: He did not prevent the press from publishing glowing praises of the Hungarian revolution, nor did he interfere with the collection of funds for Hungary on the streets of Polish cities in late October and even after the Soviet invasion. As well, he released Stefan Cardinal Wyszynski from house arrest and accepted the latter's main conditions for Church acceptance of the Gomulka regime: the reintroduction of religious instruction in the public schools, restoration of confiscated Church properties, and freedom of activity for Church charities and prosyletizing orders.

Poland was also fortunate in the character of the cardinal, very different from that of the reactionary Cardinal Mindszenty in Budapest. Wyszynski had been a student of social sciences in Paris before World War II and a "worker priest" both there and in Lublin and Cracow later. He had also pressed the Vatican to recognize the Polish acquisitions of Silesia and Poznan during the few years when the Vatican was still referring to these territories as German provinces. Wyszynski thus combined his sense of Polish patriotism with a full awareness of the exploitative nature of capitalism and a willingness to accept a socialist system, provided it would guarantee individual human rights and the historic educational and moral leadership of the Church in Poland.

By agreement with Gomulka—and knowing full well the stakes for Poland—Wyszynski followed the new party secretary in addressing another mass meeting on

November 4, the same day that Budapest was occupied by Soviet tanks and Prime Minister Nagy took refuge in the Yugoslav embassy. He endorsed Gomulka's words to the effect that the fate of Poland itself depended on disciplined obedience to the new government. According to the *New York Times* report of the meeting, he

> spoke of countries where magnificent constitutions proclaiming the rights of peoples existed alongside terrifying methods of governing the citizens. The darkest stain on this century had been the trampling of the individual and of civil rights. . . . The priority of man over matter must be declared. In the economic process, one must love man more than matter, more than a machine, more than a factory, more than the products of a factory.[6]

Despite the stark contrast (at the time) between the Hungarian tragedy and the successful assertion of Polish autonomy, the longer-term results of the two uprisings were fairly similar. Both the Gomulka government in Poland and the Kádár government in Hungary sought to improve political and economic conditions within the limits set by Soviet policy and the Cold War. In both countries, the secret police were reined in and Soviet troops were confined to bases away from the main population centers. Both governments, moreover, tolerated the practice of the Christian religion and backhandedly blamed past "errors" on party leaders of Jewish origin. Both dealt pragmatically with informal worker representatives as much as (if not more than) the official trade unions, and both left agriculture in the hands of the peasants and allowed them to sell a portion of their produce on the limited free market. Both governments also established a consultative relationship with Soviet economic and trade representatives and thereby improved somewhat their terms of bilateral trade with the Fatherland of Socialism.

Neither government, of course, was truly popular with its people, but Gomulka was forgiven his autocratic manners and Marxist dogmatism because he defended the national interests of Poland, and Kádár was eventually forgiven his betrayal of Nagy because he managed to get the Soviets to agree to more economic flexibility and market elements than existed anywhere else in the communist world.[7]

However, the decreased oppressiveness of the satellite regimes after 1956 did not create any new enthusiasm for the system as a whole. Ever since the erection of the Iron Curtain, with its rows of barbed wire, its constantly ploughed-up soil, and its watch towers equipped with telescopes and machine guns, the general population had been unable to emigrate. But there was still one place at which Germans could escape simply by taking a subway ride from East to West Berlin. Between 1949 and 1961, about three million persons (including a very high proportion of professionals and skilled workers) took that ride in one direction—to the West. In the summer of 1961, the Warsaw Pact authorities made a collective decision to build a wall which would plug this one gap. The timing may have been influenced by the fact that Khrushchev wished to "test" the metal of the new young American president, John F. Kennedy. He had been saying for several years that he would seal the border, implying with his bluster that nothing but war could stop him from doing so and that no one would be so stupid as to risk war with the Soviet Union. On August 13, the work began at dawn and was completed in a matter of days. The West protested, but indeed no one was ready to go to war over this particular fait accompli. In purely practical terms, the Berlin Wall was a great success: From August 1961 to November 1989 (when it came down), only about five thousand persons escaped across the now truly seamless Iron Curtain. At the same time, however, the simple existence of the wall constantly advertised the fact that the peoples of Central-Eastern Europe were now literally prisoners.

The ousting of Khrushchev in 1964 brought to power a less spontaneous, more bureaucratic leadership under Leonid Brezhnev, the most successful machine politician in the history of the USSR. Brezhnev was willing to let the satellites run their own internal affairs provided they consulted with him regularly, maintained the unchallenged power of the single party, endorsed the Soviet viewpoint in all relations with the West and China (which was no longer a "fraternal ally"), and accepted Soviet supervision of their military forces. He even tolerated Romania's pretensions to an independent foreign policy because the Ceaucescu regime remained both staunchly communist and committed to the Warsaw Pact.

Of all the satellite nations, Czechoslovakia was the one which had given the USSR the least trouble. The population had been largely pro-Russian in 1945 and the communists, together with the left socialists, had won 51 percent of the votes in the election (which the communists then used as the "legal" justification for their March 1948 destruction of the multiparty democracy). Although relations between the Czechs and Slovaks were strained, they were not characterized by the open hatred and sporadic violence that existed between the Poles and Ukrainians or the Magyars and Romanians. Moreover, the quality and quantity of Czech industrial production was second only to that of East Germany, but the country had had no uprising on June 17, 1953, and had been absolutely quiet during the Polish and Hungarian revolutions of 1956.

On the other hand, precisely because of its relative economic sophistication, Czechoslovakia was increasingly sensitive to the Soviet failure to recognize the importance of the computer revolution, of light metals and plastics, and of market mechanisms. Nineteen fifty-seven had been the year of "Sputnik" but, in the ensuing decade Soviet technology (not basic science) fell behind that of the West. In the 1960s, the Czechoslovak economy, dependent as it was on the Soviet, stagnated. Meanwhile, a group of sophisticated young economists produced plans for combining market-pricing mechanisms and decentralized decision-making with basic state control of production and natural resources.

Political changes also threatened the domestic stability-loyalty-stagnation

syndrome. Party Secretary and State President Antonin Novotny was a disciple of
Khrushchev and, like his mentor, had reformed the worst aspects of Stalinism in
his nation. But after the fall of Khrushchev in 1964, Novotny's personal mediocrity
became evident in his rigidity toward the young economists and the growing
demands of the Slovak party for full equality with the Czech. When Brezhnev himself paid a visit to Prague in December 1967, Novotny tried to blame his problems
on the Slovak party secretary, Alexander Dubcek. This was not a very successful
strategy since, at the time, Dubcek had the best of Soviet credentials: His father
had gone to the USSR in the 1930s to work as a volunteer in heavy industry, and
Dubcek himself had been educated in Soviet schools (including as a student of
Brezhnev's in the party leadership school). Back in Slovakia after the war, Dubcek
had been an able functionary and developed warm relations with the Slovak intellectual and scientific elite. Thus, when Brezhnev decided to ease the hapless
Novotny out, Dubcek seemed the natural choice; and by this decision, Brezhnev
unwittingly ushered in the "Prague spring."

In February and March 1968, under Dubcek's leadership, the Czech and
Slovak communists agreed upon an ambitious reform program, to be adopted at the
joint party congress scheduled for September. The program included the end of
press, radio, and television censorship; more local initiative and the introduction
of market mechanisms in the socialist economy; full autonomy and equality for the
Czech and Slovak communist parties; and free elections, including permission for
noncommunist parties to participate. Censorship was, in effect, ended right away,
and an extraordinary degree of free discussion occurred in all the media from February onward. At the same time, the East German and Polish communist parties
began to attack the new binational leadership as "counterrevolutionary" and "anti-
Soviet." The East German party was still led at the time by the hardline Stalinist
Walter Ulbricht, while in Poland Gomulka had evolved steadily toward conservative positions after having saved the country from direct Soviet rule.

Brezhnev's reaction to these developments in Czechoslovakia was at first
ambiguous. He was inclined to permit economic reforms, as long as there was no
doubt about loyalty to the one-party regime and the Warsaw Pact. (This was, after
all, the established position with regard to Hungary, where the Kádár regime had
introduced some of the reforms now being advocated in Prague.) But the Soviet
press started cautioning Czechoslovakia against the return of "bourgeois" or West
German "revanchist" influences (albeit less stridently than the East Germans and
Poles). The warning about West Germany was particularly significant, because
Czech economic plans depended on increasing trade with Germany and on
importing German machinery.

During the spring, Kádár and Tito each tried to warn Dubcek of the rising
danger of Soviet intervention. The East German, Polish, and Soviet press now
began to talk about "Zionist" influence, employing crude anti-Semitism to stigma-

tize the role of Edward Goldstucker, a professor of *German* literature, an advocate of the Dubcek reforms, and the president of the Czechoslovak Writers' Union. In June and July, the Warsaw Pact held military maneuvers on Czech soil and were very slow to evacuate Czech territory after the end of the official exercises. The national press complained bitterly at the continuing presence of the "fraternal" armies, and an emergency meeting of the Soviet and Czechoslovak politbureaus was called for August 2.

They met on the frontier between Slovakia and the Soviet Union, the Czechs and Slovaks having declined an invitation to meet in Moscow. Each delegation resided in its own railroad car and the discussions took place in the station restaurant. The Soviets demanded the re-establishment of press censorship and reiterated the various editorial warnings of recent months regarding the dangers of bourgeois influence in the Czech liberalization program. Dubcek assured the Soviet leaders of his absolute loyalty to the pact; he agreed to eliminate all press references to foreign troops and to restrain press criticism of the Warsaw Pact allies. A public show of renewed unity then took place in the city of Bratislava on August 4, marred only by some booing at the appearance of Walter Ulbricht.

Nevertheless, on August 20 some 400,000 Soviet troops, accompanied by small units of Germans, Poles, Hungarians, and Bulgarians, occupied the whole country in twenty-four hours. They kidnapped Dubcek and his entire cabinet, flew them to Moscow, and pressed President Ludvík Svoboda (still in Prague) to name a cabinet acceptable to Moscow. At the moment, however, the revulsion against the invasion was so severe, even among Czech party officials, that no pro-Moscow party members would consent to be named. Instead, the Dubcek cabinet was browbeaten into resuming office while promising to combat energetically all "antisocialist" forces. In April 1969, Dubcek was replaced by Gustav Husak, who had been his successor as head of the Slovak Communist Party and who had seemingly supported Dubcek's reform program during the brief "Prague spring" of February–August 1968.

In this intervention, as in the Hungarian invasion of 1956, international circumstances protected the USSR from any strong condemnation (let alone counterintervention) from the West. In July 1968, after years of laborious and often acrimonious negotiations, the three principal nuclear powers—the United States, Great Britain, and the Soviet Union (but not France, China, or Israel)—had signed a nuclear nonproliferation treaty which gave rise to the hope of eventual nuclear disarmament (a promise of which was included by the signers). Any condemnation of the Soviets by the West would have risked the effective destruction of the nonproliferation treaty; on the other hand, China did not hesitate to condemn the Soviet invasion as pure imperialism.

Communist morale never recovered from the August 1968 occupation of Czechoslovakia. The French and Italian communist parties had warned Moscow in advance not to invade and condemned the action unambiguously when it occurred;

there were even a few small public protests in Red Square. Indeed, there had been nothing resembling a plausible pretext for the invasion, such as had existed in October 1956 when the Hungarian "socialist" regime did in fact collapse. If even a faithful, lifelong communist like Dubcek—leading a party which had always been loyal to the Warsaw Pact, in a country which had been more friendly to the Soviet Union than any other Soviet "ally"—could not be permitted to create "socialism with a human face," what hope was there of ending the stagnation anywhere in the Soviet-led world?

However, both the Soviet chieftains and the satellite leaders interpreted the events in Czechoslovakia as a warning that standards of living must be raised. In the 1970s (taking advantage of the general détente in East-West relations), the Soviet empire bought much Western technology and also imported both food and consumer goods. This effort was greatly facilitated by the capitalist world's oil crisis of 1973. When the major Middle Eastern oil producers formed a cartel and quadrupled world oil prices, the USSR (and Romania) were able, without having taken any "hostile" initiative, to reap a windfall from the increased world market rates; the USSR could also borrow heavily from Western banks using its vast oil reserves and other natural resources as collateral. This flush of short-term prosperity, however, did nothing to address the continuing systemic weaknesses of the communist system, which became most evident in Poland. During the 1970s, the Polish government contracted for the establishment of numerous foreign industries, among them Fiat automobiles (Italian), Berliet trucks (French), Massey-Ferguson tractors (American), Grundig radio and TV (West German) and Leyland engines (British). By 1979, Poland's foreign debt of twenty billion dollars was approximately equal to the entire foreign debt of the USSR—but Poland had no gold, oil, or even caviar with which to fund its debts.

By May 1980, Polish Party Secretary Gierek was receiving the visits of both Soviet economists and David Rockefeller, the president of the Chase Manhattan Bank. On July 1, the government reduced food subsidies as a necessary means of financial retrenchment. The inevitable price rises caused a wave of industrial strikes, beginning in the Lenin shipyards in Gdansk and later spreading to hundreds of other factories. The Polish workers had become quite sophisticated in their tactics, and they were led by a very energetic, appealing, and devoutly Catholic electrician, Lech Walesa, who had been fired four years earlier for trying to organize free labor unions. Under Walesa's disciplined leadership, the strikers occupied factories rather than demonstrate in the streets, thereby minimizing the risk of clashes with the police. Their first demands were strictly economic, and they reiterated their acceptance of the Warsaw Pact and of the "leading role" of the Communist Party. The government in turn was anxious to avoid physical conflict, which would have immediately destroyed Poland's delicate relationships not only with the Soviet Union but with Western banks and industries. On August 31, the government and the strikers signed agreements which included pay increases, shorter hours, improved social benefits, freedom of expression, the release of political prisoners—and, for the first time in Warsaw Pact history, the right to strike.

As on past occasions, the party pretended that the strikers had been protesting the errors of individual plant managers and not the communist system as such. They replaced Gierek with a party bureaucrat and made numerous personnel changes (which also allowed them to drag their heels in fulfilling the expensive concessions they had just made). In late September, the various unions coalesced to form "Solidarity," a confederation which by mid-1981 would number some nine million persons (in a population of thirty-six million), including many intellectuals and priests as well as industrial and white-collar workers. At the same time, the costs of the new wages and services, together with continuing strikes and social tension, led to a considerable drop in Poland's GNP. In the interests of social peace, the USSR heavily subsidized the Polish economy in the months following the August agreement.

Both Soviet and Polish communists inevitably had to remember the events of 1956 and 1968. In February 1981, General Wojciech Jaruselski, who had been minister of defense for some years, was named prime minister and, on the whole, Moscow increasingly consulted with Polish communist army officers rather than with party functionaries. On June 5, the Soviet Central Committee warned the Polish Central Committee concerning the activities of the enemies of Polish socialism. In September, Solidarity raised the ante by publishing an appeal for political and social reforms addressed to the workers of *all* the Warsaw Pact countries. The Soviet response was swift, as the Soviet government and party combined signatures on a letter demanding immediate and decisive action. On October 16, General Jaruselski became First Secretary of the Polish Communist Party, and two months later he declared martial law (on December 13, 1981). In short order Jaruselski banned strikes, arrested the main leaders of the unrest, dissolved Solidarity as an organization, and reintroduced press censorship. Poland had found not its Dubcek but its Kádár; it had been saved from Russian invasion, and would be ruled by a mild dictatorship until the dissolution of the empire.

In spite of the dismal economic and human-rights record reviewed here, there is no convincing reason to suppose that the Soviet empire would have collapsed as abruptly as it did simply because of that record. Indeed, the vast majority of political leaders, diplomats, and social scientists in the West firmly believed, throughout the 1980s, that although the Soviet empire would continue to stagnate, falling further and further behind the West and Japan both technologically and economically, it would nevertheless survive for some decades. In fact, two new developments were responsible for the rapid collapse of the Soviet empire in 1989 and the dissolution of the Soviet Union itself in 1991. One was the renewed arms race with the United States, and the other was the naming of Mikhail Gorbachev as General Secretary of the Soviet Communist Party in 1985.

To speak of the arms race first: by the late 1970s smaller and more accurate nuclear missiles had been developed on both sides of the Iron Curtain. The result was that nuclear war was no longer "unthinkable" in the sense that massively destructive hydrogen bombs would inevitably destroy a large percentage of humanity in a few hours (the nightmare with which the planet had lived throughout the 1950s and 1960s). Europeans and Americans alike began to wonder whether the U.S. would necessarily risk world war to counter a limited Soviet strike in Europe. Strong popular opposition to the proposed placement of advanced American missiles in Germany came from local peace movements, eagerly supported by the Soviet media and the various communist parties.

While the West was hesitating, in the four-year period from 1977 to 1980 the Soviets deployed their own SS-20 missiles, which were capable of striking West European targets without directly menacing America; and during the next several years (1980–1983), the USSR stalled negotiations from its obvious position of strength. But in March 1983, President Ronald Reagan—who had often referred to the USSR as "the evil empire"—announced a new American program, the Strategic Defense Initiative (SDI), intended to build a space shield that would destroy any incoming Soviet missiles. The SDI technology would be enormously expensive (in fact, it had not even been invented yet), and the Soviets knew that they could not possibly match the American investment. They were also alarmed—like many ordinary citizens in the West—by the way in which Reagan appeared to think that a nuclear war was "winnable."

Things came to a head in November 1983, when the West German parliament voted to permit the installation of new American Pershing missiles if the Soviets refused to remove their SS-20s. The first reaction of the Soviets was to withdraw from all arms-control negotiations and attempt to throw the blame on the US and West Germany—the two countries of which they indeed were sincerely (and correctly) afraid. But in 1985 the second factor came into play—the appointment of Mikhail Gorbachev as party leader in the USSR. Gorbachev was determined to modernize the Soviet economy and to permit a considerable degree of political liberty within the framework of the single-party state. He also made a favorable personal impression on both the conservative British prime minister, Margaret Thatcher, and President Reagan, who valued her judgment. The good personal chemistry between Gorbachev and Reagan (both of whom were fundamentally sane and optimistic human beings) produced results: The Soviets now accepted the "zero-zero" option which the Americans had first proposed in 1981, and which mandated the complete removal from Germany and Eastern Europe of both the Soviet and American nuclear missiles.

Meanwhile, Gorbachev's policies of open discussion and economic reform, applied to the Soviet satellite states as well as to the USSR, revealed the complete absence of any prospects for constructive change within the Soviet world. The East

European countries all wanted to be free of Soviet garrisons (i.e., free of the Warsaw Pact); moreover, the Soviet and East European economies were in total disarray. As soon became stunningly clear, nobody free to speak his or her mind still believed in the centralized command economy, and traditional religious and national sentiments flourished with the new freedom of expression. Thus, confronted with the choice between an uncertain (but hopefully nonviolent) future and the attempt to hold the empire together by force, Gorbachev wisely chose the former. Sensing that they would not incur a Soviet invasion, the peoples of the satellite states unanimously and peacefully demanded an end to communism and the Iron Curtain. When Gorbachev accepted their demands, including the destruction of the Berlin Wall and the reunification of Germany, the Cold War was automatically over.

One more reflection remains to be offered regarding the Soviet system. In theory, it was a scientific system intended to aid History to evolve as History was inevitably destined to evolve. In theory, individuals were only the instruments of this dialectical unfolding of History, which in the communist universe had taken the place of God. Thus, in his final statement in his treason trial in 1938 (after he had been condemned to death), Nikolai Bukharin quoted approvingly the words of the German fellow-traveling novelist Lion Feuchtwanger to the effect that "world history is a world court of judgment." Bukharin truly believed that—as did Lenin, Trotsky, Stalin, Mao Zedong, and practically all revolutionary Marxist leaders until about 1960.

But in fact, the evolution of the USSR and its satellite states depended far more narrowly on the all-too-human personal traits of individual leaders than did the nations of the capitalist West. The paranoia of Stalin, the blustering enthusiasm of Khrushchev, the cold efficiency of Ulbricht, the patient resourcefulness of Kádár, the mistakenly trusting decency of Dubcek: such character traits were far more decisive in the history of their countries than any political or social theory, and such traits were far less important in those societies where economic and political power were not so fully concentrated as in the communist dictatorships.

ENDNOTES

1. The above paragraphs may appear to some readers as a mere caricature, but it is a brief and exaggeration-free summary of the litany I heard repeatedly as a student in the universities of Toulouse and Paris in the years 1950–1952.

2. For a thoroughly documented example of the French intellectual refusal to recognize the facts about Soviet Russia, see Nina Berberova, *L'Affaire Kravtchenko* (Toulouse: Actes du Sud, 1990). The book is a translation, with commentary, of her articles for the

Russian-language press in Paris in 1949, during the suit for defamation won by the former Soviet diplomat against *Les Lettres Françaises*. The latter review had tried to discredit his writings by slanderous personal accusations and had called as witnesses a number of prestigious French academicians and writers.

3. Herman Weber, *Geschichte der DDR* (Munich: Deutscher Taschenbuch Verlag, 1985), pp. 236–44.

4. The Hungarian revolution was covered in detail by the Western press. Excellent eyewitness accounts and interviews with leading personalities appeared in (among others) the *New York Times*, the *Christian Science Monitor*, and the *Reporter*. The last weekly carried some particularly fine articles by Leslie Bain, later collected in a book entitled *Reluctant Satellites* (New York: Macmillan, 1960). See also Tibor Meray, "L'insurrection hongroise et le drame d'Imre Nagy," *Les Temps Modernes*, November 1957.

5. Henryk Slabek, "Socio-Political Aspects of the Polish Peasantry, 1944–1948," and Janusz Kalinski, "Collectivization of Agriculture in Poland, 1948–1956," *Acta Poloniae Historica*, 1988, 137–201.

6. Sydney Gruson in the *New York Times*, November 5, 1956. Slightly different excerpts and translation of the original Polish appear in Konrad Syrop, *Spring in October* (Westport, Conn.: Greenwood Press, 1957), pp. 154–57.

7. Adam B. Ulam, *The Communists . . . 1948–1991* (New York: Macmillan, 1991), and Antonin Snejdarek and Casimira Mazurowa-Chatêau, *La nouvelle Europe centrale* (Paris: Imprimerie, 1986), *passim*, concerning the events in Poland of 1956 and the events in Czechoslovakia of 1968.

15

Interpreting
Twentieth-Century Europe

I f it is difficult to compress the outlines of an entire century into fourteen chapters, and even more difficult to offer a single chapter interpreting that history with an eye to the future. Indeed, the first thing that must be emphasized is that, no matter how carefully and lovingly one has studied history, there is no way to predict the future in any detail. This limitation is due to the simple but unavoidable fact that decisions are made by human actors. There is no method of foreseeing the intelligence, energy, relevant factual knowledge, economic and demographic resources, quality of education, or emotional and moral commitments of those who will assume political and institutional leadership in the future. The best one can hope for is to define parameters, recognize truly long-term forces and trends, and thus hopefully reduce the extent of the unknown.

Starting with the overall economic picture, capitalism in the twentieth century continued to prove itself (as it already had in the eighteenth and nineteenth centuries) to be the most effective productive system in human history. The authoritarian socialism of the Soviet Union claimed, with brief plausibility during the depression of the 1930s, to have invented a better productive system and a more just form of distribution. But the peacetime competition between Western capitalism and the Soviet economy in the second half of the century clearly demonstrated the superiority of capitalism.

That superiority does not depend solely on the role of the market, but also—and very substantially—on that of political liberty. As long ago as 1831, the distinguished British historian Thomas Macaulay, in his inaugural lecture at the new University of London, noted the linkage between economic and academic freedom. The entire experience of the modern West indicates that freedom of the individual makes possible the most inventive, uncoerced, unintimidated use of

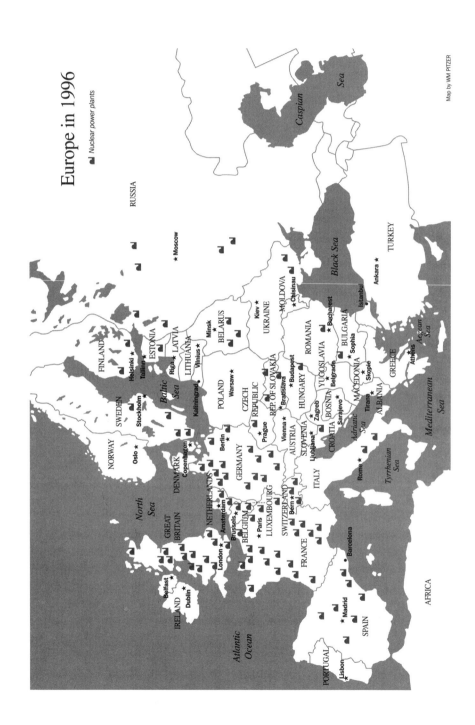

Europe in 1996

⬛ Nuclear power plants

Map by WM PITZER

intelligence in both intellectual and commercial pursuits; while freedom of the press, and of the communications media in general, constitutes a necessary counterweight to corruption, favoritism, monopolies, and all the many tendencies by which an existing power elite tries to hold on to its privileges and restrict the entry of new participants.

The experience of the economically successful authoritarian states of contemporary Asia—Singapore, South Korea, and China—may seem to contradict the above generalization. Indeed, these nations frequently claim that the development of the market economy has nothing to do with merely "Western" (not human) liberties. But their success, in its first generation, is too recent to prove the point. Over the coming decades, they will either have to offer political freedom or else succumb to the corruption and gerontocracy that destroyed the Soviet Union—and that severely limits the development of the oil sheikdoms and such nations as India and Pakistan today.

The superiority of contemporary capitalism also depends on the modifications and social controls associated with the welfare state. The alleviation of mass unemployment in the Anglo-Saxon and Scandinavian countries during the 1930s, the rebuilding of the German and West European economies after World War II, and the rapid conversion of the Mediterranean economies from landlord-dominated agriculture to market capitalism all depended on a large measure of social control, especially investment and redistribution decisions which put money in the pockets of nonentrepreneurial workers.

Capitalist prosperity depends on both large consumer markets and industrial and high-technology sales, civilian and military, to the world's hundred-and-eighty-odd sovereign states. Neither in the 1930s nor in the 1990s has unregulated capitalism been able to solve the problems of mass unemployment, "overproduction," or "underconsumption." During the first years of the world depression, the governments of England, the US, and Germany all pursued balanced budget and monetarist policies of the type now being urged by conservative economists. The depression did not respond to that treatment, and the post-1933 recovery was due to government investment in public works, infrastructure, social insurance, and rearmament.

Western prosperity between the end of World War II and the oil-pricing crisis of 1973 depended on the rebuilding of infra-structures, on wage increases which enabled the great majority to buy the consumer products, on the development of nuclear and other high-tech military products, and on the sale of arms in both the developed and underdeveloped worlds. Since 1973, energy costs have forced the developed countries to increase efficiency and productivity and to reduce waste in public expenditures. Moreover, since the dismantling of the Soviet empire in 1989–90 and the disappearance of the USSR itself in 1991, conservative economists and philosophers have increasingly insisted that the welfare state as such is obsolete.

In this regard, we should not forget that the welfare state developed in large part as the capitalist world's reply to the possibility that the Soviet revolution might lead to a better material life for the masses. It is no cause for surprise, then, that when the economic competition was won by capitalism, the spokesmen of neoclassical economics saw no further reason to coddle the Western working classes with the expensive welfare state. The ease with which capital can now be transferred electronically all over the globe, coupled with the industrialization of many countries with much lower labor costs than Europe, do indeed threaten the standard of living acquired by the European peoples only in the past four decades. Theoretically, whole industries can simply be moved to Asia now, Latin America tomorrow, and Africa the next day, as global industrialization raises labor and infrastructure costs in one location after another.

But such visions fail to realize the complexity of industrial society. Some investors have already discovered that the advantage (for the capitalist) of low wages may be more than offset by such things as the lack of local infrastructure, political or monetary instability, the need to bribe legions of police and bureaucrats, resentment or incomprehension of technical needs, and the myriad cultural differences between the home office and the electronically connected local office. Much of this potential transfer of industry from mature to developing countries will lead to the same kinds of bitter struggle that have always accompanied imperialism, be it imposed with a flag and gunboats or just with a set of banking rules.

A more realistic possibility than the massive decapitalization and deindustrialization of the West is the necessary reform of the welfare state. For example, some trade unions are fighting for the right of their members to retire on full pay (or close to full pay) at the age of fifty-five. What is needed instead is to raise the retirement age to seventy, especially since many people in good health may well prefer to work even beyond that age rather than fill their remaining years with TV games and packaged tours.

Necessary also are the work-sharing plans that present the only eventual solution to massive unemployment. If work-sharing is to be successful, it also means both general and technical education must be improved so that the great majority of potential workers will be capable of the same productivity as the elite. This, in turn, constitutes one more good reason among many to increase the social investment in education for those generations who will have to live in an increasingly automated and technological world. Then, too, when work is shared on less demanding office or computer-terminal schedules, the new situation will itself encourage people to remain in the work force longer, which means in turn that they will continue to contribute to the collective funding of their old-age pensions.

The cost of modern medical technology is also one of the factors threatening to create ever larger deficits in the budgets of the welfare state. But a perfectly feasible (albeit gradual) change of emphasis from treatment to prevention would go far to control total medical costs. It is impossible to say how many of the heart attacks and strokes requiring expensive emergency treatment would not occur if people ate more sensibly, controlled their weight, and were less competitive in ways that send the heartbeat racing and the blood pressure soaring; but it is a matter of simple common sense to observe how many people are injuring their health by smoking, drinking, stuffing themselves with junk food, leading sedentary lives, and so on. There are also the very serious and costly problems of drug abuse, which can only be reduced by preventive education and a society in which the young can always find useful employment. There is an old adage that remind us "an ounce of prevention is worth a pound of cure." It is as true now as ever, and its application is one of the necessary (and most eminently feasible) reforms of social-welfare spending in the technically advanced nations.

In any case, all democratic governments have found it necessary—and will continue to find it necessary—to maintain the essential features of the welfare state, if only to maintain the social cohesion of the countries they govern. The evangelists of unregulated capitalism and balanced budgets rarely show much concern for the deficits resulting from military expenditures, but they find reprehensible those which result from social spending. Nor do their statistics deal with the fact that military expenditures are a dead loss economically, whereas health and education multiply their (admittedly difficult to quantify) economic benefits throughout a society's future. Thus, despite all the graphs and technical vocabulary with which the subject is approached, the real issues are more political and educational than they are economic.

While the capitalist welfare state certainly counts as a factor of potential optimism for the future of Europe (as well as humankind in general), there is an immense potential obstacle to the realization of that future: the accumulating ecological and demographic crisis, a crisis which has itself been largely caused by the industrial and medical progress of the present century. As little as fifty years ago, economists and industrial managers were worried about what they saw as the unavoidable exhaustion of such natural resources as lumber, oil, and coal. And while the world's forests indeed continue to be endangered by a combination of commercial logging and the expansion of primitive agriculture and grazing, the discovery of much new oil and coal has ended the fears of imminent exhaustion of those resources, while the invention of plastics has greatly decreased the total dependence on lumber and metals. The problem, therefore, is not so much the availability of raw materials as the "side effects" of both industrial development and land use upon the biosphere—the air, water, plant, and animal life upon which all human activities ultimately depend.

Destruction of the biosphere takes place under all economic systems. The conversion of forests and steppes to agriculture, the chemical pollution of air and water by industrial operations, and the creation of smog by millions of gasoline-powered vehicles takes place whether the economy is precapitalist, capitalist, or communist. Once again, the presence of political freedom has meant that, in the democratic countries, public opinion has been able to expose and achieve partial correction of many of the worst abuses of the environment. But under the mostly authoritarian governments of the communist, precapitalist, and Asian capitalist worlds, the combination of censorship and ignorance has prevented the necessary protection of the environment.

Five years after the collapse of the Soviet Union, we still do not know how many people died at Chernobyl, or how many millions of acres of agricultural land have been poisoned by radioactive fallout throughout the former USSR, its Scandinavian neighbors, and its East European satellites. Nor do we know how much nuclear waste has flowed into Arctic waters, and eventually the world's oceans, as the result of shipping accidents and simple dumping of radioactive chemicals by the Soviet navy. Nor do we know anything more about nuclear wastes and industrial pollution in China and Southeast Asia than the governments of those developing nations care to reveal.

In the American northwest, scientists, businesspeople, and the general public have recognized the deleterious effects of clearcut logging on freshwater supplies, flood and erosion control, plant and fish life in the coastal waters, and the fishing industry. In the meantime, in much of Latin America, Africa, and Asia, peasants desperate to feed their families cut down trees and bring under cultivation land which has neither the fertility nor the rainfall to support successful agriculture.

Much of the ecological damage of the past century is a result of steadily increasing population pressures. Traditional peasants—who still constitute the majority in some of the most populous portions of the globe—consider large families as a guarantee of economic support in their own old age. At the same time, the world's most vigorous proselytizing religions—Roman Catholicism, Islam, and the fundamentalist Protestant churches—are all adamantly opposed to family planning and birth control. Only Confucian China has adopted official policies for limiting population growth, through the methods by which its leaders feel obliged to implement this policy in a technically backward country include not only massive abortions but forced sterilization and infanticide (mostly of girl babies).

The evidence is strong that, with economic development, people of all nationalities and religions begin to produce fewer children. But the outlook for voluntary, effective methods of limiting the planetary population depend upon changes of attitude on the part of religious authorities—changes of which there is no present sign. In any case, a minimally civilized future for the human race will require much more careful use of land, water, and all types of natural resources than has ever been characteristic of human behavior. Moreover, this is one of many problems that cannot be solved by the market, which is driven by short-term (and amoral) profit motives, not by concerns with social problems or long-term resource availability.

Assuming that European society will be rational enough to reform and maintain the essential character of the welfare state, and assuming as well that all governments will understand the need to preserve a livable planetary environment, there are many hopeful possibilities for the continuing vitality of European civilization in a mostly peaceful, nonimperialist world. One essential cultural factor in this vitality has always been the complex interplay between many diverse linguistic cultures and a lingua franca—Latin until the seventeenth century, French until the mid-twentieth century, and English since the Second World War. Language, taken together with the books, the religious and folk customs, the musical, artistic, and athletic cultures, and the landscape and architectural styles that accumulate among people who share the same language, are the tangible distinguishing marks of the different "minicivilizations" within general European one. Too often, linguistic cultures have been confused with the pseudobiology frequently referred to in this book. In the First World War and again in the fascist-Nazi era, the illusions of pseudobiology brought European civilization to the brink of suicide. And the reification of linguistic cultures into nationalist doctrines (almost invariably demanding a separate state) remains a difficult contemporary problem.

Of course, in itself the emphasis on cultural heritage—the desire to use one's historic language and legal institutions to contribute to the variety of a shared civilization—is a distinctly positive trait. Political democracy, the devolution of power from central governments to regional units and municipalities, the actual economic and potential political unification of Europe, all work in the direction of recognizing linguistic and cultural variety without the need to create new sovereignties, armies, currencies, nationalist prejudices, or diplomatic corps and frontier police. Full freedom of travel within the European union, as well as mutual recognition of each nation's educational degrees and professional associations, the development of the Erasmus fellowship programs, and international cooperation in scientific laboratories (such as CERN), and expensive technology projects (such as the Eurobus and satellite communications systems)—all these things are creating a Europe that is psychologically very different from the confrontational, nationalist and imperialist Europe of 1914.

Extending this fruitful coexistence of linguistic cultures is admittedly not easy. Centralized states do not easily acknowledge the justice of delegating their functions to regional autonomies. Ardent spokesmen of small, stateless nationalities do not like to recognize that there are cultural minorities within their own midst. All nationalisms—even those that are free of racism and military aggressiveness—have a strong tendency to succumb to the temptations of victimism, to seeing all their troubles as being caused not by economics or geography or competing class interests or local inefficiency, but by neighboring states.

The creation of a united Europe composed of several dozen cooperating linguistic cultures seems to me one of the essential and achievable tasks of the coming decades. Constructive models for this undertaking are the regional politics of Catalonia, the peaceful separation of the Czech Republic and Slovakia, the arbitration of historic conflicts between the Romanian and Hungarian minorities living under each other's state sovereignty, and the politics of devolution being worked out gradually among England, Scotland, and Wales. Destructive models are the bitter ethnic wars being waged in the former Yugoslavia and the former Soviet Union, and the terrorism being pursued in the Spanish Basque country and Northern Ireland with the very obvious motive of preventing peaceful, less than "total," solutions to historic grievances.

Thinking in the long term, one cannot emphasize too much the importance of freedom of *circulation*, both physical and spiritual, within the variety of linguistic and national cultures. Presumably Albert Einstein would have been a great physicist even if he had had to live his entire life in the imperial Germany whose class structure and militarism were alien to his nature. But he could pursue his education in Italy and Switzerland, and could live and work in the very international city of Zurich, which was also home to many political and artistic revolutionaries whose general spirit was closer to his than that of either bourgeois Munich or bourgeois Milan. Einstein could also spend a few intellectually rich years in Prague in the period before the First World War, when it was a center of brilliant, unorthodox Czech, German, and Jewish culture. He could return to imperial Germany, where (despite an undercurrent of anti-Semitism), the government and his colleagues gave him the best existing facilities in which to pursue his research in the midst of war. And he could show his gratitude afterward to that finer Germany by insisting that he would not attend international conferences to which German physicists were not invited.

The great Russian composer Dmitri Shostakovich was obliged to humiliate himself with public confessions and to limit his published compositions in the years 1937–1953 to works that were sufficiently melodious to please the ears of the exalted Father of Soviet Peoples. But before the establishment of Stalin's dictatorship, Shostakovich had gloried in his musical contact with the experimental composers of Western Europe (also with American jazz), and he had been intellectually stimulated by the movies and plays in several different languages for which he supplied the incidental music.

In 1949 and 1950, the Soviet government sent Shostakovich—now world-famous for his wartime Leningrad Symphony—to New York, Paris, and Warsaw as part of the Soviets' effort to portray themselves as the true proponents of world peace and international culture. Shostakovich was extremely cautious in answering questions from reporters; he knew that spies would report his every word and gesture, and of course his family was being held hostage in Leningrad against the possibility that he might defect. But these travel opportunities were certainly worth the elevated level of caution exercised by this normally sociable man in order to meet his Western counterparts and to hear their music. Probably the most important of these journeys was the one to Leipzig in the summer of 1950. This time, Shostakovich had been sent as a judge of the international piano competition being held to commemorate the two-hundredth anniversary of the death of Johann Sebastian Bach. Outwardly, Shostakovich was present as a Soviet cultural ambassador. Inwardly, it was an occasion to see for himself the somber war ruins of East Germany and to attune his spirit to that of Bach; and in the months thereafter, he wrote a set of twenty-four preludes and fugues worthy of the master whose *Well-Tempered Clavichord* he was commemorating.

Throughout his creative life, Shostakovich combined the necessary outward conformity to Soviet ideology with inward (and very "cosmopolitan") criteria of his own. Of solely Russian and Polish ancestry, Shostakovich wrote music on Jewish themes, *especially* during the 1940s when Stalin's anti-Jewish sentiments were quite evident. His symphonic work placed itself squarely in the traditions of Beethoven and Mahler; moreover, he wrote several scores for Shakespearian plays and films, and one of his last major works was a symphony of songs, on poems he chose from the works of Federico García Lorca, Guillaume Apollinaire, Wilhelm Küchelbecker, and Rainer Maria Rilke. Thus, in spite of once having been the direct object of Stalin's censorship and also severely criticized during the late 1940s campaign against "rootless cosmopolitanism," Shostakovich was able to enrich his creative life by embracing the culture of all Europe, past and present.

Having come this far in the general interpretation of twentieth-century Europe, let us assume that political liberty, constitutional democracy, and unimpeded contact among the many linguistic cultures will continue. In such circumstances, there need be no pessimism about the future prospects of European civilization. But just as economic optimism has to be modified by the threat of ecological and population crises, so cultural optimism must be modified by the evidence of an accumulating spiritual crisis in the West.

In the recent past (measured in centuries rather than in CNN newscasts), the West has given some sense of purpose—and some hope of transcendence—to its peoples in three general forms. The first of these is religious, and indeed the hope of religious salvation in its many Christian and Jewish forms has been an intimate aspect of European culture for two thousand years. (And as large numbers of African and Asian immigrants settle in Europe, forms of Islam and Buddhism are being added to the variety of creeds.) Then came the eighteenth-century Enlightenment, which along with the positive aspects of the American and French revolutions gave rise to hopes of secular salvation in the form of political democracy, human rights, and economic and educational opportunity. These hopes were generally confined to the urban business and professional classes and to those workers and rural immigrants who possessed the ability to succeed in the competitive meritocracy. Then, in the nineteenth century, various forms of socialism and anarchism—but especially the Marxism of the Second International—extended those secular hopes in the form of a noncompetitive ideal of collective control and usufruct of all resources, natural and human.

To express matters bluntly (but without exaggerating them in the slightest), at the end of the twentieth century all three of these forms of hope and purpose have lost their inspirational power. Of course, the true strength of Christianity is hard to evaluate. Statistics can tell the reader how many people attend church services, take their marriage vows in a religious ceremony, send their children to religious schools, and give a religious burial to their family members. But none of this is evidence that the persons doing these things really believe in Christian theology and morals, and the same considerations apply only slightly less to Jews.

In 1931, the highly intelligent prime minister of the new Spanish Republic, Manuel Azaña, caused a scandal when he advocated separation of church and state on the grounds that Spain had ceased to be a Catholic nation. He did not mean that people had ceased to go to mass or that the Church had lost its institutional power, but rather that the Church no longer provided the kind of intellectual and spiritual leadership that it had provided in the sixteenth and seventeenth centuries. And much the same thing can be said for Europe as a whole in the twentieth century. In Scandinavia and Western Europe, the role of churches has become increasingly limited to the registration of births, marriages, and deaths, and to intermittent ceremonials of moral exhortation and comfort. But for the vast majority, these functions have very little to do with their personal beliefs and their vital decisions.

In Soviet Russia from 1917 onward, and in Central-Eastern Europe from 1945 to 1990, the noncommunist population clung to their religious beliefs as the only permitted expression of any ideal different from the drearily repeated shibboleths of the ruling party. But even in Poland—where the Roman Catholic religion for centuries has been consubstantial with the sense of nationality, where electronic amplification is employed to carry the mass to overflow crowds in the church courtyards, and where the conservative Pope John Paul II is a national hero—the younger generations practice all forms of birth control, and the prevalent economic and cultural ideal is to become as much like the democratic, secularized West as possible.

To turn from religious to secular ideals: Marxian socialism has been completely discredited in the East because of the series of oppressive, incompetent, and hypocritical dictatorships which created what they were pleased to call "real socialism." And it has been largely discredited in the West as well, because the nearest approximation to its best ideals has been embodied in the social-democratic, mostly capitalist welfare state, not in the regimes resulting from the Bolshevik revolution.

More serious in regard to the future is the disenchantment with the heritage of the eighteenth-century Enlightenment. One of the few positive categorical statements that can be made about the twentieth century is that the welfare state of the past forty years has offered a better material life and greater cultural and educational opportunities to a higher percentage of the population than any known previous society. Materially, that society was made possible by democratic capitalism. Spiritually, it was inspired by the ideals of (potential) human perfectibility and the political and religious liberty associated with the Dutch and English revolutions of the seventeenth century and the American and French revolutions of the eighteenth.

As of the 1990s, however, that whole secular tradition is on the defensive. The most prestigious economists insist that the welfare state is too expensive to be maintained, that global economic conditions require an unregulated competitive capitalism like that of the early stages of the industrial revolution (allegedly in order to compete with the newly industrialized Asian economies, which have the low wages and lack of social protections that were indeed characteristic of European industry until the late nineteenth century).

Politically and spiritually, optimism about human perfectibility, as well as a belief in the potential of universal public education, and the importance of voting or otherwise participating in "the political process" are much less prevalent than they were in the first decades of the century. The struggles for trade-union recognition, women's suffrage, Popular Front social legislation, and solidarity with the Spanish Republic, as well as the ardent debates within the World War II resistance movements regarding the democratization of postwar society: all were inspired by the secular ideals of the Enlightenment and by versions of Marxism compatible with those ideals (including the illusion that the Soviet Union was a society embodying those ideals). Of course, in recent decades, the movements for full equality between the sexes, gay and lesbian rights, and the protection of immigrant workers against racism can also trace their ultimate sources to the ideals of the Enlightenment. But except for women's rights (and women, after all, constitute 51 percent of the population), participation in these movements has not been as widespread and militant as in the movements prior to World War II.

To me, it seems that the Second World War—and especially (but by no means only) the Nazi occupation of most of continental Europe—destroyed the ability of the European peoples to think optimistically about the future. How could presumably civilized people like those fine, healthy, disciplined young German soldiers treat the Jews, Gypsies, and Soviet prisoners of war with the cold cruelty and efficiency of the extermination units? How could presumably civilized political leaders even among the Allies decide on the carpet bombing (and, ultimately, the atomic bombing), of crowded cities inhabited by defenseless civilians? Conversely, how could the Allied leaders fail to have bombed Auschwitz? How could Stalin encourage the Warsaw underground to rise and then quietly watch while the Germans destroyed the Polish capital? The combination of such material power and such massive cruelty and betrayal had never been seen by—or, at least, never been brought to the consciousness of—so many witnesses.

If this seems to be stretching the point too broadly, consider, for example, the abstract art and music of recent decades; the vogue of violent crime and horror novels, movies, and TV series; the search for forgetfulness, ever-new physical sensations, and a submersion of the here-and-now in sadomasochist sex games, exotic travels, drugs, and alcohol; the tortured, deliberate mystifications of so much contemporary philosophy and poetry; the massive protests, albeit without any clear constructive programs, of the student political movements and especially their terrorist factions in the 1960s and 1970s; the "deconstruction" of the Western humanist heritage currently fashionable in the universities; or even the ugly mass riots among soccer fans. All of these are symptomatic of a society characterized by material prosperity, high technology, and the absence of any generous, hopeful consensus ideals for that part of human nature which cannot live by bread alone.

In Eastern Europe and Russia, the public experience of the twentieth century has been disastrous: tottering dynastic empires succeeded by the one-party Bolshevik dictatorship in Russia, by failed republics and quasifascist dictatorships in Central-Eastern and Balkan Europe after the First World War, and by the extension of the Soviet dictatorship to those small nations as a result of the second. Roughly until the 1960s, a significant proportion of the intellectuals, scientists, students, and elite industrial workers believed they were constructing socialism in spite of Stalin's purges, and in spite of the humorless bureaucrats who succeeded the generation of purged revolutionaries. But when the economy stagnated, when liberty failed to appear, and when it became unmistakably clear that "real socialism" could not offer the masses nearly as tolerable a life as did the capitalist West, the secular Marxist faith melted away. In proportion to their intelligence and their sensitivity, people privatized their personal lives and sought their solace in reading, music, sex, alcohol, religious hope (or despair), and scientific or nonpolitical artistic activity for those blessed with the necessary talents.

I do not know how many references I have read to the fact that Yuri Andropov —for many years head of the Soviet secret police—possessed a fine collection of classical recordings and was reputed to be a charming conversationalist regarding literature and the arts. I have never been sure how seriously to believe such reports, since they have also been made concerning one of his worst predecessors, Lavrenti Beria, and frequently appear in writings concerning some of the worst Nazi butchers. If these reports are true, all they mean is that, for persons who have detached themselves from all humane ideals, it is perfectly possible to be a villain and enjoy the arts.

It is too soon to judge in detail the sentiments of the Soviet-ruled populations in the 1980s and after the unexpected collapse of the empire. But certain trends are clear: complete disillusionment with the command economy and a predominant rejection of, or loss of hope in, all forms of collective economic management; hatred of the *nomenklatura* and the commissars-turned-capitalists who have expropriated the Russian economy in ways that would make the "robber barons" of nineteenth-century capitalism green with envy; and bitter doubts about achieving political democracy and capitalism with a human face (to alter slightly the phrase of one of the few truly decent men ever to rule a communist country, Alexander Dubcek).

The possibilities of creating a democratic capitalist economy in the former Soviet empire are being hampered equally by the Soviet heritage and by the doctrinaire unregulated capitalism promoted by the present Western governments and banks, in collusion with the Russian mafia. The Soviets never succeeded in creating the New Soviet Man dreamed of in the 1920s and 1930s, but they did succeed in destroying the old middle classes so completely that, in Russia since 1930 and most of Eastern Europe since 1950, there have been no middle classes capable of creating small businesses, managing markets and financial services for people of modest resources, and so on. The elimination of the middle classes was not quite so complete in Poland, the Czech republic, Hungary, and the Baltic states—and these are precisely the areas in which it has been possible to create, in the 1990s, the basis for a free economy and free political institutions.

But in terms of social and community ideals, the situation in Eastern Europe is sadly familiar to the Western observer. The Soviet perversion and exploitation of internationalist ideals has meant that the values of the eighteenth-century Enlightenment are no more flourishing there than in the West. Human rights were a banner in the struggle to throw off Soviet rule; but in the absence of secular democratic faith, traditional religion (loaded down with its own weight of prejudice against outsiders), nationalism, and racism threaten those unhappy lands even more strongly than they do the pessimistic and disillusioned sectors of Western society.

The recrudescence of nationalism, racism, and the entire panoply of Social Darwinist ideas throughout Europe has largely destroyed the euphoria which accompanied the "velvet revolution" and the nonviolent collapse of the USSR. The secular democratic ideal has always assumed that human beings, if they have enough to eat and have been reasonably well treated at home and in school, will act decently toward their fellow human beings. All the social and educational programs undertaken, both by public and private institutions, depend on that faith. But what if—as Thomas Hobbes, Edmund Burke, and Sigmund Freud, among other great thinkers, supposed—there is a certain irreducible quid of sheer meanness in a considerable number of human beings? Terrible crimes are often committed by college graduates from prosperous families. Riots by soccer fans and acts of arson against immigrant worker housing are often instigated or committed by people who have not been the victims of oppression or starvation. Many of the most monstrous Nazi criminals—the Himmlers, the Eichmanns, and the Mengeles—came from quite normal family backgrounds. And the man most responsible for the ethnic cleansing of Bosnia in the early 1990s is said to be both a psychiatrist and a poet.

Actually, the threat posed by such persons is the same whether or not we believe that only 1 percent of our fellow human beings, or a far more sizable minority, may be motivated by such murderous hostility. In a world full of nuclear, chemical, and biological weapons (and with a flourishing black market in such arms), it is already perfectly possible for tiny minorities to blackmail the peaceable majority, and it will only become easier in proportion as such weapons are "perfected" and disseminated. It is for this reason that I have always believed in the necessity of nuclear, chemical, and biological disarmament, from ground zero 1945 onward, simply to protect humanity from such catastrophes. The problem, of course, is not solely European, or white; it exists on all continents and among all skin colors. In the present context, it means that anything one can anticipate about the future of Europe (or of humanity) depends on the avoidance of nuclear, chemical, or biological war by organized states, and of blackmail and terrorism by small groups using such weapons in the name of a particular ethnic, religious, or political group.

Besides the evident need for disarmament, twentieth-century European history also shows what happens when amoral "realism" replaces all sense of solidarity and principled resistance to massive, clearly intentional evil. Of the many instances that could be cited, I will choose two: the political responsibility for the occurrence of the Second World War, and the intellectual and moral implications of the recent (and still flourishing) school of literary and philosophical criticism known as "deconstruction."

In Europe before the twentieth century, war was a normal instrument of dynastic or national policy. Philip II, Louis XIV, Frederick "the Great," Bismarck, and numerous lesser chieftains calculated their risks and launched their wars, whose costs were thought to be reasonable in terms of the contemporary technology and the minimally acceptable treatment of their politically disenfranchised subjects. The First World War was also the result of strategic calculations on the part of military and diplomatic leaders who considered war a normal instrument of policy. But by this time, the mass of the population was beginning to possess some political rights, and the war itself turned out to be far more destructive than any of the calculators had anticipated.

The covenant of the League of Nations, and the several conferences in the 1920s looking toward the limitation of arms, were evidence that world political leaders recognized the absolute necessity of eliminating war as an instrument of national policy. Then, in 1933, Adolf Hitler came to power in Germany (without a majority, but perfectly legally). His autobiographical *Mein Kampf*, his pre-electoral harangues, and his many speeches as chancellor constantly reiterated his determination to dominate the European continent, by terror or by war; and his intent to establish a German empire based on racial hierarchies. If these indicators were too subtle, Hitler's gunbarrel diplomacy and his stepped-up rearmament program were perfectly consistent with his verbally expressed intentions. Indeed, in contrast with the complex rivalries and mistaken calculations underlying the First World War, there was no doubt in the years from 1933 to 1939 that Hitler, and Hitler alone (not even his hapless ally Mussolini), wanted war. We did not have to wait for the unsealing of diplomatic papers or the memoirs of the political leaders of the 1930s; anyone who read the newspapers knew Hitler's intentions and the preparations he was making to fulfill them.

Europe had two clear opportunities to stop Hitler without a major continental or world war. These opportunities were the Spanish Civil War of 1936–1939 and the Czechoslovak crisis of 1938. In the first case, the Western democracies would have had the cooperation of the Soviet Union and the support of majority public opinion at home if they had decided to come to the aid of the legally elected Spanish government. In partial defense of the appeasers, it can be argued that the military coup in Spain unleashed a violent leftist revolution in the first months of the struggle and that, throughout the war, the Soviet government exercised undue influence on the republican governments (although this was a direct result of the Western refusal to aid the republic). No such excuses, however, can be offered to defend the betrayal of Czechoslovakia, which had a stable government fully as democratic as any in the West, plus a high-quality army and excellent fortifications—a country, in short, which was ready to take the brunt of Hitler's assault if only the West would recognize its own self-interest by coming to the aid of that thoroughly middle-class, democratic state.

The complete bungling of the opportunities in Spain and Czechoslovakia involved a stunning combination of badly calculated national interests and moral cowardice—with each of these factors reinforcing the other. The British prime minister's blindness to Nazi intentions and his exaggerated fears of communism dovetailed with suggestions about the pointlessness of risking war for a far-off little nation of which the West knew very little. And these suggestions dovetailed, in turn, with the desire to avoid any general human responsibility that might involve war. In 1936, Hitler knew he could not risk war and, even as late 1938, his own military advisers (the memory of World War I still fresh in their minds) counseled him strongly against provoking a war against the combined forces of the West and the Soviet Union. But under Chamberlain's leadership at Munich, the West saved Hitler the trouble—and created the situation in which, a year later, they could only save themselves at the cost of a world war.

Returning to the question of responsibilities, the political responsibility for the Second World War lies positively with Hitler's unquenchable appetite for aggression, and negatively with the Western appeasement governments as well as Joseph Stalin, who in August 1939 trumped the West's readiness to make him Hitler's future victim. I would not so heavily emphasize this lethal mixture of mistaken calculation and moral cowardice, except that it has been already repeated in the "minor" but vicious wars which destroyed Yugoslavia and partitioned Bosnia between 1992 and 1996. The political and economic self-interest of the European nations—and every consideration of human decency—pointed unmistakably to the need to forestall Serbian and Croatian aggression. It could have been done with little or no war in 1991 or 1992 but, as in the 1930s, the principal European powers were not ready to take risks on behalf of small, far-off peoples.

Given the enormous issues at stake in the example discussed above, it may well seem trivial at best to discuss an aspect of postmodern literary criticism in the same context. But if we are concerned with evidences of moral motivation (or paralysis), the relationship between the calculations of international politics and the interpretations of literary criticism may not be so farfetched.

One of the principal features of postmodern literary theory, and in particular of the movement known as "deconstruction," is the reduction of the role of authors and their conscious intentions. Books are not principally the product of the intellectual efforts and the moral judgment of those individuals whose names appear on the title page; rather, some unconscious linguistic or mythic "structure" is expressing itself through the writer. The work which he or she may mistakenly and egotistically think of as his or her "creation" is in fact a mere "text" without any fixed meaning, to be "deconstructed" by literary critics who point out all the ambiguities in the use of words, all the possible internal contradictions, and the many alternative ways in which the text can be interpreted.

A world which has lived through Munich, Auschwitz, and Hiroshima; through the ethnic cleansings in large parts of Africa, the Balkans, and the former Soviet Union; and through the indiscriminate bombings of terrorists on all continents, is indeed a world of moral uncertainties and ambiguities. The postmodern insistence on multiple interpretations and moral ambiguities indeed corresponds to the late-twentieth-century *Zeitgeist*. In reducing the conscious role of the author, deconstruction also reduces the elements of intellectual and moral judgment and, hence, the elements of moral responsibility (or perhaps of responsibility plain and simple). This is especially problematic given that alive and flourishing in the present world there are thousands of persons who were fascist or communist officials but later transformed themselves into democrats or nationalists, depending on the political context in which they found themselves. A single dramatic instance of this phenomenon is the career of one of the most admired founders and practitioners of deconstruction, the late Belgian-American professor Paul de Man.

At the time of his death in 1983, de Man was the revered mentor of dozens of the most brilliant professors of literature in the United States, as well as the author of several authoritative books (I should perhaps say "texts") in literary theory and literary criticism. As far as anyone knew, de Man had arrived in the U.S. in 1948 as a nearly penniless refugee and had taught at Bard College, where he married one of his students. The originality of his writings was quickly recognized and led successively to membership in the prestigious Society of Fellows at Harvard University and then to a professorship at Yale.

Four years after his death, a student who was preparing a biography stumbled on some 170 articles which de Man had published in the years 1940–42. These articles appeared in *Le Soir*, which had been the leading independent newspaper of Belgium until it was expropriated by the Nazis and edited under their auspices after the German invasion in May 1940. It also turned out that de Man had left large unpaid debts resulting from the bankruptcy of a publishing house which he had founded during the war, and that he had deserted a wife and three infant sons who had gone to Argentina when he came to the U.S.[1]

As might be expected, these discoveries led to a good deal of soul-searching and bitter debate in the university community. De Man's articles were not as rabid as the most violent Nazi propaganda, but they definitely reflected Nazi views, looked forward to a Nazi-oriented European future, and included the obligatory denigration of the role of the Jews in European cultural life. To be fair, they also contained plenty of phrases with multiple possible meanings, phrases which could —with effort—be deconstructed for their non-Nazi or even anti-Nazi implications. As for abandoning one's wife and children, this phenomenon is not as rare as we could wish, either in academe or in the less exalted strata of modern society. And so de Man's former colleagues (many of them Jewish) could, if they wished, pro-duce a defense—or at least an "explanation"— of both his wartime journalism and his personal behavior.

As a matter of fact, the existence of some of the articles had not been entirely unknown prior to the 1987 scandal. When de Man was being considered for the Har-vard fellowship, he had been asked about reports of his activities during World War II. His well-wishing sponsors accepted his statement that he had written "some lit-erary articles" in 1940 and 1941. He had ceased to write them, he said, "when Nazi thought control did no longer allow freedom of statement." Actually, de Man had con-tinued to publish until late November 1942 (by which time it was clear to any intel-ligent observer that Germany would eventually be defeated), but the Harvard author-ities either did not know or did not pursue this fact. Nor did they investigate whether those published articles that he did acknowledge contained any pro-Nazi and anti-Semitic content, or whether such articles represented his freely expressed opinions at the time. To complicate matters still further, the evidence seemed not only to absolve de Man of any personal anti-Semitism but to suggest some very decent behavior on his part toward individual Jews. One testimony was given of de Man's having provided shelter to a Jewish couple on the run from the Nazis, and several of his wartime Jewish acquaintances were certain that he had never reported them to the occupation authorities. His Jewish colleagues and students at Yale almost all defended him against any suspicion of personal anti-Semitism.

What does all this have to do with the moral issues of twentieth-century Euro-pean history? To me it shows the deplorable effects of that amorality and opportunism which have been so widespread in twentieth-century behavior, whether in power pol-itics or in a particular academic career. The fact that de Man was decent in his actions toward individual Jewish acquaintances and that he was, on the testimony of many students and colleagues, a very supportive teacher serves only to highlight his indecency in so many other respects. This same man was evidently ready to write pro-Nazi drivel in order to advance his career, desert his family (for whatever motives), hide the past as long as possible, and then lie about the details. And through it all, there need be no pangs of conscience, no moral suffering. The deconstructionist outlook makes it intellectually respectable to write (and act) as though nothing has a fixed meaning, as though nothing involves responsibility, moral judgment, or solidarity. Personally, I do not believe that any high-quality intellectual and artistic culture could long survive were this kind of opportunism and amorality to become the general rule of behavior. The vast majority of creative scientists, philosophers, and artists of all kinds have been inspired by some transcendent ideal—not simply by the wish to succeed in the survival politics of their era.

After the Second World War, the word "totalitarian" was widely used to characterize the Hitlerite and Stalinist dictatorships. The term was coined to describe the unprecedented totality of both ideological and institutional control achieved by those two dictators. Later research indicated that neither the ideological nor the institutional control had been quite as complete as it looked from the outside while those two mighty criminals were exercising power. But it still seems true that, in some ways, those regimes were indeed more "total" than even the most powerful earlier regimes with which we can compare them. To my way of thinking, what was total about them was their capacity for cynical manipulation and their utter lack of moral scruples.

If we examine the regimes of such mighty rulers as Philip II of Spain or Louis XIV of France, we find that each of them was convinced that he had received his power and authority directly from God and that he had the right to dispose (literally) of the lives of his subjects. To be a galley slave under Philip or Louis was not one bit happier a fate than to be an inmate of a Nazi concentration camp or the gulag, and the lives of lowly peasants and foot soldiers were no more valuable to them than to the twentieth-century dictators.

But two general circumstances were very different. The Habsburg and Bourbon sovereigns did recognize the human value of their middle-class subjects, their artists and scientists. Those subjects, in turn, recognized the "divine right," the religious-political framework, within which the absolute princes could dispose of their lives and property. There were no democratic institutions and no civil rights; but there was a concept of mutual responsibility between the autocratic Christian ruler and a substantial minority of his Christian subjects. Thus, Philip II could turn over accused heretics to the Inquisition and Louis XIV could exile the Huguenots, and both could miscalculate their war plans as badly as did their 1914 successors; but, for the most part, they also encouraged the individual enterprise and the intellectual and emotional autonomy of that middle-class portion of their subjects whose full human dignity they recognized. They had some scruples about the treatment of human beings, and they did not intentionally alienate or oppress those whom they recognized as loyal subjects.

But Hitler throughout his career, and Stalin at least from the time he achieved absolute power (c. 1930), had no scruples whatsoever about the treatment of their subjects. There was no equivalent of the ruler recognizing the human value of his subject (in the form of an immortal soul). Power was their sole criterion, measured in unquestioning obedience to the Führer or the "Party" as personified by Stalin. Hitler's table talk is full of scornful references to the character of ordinary Germans and, when he knew the war was lost, he proclaimed that the German people had not been worthy of their Führer. So far as we know, his suicide included a nauseating amount of self-pity, but not an iota of remorse. As for Stalin, there is no other ruler in recorded history who extracted false confessions from thousands of his faithful subjects, then had them executed or exiled to arctic camps where they were ruled over by a combination of police flunkies and hardened criminals.

If I ask myself what was the qualitative difference between these monsters and the authoritarian kings of the past (including the Russian past), the answer seems to be that the recent tyrants felt no religious or moral constraint of any kind, whereas dynastic rulers of the past at least acknowledged some responsibility, some motive (however paternalistic, erroneous, or hypocritical it might be at times), to respect the minimal humanity of their subjects. It is in this latter sense of complete instrumentality, pragmatism, and human irresponsibility that the regimes of Hitler and Stalin were indeed "totalitarian." To which I would add that overwhelming power almost inevitably takes sadistic forms—indeed, is inconceivable without sadistic intentions.

One of the crucial questions, then, concerning the European future, and the general future of the West, is whether the highly secularized societies of the late twentieth century—societies which lack any transcendent principle of legitimacy or restraint on purely human power—will be able to substitute a secular human ethic for the lost religious one. Though I was educated as a Jew and feel both fortunate and happy with that cultural heritage, I cannot in my own heart find any reason to believe in the specific claims of any of the great monotheistic religions. Like the late Russian poet Boris Pasternak, I believe we are "guests of existence," grateful guests of an inscrutable host, but no form of learning has given me grounds for definable theological belief. Besides which, any student of history knows that genocidal massacres have been committed in the name of each of the monotheistic religions. At the same time, this historian knows of no instance in which a nonreligious faith has ever convinced large segments of humanity that the life of their fellow humans—including those who worship other gods or no gods—is sacred.

In the century discussed in this book, we have seen what absolute rulers are capable of when they acknowledge no limit or restraint upon their own power. Hitler and Stalin could kill millions of people simply for *who* they were, without any relationship to what they had actually *done*. For these men and their lieutenants, there was absolutely no sanctity inherent in the human condition. In contrast, the feudal kings of the Middle Ages and the absolute sovereigns of sixteenth- to eighteenth-century Europe believed (or at least found it wise to pretend to believe) that every human body enclosed an immortal soul and that they, as sovereigns, were accountable to God. In times of war and in moments of fanatical anger, they sometimes forgot that belief; but they did not consider that, as a matter of principle, they were entitled to massacre whole categories of human beings.

Therefore we might well ask: What caused the unique destructiveness of these two twentieth-century tyrants? One can name at least three elements: first, the utter lack of any transcendent belief limiting their conception of their own power. Second, the pseudorationality of their secular programs—*Lebensraum* for the superior Aryan race, the eventual glorious future for the world proletariat. Third, the accumulated resentments of men who were neither princes, nor scions of the prosperous middle class, nor beneficiaries of democratically awarded educational opportunities. Both men were outsiders scorned by the arbiters of the society in which they had come to physical maturity—and the accumulated resentments of such persons often lead to sadism, though rarely on the scale perpetrated by Hitler and Stalin.

Personally, I am unable to believe that "objective" factors such as economic depressions or wartime sufferings suffice to explain the monstrosities of our century. Some degree of suffering has been a near-universal trait of human life, and some degree of arbitrary cruelty has been frequent in all societies. It is the complete devaluation of individual humanity, the complete pragmatism and instrumentalism in the treatment of human beings, that characterizes such phenomena as Nazism and Stalinism. The crucial problem, then, is to find some new basis for preserving the sanctity of human life. The great Alsatian doctor and musicologist, Albert Schweitzer (1875–1965), recognized this need early in the present century, before either of the two world wars. A devout but unorthodox Christian, Schweitzer was keenly concerned with the secularization of the Western world and was particularly sensitized by his awareness of the crimes of European imperialism in Africa. Without preaching any specific political solution, he spoke of the need for what he called "reverence for life." Whether such a feeling can ever act as powerfully to restrain power and encourage altruism as the idea that "we are all children of one God" is something that only the future can show.

The great British logician and atheistic philosopher Bertrand Russell (1872–1970) was every bit as concerned as Schweitzer with the need to restrain the obvious excesses of power-without-scruple. He was one of the first visitors to revolutionary Russia to recognize and condemn the utter ruthlessness which accompanied the rational economic plans of the Bolsheviks—a ruthlessness which provided Lenin with the political and moral justification for thousands of death penalties, and which provided his successor with the rationale for millions of deaths.

In one of his shorter, nontechnical books: *Power, a New Social Analysis* (New York: W. W. Norton, 1938), Russell tried to imagine how political power could be tamed. The legal and institutional requirements were available from example. Political liberty, constitutional government, and freedom of expression would make it possible for normally intelligent voters to keep fanatics from gaining unlimited power. The difficult part of the task was psychological. What could be done to educate people so that they would prefer peaceful, constructive pursuits to violence? To begin his answer, Russell defined power in the widest possible terms as "the ability to produce intended effects." He assumed that it is a part of human nature to feel the need to express one's desires, to make an impression on the surrounding world. There are many ways to make this impression. To build a chair, to paint a picture, or to converse in ways that give pleasure to one's friends or children are all forms of power; they share with the dropping of an atom bomb the ability to produce intended effects. We do not know why some people need to contribute to the happiness of others and why some people need to produce oppression and murder as demonstrations of their power. But for elementary reasons of survival, we must now find ways to motivate as many people as possible to produce peaceful effects, and we must isolate the others from access to lethal weapons.

The varied technical capacities of modern industrial and postindustrial society make it much more feasible to offer an endless variety of pacific ways of producing intended effects. Competitive business enterprises, legal battles, science fairs, musical and art contests, and athletic events provide endless opportunities to express aggression while producing effects that are gratifying to the individual and useful to society. In that sense, there is every reason for optimism as to the possibilities of the human future. But since it is also true that technology will continue to offer more and more ways to kill people as a way of demonstrating power, it is essential to achieve nuclear, chemical, and biological disarmament and to have full knowledge of what is being produced in the world's laboratories and factories.

In these final pages, therefore, I shall take the risk of summarizing what I think of as the main "lessons" to be learned from the history of Europe in the twentieth century. If I ask myself what are the features worth emulating (and also realistically applicable to other civilizations, if they so desire), they would be the capitalist market economy, limited where necessary by moral and humane considerations which are not inherent to the market economy itself; individual liberty in both the economic and political spheres; constitutional government as the guarantee of peaceful methods of social change and the means to achieve the approximate balance of competing group interests; freedom of expression as the ultimate necessary protection against corruption, favoritism, dogmatism, injustice, and the neglect of environmental problems; and the tolerance of human variety in day-to-day relations (which in Anglo-Saxon and northern Europe takes the form of cool civility, and in the Latin, Mediterranean, and Slavic worlds tends to be more exuberant).

Conversely, the most important negative lesson of twentieth-century European history is the need to reject the entire syndrome of Social Darwinism in all its forms. Nationalist, ethnic, and religious prejudices are the destructive side of that variety of linguistic cultures which constitutes one of Europe's most positive attributes. Social Darwinism as a whole is the long-term result of an unfortunate set of temporal coincidences: the triumph of individualistic capitalism in the nineteenth-century industrial revolution; the doctrine of biological evolution, which in the dominant nineteenth-century interpretations emphasized the "struggle for survival" both within and between species; the vogue of the pseudoscience of eugenics, promising an improved human race via the sterilization of the "improvident" poor; the world-imperialist triumph of white European nations which seemed to show—in the form of both destructive weapons and economic exploitation of the earth's resources—that the white "race" had reached a higher stage of "evolution" than had the black and Mongolian "races." Indeed, it was the biological racism of the fascists (as applied in Ethiopia and North Africa) and the Nazis (as applied against Jews, Slavs, and Gypsies) that made possible such indiscriminate and public mass slaughters in twentieth-century Europe. And the virus is still very potent, as varieties of racist nationalism fuel the civil wars in the former Soviet Union and the former Yugoslavia, and are an element in Middle Eastern, Basque, and sporadic European antiimmigrant terrorism. Any decent future for European civilization requires the peoples of the continent completely to overcome their deep-rooted racist sentiments.

But after this necessary warning against Social Darwinism (and remembering that bad news creates more headlines than good news), I am inclined to believe that the average human being is more decent than the agitated pages of recent history would lead one to suppose. The movers and shakers tend to be frustrated persons of high energy—and when frustrated, they can become very cruel and destructive. The Hitlers and Stalins obviously make a lot more news and create a lot more archival documentation than do the modest people who hide the persecuted and who give their money and their time to charitable, educational, medical, and humanitarian organizations. The continuity of civilization depends on the education and the "empowerment" of the potentially decent majority, together with the necessary legal restraint of that energetic minority of would-be destroyers.

Lest these words seem to reflect a species of panglossian optimism, it should be noted that neither Mussolini nor Hitler nor Lenin nor Stalin were *chosen* by majorities of their people. The fascist dictators came to power with the direct, conscious collusion of conservative forces which thought they could use them to control the democratic or revolutionary demands of populations devastated by war and depression. Lenin led the Bolsheviks in a successful minority-backed seizure of power in the capital cities of the war-ruined Russian empire. And Stalin gained power by winning the political struggle within the top party leadership after Lenin's death.

Moreover, none of the lesser right-wing dictators—Franco, Salazar, the Greek colonels, or Count István Bethlen—ever gave their peoples an opportunity to vote in free elections (and for good reason). As for the lesser communist dictators, they were freely appointed and removed by their masters in the Kremlin. And while, in the second half of the century, there have been several neofascist and utopian-terrorist movements in Western Europe, none of them have enjoyed majority popular support (as opposed to partial sympathy with some of their demands). Thus, after the sufferings of the years 1914–1945, I think it is reasonable to hope that, in conditions of peace and with constitutional government, the peoples of Europe will, both by their votes and their own behavior, avoid the horrors of the recent past.

ENDNOTE

1. For the facts, David Lehman, *Signs of the Times, Deconstruction and the Fall of Paul de Man*, New York: Poseidon Press, 1991; for a detailed analysis of the controversy, Alan B. Spitzer, *Historical Truth and Lies about the Past*, University of North Carolina Press, 1996, chapter 3.

Afterword

*O*ne of the risks, and pleasures, of writing the history of very recent events is that new documentation may chance to turn up at any moment and change both the factual narrative and the author's interpretation. Luckily, in the seventeen months since I completed the present work, I have not come across anything that compels me substantially to alter the existing text, but I welcome the opportunity to add a few nuances concerning two important subjects.

The first is the interpretation of the Holocaust presented by Jonah Goldhagen in his book, *Hitler's Willing Executioners*. Goldhagen focuses on the perpetrators of that evil event and argues—very persuasively, in my opinion—that the great majority of civil servants, doctors, lawyers, policemen, soldiers, transport and communications workers, and others who participated in the administration of the death camps did so willingly. In Goldhagen's view, the explanations (and excuses) which emphasize the elements of fear, coercion, bureaucratic discipline, and unquestioning obedience to orders all fail to account for the sheer massiveness of the killing and the smooth operation of this complex, thoroughly industrialized form of genocide. In addition, such explanations tend to treat as merely incidental the fact that the overwhelming majority of the victims "happened" to be Jews.

Goldhagen buttresses his reading of the extensive Holocaust literature with numerous citations of anti-Semitic sentiments throughout nineteenth- and twentieth-century German and Austrian literature, philosophy, and social "science." In his opinion, most historians have underestimated the popular nature of this anti-Semitism, in large part precisely because that sentiment was so widely taken for granted and so infrequently challenged in public discourse.

So far as German attitudes and actions between roughly 1900 and 1945 are concerned, I believe that Goldhagen is correct. Moreover, it is greatly to the credit of democratic Germany in the 1990s that his work has aroused such intellectually serious discussion and so high a degree of consent among persons who bear the terrible knowledge that some of their own grandparents, parents, or other family members can be counted among Hitler's "executioners."

My only reservation has to do with Goldhagen's constant emphasis on *German* anti-Semitism. The *belles lettres* and periodical literature of the Baltic and Slavic countries (other than Russia) have not been nearly so extensively studied by scholars as have the German-language publications. Also, since these countries were themselves the unfortunate victims of both Hitler and Stalin (the latter an opportunistic anti-Semite himself), most historians—including this one—have been reluctant to accuse these peoples of having been active participants in the Nazi atrocities of the Second World War.

But anti-Semitic attitudes, social boycotts, sporadic violence, and quotas denying Jews entry to the universities and the liberal professions were at least as prevalent in all of these countries (with the exception of Czechoslovakia between the two world wars) as in Germany and Austria. I believe that, if one were to analyze the literature of the Baltic and Slavic peoples as scholars have analyzed the German literature, the same anti-Semitic attitudes that Goldhagen highlights would turn out to be equally characteristic of those publications.

Moreover, though Goldhagen does indeed mention the "willing executioners" found in the occupied countries, by hammering away so repetitively at German and Austrian support for Hitler's homicidal obsessions, he runs the risk of encouraging a kind of reverse racism. His "eliminatory anti-Semitism" was a potential trait of all the Germanic, Baltic, and Slavic nationalities of Central and Eastern Europe, as well as of much of the Balkan peninsula. It is also important to note that the anti-Semitism always becomes more shrill and violent in direct proportion to the extreme nationalist sentiments and resentments involved. The reason that Hitler (and his followers and imitators) could fulminate against the Jews as both international bankers and international Bolsheviks is that extreme nationalists tend to become paranoid about *anything* international; what cannot be subsumed in the patriotic catechism is by definition the enemy. Unfortunately, however, in the last few centuries anti-Semitism has also been a constant undercurrent in Western Europe and the English-speaking world. Indeed, on the one hand (and to the great glee of the Nazis), those countries showed very little willingness to rescue significant numbers of German and East European Jews. But on the other, the influence of the Enlightenment, English utilitarianism and liberalism, and the various forms of democratic socialism and cooperativism in those same countries competed with nationalism far more successfully than in the areas where Hitler found so many of his "willing executioners."

The second subject for which I would now like to offer an additional interpretation is the nonviolent demise of the Soviet Union. Several recent books, as well as many articles in the economics pages of the European and American press, have indicated reasons for that collapse beyond those I discuss in the present volume. In chapter eleven, I attributed the increasing Soviet economic and technological backwardness after 1960 to several factors: first, to a dogmatic ideology which neglected market economics and deformed the practice of both the exact and the social sciences; second, to the censorship which made it impossible to acknowledge and correct errors before they resulted in catastrophes; and third, to the fear of letting the new computer revolution put novel and unpredictable communications technology into the hands of the general population. As for the Soviet empire's sudden, unanticipated, and nonviolent collapse, I attributed it principally to the low morale of the *nomenklatura*, who themselves had lost all secular faith in the future of "real socialism."

But I now realize that there was yet another reason for the Soviet Union's swift and total collapse, one surely as important as any of the above. Once *glasnost* and *perestroika* had failed and Gorbachev himself had weakened the power and prestige of the Communist Party, the Soviet Union's economic and factory managers— the only remaining nationwide apparatus of officials who retained their clout— simply inherited the resources of the now-demoralized and leaderless country. These managers became the informal (and later, in many cases, the legal) owners of the factories they had superintended as Soviet officials. They knew, moreover, the value of the mines, the forests, and the oilfields whose production they had been charged with regulating, and they were the persons best placed to negotiate with Western capitalists anxious to apply modern technology and marketing methods to those fabulously rich natural resources. (Similarly, the managers of nuclear-arms depots knew the scientific, monetary, and sheer blackmail value of the weapons under their control, and they proceeded to "privatize" the sale of those armaments.) Soon enough, these managers and their families (as well as their mistresses and bodyguards) came to know the pleasures of the Lido and Marbella, of Rome and Paris; and thus the most energetic and intelligent of the managerial class in the old command economy became the principal beneficiaries of the "transition" to a completely uncontrolled capitalist economy. For this very reason, they had no motive whatever to prevent the collapse of the old order.

Index